I0819126

BY KATHERINE GRANDJEAN

Kingdom of Devils

American Passage

Kingdom of Devils

Woodcut from *The Last Confession & Dying Words of Conrad Englehart* (1807). Courtesy of American Antiquarian Society.

KINGDOM OF DEVILS

A TALE OF MURDER IN THE SHADOW OF THE AMERICAN REVOLUTION

KATHERINE GRANDJEAN

RANDOM HOUSE
New York

Random House
An imprint and division of Penguin Random House LLC
1745 Broadway, New York, NY 10019
randomhousebooks.com
penguinrandomhouse.com

Maps: David Lindroth Inc.

Hardcover ISBN 978-0-593-72993-9
Ebook ISBN 978-0-593-72994-6

Printed in the United States of America

1st Printing

First Edition

BOOK TEAM: Production editor: Luke Epplin • Managing editor: Rebecca Berlant • Production manager: Nathalie Mairena • Copy editor: Diana D'Abruzzo • Proofreaders: Michael Burke, Barbara Jatkola, Muriel Jorgensen, Al Madocs

The authorized representative in the EU for product safety and compliance is Penguin Random House Ireland, Morrison Chambers, 32 Nassau Street, Dublin D02 YH68, Ireland.
https://eu-contact.penguin.ie

For Laura, Carey, and Zack

When without a king, [one] doeth according to freedom of his own will.

—William Doack, 1774

Dollars damn me; and the malicious Devil is forever grinning in upon me, holding the door ajar.

—Herman Melville to Nathaniel Hawthorne, 1851

CONTENTS

Kingdom of Devils

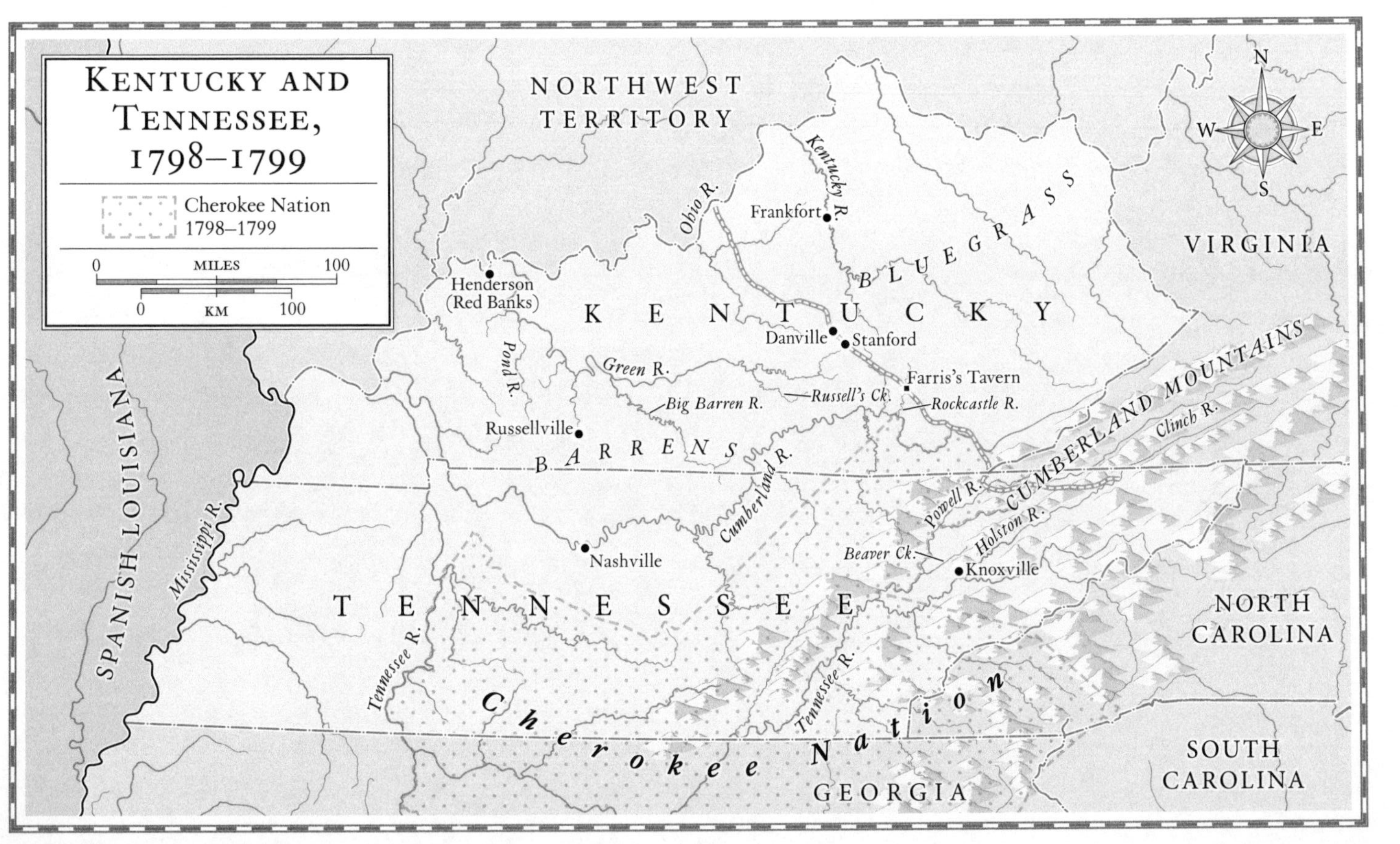

Kentucky and Tennessee, 1798–1799
Cherokee Nation 1798–1799
0 MILES 100
0 KM 100
NORTHWEST TERRITORY
VIRGINIA
N
S
E
W
KENTUCKY
BLUEGRASS
BARRENS
TENNESSEE
NORTH CAROLINA
SOUTH CAROLINA
GEORGIA
SPANISH LOUISIANA
CUMBERLAND MOUNTAINS
Cherokee Nation
Frankfort
Henderson (Red Banks)
Danville
Stanford
Farris's Tavern
Russellville
Nashville
Knoxville
Ohio R.
Kentucky R.
Green R.
Pond R.
Big Barren R.
Russell's Ck.
Rockcastle R.
Cumberland R.
Powell R.
Holston R.
Clinch R.
Beaver Ck.
Tennessee R.
Tennessee R.
Mississippi R.

PROLOGUE

THE SHAVING GLASS

Farris's tavern
Big Rockcastle River, Kentucky
December 1798

Jane Farris noticed things. She was observant. It was her duty. At the tavern, she had to deal with strangers and had no doubt learned to read them. So when the man walked in, she took note of several things about him: his great sweeping coat, his Virginia dialect, even the horsewhip he carried.[1] He was well dressed, with an air of money.

She looked, as he shook off the chill. Outside it was December, the air "frosty." "Prepare for cold weather," the *Kentucky Almanac* warned. Thin crusts of snow sometimes fell on Kentucky's rolling hills this time of year. The ground could be slick and icy beneath horses' hooves. "Christmas draws near," the almanac lilted. "Take care to get the plates and dishes, pot & spit."[2]

The Farrises kept a public house, open to all comers. It stood on the route that many people still called "Boon's Trace," a nod to Daniel Boone, who, hired by the Transylvania Company, had cut his way through the Kentucky mountains twenty years earlier. Jane might have remembered those days, when Shawnees sometimes came screaming into the settlements and sent Kentuckians fleeing to forts. "I was forted from the time I was 7 years old," one woman recalled.[3]

The wars were mostly over now. Men were pouring into Kentucky. The young United States, restless and fidgety, was bursting at its seams. People scrambled westward, squeezing through the Cumberland Gap. Perched a bit beyond the Gap in a no-man's-land of mountainous rock, Farris's tavern was well situated to cater to this parade of weary newcomers. To step into a warm tavern with a hopping fire was a relief. It must have seemed a safe haven on this desolate stretch of road.

Jane cooked. She took care of plates and dishes, pot and spit. In warm months, she might have served boiled turnip tops to hungry travelers, or a bit of warm salad tossed in bacon grease. In winter, times were leaner. Salted pork "is the only food to be got at most of the taverns in this country," one visitor complained.[4]

The man ate. If at some point he opened the little pocket book he carried, in which he made notes of his expenses, she would have seen his name: Thomas Langford.

* * *

JANE WATCHED, AS Langford settled in. She was close enough to notice his shaving glass, the little mirror he palmed. Perhaps he pulled it out to check his appearance or to smooth his hair, fearing he was a little ruffled after hours spent on horseback. She took note as he warmed up and drank with the other tipplers.[5]

She saw him hobnobbing with two men in particular. One of them was rather imposing because of his size: He was a "very large brawney-limbed, big-boned man."[6] The men Jane encountered were sometimes gnarled from years of punishing labor, or scarred from war, their bodies bent or stunted. But this intimidating character was "among the tallest class of men," above six feet. He had thick dark hair that tumbled over his forehead and was "full-fleshed in the face."[7] The other man was less remarkable. He was "light made" with a slighter build ("somewhat under common size," as one man described). His hair was lighter and his face more pleasing, though he bore something of a surly look, even while chuckling.[8]

There were several women with them. They were quieter and hovered nearby as the men talked. Jane did not know any of them. "They were entire strangers in that neighborhood," as one writer later put it.[9]

None of them looked as well heeled as Langford. "Their appearance denoted poverty, with but little regard to cleanliness," one account claimed. Some observers would later describe them as "ragged and filthy," their clothing weather-beaten and faded, as if hinting at "continual exposure to the elements."[10] But was that really unusual for those making their way through Kentucky's unforgiving mountains? At the time, it was not uncommon to see the penniless and desperate, braving the elements, as they entered Kentucky—women and children shivering in the ice and snow, wading through creeks "with out Shoe or Stocking, and barely as maney raggs as covers their Nakedness."[11]

It seemed as if the two men might have fallen on hard times. Their clothing, if dirty and worn, also appeared to some as respectable. They "were well dressed in broad-cloth coats," one man later said.[12] Glancing from across the room, Jane might have guessed that they belonged to a certain familiar, struggling class of men who "provided a constant reminder" in Kentucky's perilous early years that misfortune was "an eager, albeit unwanted, visitor."[13]

To be rough around the edges did not disqualify men from a little socializing. Kentucky prided itself, somewhat, on its leveling spirit. Any man was as good as another, affectations be damned. "If our manners are not as polished as those of the more civilized people in your part of America, you should excuse it," one Kentucky politician wrote in 1798 to a friend in Virginia. After all, Kentucky was refreshingly free of "*supple* courtiers" and grasping "office-hunters." If it also had fewer fine levées and gay balls, well, that was merely a measure of the state's "republican veracity." "When men associate with none but their equals," he wrote, "they will not acquire that refinement of manners, which is generally met with about courts."[14]

They drank. They laughed. To Jane's eye, all "appeared to be very friendly with each other." As the jokes flew, Langford downed whiskey. Jane—who was likely pouring it for him—thought he "seemed to be somewhat intoxicated."[15]

Langford lodged at Farris's tavern overnight. When the sun came up, he settled the bill with her. Then he left with his new friends, not having the faintest idea of the danger he was in. As Jane recalled, "No other person was in company with them."[16]

She must have watched them ride away, north, toward Crab Orchard. She likely did not expect to see any of them again, not anytime soon.

* * *

BUT TWO DAYS later, a wagon clanked up to the Farris house.

Jane saw what it was carrying—a body, beaten and lifeless, its head bashed and bloody. Some passersby had discovered the corpse in a valley a little way off the main path, where a soaring ridge plunged "into a hollow."[17] It had been dumped behind a rotting log. Although the man's greatcoat was missing—and his shaving glass, too, was nowhere to be found—Jane realized as she squinted at his battered body who it was: It was the guest who had shuffled into the tavern days earlier, a man later identified as Thomas Langford.

The sheriff came. Jane told him about the men Langford had been traveling with, though she could not say who they were. Or, as a newspaper put it, "Their names we have not yet heard."[18]

INTRODUCTION

"THE BACKWOODSMEN"

Cincinnati, Ohio
April 1824

In Ward 2 of the brick-faced city of Cincinnati, John Parsons Foote reclined at his desk. Before him was the latest *Port Folio* magazine. Warm winds wafted through the city's alleyways that spring, and noisy sounds of workers building steamboats, hammering and hollering, would have drifted up from the waterfront. But all of that faded when, leafing through the pages of the magazine, Foote landed on a startling piece.[1]

Others, too—in their own plush parlors and city homes—would have halted as they read. *Port Folio* readers were members of polite society: "men of affluence," refined and genteel.[2] They sat back in stuffed claw-footed chairs and lifted their magazines from gleaming mahogany tables; some read, perhaps, by the sound of a brass mantel clock ticking nearby, or the flickering light of an oil lamp, or the pleasing sight of a pianoforte. They were expecting the usual fare, a highbrow miscellany of politics and literature.[3] But when they opened the pages of the magazine that April, they were treated, instead, to a grisly tale.

It was a true story—the author, James Hall, promised—"a most wonderful one indeed," though by all accounts, it had "never appeared in print." In a haunting piece called "The Backwoodsmen," Hall told of a series of vicious murders, committed by two brothers who had once stalked the American backcountry.[4]

"Many years ago," he began, "two men named Harpe appeared in Kentucky spreading death and terror wherever they went."[5]

They seemed to come from nowhere. But they killed wantonly, furiously. "They murdered every defenceless being who fell in their way," Hall wrote. The two men left whole swaths of Kentucky littered with bodies. They stalked people on the byways. They entered people's homes. "In the night," he wrote, "they stole secretly to the cabin, slaughtered its inhabitants, and burned their dwellings—while the farmer who left his house by day, returned at night to witness the dying agonies of his wife and children."[6] Disturbingly, the killers seemed to have no obvious motive. "Neither avarice, want, nor any of the usual inducements to the commission of crime, seemed to govern their conduct," the author marveled. Only a "savage thirst for blood," it appeared, had motivated them.[7]

Readers were aghast. Nothing of this ghoulish sort could be true, they scoffed. Nothing like this marred the history of the United States!

Foote, a booster of the West and all its promise, in umbrage, took up his pen. His blistering letter soon turned up at *The Port Folio*'s office. It expressed "surprise, as well as regret" that the magazine had allowed the story to see the light of day. It charged Hall with fabricating the entire thing. "The horrible details concerning these men, are given as *authentic*," it hissed, then adding, "yet we have no hesitation in asserting that their history, as published in the Port Folio, is unworthy of belief." Surely Hall's "disgusting sketches of human depravity" were drawn from the "regions of romance," not the American past.[8]

* * *

BUT THE STORY was not invented. It was harvested, like milkweed, from the far shores of the Ohio River. It was there—the water lapping nearby—that James Hall first heard it, collected it, and thought of preserving it.

In 1820, Hall, a Philadelphian "smitten with the desire to go West," had boarded a keelboat and floated westward along Kentucky's shores.[9] On the banks of the Ohio, he met people and listened to their stories. He visited their little cabins, with "droves of chubby children" frolicking nearby.[10] "Whenever his floating lodging-house stopped on the border of Ohio, Virginia, or Kentucky," a biographer later wrote, "he sprang ashore . . . and made social calls at the settlers' houses, [to] learn the folk-lore of the backwoods."[11] He drank it all in. "At their cabins," Hall recalled, "I could always procure a refreshing draught of milk, as well as a dish of conversation."[12]

By the smoky glow of kitchen hearths, Hall first heard of the brothers Harp.* He was spellbound, transfixed, as he listened to the "old settlers" spin wild yarns about the killers. Hall, too, might have wondered, at first, if it was all true. This was, after all, the land of tall talk. Kentuckians—chuckling at the widening eyes of gullible travelers—relished nothing more than "pumping listeners full of gruesome legends."[13] But by the time he wrote "The Backwoodsmen," Hall had spent years in this western valley. He had talked to scores of local people. In 1823, he married a girl from Henderson County, Kentucky, where people remembered the murders with pinching freshness.

"These horrid events will sound like fiction to your ears, when told as having happened in any part of the United States," Hall wrote. The murders seemed "foreign," he admitted, to "the generosity of the American character" and "the happy security of our constitutions." But, he said, he "had it attested by a number of

*Their name sometimes appears as "Harpe," but in their own time was more typically spelled with no "e."

living and credible witnesses, who were acquainted with all the facts."[14]

Accused of spinning fairy tales as fact, Hall punched back. He produced testimonials, vouching that the murders were "a matter of general notoriety which hundreds of witnesses can attest." Even the editors of several newspapers local to western Kentucky stepped forward. "Some of the men who pursued the *Harps*," one wrote, "are yet living in this county" and "are well acquainted with the principal circumstances in their career."[15] Local people knew the landmarks in the Harps' murderous path. "The place is still pointed out," another letter read, ". . . near the mouth of the Saline river, where they shot two or three persons in cold blood, by the fires where they had encamped."[16]

Hall did not get every detail right. But the murders he described were real. The two brothers were real flesh-and-blood men. "That there were such men," wrote one of Hall's defenders, ". . . there can be no manner of question."[17]

* * *

THEIR NAMES WERE Wiley and Micajah Harp. In the late 1790s, they committed a fevered series of murders, their grisly scenes flung over hundreds of miles of countryside. It was a wild killing spree. They left a trail of the dead across Tennessee and Kentucky and along the edges of Cherokee country. At one point, the reward money offered for their capture amounted to more than two thousand dollars—a spectacular sum for its time.[18]

Bodies turned up along roadsides, stuffed into brush. They floated to the surface of muddy brooks. Hillsides and rivers kept coughing up the dead, confounding sheriffs. Across the crooked corners of Appalachia and the flatlands of western Kentucky they surfaced: A man last seen by the barkeep at a groggery outside Knoxville was found drifting, lifeless, in a river. Another discovered among the fallen crab apples that lined the Wilderness Road. A dead boy, staring up from a sinkhole. The Harps killed with blunt force. They killed with knives. When they had guns, they used them. There was no special method. But a telltale sign of their involvement was that the victim's body was often filled with stones and sunk into a river so it would not immediately be found.

For nine terrifying months—from late 1798 to August 1799—the Harps rained hell on society. They killed dozens of people along the way, almost all of them men. As the murders unfolded, the little villages of the American frontier shook, convulsed by waves of panic. People shut themselves into their houses, petrified. "Their relentless and furious rage," the son of a Tennessee deputy later wrote, "alarmed and terrified . . . the whole country."[19]

Who they were is a bit hazy, unfortunately, and clouded by folklore. But in some records, they seem almost to step off the page. Micajah Harp was huge, "robust," standing high above most men. "His frame was bony and muscular, his breast broad, his limbs gigantic," one man remembered. He had short black hair creeping down over his forehead and a "downcast countenance."[20] Such was "Big Harp," as he was sometimes called.[21] Wiley, or "Little Harp," was smaller—"meagre in his face" with hair "not quite so curly as his brother's." Very "ill looking" fellows, both of them, according to descriptions that were published during their stint as notorious outlaws.[22]

The Harps' deeds eventually became the stuff of legend. James Hall was merely the first to cast their story into print. Others followed. In the nineteenth century, the brothers were the subjects of folk ballads, memoirs, and tall tales. Herman Melville, in *The Confidence-Man,* called them "Thugs." In the novel's opening scene, Melville pictured a peddler aboard a Mississippi steamboat hawking cheap, pulpy prints about the exploits of "the brothers Harpe."[23] The novelist William Faulkner thought he spied their ghosts haunting the thickets of old Mississippi. To set the scene in *Requiem for a Nun*, he conjured "the legend of the mad Harpes."[24]

Every bit as bloody as Lizzie Borden, as wild as Bonnie and Clyde, the Harps loomed large in the American imagination before the Civil War crashed like a wave over Southern folklore. After that, memory faded. Some of the last studies to cover their crimes in any detail were published a century ago. Still, if you google them today, you will find that murder aficionados count the Harps as "America's first serial killers." But no one—no historian or folklorist or true-crime buff—has ever explained why it all happened.

To some, the Harps look like marauders—wild highwaymen bent on plunder. To others, they just look bloodthirsty. When people wrote about Wiley and Micajah in the nineteenth century, they often painted them as incomprehensible, inexplicable, motivated by pure bloodlust. "A hellish thirst for carnage," as one writer put it.[25] But that is too simple.

Most writers have settled for marveling at them in awed bewilderment. "Their history is wonderful," as James Hall wrote in 1828, not only because of the "number and variety," but also "the incredible atrocity of their adventures."[26] There is more to the story, and it's the question that has gripped me: *Why did they do this?*

* * *

ON THE TOWN green in Danville, Kentucky, there is a replica of an old jail where the Harps were once held. I went there one summer as I began to retrace their steps. Inside were a few lonely objects: an old shackle that had rolled to the middle of the dirt floor, a wooden table, a candle, a pewter plate. In the back corner, staged mutely in a chair, was a headless mannequin in a lacy white gown. Presumably she was meant to represent one of their victims. But she also previewed my own haunting. On the glass viewing window, someone had pasted a little sign: UNHAPPY WITH HER DEMISE, HER RESTLESS SPIRIT SEARCHES FOR BIG HARPE!

I first encountered the Harps about eight or nine years ago. I was teaching a seminar on early American violence. In that course, I assigned Richard Maxwell Brown's "Historical Patterns of American Violence," a galloping overview of the nation's most violent episodes, written during the upheavals of the Vietnam era. Brown and the other writers in that collection, which was commissioned by President Lyndon Johnson, were not particularly interested in the history of murder; they wanted to track patterns of collective violence and protest. But there I found them, mentioned in passing: "the brutal Harpe brothers," who "accounted for anywhere from about 20 to 38 victims in the frontier states of Kentucky and Tennessee."[27] I had never heard of them. Almost everything else that Brown said about the story, I later found out, was wrong. But I knew right away that I would write about it.

The Harps hooked me. At first, I was drawn to the story because it promised to lure me into the shadowy corners of an early America seldom visited. But, quickly, it became an obsession with trying to understand the brothers and their crimes. I have now chased the Harps as much as any lawman ever did. I have followed them into archival collections across six states. I have talked my way into the vaults of county courthouses, where the wormy record books were held together with duct tape. I have begged circuit clerks to scour their closets for centuries-old depositions. I have driven through torrential summer rains in western Kentucky to find the site where a lonely cabin stood in 1799.

It takes some arrogance—or, maybe, foolishness—to think you can decode the meaning of any murder, let alone a string of deaths that occurred centuries ago. Why people commit murder is an extremely complex question. All murders are not the same. Each story has its own quirks, its own signature, its own constellation of causes—a brutal combination of individual psychology and societal influences and pressures. "Murder is not a natural occurrence, a weed appearing every so many thousand persons," the historian Eric Monkkonen writes in *Murder in New York City*. "Rather, it is the culminating event in a series of interactions, some over years, some over seconds," all of it "tempered" by "broad political and state-based . . . patterns."[28]

Some killers confess. Some tell their motives. "I resigned myself fully to Satan," one man wrote in 1807, after he killed a girl he'd gotten with child by pushing her into a river.[29] But the Harps do not give up their secrets quite so easily. They left behind no diaries or letters. I have pieced this story together from court records, newspaper accounts, land records, government documents, local histories, and the recorded memories of people who knew them. All of what follows is based in fact. Every quote, and every detail, is taken from a letter or a deposition or some other document. Happily, there are some rich pockets of material, as well as some dazzling undiscovered fragments. But the body of evidence we have inherited, after two hundred years, is painfully incomplete. It is distorted by generations of florid storytelling and mostly bereft of the kind of salacious firsthand testimony that any true-crime writer would want. Recovering Wiley and Micajah Harp is no easy thing.

Still, there is something strangely seductive about them. In their very elusiveness—their maddening slipperiness—is a cruel magic. The Harps are an imperfect puzzle: Pieces are missing, but it is hard, nonetheless, to resist the impulse to solve it. Even in the blank spaces, there is a temptation to peer in and imagine what was once there. "The historian obtains a peculiar pleasure," Robin Winks writes in *The Historian as Detective*, "from discovering unanswerable questions . . . [from] knowing that one will never *know*, that one will never reach the other end of the sea, because it is endless."[30]

* * *

ONE GLARING CLUE to understanding the Harps is the moment that created them. These were the heady and unpredictable years just after the American Revolution. The United States was still in its infancy. People were smarting from the contortions of war and struggling to adjust to a new kind of society. When the Harp brothers took off on their murderous spree, only two presidents had yet occupied the nation's highest office. No one knew entirely what a president, or the republic itself, should be.

It was, in many ways, an exhilarating time. A breathless novelty filled the air. Americans had witnessed the unthinkable—the end of monarchy, an entire way of life toppled, much as the gilded statue of King George III had come crashing down in New York City in July 1776. It was an awakening—a new beginning—as if, as Thomas Paine wrote, "every corner of the mind is swept of its cobwebs, poison, and dust." Paine saw, correctly, that the American Revolution was much more than a victory over Britain. It had rewritten the way Americans thought about themselves. "Our style and manner of thinking have undergone a revolution, more extraordinary than the political revolution of the country," he wrote. "We see with other eyes; we hear with other ears; and think with other thoughts, than those we formerly used."[31]

Independence fired every man's imagination, filling him with a crackling new sense of possibility. It freed him from the shackles of the past. It gave common men a sense of importance—and worth. As English visitors reportedly complained, even Americans "in the humbler walks of life" possessed "a certain surly independence." If you hired them to perform some service, they did it with the attitude of granting a favor. Even "while they pocket your money," one man wrote, "they remind you that they are your equals."[32]

But there were dark sides, too. The American Revolution was not only liberating. It was also deeply destabilizing—a profound breach from the past, both politically and socially, and it looms behind the Harps unavoidably, like a great shadow. It shook people free from their families and villages and sent them bolting, isolated, into new territories. It released torrents of migrants into the West, ready to claim Indigenous land. It created chaos in property markets. It taught men a new ethos of ruthless, individual competition. Even as it boosted hope for every man's success, it stacked the deck against them, fueling their anger. Unspooling the mystery of what sent the Harps reeling exposes hidden, violent legacies of the American Revolution.

Menace lurked in the cracks, where men's new sensibilities and hopes were frustrated or disappointed. The Revolution promised new chances at life, liberty, and the pursuit of happiness. But not everyone could achieve those things. What happened to those who didn't?

* * *

BY THE TIME Hall was writing twenty years later, the dust had settled. Many of the convulsions of the founding era had faded. The Harps had already become unmoored from their own times.

Those times, and their troubles, seemed far behind. An "Era of Good Feelings" was under way. In 1817, when James Monroe kicked off his presidency with a friendly tour of the United States, all the rancor of the past seemed to melt away, replaced with a "burst of National Feeling." Darker aspects of the nation's early history, by then, had been pointedly forgotten, the Revolution bathed in a rosy glow. Monroe himself—whom one newspaper called "the last of the revolutionary farmers"—represented the passage away from the Revolutionary generation's lived experience, into a haze of nostalgic memory. "He wore a plain blue coat" and a "hat and cockade of the revolutionary fashion," the New Haven *Herald* reported, "well calculated to excite in the minds of the people, the remembrance of the day which 'tried men's souls.'"[33] Already, the day which tried men's souls seemed long ago.

What was it in the Harps' tale that so bothered *The Port Folio*'s readers? It was not so much the plain violence of the story. It was more that Hall was resurrecting things that many preferred would stay buried. So thorough was their forgetting by 1824 that the Harps did not even seem legible within the confines of American history. How was it that the sweet land of liberty could have produced such men?

For all the fascination that has, at times, been lavished upon the Harps, there has always been a strange hesitation to stare at them too closely. All along, there has been a kind of squeamishness about what might be discovered there, as if something we don't want to know might be unlocked or exposed. As if there was something uncanny and recognizable in them, and the mere act of looking for too long might awaken whatever it was. "The truth is," the *Boston Spectator* admonished in the 1820s, "that many an act of vile atrocity would never be repeated" if not for stories "reminding men . . . [of] those who dare to do it."[34] But it was more than that. When he encountered the Harps in *The Port Folio,* John Parsons Foote was but a few hundred miles—and a quarter century—removed from them. But, still, he could not bring himself to look at the story straight on.

The saga of Wiley and Micajah Harp has never been complete. A lot has disappeared over the years. Other parts were never there because no one went looking. But what's been missing from the Harps' tale is telling. It is easy enough to paint the two brothers as opaque—or plainly evil, acting out of "a fiendish delight in human misery."[35] But to do that, as so many have, is to miss the deeper lessons of their story. Inside it hides an allegory—a kind of parallel American founding. The beginning of something darker, more sinister, and, perhaps, still with us.

EAST
TENNESSEE

Come all ye young men a warning take by me,
Love your wives, and mind your work, and shun bad company;
Quit gaming, and fine whores,
Pay off your tavern scores,
For they'll be staring at your daring,
When you can spend no more.

—from "The Confession of Thomas Mount," 1791

CHAPTER 1

LIBERTY AND PROPERTY

Beaver Creek
Knox County, Tennessee
Fall 1797

On a brisk autumn day, Wiley Harp went into town. He strolled among the buildings, squat and wooden. Knoxville was square, all blocky lots, a giant chessboard teetering on the muddy edge of the Holston River. Close to the center of the board was the courthouse. It was one of the town's grandest buildings, but even so, it was an ugly thing, already falling apart. It would later burn down, possibly at the hand of an arsonist.[1] This was the place he was looking for.

Outside, clumps of men stood talking. There was laughter and shouting. Peddlers hawked whiskey, and tied-up horses twitched restlessly. On court days, when people gathered in the square, the town felt festive. A "promiscuous throng" clogged the streets.[2] Women yelled from doorways, and others sang as "the crowd whooped and danced."[3] Wiley moved through them. His brother was by his side, along to help with his business. Clutching a piece of paper tightly in his hand, he stepped into the courthouse and waited his turn.

It was 1797, and the United States was filled with a jittery and boundless energy. Not long ago, America had fought for and won its independence from Britain. People had scattered; loyalists had fled. Old resentments were fading, or, at least, sinking beneath the surface like old shipwrecks—invisible, submerged. America had its eye on the future, even if it continued to nurse the bumps and bruises of the past. The new republic was finding its way, groping forward, but there were stumbles. Fallout from the Revolution was not entirely settled.

Years had elapsed since delegates gathered in an airless hall in Philadelphia—latching the windows shut for secrecy—and drafted the United States Constitution. If the republic had held together since then, it was largely attributable to the people's affections for the first man to be elected president, the imposing war hero George Washington. Though his presidency had endured its rocky moments, Washington was largely beloved. Women tossed flowers at his feet. Men toasted him. In 1796, church bells rang in one New England town to celebrate his birthday, while men belted out, in song, "God Save Great Washington."[4]

But now the nation had a new president—its second. When John Adams gave his inaugural address earlier that year, he could feel the crowd lamenting Washington's departure. "A Solemn Scene it was indeed," he wrote later. The only happy one in the room seemed to be Washington himself. His "Countenance was as serene and unclouded as the day," Adams remembered. "He Seem'd . . . to enjoy a Tryumph over me. Methought I heard him think Ay! I am fairly out and you fairly in! See which of Us will be happiest."[5]

Adams had reason to be anxious. With his arrival, the national mood shifted. His presidency would not be a time of optimism and confidence. It was, instead, a time of contraction. War threatened; markets tightened. "[Washington] is fortunate to get off just as the bubble is bursting," Thomas Jefferson wrote upon Adams's election, "leaving others to hold the bag."[6]

But at the courthouse in Knoxville that day, the mood was hopeful. The court was busy. Wiley waited his turn. When the justices beckoned, he stepped forward and announced his business with the court: He was there to register a deed.

He handed the document to the men on the bench.

Was it valid? they asked.

Standing behind him, his brother, Micajah, nodded, and swore, yes.

It was 1797, the year that Wiley Harp became a land owner. For the first time in his life, he owned property.

* * *

WILEY HARP WAS in his late twenties. He was a slight man of meager build, not quite short, though not nearly as tall as Micajah. Although he was the younger brother, Wiley looked older. He had blue eyes. His hair may have been a darkish auburn; it could look lighter or darker, even "reddish," in different light. He was not bad looking; by some accounts, he was even "handsome" with a "pleasant agreeable appearance." Nothing about him was especially distinguishable or unusual. He wanted the things that all young men wanted.[7]

He was newly married. His wife was a pretty girl named Sarah—though she was invariably called by her nickname, "Sally." She may have been a preacher's daughter. (This was a piece of lore that would later attach to her, though it's difficult to confirm.) By all accounts, she was a "fine girl," the daughter of "a man of fine irreproachable character" who lived outside of Knoxville. Some people even remembered her father as a "gentleman." All the descriptions of her agree: She came from a respectable family, and she was beautiful—"really pretty" and "delicate."[8] Wiley must have been pleased to marry such a woman.

They signed the marriage bond as June bloomed in 1797, promising that there was "no lawful objection why Willie Harp and Sarah Rice may not be joined together in the holy estate of matrimony." The bond was dated in "the XXI year of our Independance."[9] It was the first year of his.

Two months later, he bought his land. It was not much, only one hundred acres. But since he had likely been renting (or squatting) before this, it was quite a moment. He and the seller drew up the deed on August 4, 1797, a rainy day. Wiley paid two hundred dollars. The land, a lush little plot on Beaver Creek, lay a bit northwest of Knoxville. It was a stone's throw from Cherokee hunting lands. Just over the Clinch River, very close to Wiley Harp's parcel, was Indian country.[10]

Only a few years earlier, Wiley's little patch of ground had seen carnage. Not far away stood the remains of Cavett's Station, a fort that Cherokees had left in "smoking ruins," the "mangled bodies" of the Cavett family strewn about, in 1793.[11] As Americans speared westward, Cherokees had mercilessly tried to beat them back. Whole Cherokee towns, in turn, were put to "fire and slaughter." "I am still among my people, living in gores of blood," wrote Doublehead, a Cherokee warrior, in 1793. For seventeen years, from about 1776 to 1794, the wars had raged, with scores of people "shot, hacked, scalped, burned, and taken captive."[12]

These were the scenes that haunted the ridges near Knoxville. For now, the bloodletting seemed to have quieted. But the place where Wiley planned to settle with his new bride was still a murky borderland. Cherokees now felt comfortable enough to ramble into town for a little recreation ("they frequently resort among our inhabitants," the governor wrote in 1796), and some American hopefuls were even fearless—or desperate—enough to begin putting up shanties inside Cherokee Nation, squatting.[13] But the punishing years of the Cherokees' "long war" cannot have felt very distant.

Nonetheless, as Wiley looked to set down roots, East Tennessee was booming. With the violence of the Indian wars subsiding, migrants were streaming into the region's creeks and river valleys.[14] "It is not unfrequent to see from two to three hundred people coming in a gang," wrote an observer in Knoxville in 1795. The countryside seemed ready to burst. Georgia and the Carolinas appeared to be "emptying themselves into it."[15]

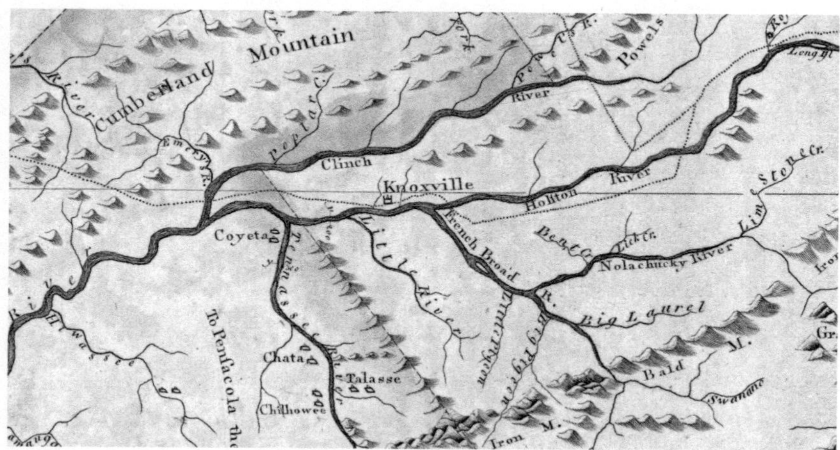

Wiley Harp's land was north and west of Knoxville near the Clinch River. Beyond lay Cherokee country. From *A Map of the Tennassee Government* (John Reid, 1796). Courtesy of the Library of Congress, Geography and Map Division.

Knoxville in 1797 was a rough, young town, founded only a few years earlier. Barracks, attached to the fort that founder James White had built on high ground in 1786, were still standing and used now as a meeting place for the Assembly. By the time Wiley Harp arrived here to file his deed, there were about forty houses and businesses, arrayed in a grid. The town had a printing office, where the *Knoxville Gazette* was published. There were shops and markets. You could buy chocolate, coffee, gunpowder, stationery, window glass. You could buy Irish linens, hyson tea, pepper, and allspice. It had no church. But there were taverns, ordinaries, and tippling houses aplenty. In the north end, there was a graveyard.[16]

The people had a reputation for rowdiness. "They are of a class that have nothing to lose," wrote one visitor.[17] To the wayfaring preachers who sometimes rambled through, they seemed godless. On Sundays, instead of going to church, they sang and danced and played cards. They swore. A merchant, visiting in 1798, was shocked. "Thinks I, is this that promised land?" he wrote. "Is this that noble Tennessee whose great fame has filled the mouths and fired the breaths of many?" There were good men in eastern Tennessee, he conceded. But there were "more bad ones." A joke in town was that the devil, now too old to travel, had retired in Knoxville, where he hoped "to spend the remaining part of his days in tranquility, as he believes he is among his friends."[18]

They were not entirely unchurched. In 1796, when delegates crammed together in a War Department office in Knoxville to write the state's constitution, they stitched into it a clause to ensure that its leaders were men of faith: "No person who denies the being of God," it read, "or a future State of rewards and punishments shall hold any office."[19] Only a few years after the Harps moved onto Beaver Creek, ecstatic revivals would sweep the valleys, with thousands flocking to massive camp meetings in hopes of receiving God's grace.

Outside of Knoxville's limits, it was mostly a landscape of small farms. People made their living simply—by growing corn, raising stock, making whiskey. The Appalachian Mountains ran in jagged gashes through eastern Tennessee. Emerald-hued valleys, watered by a tangle of boisterous blue streams, beckoned newcomers. But these valleys were broken up by sharp, towering ridges. "The face of the country is much broken," one man described.[20] It was not terrain that encouraged grand plantations, so people collected herds of livestock and built stills. They found other ways to make the land feed them.

Some families lived very sparely. Sifting through the surviving inventories of what men owned, you get a sense of their material lives. Plow irons and pewter basins. Washtubs and churns. A few more stately properties appear, lifelike, in the records, like that of John Kearns, who owned six slaves, one hundred cattle, thirteen horses, and an assortment of geese, beehives, and fancy furniture. But more typical was William Roseberry: When he died in 1794, all he left behind was a bay horse, an old black cow, a yearling heifer, and a promissory note for twenty-three pounds. The entire estate sold for a mere $42.50.[21]

But the men here were jealously proud of their independence. "Every Man who arrives here and determines to become a Citizen," wrote the politician William Blount in 1797, "appears to feel and I believe does in reality feel an Independence & Consequence to which he was a Strainger in the Alantic States." Here was opportunity for "Plenty & Health if not . . . greater Riches."[22]

Touring the southern backcountry in the late 1790s, British traveler Charles William Janson was less sanguine but no less struck by men's love of liberty. "The lower class in this gouging, biting, kicking country," he wrote, "are the most abject that, perhaps, ever peopled a Christian land." They lived in wretched houses, just pine logs piled on top of one another, Janson marveled. They farmed only enough land to fill their mouths with a bit of corn and cabbage. But, despite "these accumulated miseries," he pronounced, "the inhabit-

A backcountry cabin. From Lewis Collins, *Collins' Historical Sketches of Kentucky* (1847). Courtesy of the Library of Congress.

ants of log-houses are extremely tenacious of the rights and liberties of republicanism. They consider themselves on an equal footing with the best educated people of the country."[23]

Maybe Wiley Harp did, in reality, feel an "Independence & Consequence" clutching that deed. Land, here, was the foundation of manhood. Property was patriarchy.[24] It was what every young, hopeful man riding into Tennessee was seeking. Plenty and health. Independence and consequence. Liberty and property.

* * *

NO ONE KNEW Wiley Harp's name in 1797. He looked like every other anonymous young man waiting patiently at the courthouse. People strode by without a second glance. No one could have imagined what lay in store. He was plainly ordinary, one of thousands of men pushing their way into the western hills—a tiny speck in a sea of humanity, most of whom lived and died namelessly and who no one remembers now. Nothing outwardly suggested he was fated to be different from any of those other unremembered souls.

His very plainness makes him difficult to trace. Much of Wiley's life before this moment is blurry. No one knows precisely who the Harps were. Where did they come from? Where were they raised? These are vexing mysteries. "Whether their real names were Harp or not, no one knew," one writer complained in 1842, "nor was it ever ascertained where they had been born or brought up, or who were their relatives."[25] Wiley and Micajah Harp, as children, resist being found. But there are clues.

The brothers were born close together in the late 1760s.[26] They came from North Carolina.[27] It was the land of the pines; even from several leagues offshore, sailors could smell the pine radiating off the land.[28] They might have spent some part of their childhood in Granville County, a patch of Piedmont bordering Virginia. In the 1770s and 1780s, there was a cluster of Harps in Granville, most of them in the Epping Forest district. (Henry Harp, John Harp, Sampson Harp, two Thomas Harps, and a Thomas Harp, Sr., are all listed as taxpayers in Granville County for the year 1788.) There were Harp marriages there.[29] Micajah and Wiley are not named in these records, but they may be among the anonymous little ones listed in the censuses.

There is no proof. There is no parish vestry book, no baptism record, to prove that these are the right Harps. But there are strong reasons to believe they had ties to this part of North Carolina. One early writer placed their origins in almost this very spot—the northern Piedmont, close to the Virginia line. Another wrote, too, that they "came from the borders of Virginia."[30] Although there were a few other Harps scattered here and there across North Carolina, nowhere else does the census data quite match the surviving traditions about their family origins.

Granville County was named for John Carteret, second Earl of Granville, an heir of one of the original Lords Proprietor of Carolina. The Harps who settled there lived simpler lives. None of them owned any slaves. They were probably Scottish, perhaps having arrived as recently as the 1760s or 1770s.[31] Granville lay on the great trading path to Cherokee country, and several Scottish trading firms were operating there in Fishing Creek, not far from where some of the Harps ended up. Those firms drew Scottish migrants, and it is possible that the family had come as part of a recent crush of immigrants to Britain's mainland colonies.[32]

If they grew up in this part of North Carolina, life was very bare and simple. A traveler cutting through Tarboro in the 1770s called the people "wretchedly ignorant." They fed their hearth fires with scraps of pine—roots and knots. The tarry smoke yellowed their skin. They wore cotton rags.[33] The Harps who lived in the Piedmont may not have been among the very poorest. At least one of them, John, owned land—a small grant on Long Creek. But the others were counted as single "polls," no land, with just one or two cattle.[34]

To conjure even a glimpse of Wiley Harp's childhood requires some imagination. But the brothers would have lived modestly, perhaps in a house with only one room, bedecked with very little furniture. When they were young, the two boys probably fished, up to their ankles in gurgling creeks. They fell asleep to the sound of frogs making music in the marshes. They slumbered on beds of straw or corn husks. They cut tobacco from its stalks.[35] They would have spent much of their time outdoors. Children were allowed to roam freely. Parents did not hover over them. Little boys and girls raced through the towering pines with little oversight. Occasionally, toddlers rambled into the woods and got lost.[36]

There are some hints that in this earlier part of their lives Wiley and his brother had lived through troubled times. It is tempting to try to discover in their youth some dim outlines of their characters—of the men they would become. Even in the eighteenth century, people recognized that children might bend, like river reeds, in the direction in which the current swept their young lives. "Children like tender [willows] take the bow," wrote George Washington's first biographer in 1800, "and as they first are form'd, forever grow."[37] But the portrait is too faint for that. All that can be said, perhaps, is that Wiley, in 1797, was seeking a bit of stability, solidity, of a kind he may not have known fully in the past.

* * *

AS CHILDREN, THE Harps lived under a king. All authority in the colonies and elsewhere descended from George III, cloaked in his royal robes of velvet and ermine and lace.[38] Each of North Carolina's counties was but a tiny fragment of a vast empire.

But then, the empire began to crack.

It began in the 1760s, in scenes very distant from the Carolina hills: Rioting in the seaports. British soldiers marching in the streets of Boston. Tea dumped into the harbor. In 1775, when Wiley and Micajah Harp were still boys, shots were fired in Massachusetts, and the war ignited. "You have begun to burn our Towns, and murder our People," Benjamin Franklin wrote to his friend William Strahan, a member of Parliament, that July. "Look upon your Hands! They are stained with the Blood of your Relations!"[39]

When the Harps were still young, war came to the Carolina countryside. It smoldered slowly at first. But then it burned hot. Even as Wiley walked the streets of Knoxville years later he might have borne the scars. What streams swept the Harp family into Tennessee are obscure, but one of them might have been the Revolutionary War.

What did this look like to a child in the pines of North Carolina? At first, the youngest Carolinians likely knew very little. Chatter trickled into cabins, arriving with neighbors. Little ones listened. Perhaps they overheard adults whispering at night by flickering fires. Fidgeting in church pews, children sat through sermons touching on the crisis. One boy in nearby Virginia eavesdropped on a conversation between his father and his preacher. "I heard our parson tell my father that the people was Deluded," he later recalled. What did the parson think of the rebels? "They was not only rong but fools."[40]

But soon the war crept closer. No more was it a whisper or the idle prattle of churchgoers. Soon, it was right on the doorstep. It arrived in the form of men who came to your house and forced your father to swear an oath—or else. Or as thieves who rifled your cupboards while your mother cowered on her knees. The Revolution did not always look like redcoats marching in lockstep on the mucky roads outside of Boston or like minutemen massing on Lexington Green. In the Carolinas, it turned into a nasty, bare-knuckled civil war.[41]

Some of its horrors, banished from our collective national memory, are hard to fathom today: Men were shot on their own porches, beaten, lynched. Women and children were dragged out of doors as loyalist raiders and patriot gangs scoured neighborhoods for known enemies. "King's men" and "liberty men" alike saw their property destroyed, burned, or pillaged. They "pursue each other with as much relentless fury as beasts of prey," an American general marveled.[42] Taverners like Owen Griffin, who offered room and board to officers of His Majesty's Navy, were visited by posses of "rebels" who entered loyalists' homes and torched most of what was inside.[43] Travelers cutting through the backcountry in 1782 found a scorched, barren landscape of abandoned farms. "We saw nothing but burned houses and open fields," one wrote.[44]

The terror of seeing one's house broken open and ransacked is palpable in some accounts. Near Friedberg, North Carolina, in 1781, four men smashed windows in Christian Frey's house and then stormed inside. Frey tried to speak to them "gently," but one of them bashed him over the head. They struck his wife. They used a rock to crack open his cupboards and then took his money "and whatever else they wished." Frey tried to flee, but a man guarding the door struck him, and when he finally escaped, the robbers shot after him. His wife, Sarah, hiding behind a door, crumbled to her knees. She thought he'd been killed.[45]

Children were not spared. Many saw terrible things. When a gang of men came to her house looking for her husband, one mother watched miserably—her hands tied behind her back—as her children were whipped so that they might give up "the place of their father's concealment."[46] At another family's door, a loyalist captain asked: Is your father at home? No, said the "small boy" who'd answered the door, upon which the visitor, agitated, allegedly drew his pistol and shot the child.[47]

It is possible that Wiley and Micajah saw fighting, even as young boys. Although there is no proof, it has long been rumored that the young Harp brothers participated. Many children did. When scuffles broke out in the streets, they joined riots. (One young man in New Bern, North Carolina, "hurled a lightwood knot" at the royal governor.)[48] Children piloted armies and served as lookouts, whistling when danger approached. They were also soldiers. Officially, boys had to be sixteen to enlist. But America was a young country, desperate for recruits. Boys as young as twelve served. And poor children, who were seen as more disposable, were often pushed forward.[49]

The Harps' father, allegedly, was a loyalist. According to traditions that have circulated since at least the nineteenth century, he had "fought under the British flag" and then, unable to shake off this blight, fled North Carolina. "He tried to turn his coat," one writer later suggested, "but his neighbors had too long memories" and "he was forced to flee for his life."[50] Folklore has it that by the 1790s, the Harp family, exiled as Tories, had been in the Tennessee mountains for years.[51] The evidence for this, unfortunately, is painfully thin. (Almost all of it derives from a book written much later, in the 1850s, by a man who claimed to have known the Harps' wives—though he waited to publish, conveniently, until everyone involved was dead.) But it is plausible. Many loyalists drifted westward, seeking anonymity. Some ended up living in Cherokee country.[52]

Former Tories who were unable to shed their loyalist reputations sometimes received an unfriendly reception in early Tennessee. Local histories tell stories like that of Nicholas Pyle, who was beset by the "unfriendliness of his neighbors" until he redeemed himself by fighting in the War of 1812. Another former loyalist, Dudley Redd, told his neighbors that he had been a Continental soldier. But he was outed by "an old negro man" who had once served alongside an officer in the British army.[53] Even in the West, it was hard to outrun the past.[54]

By the time Wiley bought his land, his father was apparently long gone. If he had ever been in Tennessee, he was not there in

1797. There is no mention of him—or of their mother, or any siblings, or any other blood relations—in any record. They were alone.

* * *

"HE PROVED IT in open court," an archivist said to me, pointing to the spot in a fragile record book where the clerk had captured the moment Wiley registered his land, a proud day in his life. There it was, a snapshot: "Willey Harp," one hundred acres, his own little creek-side kingdom, its purchase witnessed "by M Harp."[55]

As I started to retrace the Harps' steps, I went, first, to Knoxville. I knew the Harps had lived here once, before the murders began. "In the year 1797 or 1798, two men came into the county of Knox, and settled near Beaver creek," one early chronicler wrote. "They . . . said their names were HARP."[56] But there was little else—almost nothing to suggest what might have happened to them here. So I started digging. I found Wiley's wedding bond. I found his deed. I found the two brothers, sauntering into court in 1797, the rest of their lives awaiting.

After that, I went to find his land. I wanted to see the place where Wiley Harp had once lived—the place he had staked his savings on. I rented a car and drove north, out of the city. I drove over Beaver Ridge—gnarly, dark, steep, and green. On the other side was a lush, verdant plain, and somewhere beyond that, the creek. I found a spot, up against the ridge, and gazed out over the landscape. I don't know if I was standing in quite the right place. The black oaks and brush fences and boulders of the eighteenth century are all gone. But I knew I was close.

Everyone in Wiley's world wanted land. Why men so badly wanted land can only be grasped by knowing what it meant to them: the quickest way to personal independence, or as one historian puts it, "freedom from the will of others." If you had land enough to be self-sufficient, you were free; if you didn't, you weren't. You were dependent, beholden to the whims and orders of other men. You could not be trusted to vote. You could not even be trusted to think for yourself.[57]

Property, to Americans, had always been sacred. "There is nothing which so generally strikes the imagination, and engages the affections of mankind," wrote the English jurist William Blackstone, "as the right of property."[58] Its jealous protection was a fundamental part of English law and political culture, reaching well into the distant past. To be deprived of one's property, without consent, was slavery. It was precisely this idea—electrified by a few pences' worth of taxes on molasses or paper—that had propelled the coming of the American Revolution. "Liberty and property!" had been the rallying cry of the revolutionaries.

But after the Revolution, the obsession deepened; it metastasized. Americans were gripped by a sort of collective madness for western land. "The Land Mania is a frequent disease in every part of America," one writer mused in 1798. "It broke out with peculiar violence" just after the war, he wrote, and had remained "the epidemic of our country ever since."[59] Speculation ran wild; "anybody with capital or access," it seemed, "was getting involved in the land business."[60] And many an American feverishly rushed westward, intent on claiming his own little slice of independence in the form of landed property.

But in the early West, property—and liberty—were anything but secure.

Wiley Harp's land rested on shaky ground. In the 1790s, virtually all of Tennessee was a quicksand of rotten land claims. In this era, nearly every patch of private property in eastern Tennessee descended from North Carolina, its parent state. Much of it had been bought, sold, or promised away in crooked dealings long before Tennessee became its own state in 1796. Land speculation among North Carolinians was famously ruthless—even "predatory." It was wild, frantic. It muscled out ordinary settlers. Or worse, it fooled them. "Unscrupulous land agents . . . defrauded hundreds of would-be buyers," one historian writes. "Instead of acquiring clear titles, many settlers paid exorbitant fees only to discover that their payments had been mislaid or that others had previously patented their claims."[61]

Buying land was often a nightmarishly long and difficult process that favored flush investors and weighty land companies over average Americans. Where western lands were first being opened for settlement, you had to buy directly from the state. It could take years. First, you located the land you wanted. Then you went to one of North Carolina's land offices (which stood, very likely, tens or hundreds of miles away), entered your claim, and paid. After waiting a short stint, you would be given a "warrant." Then the land could be surveyed. Only when survey copies reached the secretary of state's office would North Carolina issue a "grant" and make note of the fee paid: Now the land was yours.[62]

Fraud plagued North Carolina's land grants. For those in power, it was not difficult to manipulate the system. There were many ways to do it. In one nefarious scheme, James Glasgow, North Carolina's secretary of state, issued hundreds of duplicate and blank land warrants, ostensibly because the originals had been "lost." (And these replacements were easily altered or filled in to move the grants into new hands.)[63] Forgery, too, was rampant in North Carolina's land offices. One baffled North Carolinian discovered in 1787 a warrant for 274 acres in his name. He had no recollection of signing it. "I Never Conveyed that Property to any person," he wrote. "Neither was it my hand Writing." (Then, too: "I mean to be paid for it.")[64]

Some of the worst confusion arose from the fact that North Carolina had paid its Continental soldiers in land—land that would become Tennessee. In many parts of America, western land was used to persuade men to enlist. Soldiers were not paid well, and Continental currency plummeted in value as the war dragged on. But there was plenty of western land. Privates in New York could claim six hundred acres. Virginia promised two hundred acres to ordinary soldiers and as much as fifteen thousand to officers. North Carolina at first offered two hundred acres, but in the early 1780s, it raised its grants for three-year enlistments to 640 acres, plus an annual bonus of five hundred dollars and a "prime slave." Land warrants, in many ways, purchased the American victory.[65]

But the military bounties, too, were rife with corruption. Even in legitimate circumstances, veterans were seldom the ones who settled their grants. The process of claiming land was complicated and lengthy, and as a brisk market in warrants took off, many soldiers—desperate for money—sold their "scrip" for pennies to speculators, who looked to flip it at pricier rates.[66] The military claims were also vulnerable to illegal activity. This was due to a yawning loophole in the law: Before issuing a warrant to a former soldier, the North Carolina secretary of state, James Glasgow, was supposed to verify the man's service. But alternatively, rather than waiting for confirmation from the statehouse, a warrant could be confirmed much faster if a military officer simply vouched for the fact that the man had served. All the officer had to do was sign.

While staying in Nashville in September 1797, only a month after Wiley Harp bought his land, a man named John Love saw something shocking. Two veteran officers were drunk. They were signing papers. William Tyrell, a notorious land jobber, hovered over them. He brought out peach brandy and loaf sugar and "a large Bowl of Apple Toddy." He pressed one of them, a captain, "to drink, which he did very freely." Then he pushed him, again, to take up his pen. When one finally refused to sign any more, Tyrell looked him dead in the bloodshot eyes, said "Damn you," and left.

The two officers had been signing military warrants, entitling Continental soldiers to land. But they were fake. Each paper vouched for the imaginary service of a phantom Carolinian. (These claims could then be signed over to the highest bidder, or even to Tyrell himself.) Together, that day, the two drunken officers signed nearly five hundred dummy warrants.[67]

All of this left a mess. It was extraordinarily difficult to get a clear title to land. Around the turn of the nineteenth century, Tennesseans "faced an overwhelming number of land problems." Lawsuits lined lawyers' pockets. Petitions poured into the legislature. Newspapers spilled over with judicial notices of eviction, broadcasting the loss of property among those who failed to pay.[68] There were other places in the early republic where it was difficult to get a secure claim to land. But here, the problem was endemic.[69]

* * *

BUT, FOR NOW, the sun shone on Beaver Creek. The war was in the past, a fading memory. Wiley's land appeared secure. There was no telling when a stranger might come knocking, waving a deed that overlapped with Wiley's. But that was the bargain everyone made, living here.

The two brothers seemed to be entering a new phase of life. That September, Micajah got married, too. ("*A good wife & health / Is a man's best wealth*," counseled *The Lover's Almanac*.)[70] He may have met his wife, Susana Roberts, when the brothers moved onto Beaver Creek. (Nothing suggests that Micajah owned any land; he was likely living in his brother's house.) Little is known about Susana's family, though she is usually described as a simple girl of presumably little means. But Micajah's new father-in-law must have approved of the match. He witnessed the marriage bond.[71] John Roberts was present again when Micajah and Susana went to a justice of the peace and asked him to marry them. "There was an old man in the company that came along," the justice of the peace's son remembered.

It was a hopeful time. They were in good spirits. They laughed and celebrated in the warm September light. John Roberts sang a tune with a memorable chorus:

There is no land, you understand
Like the Bend of the Tennessee.[72]

Both couples went to housekeeping. They ate boiled cabbage and smoked meat, fried in a pan. They slept on straw beds in a house that smelled of damp earth. They lived quietly.[73] Not far away, the creek slunk by, day and night, its waters tranquil and low.

* * *

THEN THE TROOPS CAME.

That fall, as the air tightened with a chill, the hills around the Harps' house began to fill with people. They came in clumps, squatting. First a few. Then more. Almost overnight, there were hundreds, then thousands—babies, toddlers, whole families. They camped on the ridges, in the orchards, at the edges of creeks. They seemed to have nothing; some could barely eat. They did not belong, that was plain enough. But where they were coming from was not clear at first. Soon, though, the Harps must have understood.

They were coming from the west, across the Clinch River. They were not Cherokees. But they were coming from Cherokee country.

CHAPTER 2

UNREST

The President's House
Philadelphia, Pennsylvania
December 1797

The city was noisy. Even at night—even with the windows shuttered against the cold—it was loud. Street vendors wheeling their carts. Oystermen crying, *Oysters!* Watchmen shouting out the hour of the night. Horses cantering over cobblestones, and carriage wheels scraping the ice. It was difficult to sleep.[1]

John Adams awoke each morning in a house on Market Street. It was a pretty house, brick, three stories tall, with two pointy dormers poking skyward like raised eyebrows. It had an icehouse, a bathhouse, and stables. In the east yard, a garden bloomed. The house was older than the United States. During the war, a British general had lived in it, and it had been the toast of the town's loyalists, the scene of raucous balls and cockfights. Then it was bought by Robert Morris, a senator, who, when no other place could be found, offered it as the president's mansion. "It is the best they could get," George Washington wrote, dryly, in 1790.[2]

The president was greeted as he rose by the sights and sounds of a busy port. Only a few blocks away were the banks of the Delaware, where fishermen came ashore wheeling their catch to market, and ships docked and disgorged their barrels of stuff. The streets teemed. Chimneys pumped smoke into the air. Men scraped manure from the gutters below. Congress was convening. Politicians were rolling into town, jostled in their coaches.

On the morning of December 2, 1797, a bright Saturday, three men rapped on the door of the president's mansion. They were congressmen representing Tennessee. One was a gangly young politician named Andrew Jackson, a newly elected senator.[3]

It was not every day that congressmen sought an audience with the president. No one in 1797 approached such a thing lightly—nor was anyone sure yet how to go about lobbying fellow politicians, let alone the president. The etiquette of politicking was hesitant. Highly aware that anything George Washington did would create a precedent, his close aide Alexander Hamilton had once suggested that the president should only meet with congressmen under highly scripted circumstances. "The door of access ought not to be too wide," Hamilton thought.[4]

But the Tennessee men were resolute. They had an urgent matter to address with the president on behalf of their constituents.

William L. Breton, "Residence of Washington in High Street, Philad.," in John Fanning Watson, *Annals of Philadelphia* (1830). Courtesy of the Library Company of Philadelphia.

Adams ushered them in.

One wonders what John Adams thought of the young, unvarnished Andrew Jackson. Tall—at six feet, he towered over Adams—and impassioned, with a shock of stiff hair and a gaunt, chiseled face, Jackson was just thirty years old. But he already bore the scars of a difficult life, some of them physical (an English soldier had cracked his skull when he was captured, at thirteen, during the Revolutionary War) and some psychological (he'd been orphaned, after a "brawling, defiant boyhood," at fifteen).[5] His emotions flared easily. "His passions are terrible," wrote Thomas Jefferson, who, as vice president, had watched Jackson sputter on the floor of Congress. "He could never speak on account of the rashness of his feelings. I have seen him attempt it repeatedly, and as often choke with rage."[6]

When Jackson was choking with rage, it was often over perceived slights to Tennessee. He had long ago soured on George Washington, who he felt had turned a blind eye as president while Cherokees made the Appalachian valleys run red with blood in the early 1790s.[7] Jackson never forgot. Thirty years later, as president himself, Andrew Jackson would stride into Congress and throw his terrible passions behind the Indian Removal Act. It was aimed, in part, at the excision of Cherokee Nation. He told the Cherokees that, for their own good, they would have to go. "Listen to me . . . ," he wrote to the tribe in 1835. "You cannot remain where you now are."[8] Jackson said he hoped their removal would be "voluntary."[9] But in the end, the army moved in. Thousands of Cherokees were removed forcibly from their homes by soldiers.[10]

But that was decades away.

Today, Jackson had come to the president's house to protest a very different thing: *Please*, he implored Adams. *Do not use the army against Tennesseans.*[11]

* * *

JOHN ADAMS WAS a miserable president. He complained, often. He was prone to fits of rage. His temper, Alexander Hamilton wrote, was "ungovernable."[12] He felt unwell. "I am Old—Old very Old and never Shall be very well—certainly while in this office," he wrote at one point.[13] His teeth ached. He had a palsy. His body had plenty of its own twinges and pains. The presidency only added to his afflictions.[14]

His presidency had begun inauspiciously, almost as soon as he arrived in Philadelphia. George Washington had not yet left the house on Market Street, so Adams took a room at an inn while the Washingtons tied up their affairs. When, at last, he moved into the president's residence, he found it was in bad shape. After the Washingtons left, the servants had gotten drunk and left everything a mess. Carpets, china, linens, curtains—all would have to be bought anew. "What a Scene!" he wrote to his wife, Abigail, then adding: "There is not a Chair fit to sit in."[15]

Abigail, too, found the presidency taxing. When she joined her husband in Philadelphia, she found she disliked it. She thought it every bit as "vile" and "debauched" a city as London.[16] It was also hot. "The whole city is like a Bake House," she wrote that first summer.[17] In the heat, she found it difficult to keep up her social duties, which were many. Washington had entertained as president. So the Adamses did, too. Abigail received guests for two or three hours each day. She hosted grand dinners and planned parties. It was exhausting.[18]

"The task of the President is very arduous . . . ," Abigail wrote shortly after arriving. "I do not wonder Washington wishd to retire from it."[19]

Adams's first year as president was, in many ways, bleak. His reasons to lie awake at night multiplied. As he came into office, America's brittle relationship with France, its longtime ally, cracked. Angered by American neutrality in its ongoing war with Britain,

France piled insults onto the United States, first by allowing French ships to plunder American vessels and then, in 1797, by refusing to receive the American minister in Paris.[20] All of it rankled Adams, deeply. "We are not a degraded people," he told Congress shortly after being elected.[21]

But things got no better as the presidency wore on. The nation roiled. It churned and lurched in a choppy sea of political dramas. The threat of war with France hung over everything for almost the

John Trumbull, *Portrait of John Adams* (1793). Harvard University Portrait Collection, Gift of Andrew Craigie to Harvard College, 1794. Courtesy of Harvard Art Museums.

entire time Adams was in office. Awkwardly, under his leadership, the United States stumbled into a kind of "half war" with France, pouring millions into readying itself—without actually declaring it. ("Folly & madness," thought one politician. "We are preparing for a war wh[ich] does not exist.")[22]

Taxmen, meanwhile, poured into every by-lane and alleyway. They sniffed at every windowsill. To pay for a ballooning army and navy, Congress passed a new tax that required the invasive appraisal of every piece of property in the United States, down to counting windowpanes. (Even Abigail Adams thought legislators could not have imagined the "trouble" such a thing would entail. To "measure every House Barn out House [and] count every square of Glass . . . is a Labour indeed," she wrote when assessors descended on her own house in Massachusetts.)[23] Such intrusions bred unrest. Would Americans tolerate "herds of collectors smelling into farm houses as well as grog shops?" asked one writer in the *New London Bee*.[24] Before Adams's term was out, a small rebellion blossomed just outside the capital. When taxmen arrived, Pennsylvanians threw hot water in their faces.[25]

National politics, too, grew poisonous. During George Washington's presidency, an opposition party (the "Republicans") had emerged, spawned by the venomous atmosphere within Washington's own cabinet, a regular sparring match in which Thomas Jefferson and Alexander Hamilton were "daily pitted . . . like two cocks," Jefferson wrote. (Stifled while in the cabinet, Jefferson had secretly worked behind the scenes to build an organized opposition, even launching a newspaper, *The National Gazette*—a mouthpiece for Republican views—whose editor he paid, rather brazenly, out of the State Department's budget.)[26]

By the time he took office, Adams faced an unabashedly partisan press. Hissing critiques, filling the pages of Republican newspapers, were delivered to his desk by the day. This barrage led to what remains the most notorious legislation of the Adams years. In a fever in the high summer of 1798, the Federalists in Congress passed the Alien and Sedition Acts, the latter of which—gleefully flouting the First Amendment—made it a crime to write or even speak critically about the government. Adams defended it as a "war measure." But it was an obvious move to silence Republicans. Thomas Jefferson thought the Sedition Act was "so palpably in the teeth of the constitution" as to prove that Federalists had "no respect" for it.[27]

Adams later distanced himself from it. "I recommended no such thing," he wrote much later, though he admitted, "I knew there was need enough . . . and therefore I consented."[28] Of those prosecuted for violating the Sedition Act (before it expired in 1801), almost all were Republican newspapermen. (One, however, was the poor driver of a garbage scow, Luther Baldwin, who was drinking with friends when he heard John Adams being saluted with cannon fire as Adams rode through New Jersey. One of his companions joked, "There goes the President and they are firing at his a—." Baldwin replied: "I do not care if they fire *thro'* his arse!")[29]

The Adams presidency, in short, bloomed with disasters. "From every side we are in Danger," Abigail wrote. "We are in Perils by Land, and we are in Perils by sea; and in Perils from false Breathern."[30]

One episode, though, has escaped notice. It is missing from nearly every book about his presidency.[31] It is also absent from every narrative about the Harps, though it touched Wiley's life very closely. This was what brought Andrew Jackson to the president's doorstep: John Adams was not destined to use the army against French soldiers. But in 1797, he did use it against Tennesseans. In an attempt to protect Cherokees from the incursions of white settlers, Adams raised troops and prepared to send them right into Wiley Harp's backyard.

It was the first shoe to drop in Wiley's year of misfortunes.

* * *

THE HARPS LIVED a breath away from Cherokee lands. They had only to row down Beaver Creek and across the Clinch River to get there.

Gazing westward from Wiley Harp's cabin, you saw the hills of Cherokee country. As Sally Harp hung up her coats and gowns at night, she watched the sun set on Cherokee land.[32] In Wiley's neighborhood, people fished in Cherokee streams. They hunted in Cherokee fields. They sent their cattle and horses to range in Cherokee woods. All of this was illegal, but they did it anyway. They poached things when it suited them.

Where there is now a patchwork of sleepy Knoxville suburbs punctuated by golf clubs and Walmarts and hardware stores, Cherokee country in these years was a lush, green place broken by sharp ridges and deep valleys and creek beds full of tumbled stones. There were pine stands, hickories, black oaks, and tall poplars. There were high grasses and low grapevines. The paths were mostly narrow, wide enough for a horse. If you pulled up the sourwood or the grass beneath your feet, you would find thick black soil with limestone below.[33]

Ten or fifteen thousand Cherokees lived here amid the smoky blue peaks. Dozens of Cherokee towns—each buzzing with roughly three hundred people—studded the riverbanks. Snug up against East Tennessee, Cherokee territory stretched hundreds of miles to the west, raced up into present-day Kentucky, and swung low, on its southern side, into lands later claimed by Georgia and Alabama. These homelands had already been shrunk by a parade of treaties. But Cherokee people had been living here, in the nooks of the Great Smokies, as long as anyone knew.[34]

It was not quite "Cherokee Nation," though some called it that.

It was more of a loose confederation of towns, each with its own leader, some more belligerent than others. Not unlike the new United States, Cherokee country was weathering its own bumpy process of state-building and metamorphosis. Decades later, in the 1820s, the Cherokees would pen their own national constitution and elect a "principal chief," a Cherokee president of sorts. They would invent their own written language and publish a newspaper, *The Cherokee Phoenix*. But as of yet, Cherokees had none of those things. Towns went their own way, sometimes dramatically. "Sometimes part of the tribe was at war," one historian writes, "while part was not."[35]

In 1797, the Cherokees were in something of a state of disarray. During the Revolution, almost all Cherokee towns had sided with the king. After the war when Americans claimed the tribe was "defeated" (though Cherokee leaders, frozen out of treaty negotiations, objected), they lost tens of thousands of acres. Some of the most important Cherokee towns were given up to Americans. Thousands of people were left without homes, forced westward into new territory. Some of them, displaced and angry, kept up the violence long after the Revolution ended. The war, in many ways, roared on. "The Revolutionary War in the Western Country," wrote one migrant, "did not close before the year of [1795]."[36]

Although some of that upheaval was subsiding, Cherokee life was changing rapidly. Riding through Cherokee country in 1797, you might see fields of cotton. You might see log houses, just like Wiley Harp's, with axes perched on porches and spinning wheels inside. In their gardens, Cherokees grew watermelons, apples, plums, and peaches. Some Cherokee women cooked pork and beef, churned butter, and made cheese.[37] A few wealthy Cherokees had even begun to build plantations, though they were a very new thing. "He owns a large plantation," a visitor wrote about the Cherokee leader James

Vann in 1799. But it was new and rough: The "fields are still full of dead trees."[38]

In the fields and along the pathways snaking through Cherokee country you might encounter slaves. James Vann's slaves come through as vivid characters in surviving records. Isaac played the fiddle and knew hymns. He taught the Cherokee language to Brother Byhan, a Moravian missionary. Ned, who could read, kept a little pamphlet addressed to the "Christian Negroes of Virginia." Some yearned to hear the gospel. "I talked with old July and his wife early in the morning about Jesus' suffering," Brother Steiner wrote in 1801. In return, they gave him bread, milk, cooked corn, and catfish. They served him sunfish from a creek that flowed into the Chickamauga. The missionaries also preached to Vann's slaves, perhaps at his urging, about the "necessity of yielding ourselves to become the property of the Saviour."[39]

It was an odd moment in Cherokee history, a kind of in-between time. Historians have sometimes imagined it as a nadir, one of the lowest points in Cherokee life. But it was also a pivot. Some of the changes unfolding in 1797 reached back nearly a century to the arrival of the first fur traders. For generations, traders had been marrying Cherokee women, knitting their traditions into Cherokee families. In recent years, the United States government, too, had been hurrying Cherokees down new roads. Under President Washington, the government began a program to "civilize" Indians. Agents rushed into Indian country bearing plows, looms, and cotton cards.[40]

What Wiley thought about living so close to Cherokee Nation is hard to say. Among his ilk, loathing of Cherokees ran deep. "Many of the whites are disorderly & licentious and would be very glad to seek an opportunity of kicking up a dust with the Indians," one visitor wrote.[41] "They all hate the Indians," another echoed.[42] But for some others, Cherokee country possessed a strange magnetism. Some of the Harps' neighbors were unsavory characters who took advantage of the unpoliced border. One of the "cut-throats" who had drifted into the Cherokee orbit, for instance, was John Rogers, a former loyalist raider. One government agent called Rogers a "Villain," "one of the greatest Rascalls [the Cherokees] ever cherished amongst them." In later years, Rogers became quite important to the tribe. He would be selected in 1808 as an ambassador to the United States. But in 1797, he was allegedly a cattle thief. He also ran the ferry on behalf of the Cherokees, a stone's throw from Wiley Harp's house.[43]

There was a certain class of opportunistic white men—a flotsam and jetsam of ne'er-do-wells and petty traders and price gougers—who hovered close to Cherokee country for their own purposes. Some were looking for easy sales. (One Cherokee woman, hard-pressed, forked over several pounds of chestnuts in return for a "used petticoat.") Anyone who wanted to trade with Indians was supposed to be licensed by the United States. But many weren't. "There are Numbers of white people in the nation," one man wrote, "who . . . Carry on a Triffling Commerce with [Cherokees]" but were uninterested in "any further . . . understanding between whites and Indians."[44] There is some possibility that the Harps belonged to this crowd, engaged in "Triffling" trade with Cherokees.[45]

As Wiley alighted on Beaver Creek, the federal government was trying to curb some of this illicit dealing. It was building public trading posts called "factories," where Native people could bring in their pelts and, in turn, purchase goods "at lower prices than those charged by private traders." (One was at Southwest Point, near Sally Harp's father's house outside Knoxville.) Factories, it was hoped, would not only reel Indians into a financial relationship with the United States but also tamp down on bad feelings and frontier scrapes by "driv[ing] unscrupulous private peddlers . . . out of business."[46]

When the people came pouring back over the Clinch River in 1797—a kind of reverse migration, out of Cherokee territory—that, too, was the work of the federal government. Though Wiley Harp probably did not know it, not right away.

* * *

ABOUT A YEAR before Adams became president, while Washington was still in office, the federal government had discovered—an unwelcome surprise—that there were American settlers living on Cherokee land. Hordes of them, well beyond the treaty line. George Washington took this news with "great uneasiness." Intruders on Cherokee land threatened to provoke "very serious consequences," putting at risk the very "peace of that Country and the Union," as one cabinet member put it.[47]

Squatters settled much of the American West. From its earliest days, the American government struggled to keep illegal settlers from sprinting beyond the nation's formal bounds and simply taking up residence. (George Washington himself once confessed that he thought "[no]thing short of a Chinese Wall" could stop this.)[48] In 1785, for instance, Ensign John Armstrong had found thousands of people living, with no claims, on federal land beyond the Ohio River. He put up notices warning people off, but they still came. Soldiers burned the squatters' homes. They arrested people. But after Armstrong's men left, the settlers rebuilt.[49]

About five hundred families, reportedly, had set roots inside Cherokee boundaries. Some had been there for a very long time, claiming rights descended from North Carolina (which had, years earlier, madly promised away untold acres to its west). But new hopefuls were arriving all the time, "the number of Intruders on

Indian land daily increasing."[50] The shores of the Little Tennessee were infested with white squatters, many of them "raising vast herds of cattle."[51] Federal laws forbade Americans from crossing the boundary to graze cattle, or even to hunt wild animals. You could be heavily fined or imprisoned.[52] None of that seemed to bother Tennesseans, who were brazenly building cabins, fencing corn, and driving horses on Indian land.

Washington wanted them out—immediately. "Dislodge them," snarled James McHenry, Washington's secretary of war, in a letter to John Sevier, Tennessee's governor. "The President expects that you will bring into action all the means in your power." Sevier was warned in no uncertain terms: If he failed to shoo these people off, then the president would "resort to military force."[53]

Washington's haste to remove these settlers may seem, at first, surprising. Looking backward through the rest of American history—decades in which millions of Indians were chased from their homelands, penned into barren, wind-swept reserves, and hustled into selling land—makes it hard to grasp Washington's thinking. But in the 1790s, the United States was in a very different position. It was not yet the juggernaut that would send countless armies bearing repeating rifles against the tribes of the Great Plains.

Washington was worried, first and foremost, about war. He knew this was a powder keg, poised to spark. "He views their intrusion as a sure prelude to hostilities," the secretary of war confessed.[54]

By 1796, Washington had no more appetite for hostilities. Federal armies, under his orders, had already fought grueling wars against Native peoples. As president, he had sent thousands of American soldiers to their deaths in the Ohio country and spent millions of dollars—all to crush a Native confederacy that stubbornly kept killing settlers who wandered into Indian country and squatted. (Along the way, the U.S. Army had experienced some of the worst defeats in its history, including an embarrassing calamity in November 1791 in which 630 soldiers died and three hundred more were wounded. Hemmed in by Native fighters, soldiers had fled, willy-nilly. "The whole Army Ran together like a mob at a fair," one colonel wrote.)[55]

These are not the stories Americans choose to remember. But during Washington's presidency, confidence withered—and coffers were drained. Coming out of its own War for Independence, the United States had been cocky. (As one historian puts it: "The patriots had just defeated the most powerful country on earth; if necessary could they not turn around and score a similar success against Indians?")[56] But then it was humbled, repeatedly, by Native people, shedding American blood. The government had been cowed, slightly, into a more cautious, pacifying stance.[57] It wasn't that George Washington wanted to prevent westward expansion. Far from it—he himself had dabbled, enthusiastically, in speculating. But he and his cabinet needed it to be orderly. If Americans settled neatly and obeyed the law, then the purchase and transfer of Native lands into American hands could happen peacefully, without costly and harrowing wars.[58]

If war erupted, it might suck in not only the Cherokees (formidable in themselves), but others as well—the Spanish, the British, other tribes, all waiting to pounce. As if to illustrate this threat, a sitting senator from Tennessee, William Blount, was at this very moment (though Washington didn't know it yet) engaged in a brazen scheme to enrich himself by secretly plotting, with some Cherokee assistance, to join Great Britain in attacking Spanish territories—for his own gain, rather than the United States'. His treachery went public in July 1797 when an intercepted letter, outlining the plot, was read openly in the Senate. ("When you have read this letter over three times," Blount had written to a co-conspirator, "then burn it.")[59]

Meanwhile, Congress investigated the newly discovered settlers.

How on earth had thousands of people—some with legitimate land claims—ended up living inside the Cherokee border?[60]

One problem was this: The line had never been marked on the ground. Head-scratching Tennesseans claimed to wonder, honestly, where it was located. The Cherokee–United States border was described in the Treaty of Holston in 1791, and allegedly everyone knew where it lay. But six years later, it had never actually been surveyed. In the spring of 1797, after the federal government became aware of the intruding settlers, it frantically sent a surveying team—led by Benjamin Hawkins, George Washington's newly anointed superintendent of Indian affairs—to run the line.[61]

Hawkins's alarm soared as he trudged through the Tennessee hills. He was confronted by a "holy pack of insurgents." He had run-ins with people—"brutes," as they were dubbed by a friend of his—who hissed at him for spoiling their property claims. They called him a liar. They told him he was wrong about the line's whereabouts. Hawkins, in turn, gave them no comfort. When some asked whether they would be allowed to keep their crops if they were found to be growing on the wrong side of the line, he answered stiffly: "No indulgence ought to be expected."[62]

Hawkins had no sympathy for those he found living over the boundary. He saw them as "victims of their own folly." Worse, he saw them as evil, lawless—symptomatic of Tennessee's cancer of disorder. "A *something* crept into the State of Tennessee, which leaped over the bounds of decency and law," he shuddered to a friend. ". . . It had already taken such a growth when I arrived there as to be alarming in a high degree."[63]

Many Cherokees agreed: These valleys and streams belonged to them. "We are the first people that ever lived in this land," Old Tassel had once said. "It is ours."[64] Cherokees lived cheek by jowl with Tennesseans; they drank at the same pothouses, rented out horses to needy farmers, and collected toll money from them at the ferries.

But tolerating intruders was another matter. "There are land speculators among you who say that we want to sell our land when we do not," Doublehead protested in 1801.[65] After inking treaties with the United States, Cherokees expected the federal government to keep its promises.

"His word should remain," one Cherokee spokesman said about George Washington.[66] But when Washington left office, it fell to John Adams.

* * *

ADAMS SENT FEDERAL troops.[67] They arrived in the summer and fall of 1797. If Sally Harp went to town to buy soap or tea at King & Crozier's grocery, she likely saw soldiers in the streets of Knoxville—throngs of them.

They were not friendly. In a circular that was passed from hand to hand and house to house, the soldiers announced their presence: We don't doubt, it notified the intruding settlers, that "in a given time you will remove to that side of the line to which we have a just claim." Mostly, the tone of this handbill was conciliatory. But it was also threatening. "How much better it is," it advised the people, "to observe a strict obedience to the laws, than . . . to involve your fellow-citizens in the tumults of anarchy, and probably in the horrors of war."[68]

Tennesseans hated the soldiers. The people gave him hell, said Colonel Thomas Butler. ("You can have no Idea," he told a friend.)[69] One observer—whose brother had claims in the disputed territory—thought the hated soldiers were "held more generally in Contempt by the Citizens than ever I saw."[70] The secretary of war suspected that local people tried deliberately "to create difficulties to the removal of the settlers."[71] He was right: One landlord "ordered tenants on his own land in the disputed area not to move off," and openly railed against the invading "*Military Gentry.*"[72]

In the fall, as corn ripened and harvest-time neared, troops swept the farms. They burned cabins. Families were sent fleeing. Many simply "encamped in the woods" just over the Tennessee line. The ridges took on the character of refugee camps. "They were scattered over a rising ground," wrote a visitor who passed through the encampments. ". . . They seemed to lament their situation, in being deprived of going to settle the land which they had justly and fairly bought." Some were belligerent. Some, even, were "prepared to defend themselves against the soldiery with the point of the sword."[73]

Editorials ran in the *Knoxville Gazette:*

"Legislators of the great American Republic!" one cried. "Is it nothing to you to see our wives and children . . . beggared by your unconstitutional laws? . . . Do you feel no remorse at our impending ruin? Are you callous to our sufferings? Accustomed to wallow in luxury, you cannot feel for the distresses of the poor."[74]

Months passed. No one knew who might be next. As many as three thousand people were chased off their farms by soldiers.[75] "The people on what is called the indian lands, appear to be in great distress," Governor John Sevier wrote breathlessly in November. "Some have removed, and others have not, and say they will not, and again others that did remove, have returned, what will be the consequence I am not able to foretel, but I really fear the event."[76]

Wiley Harp left behind no letters. He kept no diary. No scrap proves what he thought about any of this. But he cannot have missed it: the soldiers—twelve hundred of them—camped just outside of Knoxville. They drilled and drummed and played military songs. They set fires. Meanwhile, the hills around Knoxville hummed and seethed. As Wiley Harp went about establishing his household, President Adams's decision to send troops to East Tennessee was what everyone here was talking about. "This was the bone of contention," one man wrote, "which was the subject of conversation in every place I went into."[77]

Everywhere Wiley Harp looked, he saw the cruel, quaking uncertainty of property. How quickly things could be taken away, lost. Not even the ground beneath your feet was fixed. There were no guarantees in this world, only risks and gambits and hope.

* * *

THAT LESSON, IN fact, soon struck very close to home. Although the moment has to be imagined (no narrative captures it), it must have gone something like this: One day that fall, Sally Harp's father heard a knock at his door. Frosts had set in, leaves stirred on the ground. "Hard frost at night which killed vines in the garden," the governor noted in his diary.[78]

John Rice lived on East Tennessee's western edge. His home stood on the Tennessee River, where the river curved south like a quivering smile. It was not far from Knoxville, only a boat ride from his daughter's new home. But it was the very edge of the United States. Not far off, he could hear the sounds of men felling trees, sawing wood, and hammering as they turned the blockhouse at Southwest Point into a federal fort.[79]

Standing before Rice when he opened the door were soldiers. He had built his house illegally, they said. This little bend of the Tennessee, the soldiers informed him, did not belong to him. It belonged to the Cherokees.[80]

* * *

NOW A FUSE began to burn. Without doubt, this was a shattering event. It was the president's dart landing right in the heart of the Harp family. Wiley and Sally had only just been married. Now her father was in serious trouble. Quite possibly, he was among those violently ejected by Colonel Butler's men. If Wiley had expected his new father-in-law to provide some ballast as the newlyweds entered family life, this new misfortune now shook the whole family.

Beyond Micajah, Wiley Harp had little family of his own. By hitching himself to Sally's kin, he likely hoped to marry into security. In the backcountry, this was something of a tradition—pulling oneself up not by bootstraps but by taking a wife. Many a young man hoped to collect a generous "marriage portion" from his wife's father.[81] "For the young man of little means," one historian writes, "the choice of marriage partner was a strategic one."[82] Winning the heart of the right woman brought access to the sorts of things needed to become independent. To send their daughters into good married lives, fathers-in-law sometimes gave land. They gave loans. Even the poorer sort might give a cow or two. When Polly Finley wed David Crockett (the congressman and folk hero who lit up Tennessee a generation later), her father gave cattle. It wasn't much, but with that modest start, Crockett rented a "small farm and cabin" and hoisted his beaming bride over the threshold.[83]

Nothing proves that any real money changed hands when Wiley and Sally were married. But one senses that their match had this essence to it. Wiley bought his land from a man named "John Rice"—almost certainly Sally's father. They might have arrived at some sort of favorable arrangement through which Wiley was to pay for it. Wiley very likely saw the Rices as a stepping stone to a more respectable life. ("I think he was buying *her*," one historian told me, pondering this set of circumstances.)[84] Once it was revealed that John Rice's own property was in jeopardy, however, that prospect evaporated, quickly.

It is impossible to tell exactly what happened to Rice. Nothing hints at where he went. Was he escorted off his property by soldiers? Did they block him from harvesting his crops? Plenty went hungry that year. Others were arrested while attempting to sneak back onto their farms. (One man who was evicted suspected the government of trying to "starve me and my family.")[85] The extent of his misfortunes can only be guessed, but when the troops came, there is no doubt: John Rice faced expulsion.

Now—right about here—Wiley's life began to shift. "The President actually sent a detachment of the army into the country," one man wrote, gobsmacked.[86] Wiley, too, must have felt a certain disbelief. Clouds had rolled in, darkening his prospects. This was a bad turn in his life, a tilt in his fortunes, a rug pulled, and the hardship was more than imaginary. Whatever happened precisely, Rice did not suffer alone; Wiley suffered, too. The proof of that survives even now—one stark, enduring clue that hints at the Harp family's distress. And it has been there all along, tucked away unnoticed in a box of the governor's papers, overlooked, apparently, by anyone writing about the Harps.

One day, deep into the crisis, Governor Sevier pawed through piles of petitions, stacked high in his Knoxville office. A blustery frontiersman with sharp blue eyes and a flushed complexion, Sevier was one of those men around whom early western history spun. He had made his bones, years earlier, by fighting Cherokees, marching seething bands of militiamen into their villages, guns blazing. Fancying himself "judge and jury as to the need of an Indian campaign," as one historian described, he did not wait to get approval from his superiors. "When he felt that the Cherokees needed chastising, he called out his men and chastised them."[87]

Sevier rarely shied from locking horns. In 1803, he came within moments of dueling with Andrew Jackson. (A shooting was averted only when he and Jackson began screaming at each other so loudly that Sevier's horse ran off—with his guns.)[88] He had defied orders from higher-ups in the past when it came to Cherokee land. When Old Tassel complained in the 1780s that Carolinians were trickling into Cherokee territory, the governor of North Carolina had ordered Sevier—then a militia leader—to sweep them out. "Pull down their cabbins and remove them, paying no attention to their entreatys," came the order. Sevier plainly ignored it.[89]

But he had behaved differently this time.

Almost uncharacteristically—perhaps because he was chilled by the thought of an American army descending, with bayonets gleaming, on his own constituents—he had tried, at first, to enforce President Adams's wishes. He warned the intruding settlers to remove. He made proclamations. He wrote to them several times and urged them to comply. "However well persuaded I am that many of you have resided a number of years on your present plantations, and agreeably to the laws," he told them in August 1797, they would have to go. A federal reckoning was coming, like it or not.[90] But, as days ticked by, Sevier wavered. He saw people suffering. He became defiant.

After months of harrowing pleas, Sevier sat down at his desk. No longer would he allow the federal government to bully his people. He began writing "passports"—permits of sorts that allowed the expelled settlers to enter back into Cherokee country. These were not meant to give permanent blessings to return. They were just temporary little slips, permitting displaced Tennesseans to trudge across the border and attend to their property. It was all Sevier could think to do. But for those evicted, it was a small lifeline.

Among them was a passport for John Rice and Wiley Harp.

* * *

I HAD SUSPECTED for a very long time that Wiley was knocked back on his heels, somehow, by this crisis. The passport is proof. When I found it, it hit me like a jolt.

The passport names Wiley, John Rice, and three other men. They must have petitioned the governor together to ask for such a permit. (The petition is lost.) Carrying it, Wiley and the others were to be allowed to "pass & repass over the boundary line between U.S. & C.N. [Cherokee Nation]." They could pass for two reasons—to "remov[e] property from Indian lands" and "to take care of grain now growing."[91]

That Wiley's name appears is, at first, curious. His own land on Beaver Creek was on the right side of the border. Why, then, was he included? There are only a few possibilities, all of them ominous.

One is that he had been drawn into the spiral that was sucking down Sally's father. The passport signals, at the very least, that John Rice's problems had metastasized, spreading to his son-in-

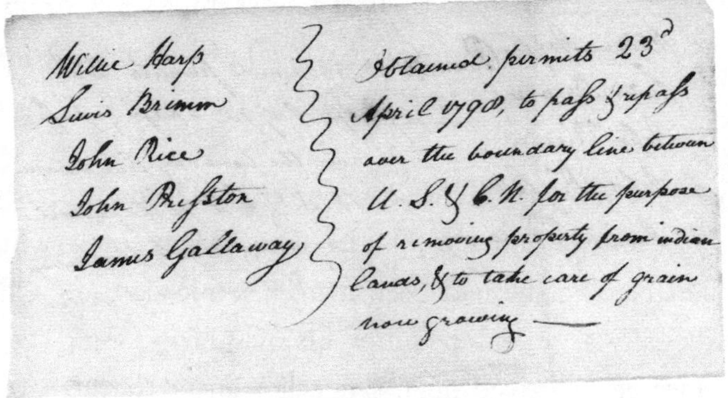

Willie Harp
Lewis Brimm
John Rice
John Preston
James Gallaway

[illegible] permits 23d April 1798, to pass & repass over the boundary line between U.S. & C.N. for the purpose of removing property from indian lands, & to take care of grain now growing —

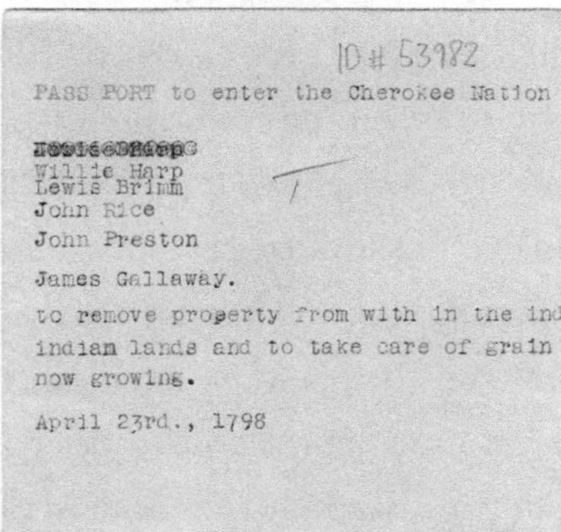

ID # 53982

PASS PORT to enter the Cherokee Nation

Willie Harp
Lewis Brimm
John Rice
John Preston
James Gallaway.

to remove property from with in the ind indian lands and to take care of grain now growing.

April 23rd., 1798

A passport granting Wiley Harp and others permission to cross into Cherokee Nation. Courtesy of Tennessee State Library and Archives.

law. Being ejected from his land would have jeopardized Rice's whole livelihood. Although Rice was by all indications a man of means, missing even one harvest could yank a farmer into debt irreversibly. Rice might have pulled Wiley in to rescue whatever corn or livestock he could salvage from inside Cherokee Nation. He might have gone to live with Sally and Wiley, a new burden. He might have strained Wiley's own resources as a new householder in ways we cannot see.

But it is much more likely that Wiley's own property was threatened. Had he been told—wrongly—that his land was in jeopardy? Some evidence suggests that Benjamin Hawkins's first survey was wrong—or, at least, disputed. "It is almost impossible to know exactly where a line (drawn only upon paper) will actually strike when it comes to be measured," one man wrote.[92] Was Wiley warned off before the final survey?

Or, was the property he wanted to retrieve "from Indian lands" on four legs? Given how close he lived to Indian country, it is entirely plausible that he had been using the meadows of Cherokee Nation illegally as an extension of his own farm. Some settlers in East Tennessee practiced open-range herding—they treated "the unclaimed woods" (including those belonging to the Cherokees) as a commons on which to range stock.[93] Had Wiley loosed his cattle across the river, only to be cut off from them—and the hundreds of dollars they were worth—when troops arrived?[94]

One final, explosive possibility remains: Had Wiley Harp been squatting inside Cherokee Nation until recently—before buying his own parcel? The clues on the passport itself tilt heavily toward that scenario. All the other men named on the passport were John Rice's close neighbors. They all lived on the same little river bend.[95] Had Wiley been living there, too, before taking Sally to Beaver Creek? Had he hastily left behind his own possessions or cattle just as John

Adams's soldiers began drumming people out? Had he bought the land on Beaver Creek just in time to escape a violent eviction?[96]

No matter what was unfolding, the passport captures the family's desperation. They would not have written to the governor unless they faced grave troubles. If, for Wiley himself, this was not a fatal blow, it undoubtedly sent his household reeling. The timing of the expulsions was pinching and cruel. They happened at harvest-time. Wiley and Sally had only just moved onto Beaver Creek. They could not have had a full crop of their own that year. They may have hoped to rely on her father for help or on whatever land Wiley had been sowing before this. But once the troops came, all of that disappeared.

Governor Sevier hoped to give some small relief. But it's unclear whether John Rice or Wiley Harp ever laid eyes on their passport or even knew of it.

The passports were no magic cure. The federal government blithely ignored them. However many passports he might like to scribble out, John Sevier would not be allowed to override the president's orders. Two days after the governor scratched Wiley's name onto a pass, soldiers effectively canceled it: Colonel Butler sent dragoons back into the disputed lands. He gave them orders to remove everyone who was found "cultivating or otherwise laboring on the Cherokee lands"—whether or not they had passports.[97]

People came to blows. The displaced settlers wounded a soldier. They shot horses. Some were sent to jail in Knoxville.[98] Under cover of darkness one night, federal troops burst into a man's home and arrested him. When the troops took possession of a bluff on the Tennessee River inside Cherokee bounds, a party of 150 "Indians"—or were they?—appeared, their faces "blacked," to express their dismay. "It appears that the Indians can no more comprehend than the citizens," the *Kentucky Gazette* reported, wryly, "by what authority the troops of the United States take possession of their lands."[99] If the Harp brothers took part in these scuffles, we can't know.

But now, Wiley's life had begun to fray.

* * *

HE DRANK. HE GAMBLED.

The devil, that old resident of Knoxville, began to make Wiley Harp his friend. And Micajah, too. The brothers went into town often, "drinking & carousing & gambling." As one acquaintance remembered it, they "resorted to low places, & with dissolute unprincipled men." Grog shops, quarter races, card games.[100] They associated with "loose individuals" and lazy, "helpless *nobodies*" who scorned the law.[101]

Just when did Wiley Harp begin to go sideways? The problem is, it's hard to tell. East Tennessee was a wild place—a place that turned men mad. But it is difficult to rule out the possibility that he might have arrived here already somewhat sour.

Soon, there were whispers that the Harps were thieves. One man swore they had arrived in Knox County with a stolen horse. They sold cattle and hogs to the butcher in Knoxville; some thought they had stolen the animals from their neighbors. But what looked like "all kinds of roguery," in retrospect, may simply have been evidence of Wiley Harp's new struggle to stay afloat.[102]

CHAPTER 3

THE QUARTER RACE

Outside Knoxville
East Tennessee
Late 1798

One morning in 1798, Edward Teele, who lived about a mile from Knoxville, went out to his stables and found a nasty surprise. All of his horses were gone.

Around him, beyond the barnyard, was a maze of crouched hillocks and soaring ridges. In the distance swelled "a green ocean of mountains," rising in "tremendous billows." Mists clung to the hilltops.[1] Down below was a warren of nooks and caves and hidden little dells, an endless labyrinth that would have to be searched. But as he scanned the countryside, a suspicion about the horses' whereabouts crept into his mind.

If you lived along the edges of Cherokee country, it was not unusual to discover that your horses were missing. Horses here had a way of disappearing. They vanished like ghosts, evaporating, improbably, into the Appalachian night. Cherokee men often were the culprits. In the late 1790s, gangs of Cherokee horse thieves, or "pony clubs," were emerging, bedeviling authorities. Old ways were eroding, and stealing horses proved manhood, just as war and hunting once had.[2]

It was this headache, more than all the others, about which federal Indian agents complained. Vanishing horses were "the Chief complaint of the People against the Indians," one agent moaned. ". . . It is apart of the Indian Business that gives me more trouble than all the rest."[3] So many stolen horses flowed into Cherokee country that federal agents occasionally sent men to collect them. (This seldom worked: "I believe but few will ever be returned," he reported.)[4] Thefts exasperated lawmen. "What in the name of reason do they want?" the agent wrote about the Cherokees. "If horses," then why not just breed them?[5]

But Cherokee men were not alone in rustling horses. American men, too—sometimes with the assistance of Cherokee partners—snuck horses through the glades and grottoes of Cherokee Nation. It was easy enough to steal a horse in Tennessee, bring it into Cherokee country, and then, in turn, sell it to some unsuspecting Georgian—or the reverse. "The number of horses carried thro' and into this country is almost incredible," wrote another agent in 1807. They came from all directions: "from Georgia, both the Carolinas, and Kentucky."[6]

It was easy money, like grabbing baubles from a jewelry box. But this was no petty theft. What made it so seductive for thieves also made it catastrophic for victims: Horses, in this world, were wealth. Some men in East Tennessee held nearly all their wealth in horses, even if they owned little else.[7] A good horse could fetch hundreds of dollars. In fact, horses—although snorting and alive, heaving flesh and blood and breath and hooves—*were* dollars: "A considerable part of the land purchased in this country is paid for in horses," one man wrote. "They serve as a kind of currency for this purpose all over this western country."[8]

But horses, as much as land, were precarious. They ran away. They died. Or worse, they were stolen. For so much wealth to be held in moveable property—with the risk of it cantering away overnight—was dangerous. It bred uncertainty, volatility. It was for good reason that horse stealing in these years was a capital crime.

When he found his barn empty, Edward Teele did not suspect the Cherokees. He suspected the Harps.

Maybe he knew that Wiley was in trouble, or maybe he had heard, as others did, that the brothers had already stolen their neighbors' hogs and sheep. Or maybe he'd had some prior squabble with them. (Teele, who "carried the mail," had worked as a courier for the War Department even as it was expelling settlers from Cherokee land.)[9] He rounded up a few other men. Then, he went looking for Wiley Harp.

No one was home at the Harp house. So Teele and his men searched the yard and the woods. Nearby, they found a place where some horses had been tied up and, beside it, a trail. Horses' hooves bite into the ground as they walk; Teele's posse followed a broken path of crushed grass and peavine leading across the Clinch River. They passed into Cherokee country.

In a cavern in some gulch of the Cumberlands, there were the horses. And there, too, were the Harp brothers.[10]

Teele took back his horses. He tried to take the Harps, too, but somewhere between the Clinch and Knoxville, they broke away and ran.

* * *

FOR A GOOD WHILE—perhaps a year or so after moving onto Beaver Creek—the Harps lived very quietly. "They planted and cultivated a crop . . . and lived in peace and friendship with their neighbors," one Tennessean recalled.[11]

If we could peer into the Harps' cabin during that first year, many of the scenes might look very plain, like any family's chores. "What is there to be sowed," a farmer asked himself each morning, or "to be hoed"?[12] For the year 1798, the *Kentucky Almanac* foresaw "warm sunshine," then June rains, threatening haying. "Cool winds" would dry the corn in October.[13] Autumn, meanwhile, was killing season. Men prowled into the forest, where their hogs foraged freely, and rounded them up. Then they were slaughtered and bled, so the pork could be preserved for the coming year.[14] Sally would pack pieces of meat in salt to be cured. Wiley, later in the season, would hang them in the smokehouse and kindle a "small, smoldering fire" to burn beneath.[15]

But inside the walls of the Harp house, all was not well. As 1798 dawned and hearths were stoked against the new year's chill, nothing was settled at the border. Federal troops continued to chase people from their farms. They arrested people. They toppled fences and left behind charred log piles, where houses had once stood. "The troops has had a leborius time this Winter in moving the settlers," one soldier wrote that January.[16] Cut off from everything inside Cherokee country, both Wiley and his father-in-law might have fallen very short on that year's harvest or lost money on the animals they had been herding.

But that was not all. If the family was pinched by the troops' arrival, their troubles had just begun. Other difficulties followed: a brisk cascade of dominoes knocked. From the outside, the Harps might have seemed to be living in "peace" as the wheel of the year turned in 1798. But, in fact, the opposite was true: Things were rapidly coming apart. Tempers ran hot. Money ran short. In the months leading up to Edward Teele's discovery of Wiley and Micajah's theft, pressures piled up like a heavy snow on the cabin's roof. Wiley must have lain awake at night, as if listening to the joists creaking above his head.

This part of the Harps' story has long been obscure. When James Hall introduced the two brothers to *The Port Folio*'s readership in the 1820s, he did not even mention Tennessee. He gave them no past at all. In his rendering, it was as if they fell from the sky, ready to wreak havoc. Other writers, too, have brushed past Beaver Creek, as if whatever happened here cannot have been very important. But it is a critical piece of the puzzle. Although the clues are not perfect—when you assemble them, it is sometimes difficult to know how one dot connects to the next—it is nonetheless starkly obvious that this part of their lives holds crucial answers.

To recover the Harps' experiences is to see the roots of violence here in new ways. The Harps lived in a violent world, in a distinctive place and time: There is no denying that the backcountry during their lifetimes was bloody. Of all the hard-knock places in the early United States, the western territories were especially brutal—a kingdom of devils. "I often pause and ask myself," one man confessed, writing about the Revolutionary backcountry, "whether men are not already devils, and this world a bit of hell set apart for their temporary residence."[17] Americans have sometimes imagined that the violence simply flourished naturally here, like an unruly tangle of wildflowers among the mountain hollows. But that is far too simple.

One of the ways to understand the volatility of East Tennessee in these years is to recognize the chronic insecurity of property, of all kinds. "Every man is for himself alone," someone once wrote about the West.[18] Each scrambled to get ahead, and he staked everything he had. But everything he owned could disappear, all at once. He might wake up and find his horses pilfered. Or that his land claim was fraudulent and worthless. Or that soldiers had come to whisk away his things and his wife and children. Like much of the young United States—even more so than other parts of the republic, in fact—it was a land of risk.

In the end, it wasn't a federal soldier knocking on his door. It wasn't land fraud that forever knocked Wiley for a loop, at least not directly. Those things mattered, deeply. But the final blow was a small piece of paper, just a little bit of script. Poking around in a box, in Knoxville, one day, I found it.

* * *

I WAS NOT expecting it. No previous history mentions it. But there it was, an astonishingly simple, if hidden, piece. Standing in the county archives, I plucked a jaundiced document out of a sleeve of court records. At the bottom, both Harp brothers had signed. My eyes jumped to the date: It was marked December 1797—not long after Wiley's move to Beaver Creek. I did not know, at first, what I was looking at or exactly what it meant. I didn't know it was the thing that threatened to unravel Wiley Harp's whole life.

In my hand was a promissory note—an IOU. In it, the Harps acknowledged their debt to a man named Joseph Carnes. They owed Carnes two hundred dollars, a hefty sum. They pledged in the note to pay him back, and quickly. "We or either of us do promise to pay," the note read. Carnes was to get his two hundred dollars' worth in horses—"one Two or three Horses," depending on their quality. By the terms of the agreement, the Harps were to pay Carnes within a fortnight—two weeks. It was December 7.[19]

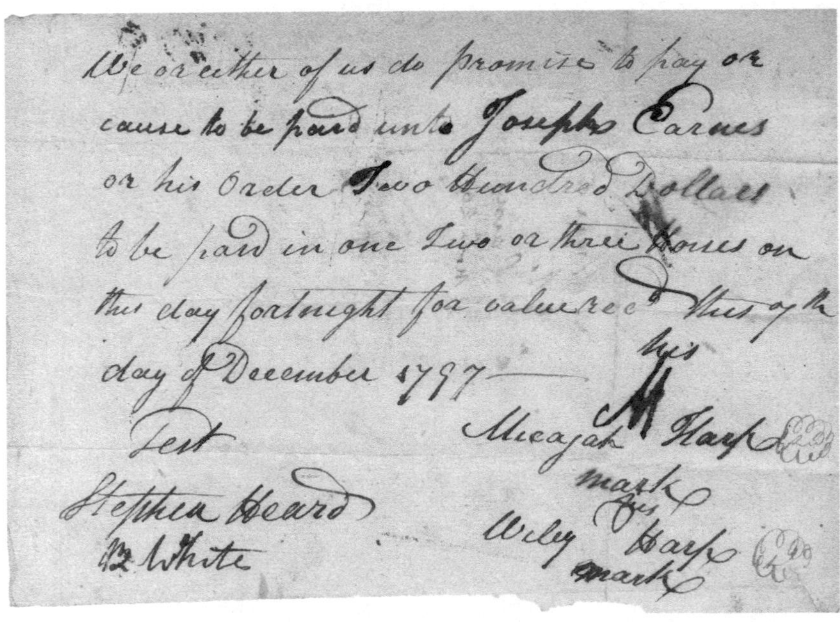

We or either of us do promise to pay or
cause to be paid unto Joseph Carnes
or his Order Two Hundred Dollars
to be paid in one Two or three Horses on
this day fortnight for value rec^d this 7th
day of December 1797
Test
Stephen Heard
[illegible] White
Micajah his M mark Harp
Wiley his mark Harp

A promissory note signed by Micajah and Wiley Harp on December 7, 1797. Courtesy of Knox County Archives, Knoxville, Tennessee.

Why the Harps borrowed money from Joseph Carnes is a mystery. One possibility is that Wiley Harp had used it to buy his land. Two hundred dollars, after all, was the exact value of his entire plot on Beaver Creek. Or maybe he had lost a bet, possibly to Carnes himself. Or maybe he needed the money because John Adams had sent him and Sally's father reeling. Whatever led Wiley Harp to set his signature to that note, whatever purchase or calamity preceded it, his debt was not terribly unusual. All of eastern Tennessee—all of rural America, really—was, in these years, a delicate web of private credit, this or that thread of which anybody, at any time, might pull.

Debt stalked everyone. Rich, poor, highborn or low, it did not discriminate. Thomas Jefferson struggled with debt all his life. "I am miserable till I shall owe not a shilling," he wrote in 1786. But he died drowning in it.[20] Credit, for better or worse, was the glue that bound communities together and allowed them to ride out the challenges of bad markets and scant money. When there was no cash or when crops failed, people absorbed those blows together—or looked the other way if a neighbor fell on hard times. Borrowing made it possible for men like Wiley Harp to become land owners. But it was also dangerous—and volatile.[21]

Credit was stretched to wild lengths wherever western lands were being settled. Beneath the cabins and pastures and rail fences of Tennessee were roiling oceans of debt. Even the major land speculators—the men grabbing up thousands of acres, rather than one or two hundred—had very little "fluid capital" and were forced to operate on credit. Given the acreages involved, land taxes soared to enormous sums, and parcels sold off slower than hoped, forcing them to borrow heavily.[22] Then, people panicked. The slightest ripple, the tiniest shiver, a wince in the network of debtors and creditors, and the entire edifice might come tumbling to the ground—that was the peril in 1797 of taking on debt.

The markets crackled with panic in the 1790s, and one reason was that people sensed debt was becoming more impersonal. Once upon a time, credit had been brokered by trust, by a man's standing. But now, paper credit could be passed on, "assigned" to third or fourth parties. Promissory notes circulated like money, often landing in strangers' hands. If you wrote a note promising to pay your neighbor two dollars, he might use it like cash to buy whiskey or to settle his own affairs. The new holder could then come find you, or even sue you, to collect. No longer was credit governed by personal relationships.[23] In the 1790s, an increasingly commercial and speculative economy was drawing men into financial entanglements that were not always of their own making. Soon, distant market forces from as far away as Europe began to intrude on places like Beaver Creek.[24]

It is possible that Wiley Harp's troubles were touched off by a financial panic: A crash happened in 1797. Its origins lay in faraway London, where in February, the directors of the Bank of England—spooked by the fear that too many banknotes were circulating to be covered by the gold in their vaults—froze specie payments. In no time, "the delicate web of Atlantic credit quickly unraveled."[25] The crunch hit England first: Farmers made runs on country banks. "The whole complicated Machine knocked up at once," Thomas Paine wrote in April 1797.[26] Then American borrowers felt the burn. As credit seized, European lenders called in their debts, and even the wealthiest speculators began to go bankrupt. As Wiley Harp moved onto Beaver Creek, the land bubble was popping.[27]

Big men felt it first. Atop the house of cards were teetering heavyweights like Robert Morris, perhaps the richest man in the United States. Morris's wildly leveraged land schemes—a veritable shell game financed by "millions of dollars' worth" of dubious notes, sucking heaps of cash out of new investors simply to pay off old ones—now sent the whole thing crashing, disastrously, down.

As the faucet ran dry in Europe and those notes came due, Morris had nowhere to turn. He and others like him began to duck creditors. They stuffed suitcases and fled to the countryside, buying time. Morris holed up at his country estate, barring the doors to visitors. But eventually, he landed, bankrupt, in Philadelphia's Prune Street Jail in 1798.[28]

But highly monied men were not the only ones to feel the pain. Hard-pressed, the whales of American finance in turn leaned on those dependent on them—smaller fish farther out in the sea of credit. They called in debts. They sued small borrowers. When they failed, they pulled investors down, too. Thomas Jefferson shuddered at the wreckage left by reckless speculators who'd spent years merrily tossing dice: "The credit and fate of the nation," he groaned, "seem to hang on the desperate throws and plunges of gambling scoundrels."[29] Meanwhile, the panic spilled outward, from wharves and countinghouses into the countryside. As small-time merchants and shopkeepers and local grandees came under duress, they cranked up the heat on their own debtors—men like Wiley Harp.[30]

Joseph Carnes was no loan shark. He was no great speculator. He was just another Knox County resident, someone a little better off. But he had financial ties to big men. He may have needed money himself. He had just been sued by William Tyrell, one of the wildest land jobbers in Tennessee. (It was Tyrell who had poured liquor down the throats of military officers that fall to get them to sign fraudulent papers.) That debt remained unpaid. In other lawsuits that likely concerned land disputes, other men also recovered sums against Carnes in 1797 and 1798.[31] His own debts mounting, Carnes had sold off two 150-acre parcels on Lyons Creek. His assets were stretched.[32]

Then, the Harps did not pay.

Fourteen days passed, a fortnight. The wind blew cold off the hills. Ice coated the roofs of the cabins in Knoxville. On the fifteenth day, December 22, Carnes got on his horse, rode to the courthouse, and entered into a bond to sue the Harps.

Around Christmas, a man knocked on Wiley Harp's door and handed him a summons: He was being sued. Court was in January.[33]

* * *

JANUARY CAME, AND the court opened. But the Harps did not attend.

For much of that winter, it is difficult to tell what Wiley Harp was doing. Or even where he was. Perhaps he was hiding, waiting until the court gaveled to a close and shuttered to business until spring.

The man responsible for dragging the Harps into court was the county sheriff, Robert Houston. It's hard to know how committed he was to the task. Sheriffs did not always work with perfect speed. Some lacked the appetite for the confrontations the job inevitably provoked. Even a simple subpoena could explode into a violent fracas. In 1794, one of George Washington's federal marshals was killed—the first federal officer to die in the line of duty—while trying to serve court papers to a Georgia man who locked himself in a room and then fired through the door. (The man later escaped.)[34]

Recovering a debt, then, was not easy. Even after a lawsuit was filed, it could take months or years. Suing was a measure of last resort—a sign that the usual hectoring and bullying had failed. A debtor who was being sued could have his property seized, or even his person, to guarantee his appearance in court. But debtors were wily; they found ways to avoid these things. They hid in their houses. They dodged the sheriff. There were many ways to put off the moment when one was made to pay. Some debtors just packed up and moved away.[35]

There were good reasons to run. If a debtor could not pay up, he might be tossed into jail indefinitely. If they could not make good, the Harps would be thrown into the county jail in Knoxville, a short skip across the street from the courthouse where Wiley had registered his deed. Once there, they would have to rely on their wives and other acquaintances to bring food and other necessities. The state felt no obligation to provide for debtors or even to feed them.[36] Although debtors' prison was not meant to be punitive, it was notoriously miserable. The idea was to squeeze the debtor—to make him so uncomfortable that he would cough up any remaining assets, even if he had to lean on friends and relatives. If he landed in jail, the problem for Wiley was that he did not have any. Having just moved onto a new piece of land in a place where he appears to have had very little kin (other than his father-in-law, who was also in trouble), he did not have much to fall back on.

He did have his brother. Wiley and Micajah seem to have done nearly everything together. When Wiley made any move, Micajah was always right behind him. He was the bondsman for Wiley's wedding, the one who vouched faithfully that there was nothing preventing his brother from marrying Sally. He witnessed the deed when Wiley bought land. He co-signed the promissory note to Carnes. They behaved as if they were two orphans who had lost everything and everyone else, which may well have been the truth. But as the one who owned property, Wiley stood to lose the most.

Debtors were stalked by a sense of impending doom. What Wiley Harp may have felt that winter can be inferred by what happened to another debtor—a man named John Ryer, a butcher who could not keep his accounts afloat. He bought cattle on credit, then sold the meat on credit "and could not collect the money." His creditors began to sue. When one threatened him with imprisonment, he panicked. To avoid being arrested, he began carrying pistols "to keep off the public officers"—at least until after the court met.[37] "I went armed with a brace of pistols, with a determination not to be taken," he said later.

In May 1792, while out at a pothouse drinking with friends, Ryer shot and killed a deputy sheriff who tried to arrest him. He fled, but was caught, and hanged on October 2, 1793. "I always bore the character of a decent honest man," he said at his execution.[38]

* * *

ALTHOUGH MICAJAH WAS often by his side, Wiley's brother did little to lighten his load. Micajah Harp was a bit of a wild card. He was unpredictable. Nearly everyone who saw him thought he had a slightly feral look in his eyes. "Micajor was a large Daring looking man," one man wrote. He had "sunken, black eyes" and a face that deadened into a "fierce vacant look" when he felt cornered. He liked to fight.[39]

Micajah had only recently been married to his own wife, Susana. But he soon took up with another woman named Betsy Walker. She was younger, and prettier, than his Susana. Whereas Susana was described as rough-looking and "raw-boned" with dark hair and dark eyes, Betsy was her contrast. According to one woman's memory, Betsy was somewhat "handsome" with light hair and blue eyes.[40] If Susana was upset about this new woman coming into her husband's life, it appears she nonetheless accepted it.

All three lived together. "From the time he took home this second woman," one Tennessean wrote, "he lived and co-habited" with both Betsy and Susana. It was a strange arrangement, but it lasted. In 1798 both women became pregnant. Where, exactly, they made their "home" is unclear because Micajah never owned any real property.[41] Were they all living on Wiley's land at Beaver Creek? Was Wiley, in some way, responsible for all these people?

* * *

SEVERAL CYCLES OF court came and went. Judges fired off new writs for the brothers' arrests: Alias capias. Pluries capias. The

Harps never appeared. By the time summer arrived—hot and soggy, bringing June rains for days on end—Carnes's lawsuit had been on the books, unresolved, for six months.[42]

As the temperature warmed, tempers did, too. Wiley and Micajah had thus far successfully ducked the summons, treading water. (*Not found*, the sheriff noted flatly on the back of the warrant each time he went looking for them.)[43] But, plainly, they could not put it off forever. In July, the court was scheduled to resume sessions, which meant there would be renewed efforts to find the two brothers and to shepherd them, as forcefully as necessary, to the courthouse. One way or another, the prickly tension of the lawsuit hanging over their heads seems to have led to a violent encounter Micajah had that summer.

In the summer of 1798, Micajah Harp got into a fight. He had a run-in with a man named Joseph Roberts. What sparked the fight is fuzzy, but it was a serious clash. (At first, it looks like a possible dispute with one of his wife's relatives; Susana's maiden name was Roberts. One imagines her kin may not have been thrilled about his taking a second "wife.") Anything could have set it off. Brawling was a part of life, likely to break out at any time in any tavern or town square where men met and traded insults. The backcountry was inescapably violent, a place where the slightest slight could come to blows. If you called a man the wrong name or "knocked a peach out of his Hand," he might answer with his fists.[44]

Among some, ferociousness was a point of pride. Visitors traveling through parts of the West wrote of men who filed their teeth sharp—the better to bite off ears. One grinning Carolinian, lisping through pointy teeth, proudly ticked off a list "of the noses and ears he has bitten off, and the cheeks he has torn," a traveler gawped. Others, too, gleefully bragged of breaking jaws and maiming opponents. They gouged out eyes. "Whenever these people come to blows, they fight just like wild beasts, biting, kicking, and endeavouring to tear each other's eyes out with their nails," wrote one observer, horrified.[45]

Sometimes the fighting was vaguely performative, a ballet of smashed jawbones and bruised knuckles. In Micajah's world, men fought each other for status. Some acquired reputations for it. Here, it was possible to become, as one Kentuckian did, "more famed as a pugilist than for any other quality he possessed." In 1799, one scrapper arrived in Greensburg, Kentucky, for no other reason than to challenge the "stoutest man in Green County" to a fight. The challenge was accepted. "Coats thrown aside, a ring formed," and the two men went at it until the challenger cried, "Take him off! Take him off!" and the two retreated to a tavern, where they "washed the blood from their faces."[46]

But just as often, men simply burst into slugfests, fists flying. Bloody scenes of wild mayhem stained the tavern floors. Almost a quarter of all the grand jury cases in Sumner County, Tennessee, between the years 1790 and 1800 centered on assault and battery.[47] The district courts, too, teemed with assault cases. In about that same period, roughly one third of the men brought to the bar as defendants in the Superior Court of Hamilton District (where the Harps lived) were charged with assault and battery. Eight others faced murder charges.[48]

Was it the place itself that made men behave this way? Was it the brutishness of living on a frontier where they had faced the wrath of Cherokee raiders and fought horrific wars to claim Native land as their own? Was it the frailty of a government unable to corral its unruly citizens? Was it the people who came here—raw, backwoods people steeped in violent cultural traditions, who, as some historians have claimed, "found quick recourse in their guns, knives, and fists"?[49] Or was it, perhaps, that the men in eastern Tennessee were living on a razor's edge, puffed with aspirations but with very little security?[50]

The roots of all this bloodletting have long been hazy. It used to be fashionable simply to paint Appalachian people as strange. They long ago acquired a reputation for being peculiarly violent: a "people hot-blooded" and "high-tempered," lawless, and untamed.[51] Some have supposed there must be something in the people's heritage, as if some poisonous blood ran through their veins. "Mountain blood is likely to be hot," one early writer judged.[52] A popular (though controversial) theory over the years has been to point to the fact that many Appalachian folk were descended from Scots and Scots-Irish migrants, who, burnished by generations of rebellion in the British borderlands, must have brought the pugnacity with them, as if tucked into ships' holds with other belongings. "They were a fighting race," one writer declared in the 1910s. ". . . They took to the rough fare and Indian wars of our border as naturally as ducks take to water."[53] But these explanations have always left a lot to be desired.[54]

Others blame the frontier itself, which is fair enough. Micajah Harp awoke, each day, in a crude little cabin of the sort suited to those who enjoyed very little permanence in their lives.[55] He knew only the ricketiest of governments. Even the courts—and the sheriffs who languidly roved about, toting scribbled writs—were but a thin tissue against the chaos. He was surrounded by men scraping by, many of them baptized by the gutting blows of warfare and then loosed, dangerously, from the constraints of established community. Like all frontiers, this one "was full of places to lurk, to hide, and to flee."[56] But still, it would be blinkered to write off all the broken-nosed broils and blood spilled as mere symptoms of frontier life. Even that is a little too easy.

Filling in the blanks around Wiley and Micajah makes it easier to see: The relentless insecurity plaguing early Tennessee made it a breeding ground for mayhem. Where men's fortunes are at the mercy of their neighbors, and the state is too weak to protect property, people often become violent.[57] They take matters into their own hands. They pick fights. They show, to anyone willing to look, how vicious they can be. That may be the starkest lesson of East Tennessee in these years: Its violence did not grow—like some indigenous weed—from cultural tradition or custom. It grew, at least in part, from unpredictability, and risk, and failure, and the rage they engendered.

Micajah fought off Joseph Roberts. Whatever sparked the clash, Micajah eventually walked away. But the fight angered him deeply. Something about it had gone beyond the usual black eyes and split lips; something about it made him indignant. As the summer heat spilled over the mountains in 1798, he found a lawyer—a bold step, given his own legal troubles—and complained: He wanted to bring charges. He accused Roberts of trespass, assault, and battery.[58]

There is one curious detail in his complaint: Along with bodily harm, he also charged Roberts with "false imprisonment." It's a strange clue; what does it mean? Had Roberts refused to let him leave a tavern during a brawl? Or had he shut Micajah into a room against his will, hoping he would cool down? Those are possibilities. But "false imprisonment" probably implies something more significant. It could very well mean that Micajah's row with Roberts was tied to the Harps' other troubles. It might even be that Roberts had tried to arrest him unlawfully—perhaps for an alleged theft or for trespassing on Cherokee lands.[59]

Or to collect Carnes's money. The most explosive and tantalizing explanation for the false imprisonment charge is that Roberts was not, in fact, Susana's kinsman but, rather, someone sent by Joseph Carnes to seize Micajah so he would be forced to pay up. Impatient creditors—unwilling to wait, any longer, for the sheriff—occasionally hired henchmen to muscle their way into a private home (which sheriffs were forbidden to do) or to capture a debtor on a Sunday (also forbidden) so he could be held until the next day.

Even the holy day, for some, was no protection against the possibility of being "abducted and turned over to a sheriff on Monday."[60]

After Micajah complained, a warrant was issued for Roberts's arrest: The sheriff was ordered to "take the body of Joseph Roberts" so he could appear in court that October "to Answer Micajah Harpe of a plea of . . . Assault and Battery."[61] But the case never made it to court. It was destined to be tossed out by judges because Micajah Harp failed to pursue it. Everything unraveled too quickly.

Luck was briskly running out.

* * *

EVEN AS MICAJAH was being roughed up, Wiley appears to have been mulling a way out. All of the agonies of the past year bore down on him: the coming of the troops, the evictions, the loss of the future he'd imagined, and, worst of all, the inescapable burden of the money he owed. And all along, he had been unable to dig himself out, even skipping court. (The July sessions passed, too, with no sign of the Harps.) Sally Harp was, by now, expecting their first child—yet another pressure. He was increasingly desperate. But he had one last move to make.

Around this time, he went to the race-paths. He watched the horses. A man who saw him there that day would later tell the story to a Tennessee newspaper.[62] If ever there was a place that embodied all the violent jockeying and grit-toothed stakes-placing of making a life in East Tennessee, it was this racing field—a grubby patch of meadow outside town where men went to race horses. Even to come here, for Wiley, was chancy: To venture out into a crowd when he had skipped several rounds of county court was a bit of a risk. But he did it anyway. This was, perhaps, his last chance. Was he reckless? Maybe. He pressed his luck.

He was hardly alone in doing so. "The whole life of an American is passed like a game of chance," Alexis de Tocqueville once wrote.[63]

Democracy and chance, he thought, were kindred spirits. They went hand in hand. "Those who live in the midst of democratic fluctuations," he wrote after touring the early republic, "have always before their eyes the image of chance," and they seemed to embrace "all undertakings in which chance plays a part."[64] You hoped to win. But losing was always possible. It was a thing that haunted you at every turn. America was a nation of men pressing their luck.

Trying one's luck at the races, even to great risk, was, for some, a favorite tradition. Horse racing had existed for generations in the South. In seventeenth-century Virginia, it was the "most popular form of amusement." Tobacco exhausted the soil quickly, so Virginians took to turning their fallow fields into racecourses.[65] In its early days, it was a gentlemanly sport, though all sorts watched. "What really stirred a Virginia or Carolina planter's blood," writes one historian, "was the chance to gamble impressively large sums. In doing so, a wealthy man demonstrated how reckless he could afford to be with his income and thus how richly he deserved to have the respect of his neighbors."[66] But not all racing was for the gentry alone. Once it crossed the mountains into Kentucky and Tennessee, it began to draw more mixed participants.[67]

Many races here were informal affairs. In Lexington, Kentucky, people simply gathered on the commons and raced horses down the town's main street. (This became such a riotous nuisance that in 1793, Lexington sought ways to "remedy . . . the growing evil.") Other stakes races took place in open fields outside of town. Some were onetime advertised events, like the day race at "Major George Blackburn's course, Equiria" in 1796, while others took place over several days. Advertisements posted the rules: "A purse race at Lexington on the 2d Thursday in October next," the *Kentucky Gazette* trumpeted. "Three mile heats," best two in three. Horses were entered the day of the race by a man at Collins's tavern; every man entering a horse paid two guineas. Fifteen minutes' rest was allowed between heats, "for rubbing."[68]

Wiley pushed through the crowd. He looked for the man entering horses. It was loud, raucous. All manner of men lined the race-path, pushing and shouting. Slaves and Indians and gougers, rubbing arms. A few hawked liquor. Some of the spectators were soused, sloppy. Bursts of wild jubilation and cursing rose up and exploded like firecrackers over the shifting mass of heads and shoulders and elbows. As any race ended, one witness wrote, the outcome was "always proclaimed by a tornado of applause from the winner's party," punctuated by men wildly "hallooing, jumping, and clapping their hands in a frenzy of delight."[69]

Quarter races were spectacles of hazard. Every race—a quarter-mile dash, usually between two horses—was a contest of the horses' speed but also of the riders' pluck and daring. Even as they sped down the track, riders tried to drive their foes off course. They shoved and jabbed at each other. In Virginia, a rider was "free . . . to use whip, knee, or elbow to dismount his opponent or drive him off the track."[70] Crowds roared loudest "if the horses . . . happened to jostle and one of the riders [was] thrown off with a broken leg."[71]

And there was betting—lots of it. Fistfuls of guineas changing hands. The betting could easily consume you. "Attend to your business and think not of horse racing," one man advised a friend. "You will lose time and money by it." You could be ruined by it. In 1785, a Mississippi man ran away to escape the crush of his debts. He owed one man an astounding $450, stemming from just one bet on a horse race. Congressman Andrew Jackson, too, had a taste for racing and breeding. He twice bet nearly all he owned on gambling events. The duel he fought in 1805, in which he killed a man, arose from a bet on a horse race.[72]

"Gaming is an enchanting *witchery*," wrote the author of *The Compleat Gamester*, an English guide to all manner of gameplay. Wagering on races was seductive. The notion that something could be had from nothing, that money could be made from such alchemy as stirring up the magic dusts of "*Idleness* and *Avarice*"—it was alluring. The intoxicating thought of winning salved the risks that were involved. But risks there were. "Above all other Vices," the habit of gambling rendered a man "always unsatisfied with his own condition; he is either lifted up to the top of mad joy with success, or plung'd to the bottom of despair by misfortune, always in extreams, always in a storm."[73] Gambling was a kind of madness.

"Is it not extreme folly for a man that hath a competent estate to play whether he or another man shall enjoy it?" the *Gamester* asked. ". . . I think it [is] madness in the highest degree."[74]

On this day, Wiley Harp entered a horse.[75] It was his horse, though maybe not a very good one. John Swaney, a race rider, watched him do it. Then, with his brother Micajah, Wiley staked nearly everything he had on the race.

His heat came up. His horse lined up alongside Samuel Gibson's. The race began.

A quarter mile is not far. It was over quickly.

In just a few brief moments, he lost everything.[76]

* * *

WHEN CRIMINALS FACED the scaffold in the eighteenth century, they sometimes offered little autobiographies, confessing all their crimes. In a "dying speech" before they were hanged, or even in a printed tract that could be purchased for a few pence, they explained how their lives had gone adrift. Some recalled a litany of wrongdoings and follies and misbehaviors, turning their life histories into cautionary tales for others.[77] The public hungered to know how men went astray. "It is a maxim, as old as ancient Rome," said one man condemned to die in 1780. "No man becomes a devil in a minute."[78]

Nothing like this exists for Wiley Harp. His own descent is

barely, faintly visible. It has to be fit together from fragments. But even those glimpses hint—as others implied of their own lives—that he did not become a devil in a minute. In the eighteenth century, most people believed that even the worst sinners could be redeemed, that God might save any man and lift him toward heaven. But here and there, in the scaffold speeches of Wiley's era, lurks a detectable belief that some men could not be cured once they had turned to thieving or killing. "Pray for me good people," said one man on the eve of his execution in 1791. "I am wicked, and there are many others in the United States perhaps as wicked as myself."[79]

Once he lost the bet, Wiley had exhausted any legitimate means of paying off his debts. Now, on the heels of that folly, it appears that he and Micajah turned, fatefully, to horse theft. "They stole several fine horses from Edward Tiel," the deputy sheriff's son later wrote, misspelling Teele's name. This decision, too, might have been a last stab at resolving the original debt to Carnes. (They had, after all, promised to pay him "in horses.") But this, too, failed: Teele followed the brothers into the caverns that reached to the west of Knoxville, a looping maze of "subterranean chamber[s]" with "high and well-turned arches" and dripping roofs. And then he found them.[80]

If there was a moment that turned Wiley Harp, irrevocably, to wickedness, it may have been the day he was caught in the Cumberlands with Edward Teele's horses. All of his debts, his final wagers, his being "broken up" at the races, had led him into that cavern, perhaps in a last, desperate attempt to pay off what he owed. But instead, it was a dead end. Although they broke free and ran away, Wiley and Micajah must have known that it would be impossible, now, to resume quiet householding on Beaver Creek.

Horse thieves faced merciless punishments. For those convicted, there was little hope of returning to respectable life. At worst, they could be hanged. At best, they might be mutilated, their ears nailed to a pillory and cut off and their faces branded with a hot iron. The sheriff would sear an *H* three-quarters of an inch high, into one cheek and a *T* into the other.[81] Convicted horse thieves were recognizable forever after, no matter where they went. One traveler in 1806 wondered: How might a stranger be able to tell whether a public house in western Virginia was of "good" or "vicious" character? The answer: Check the tavernkeeper for "*a possession, or an absence of ears.*"[82]

So, when caught, they ran.

* * *

A FEW MONTHS later, a sheriff knocked on the door of Wiley Harp's house. No one answered. No one appeared. The garden was thick with weeds. Wiley Harp would not be coming to court to answer Joseph Carnes's lawsuit.

Hell was already upon him.

* * *

IN THE WANING days of 1798, a body bobbed to the surface of the Holston River. It was bloodless and blue, possibly half-frozen after being submerged in icy water.[83]

A stream of constables and onlookers flitted in to have a look at the waterlogged corpse. When the dead man was pulled from the water, he was recognized as someone named Johnson who dwelled somewhere in the hills northeast of Knoxville. He had last been seen at Hughes's cabin, a "rowdy groggery" that was stooped along the road toward Southwest Point, a place frequented (the governor's son later said) by men of "suspicious character."[84]

Had he been gambling—involved in some card game gone bad? Was he the victim of a heated dispute, fueled by liquor, that followed him out of Hughes's place into the lonely road home? Or was he simply "robbed," as one man later suggested? Why Johnson was "taken into the woods & killed," his body then pitched into the river, was apparent to no one at the time. But in retrospect, one Knoxvillian would recall, notably, that the Johnson murder occurred not very long after Wiley Harp's bad day at the races.[85]

His injuries were odd. He appeared to have been gutted somehow. In his belly was a deep, cavernous gash, as if he had been "ripped . . . open." Only later—much later—would some men begin to suspect what had happened: In a possible attempt to conceal the murder, Johnson's killer—or killers—had "cut his bowels open, filled his body with rocks, & sunk it."[86]

Although no one knew it yet, Johnson may have been the first to die.

KENTUCKY

He led her over mountains and valleys so deep
He led her over mountains and valleys so deep
Polly mistrusted and then began to weep, saying,
"Wiley, oh Wiley, I'm afraid of your ways,
Wiley, oh Wiley, I'm afraid of your ways,
The way you've been rambling and leading me astray . . ."

—from "Pretty Polly," traditional

CHAPTER 4

NO WANT OF HELLS

The Wilderness Road
Big Rockcastle River, Kentucky
December 1798

Thomas Langford was missing one of his front teeth. It was an unremarkable thing—no one would have mentioned it—until he was found dead.

He came from Pittsylvania County, Virginia, a place defined more by its tobacco fields than its towns. He was the son of a wealthy farmer and assemblyman. "Young Langford," a relative remembered, was "a portly, fine appearing young man."[1] He was respectable. While traveling, he carried with him a looking glass and a shaving kit. He rode a solid horse. His pockets jangled with money.

In 1798, Langford set off for Kentucky with a companion, David Irby. They shared expenses. Langford put them into his account book: cheese, ferriage, half a bushel of oats. It was good to have a traveling partner; they were headed through "the Wilderness," a rough, mountainous stretch that led to the more settled parts of Kentucky. Most men did not try passing it alone. But for some reason, Langford and Irby parted ways. They planned to meet later in Frankfort.[2]

What was Langford doing there? He may have been seeking land. Kentucky, like Tennessee in these days, was full of men on the make. Only recently, it had been a place of grinding frontier warfare, as Shawnees and Cherokees and Miamis lit fires in the way of American expansion. But in 1794, a federal army had crushed the Western Confederacy, an alliance of Native peoples. When the Treaty of Greenville was signed in 1795, promising an end to Indian raiding, it released gushers of migrants. In the 1790s, Kentucky's population almost tripled. People came, dragging their carts, their children, their slaves.[3]

On the Wilderness Road, Langford looked for a place to stay. He spotted a public house, on the banks of Big Rockcastle River. It must have seemed a happy oasis: You could have a warm dinner for a shilling and a half, a cold one for a little less. Breakfast, with or without tea, coffee, or chocolate. Lodging in "Clean Sheats," six pence.[4]

He stopped.

* * *

THE WAY INTO Kentucky, for most migrants, was the Wilderness Road. It was a crude filament curling through the Cumberland Mountains. Once little more than a bridle path, it had been widened, over the years, into a wagon road. "THE WILDERNESS ROAD . . . is now compleated," boasted a 1796 announcement in the *Kentucky Gazette*.[5] But it wasn't, really. It was dreadful, a punishing trial of rocks and hills, one of the worst roads in the country.[6] "Certainly the worst on the whole continent," one traveler judged.[7]

Parts of the road were unsafe. Only a few years earlier, families had sought escorts and traveled together in caravans to ward off Cherokee attacks. Now the threat, mostly, was other Americans. To enter Kentucky, one rode first through the Powell Valley, which was infested with thieves. Preachers, riding circuit, shied away from the "rough company" who reputedly lived in these hills. The people here were "desperate characters," wrote one Methodist minister. They watched the road into Kentucky and robbed travelers.[8]

Leaving Tennessee, the Harps passed through here first. After everything had fallen apart in Knoxville, they fled. There was nothing to do but to wipe the books clean—to leave their debts and problems behind. So they took horses and guns and their pregnant wives and went north into Kentucky. Like everyone else, they fol-

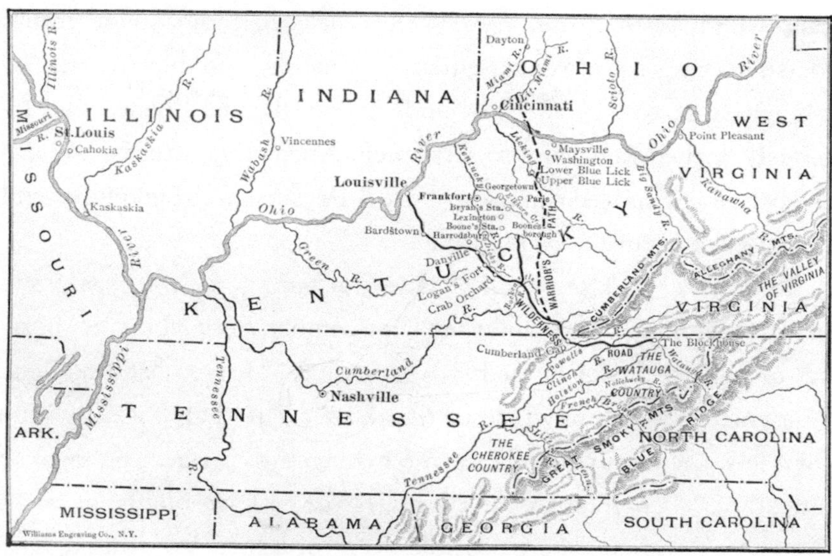

The Wilderness Road. From Henry Addington Bruce, *Daniel Boone and the Wilderness Road* (1910). Image courtesy of Tennessee State Library and Archives.

lowed the Wilderness Road. They passed the tollgate at Cumberland Ford. Nine pence per person and another nine for every horse.[9] There were not many places to stay. At night, they slept in the woods. On rainy days, they were soaked. "In the mountains it does not rain, but pours," one traveler wrote.[10]

They passed others, trudging along. Whole families, the weary fathers leading packhorses, the mothers quieting toddlers. Some lacked shoes or money. Amid this stream of scowly faces, the Harps probably looked unremarkable, like any other family. But the people they passed were not running away. They were running toward something, full of hope. "Ask these Pilgrims what they expect when they git to Kentuckey," one man wrote. "The Answer is Land." Have you any? you might inquire. "No," they would answer, "but I expect I can git it."[11]

Most were destined for disappointment. Land ownership was fraught here, too. As in Tennessee, the mad scramble for claims caused endless confusion. By 1797, Kentucky had issued land grants for something like twenty-four million acres—double the size of the entire state. Lawsuits abounded. Even Daniel Boone, who famously opened Kentucky to settlement, spent the latter part of his life battling disputed claims in court.[12] Dreams of the good life, and promises of security, evaporated.

Kentucky was a state full of failed, or failing, men. It was growing breathtakingly fast, and they kept coming, hopped up on boosterism and dreams of landed independence. "Heaven is a Kaintuck of a place," someone wrote in the 1810s.[13] But that was only true for a few, the fortunate, those who managed to carve out a farm or an estate.[14] It helped to get there first or to have plenty of cash. For those few, riches were possible: Some of Kentucky—unlike East Tennessee—was on its way to becoming a landscape of gracious plantations tended by slaves. (By 1800, about one in five Kentuckians was enslaved.) Beneath their feet were the black and vermillion soils and the bluegrass and the snow-white limestone that made Kentucky uniquely suited for horse breeding and bourbon.[15] But for most comers, the land crunch put those things out of reach. Many ended up working for someone else, as tenant farmers or salt workers, "exausted and worn down with distress and disappointment."[16]

It was also a haven for the politically disaffected. "This State is considered as the ultimate refuge of those . . . who will not submit to the Oppression & Tyranny [of] Federal Measures," a prominent Kentuckian confessed.[17] President John Adams had never been popular here. ("In no part of the Union were his measures denounced with more bitterness, nor his downfall awaited with more impatience," one Kentucky historian later wrote.)[18] But he was never less popular than in the fall of 1798.

The Harps entered Kentucky at an electric moment. Politically, it was in a tumult. The Federalist war program—especially the Sedition Act, which made it a crime to speak out against the federal government—had touched off a frenzy of "Political Fever." For months, Kentucky blistered with protest. "The minds of the people here are all fired respecting the proceedings of Congress," a Kentucky legislator wrote that summer.[19] Thousands had gathered in a sweaty "mass meeting" in Lexington on July 4, 1798, to register their dismay. The fire spread briskly from there. Protests erupted in many counties.[20] "Our liberties are in danger," Clark County proclaimed.[21]

That fall—around the very time the Harps headed north—Kentucky's legislature passed the Kentucky Resolutions, nine resolves flouting the federal government in historic fashion.[22] In angry language, they vehemently condemned the new laws—the Alien and Sedition Acts—aimed at muzzling the government's critics. And only a few lines into the document was nestled a little poison vial, a statement so dangerous that, if carried to its logical conclusion, had the power to destroy the nation: When the federal government overstepped its powers, it declared, "its acts are . . . void, and of no force." The states could simply turn their cheeks and ignore federal law.[23]

It remains one of the most profound acts of protest in American history. "KENTUCKY!" proclaimed a writer in the *Palladium*. "In vain the *Harpy Claw* is extended over thee . . . Entrenched behind the *Constitution*, thou shalt continue to flourish."[24]

Wiley Harp may have known nothing about this. Or he may have heard men talking about it as they moved north. Either way, there is something fitting about the fact that he chose Kentucky as the stage on which to perform his own grand acts of disaffection.

* * *

LANGFORD WAS TIRED. Shuffling into the tavern, he looked forward to a bit of rest. To anyone looking closely, he might have appeared slightly frayed. The hem of one of his leggings was torn;

perhaps it had caught on a stirrup. Hoping to make arrangements, he looked for the public house's owner.

The tavernkeeper was John Farris. In his mid-forties, Farris had been in Kentucky for at least fourteen years, and in that time, he had seen a lot. He was the sort of wizened Kentuckian who had watched the fragile forts and blockhouses of what was once western Virginia become transformed into a state of its own. In the early 1790s, he had ranged the frontier as a scout with the Kentucky militia. He had worked as a constable. He had also been in brawls and gotten into trouble selling liquor at the races.[25] But it was likely Farris's daughter-in-law, Jane, the young wife of Farris's son William, who welcomed Langford.

Inside, the visitor was greeted by unfamiliar faces, lit dimly by the glow of the hearth. In taverns like this one, men of all walks mingled. Laborers, travelers, drifters. Public houses were required by law to accommodate travelers, but they catered to local men, too. Prices were strictly regulated to discourage greedy publicans from gouging their customers. (If your inn was the only place to stop for miles, it was easy to take advantage.) Anyone with a few pence to spare could down a dram of rum or brandy.[26]

If Langford ate, it was with others. Dinner was served communally, almost always around a common table.[27] Drinking was also collective. If you drank punch, it was served by the bowl—you simply passed it around. Such communion encouraged loose chatter. "There is no shyness of conversation," a British traveler noted about American public houses. "People of different countries and languages mix together, and converse as familiarly as old acquaintances."[28]

Perhaps it was here, around Farris's table while supping on a bit of bacon and Indian bread, that Langford met some of Farris's other guests: two brothers, also traveling.

He introduced himself.

From a distance, Sally Harp took his measure. Riding through the mountains had left him a little dusty, rough around the edges. But she could probably tell from the look of Langford that he was well-off, "a man of much respectability," as one description put it.[29] He wore a great sweeping coat. He had delicate handkerchiefs stuffed into his pockets.

Langford looked, too. He probably did not warm quickly to the two brothers. Maybe he did not know what to make of them. They had three women with them. All were pregnant. They looked poor. They wore dirty clothes. They had two horses and a couple of rifles but few other possessions. Maybe he found them, at first, "squalid and miserable."[30]

But he became friendly with them. One of the women, Susana, noticed the torn hem on his leggings. She mended it. They began to have a good time. He joked with them. Then he got drunk with them. The Harps treated him to a little bottle of whiskey at their expense.[31]

Traveling, in the eighteenth century, was tricky. It meant relying on strangers; there was no other choice. You needed their hospitality, their company. But you had to be careful about whom you trusted. Confidence, misplaced, was dangerous. It was all a bit speculative: looking people over, gauging their characters. The Harps existed at the very origin of a pattern in American life, in which a relentlessly mobile population, and an increasing number of interactions between strangers, gave birth to a certain art of duplicity—an emergent class of characters who could manipulate appearance and identity "in a calculated effort to lure the guileless into granting them confidence."[32]

Confidence was to become the chief problem of the times.[33] It was not quite the era of the "confidence man," as Langford laughed and drank with the two brothers. That term would not be coined until the 1840s, when a trickster named William Thompson began conning well-heeled New Yorkers out of their pocket watches. It would be years before card sharps prowled the Mississippi steamboats, trolling for marks. But as the young United States moved and swerved and lurched into new territories, its farm boys moving to the cities, its population ever restless, it was becoming more anonymous. Hustling, counterfeiting, deception: These would be the tides of the coming years.[34]

At various points during their coming spree, the Harps took on other guises. Once they left Tennessee and began meeting people on Kentucky byways, they learned to play different characters. There are several stories about them pretending to be peace officers, or ministers. Once, sitting down to a meal in a part of Kentucky where "no one personally knew them," Micajah said a long blessing, and the host mistook them for itinerant preachers. On occasion, they even claimed to be searchers, looking for the dreaded Harp brothers. But that was later.[35]

Langford asked: Where were they headed?

To the settlements beyond Crab Orchard, they said.

Well, why not go together? he suggested. It was at least a day's journey. They could camp together.

This idea seemed to make good sense. All feeling "very cheerful with each other," they decided to travel on together.[36]

In the morning before departing, Langford found the brothers arguing with the lady of the house. They were quibbling over the cost of their meal. Langford squirmed. It was not polite. "Mrs. Farris," he said, "I would not offend you for all that's in my saddle bags." And that, he boasted, "was worth five hundred pounds."[37] He may have pulled out a handful of silver and paid for his new friends' meals. Then the party left.[38]

Maybe Sally Harp knew, then, what would happen next.

* * *

MURDER AND ROBBERY! shrieked a Georgia newspaper in 1796. A store had gone up in flames. The boy inside, keeping watch over the goods, had been murdered—his throat cut. Nine hundred dollars in banknotes and silver were missing.[39]

In 1792, Elizabeth Reeves walked home, alone, after visiting a friend on the outskirts of Philadelphia. She did not make it. Her body was found face down in the mud at the dockyards. Her comb and ribbon lay nearby. She was beaten, bruised. Her teeth were knocked loose. She was seventeen.[40]

Thieves killed Marcus Lyon, a merchant, on the turnpike in Massachusetts in 1805. They bashed him over the head with a pistol, then dragged him to the edge of the Chicopee River, where he was found dead, floating among the reeds. He was still wearing his coat and mittens.[41]

The early republic was murderous. When you trawl the newspapers of the time, the bodies seem to pile up. Americans killed for all sorts of reasons, many of the ones you might expect. Men killed their wives in nasty squabbles over money or fidelity. They killed their business partners. They fell into drunken brawls or duels or shot those who slighted them. They killed for revenge or for financial gain. They killed people they knew, and they killed strangers. Every murder is different, like a fingerprint. If you read carefully, though, you begin to see a thread—a kind of shadow that lurks behind many of these stories.[42]

Murder rates have risen and fallen throughout American history. In this period, they rose nearly everywhere.[43] Some parts of the early republic—like the mountain backcountry that produced the Harps—were undeniably more dangerous than others. But all over the country, homicides crept upward. The causes are multivalent and complicated. In his sweeping study of homicide in American history, the historian Randolph Roth finds that when political instability reigns—when people distrust government and its ability to address wrongs, and Americans lose faith in the legitimacy of the social hierarchy—the number of murders rises.[44] All of that describes the Harps' moment.

But something else was happening, too. Something new. In ways that historians have not quite grasped, some of the murders of Wiley Harp's era are tied to the very core meanings of the American Revolution—the defining features of the republic itself. Appalachia's disease may only have been a more severe case of something that infected men across the United States in the wake of the American Revolution. Everywhere, in the new republic, men struggled. Shaken free of traditional safety nets, loosed into new places without family, and drunk on a giddy cocktail of new markets and new expectations, they stumbled. Then they fell.

One of the most sensational multiple murders of the early nation occurred in Connecticut. In the wee hours of December 11, 1782, a shopkeeper named William Beadle struck his sleeping wife and four children in the heads with an axe. Then he slit their throats. He covered the children with a blanket and his wife's face with a handkerchief. Then he sat in a Windsor chair, pointed two pistols into his ears, and fired them.[45]

The murders seemed, at first, incomprehensible. People scrambled to understand. Beadle had appeared, in life, to be entirely rational. A jury of inquest found that he was of sound mind.[46] Quickly, though, it became clear that Beadle's problems were ones of pride and finance. He had not been born into wealth or status, but he had made something of himself, despite humble beginnings.[47] By the time he opened his shop, he had acquired about twelve hundred pounds' worth of wealth, which he guarded very carefully. After all, his assets were what made Beadle a person of consequence.[48]

But not for long. The Revolution ruined him financially. Beadle was a patriot: He had even pledged money to relieve Boston, after the port was closed in 1774.[49] But his investment in the new nation was disastrous. He made one very grave error: He kept all of his wealth in cash. Instead of buying real estate, he hoarded Continental currency, piles of it, and as the war progressed, it plummeted in value. Beadle was enraged: "Continental Trash" had cost him his entire fortune. "Continental currency taught him that wealth could take to itself wings and fly away," attested one memorial.[50]

Beadle, slowly, broke. He could not bear "being thought by his friends poor and dependent."[51] He could not stand the loss of face. That, ultimately, was what moved him to kill himself and his family.

"If a man, who has once lived well . . . ," he wrote shortly before the murders, "falls by unavoidable accident into poverty, and then submits to be laughed at, despised and trampled on . . . he must become meaner than meanness itself."[52]

He was not alone. The annals of murder in the early republic are, in fact, filled with men who had once lived well but fell on hard times and could not abide poverty—or, worse, being laughed at and trampled on. They had tasted prosperity. They aspired to respectability. They believed it possible, attainable. But when those hopes crumbled, like so much Continental cash, they crumbled, too. A lot of those bodies—swallowed up by the fields and pastures of the early United States—they were the victims of social and economic disappointment.

Consider a sample of sixty-three murder cases drawn from the years 1776 to 1810. All were committed by white men whose names appear in well-known anthologies of those convicted and executed during this period. Reading deeply about their cases—plumbing court records and confessions and newspapers and local histories—reveals that about one in five was experiencing, like William Beadle, some type of social or economic frustration. (Beadle, of course, along with scores of others, does not appear in this sample. He was dead by suicide before any court could pass judgment.) Excluding the cases about which there are almost no known details (other than, say, the victim's identity), the rate rises even higher—about 25 percent.[53]

To understand the rage the Revolution sowed in its wake, one needs first to grasp what it meant to men. It was not simply a matter of defeating the British. The American Revolution was a social experiment as well as a political one. Society, in its wake, was different—remade, with a new social compact. Its promises are all contained in the Declaration of Independence: Equality, at least of opportunity. Liberty. The right to pursue one's own happiness. The very power of the American Revolution was that it gave hope to ordinary men. It gave them a reason to believe, as the struggling young man (and future Supreme Court justice) James Iredell put it, that they could "get into the [marvelous] Road that leads to Happiness and Independence."[54]

Under monarchy—the world of Wiley Harp's birth—most men were merely subjects. Every man knew his place—what he owed to his betters and what was owed to him by those below. Britons obsessed over rank. There was a gentry class, which, in the colonies, was a tiny minority. Then there was everyone else: farmers, apprentices, servants, slaves.[55] No one expected to move dramatically up or down. Common people, for the most part, accepted their lot. They rarely aspired to the life of their betters. The small farmers in Epping Forest district, North Carolina, where some early Harp migrants lived, did not hope to become gentlemen. They had not been born to that.

One of the great advantages of monarchy was its predictability: You gave your allegiance to the king and the men above you, and in return, you were protected. You were not necessarily free or independent. But if you got into trouble, you could appeal to a patron for help. (The gentry's obliged relationship to the humbler classes is captured in a famous scene from the life of a Boston shoemaker, George Hewes: In the early 1760s, Hewes repaired a shoe for the wealthy merchant John Hancock, who, in turn, invited Hewes to have the privilege of calling upon him briefly. When Hewes arrived, heart in his throat, Hancock rewarded him—in a gesture of gentlemanly obligation—with a crownpiece.)[56]

But the end of monarchy meant, in theory, the end of the chain of social dependency in which men were beholden to those above them. One of the key intellectual changes of the era was the notion that no man was born better than another. In a republic, citizens were born free and equal. Tearing down monarchy meant rejecting the idea that any man was more noble, or royal, simply by pedigree. "All men being originally equals, no *one* by *birth* could have a right to set up his own family in perpetual preference to all others for ever," Thomas Paine argued in *Common Sense*.[57]

These were beautiful, radical sentiments. For American men, this was a new deal. No longer were they stuck, "destined to be what their fathers were," as one historian writes.[58] In the new order, they were free to pursue happiness—to compete, freely, as individuals. Moving forward, many hoped that the social order might be more fluid, that men might succeed or fail according to their own talents. And everyone hoped himself a talent. Now, a man would forge his identity "from his own achievements, not from the accident of his birth."[59]

But as the Harps' and others' experiences suggest, there were dark sides to the new regime. The untethering of men from monarchical society was deeply destabilizing. It did not help matters that the economy, too, was becoming increasingly market-driven and competitive. Even men like Wiley Harp were beginning to feel the intrusion of faraway market forces: A ripple from the Bank of England in London might wash ashore on Beaver Creek. The Revolution's ideals and the economy reinforced each other in a heady mix of expectation. Freedom and participation in the market economy were linked "so completely that later apologists scarcely could believe they were not the same thing."[60]

What this meant was that there would be winners and losers. Competition became the new way of living. Patriots and loyalists—as categories and identities—might start to fade. But there would be those who soared, in the new republic, and those who sank. "The world is nothing but a contra-dance," Daniel Webster, a future congressman, wrote in 1802, "and every one, *volens, nolens,* has a part in it. Some are sinking, others rising, others balancing, some gradually ascending towards the top, others flamingly leading down."[61]

Historians have not linked these changes in American life to patterns of violence or murder.[62] But it is hard to escape the sense that they are related. Reading the stories of murders in the early United States, you encounter men sucked under by this new order—failing, facing ruin, turning to violence. It is not the only pattern. But it is there. When men went about explaining their crimes, they themselves often talked about property loss, or debt, or punishing lawsuits. In 1791, a New Jersey farmer beat to death a man who had forced him to settle a lawsuit, "greatly to my wrong."[63] Another shot his neighbor in the head in 1794, after a long legal dispute over property boundaries.[64] In 1805, a South Carolina man hired killers to shoot the man who had begun a ruinous lawsuit against him.[65]

It was not simply the rich or those who briefly grasped at wealth. Hugh McLean, a working man, had fought under George Washington. But he did not do well after the war. At age fifty in 1789, he was a "poor laboring man" and an alcoholic. When his wife called him drunk and worthless, he stabbed her with a kitchen knife.[66] John Banks, too, killed his wife. He blamed her for his financial troubles. He was a simple laborer, but, "by industry," he had managed to save thirty dollars—a substantial pot of money. He rented a cellar in New York City and invested in fruits and nuts for Margaret, his bride, to sell. But Margaret drank and picked fights. She squandered his money. "She . . . ruined me twice," Banks said in 1805, after he killed her.[67]

Some were able to explain how the anger ate away at them after losing everything. "After misfortunes and abuses increased upon me," Josiah Burnham said in 1805, ". . . my temper became quick and furious—my disposition *remarkably* changed, and *not* for the better." Swindled by a friend and entangled in property lawsuits for fourteen years, Burnham lost nearly everything and was ridiculed by neighbors. His wife left him. In debtors' prison, he snapped and stabbed two men.[68] Several others killed sheriffs who were attempting to drag them to court to answer debts. Underlying their fury was the sense that, as one man put it, even in "this Land of boasted Freedom," the decks seemed to be stacked against their success.[69]

One of the oddest—and most telling—clues, unlocking the violence of this period, lies with the men who killed their families. The early republic saw a bizarre rash of familicides.[70] Beadle struck first, but others followed—almost a dozen of them, at least, in wildly different places. In 1785, Philip Pepple, an "unhappy man, frightened . . . by the spectre [of] poverty," slew his family.[71] One evening in 1799, John Jacob Werner, a bookbinder, read prayers to his family and the next morning tried to kill them all. (Two children and his wife survived.)[72] In 1805, a tenant farmer named Abel Clemmons murdered his wife and eight small children while they were sleeping. They were planning to move to Ohio imminently.[73]

Familicides are very often about lost status. They are about shame. "The father is almost always considering suicide as the only escape from some sort of financial crisis," Richard Gelles, a sociologist, has said about modern familicides. "Murdering his family members, then, becomes a way of rescuing them from the hardship and shame of bankruptcy and suicide."[74] The family murders of the early republic suggest that this pattern began early on in the United States. Werner, the bookbinder, drank so much "he had reduced himself and family to a state of want." He was also being sued; the lawsuit was to be decided—against him, he feared—on the day of the murders. James Purrinton, a farmer in Maine, had been "rapidly improving his estate," but in 1805, a drought hit and he feared "his family would suffer for want of bread." On July 8, 1806, he killed them all. The "diminution of his property or prospects, was a disappointment" that he simply could not bear.[75]

In America, men compete. That is the basic ethos. To be American is to cherish the idea of material success, which, you understand, will be chased by everyone, competitively.[76] But what happens when men fail to realize the dream? Or worse, when they feel it has been robbed from them, or withheld unfairly? It was not only in the tangled backwoods of Tennessee that Americans confronted this problem. It percolated up in other parts of the republic, too. In a society that promised the possibility of social ascent for all, the losers did not always go quietly.[77]

In Wiley Harp's lifetime, the United States was just beginning to embrace these values. Without seeing his experience being sued, gambling, and failing in eastern Tennessee, he does not look like a part of this pattern. But with it in view, he represents the origins of something distinctly American—the ethos of individualism, liberalism, and the power of the market colliding with the realities of failure and loss of face. A sullen army of men in the early United States seethed about their misfortunes. Sometimes that seething manifested in beatings, bludgeoning, stabbing—or killing.

These were the wages of citizenship. It could be grand and profitable. But "*if [God] chuses to frown*," William Beadle wrote, "I know by Experience that there is *no want of Hells* in this state of Things."[78]

* * *

CATTLE DROVERS FOUND Langford's body. On the side of the road they spied pieces of "human scull, fresh mangled." Smelling blood, some of the cattle bolted into the woods. Just off the main path, concealed beneath some brush and rotten wood, lay a dead man.[79]

The coroner came. Only recently had Kentucky come to have coroners. Less than a year earlier, the state had passed a law detailing the county coroner's duties, including what to do when any person was found slain: If a man were found dead "in the fields or woods," the coroner was to conclude whether or not he had been killed in that spot, and if not, to "follow [the] steps" of those who had brought the body there. Was the dead man a stranger? Was he known? Where had he been? "It shall be enquired also . . . where he lay the night before," the law advised.[80]

Others would come, too. Typically when there was an unexplained death, the constable gathered a jury of inquest to investigate. Twelve men were called to "appear at the place where the Body lies" and determine the manner of death.[81] The coroner—if there was one in the county—presided, as these men peered and poked and pondered wounds, or the position in which the body lay, or even what sort of clothing the person was wearing. Had he been strangled? Stabbed? By whom?

It was not hard to tell how this man had died: His head was crushed near his right temple, as if he had been struck with a heavy object. He probably had not seen death coming, at least not for very long.[82]

The corpse was taken to the nearest public house, just down the road: John Farris's tavern. There, they recognized him. It was Thomas Langford, a recent guest.[83] Farris confirmed the man's identity. "It is said that the murdered person is Mr. Thomas Langford, of Pittsylvania county, Virginia, who was on his way to Kentucky with a large sum of money," *Stewart's Kentucky Herald* reported.[84]

Langford was buried.[85] But David Irby, who had been his traveling companion, heard about the murder and could not believe it was his friend who had been killed. So he and John Farris found the gravedigger who had put Langford in the ground, and they went to the gravesite and dug him up. Irby brushed off the dirt and "inspected" the body. It was him. "The whole visage of the person" looked like Langford, he said. But he knew him, especially, by one distinctive feature: "the loss of a tooth in the front part of his jaw."[86]

Meanwhile, Langford's loved ones began to mourn him. He was missed. "Mr. Lankford was a man of much respectability," one memorial noted, "and his loss is sincerely lamented by all who had the pleasure of his acquaintance. But to his father and relatives his death is a source of the deepest affliction."[87]

* * *

THE HAND OF justice hardly ever moved swiftly in early Kentucky. Constables dragged their feet; sheriffs slept through duties. Trials were delayed. The law moved slowly, if at all. But not in this case.

The Harps were immediately suspected. Langford's body was found on December 14, only two days after he had been seen leaving the tavern with the brothers. Captain Joseph Ballenger, a wealthy merchant and former Revolutionary soldier, was tasked by the attorney general with finding the suspects. About six days after Langford's body was discovered, Ballenger and his men mounted horses and began the chase.[88] "Mr. Ballenger is in pursuit of them, with a determined resolution never to quit the chase," one newspaper reported.[89]

Ballenger was formidable. He loomed large, the sort of character around whom whole counties gathered shape. Around town, he was called "Devil Jo." Through his wife, Ballenger was related to one of the premier families of Kentucky. Jane Logan Ballenger was the daughter of Colonel John Logan, who, after moving to Kentucky in 1779, had fought in countless expeditions against western Indians and was now Kentucky's state treasurer. The Ballengers were a prominent couple. "He was really a gentleman, and his wife was a lady," one traveler wrote after visiting with them.[90]

Ballenger was a sometime sheriff, which may be why he was chosen to head the search party. But as a merchant, he also knew the terrain reaching well beyond his own county. He had several times traveled to Spanish Mississippi to buy and sell slaves. He also kept a tavern in Stanford where guests could swig a half pint of whiskey for a shilling, brandy for a few pence more. It was one of the few gathering spots nearby, a good place to round up men—and news.[91]

He knew who he was looking for: Plenty of people had described the men and women last seen at the tavern with Thomas Langford. (Jane Farris well remembered watching him drink and leave with the Harps.) At a time when most people were hunkering down for the cold season, Ballenger put his face to the wind and rode the dips and swells of Kentucky's undulating hills—one writer called them "agreeably uneven, gently ascending and descending at no great distances"—which, at this time of year, might have been dusted with snow.[92] He haunted the lonely barns and smokehouses where farmers were curing meat for the coming year.

Ballenger's men knocked on the doors of small cabins where the people inside were huddled around fires, warding off the cold. They inquired about travelers. Then, somehow, Ballenger stumbled into some dumb luck. At one house, he heard that a party like the one he was seeking had been spotted near the head of Rolling Fork. A man told Ballenger that he encountered them himself; he had paused to warm himself by their fire, but something had spooked him.[93] Ballenger's men rode off that way.

On Christmas Day, less than a week after setting out, Ballenger found them. It was an incredible thing, given all the hiding spots into which they could have disappeared. Did he see a thread of smoke rising above bare trees? Tracks in the snow? When Ballenger arrived, he caught them off guard. They were eating, according to one report, hunched over something simple like corn and broth. They had not dreamed of being discovered. Maybe they did not even know they were suspected of Langford's murder. Ballenger's men surrounded the humble little camp. The Harps barely resisted.

Ballenger took all five—Wiley, Micajah, Susana, Betsy, and Sally—into custody.[94]

Not only did they have Langford's horse and much of his money ("about 50L," according to the *Georgia Gazette*), they had all sorts of his things: His coats. His breeches. His whip. His Freemasons' apron. His handkerchiefs. His shaving glass. They had even kept his little pocket book with its notes about how much he had paid for cheese. Inside the flap was his name: *Thomas Langford.*[95]

* * *

BALLENGER TOOK THEM to Stanford, where he lived. It was an unremarkable little place, just up the road from Crab Orchard. It had a violent history of its own and had weathered relentless Indian attacks years earlier. But in 1798, when the Harps arrived, Stanford was quiet. It had a plain face. Stout log houses, a tanning yard, a few taverns. "Little can be said in favour of the Town," one traveler wrote in 1796.[96]

Ballenger kept them in his own house. He held them there for ten days, while awaiting the Lincoln County court to convene. It was the same public house where men gathered to drink "rum, wine, and French brandy," among other things, by the half pint. But the prisoners were kept under careful watch. Eight men guarded them, at all times. Days came and went. The new year arrived, 1799. A blacksmith came with handcuffs, two pairs, specially made for Wiley and Micajah, and put them on.[97]

The Harps, for their part, refused to despair. They passed the hours in song and kept themselves amused. Micajah sang "finely." "They were lively whilst in confinement," Ballenger's young son remembered, "and did not seem in the least depressed."

Little John Ballenger must have gotten a good look at them, while they were in his father's house. Many years later, he vividly recalled their appearance: Micajah was "upwards of six feet high and remarkably strong and active." He had a "black bushy head of hair, which fell over his ears & shoulders." He seemed larger than life—"savage," even. Wiley, on the other hand, was smaller, with lighter hair. To Little John, he looked "pleasant."[98]

* * *

ON JANUARY 4, all five were indicted for murder. All gave their family name as "Roberts" (Susana's maiden name), except Betsy, who gave her real name—Elizabeth Walker.[99] The prisoners were allowed to speak in their own defense, but that testimony is lost. The evidence was damning. Langford's sundry belongings, found with the Harps, were trotted out. (Jane Farris singled out one item she knew belonged to the decedent: "the small shaving glass.")[100] They were ordered to appear before the district court in the spring to stand trial for murder. In the meantime, they would be sent to the jail in Danville, Kentucky, about ten miles away.[101]

On the way out of court, Micajah Harp turned to Ballenger.

Give me a chance to escape this, he said. I'll fight the three best men in the crowd. If I win, you let me go.[102]

If Ballenger heard, he ignored it.

* * *

THE HARPS ARRIVED in Danville, under guard, on January 5, 1799. They must have looked a sorry lot. All three women were very pregnant. They were taken to the jail, a crude little building made of thick-hewn logs. It had just two small, dark chambers with dirt floors. The wind trilled through the walls in places. They would pass several months here, awaiting trial.[103]

The jailer's name was John Biegler. He brought wood for the fire to keep them warm, and he fed them. He must have worried for his own safety, or he was nervous they might try to break free, because on January 20, two weeks after the Harps arrived, he bought "Two horse locks to chain the men's feet to the ground, 12s. and 1 bolt, 3s." It wasn't enough. In February, he purchased a lock for the jail's front door. Eighteen shillings. Two weeks later, he bought three pounds of nails. Four men, two at a time, guarded the prisoners.[104]

Often crudely constructed, county jails were like sieves. It was easy enough to bribe a jailer or recruit a friend to jostle the door open after nightfall or even to pick a lock and slip out, undetected. Lawmen were forever fretting over the security of their jails. In 1797, the governor of Tennessee begged a sheriff to secure the Knoxville jail. Its prisoners seemed to be plotting an escape. How did he know? "I am told they were heard at work Last Night," he wrote, "appearingly filing their Irons off."[105]

Biegler had reason to worry. After he clapped the Harps into jail, another body turned up near the Wilderness Road. "The body of a man was discovered," the *Palladium* reported. "Concealed under the water" of Robinson's Creek, "with some old wood thrown over him," he had been dead for some time. "On the body being examined," the newspaper divulged, "there were five holes discovered in his head." Although the report does not name the Harps, whoever examined the body connected the man's death, immediately, with Langford's. "It is supposed he had been killed about the same time that the unfortunate Mr. Langford was, and that they both met their fate with the same instrument of death."[106]

A month passed. On February 7, Betsy went into labor. Biegler ordered hyson tea—a quarter pound of it—and sugar and ginger. He called in a midwife. It was a difficult birth; she labored for two days. But in the end, she bore a healthy baby boy, Micajah's son. In early March, they repeated the ritual when Susana was brought to bed. Hyson tea (a little less of it this time), sugar, midwife. She gave birth to a baby girl, Micajah's daughter. Strange little family they were, these seven lost souls.[107]

It was a cramped space, that little room. It was dark. They didn't

A replica of the Danville jail at the Constitution Square Historic Site in Danville, Kentucky. Photo by the author.

wash. The babies squalled. And the trial neared. By 1799, some states had begun building penitentiaries, blocky buildings with solitary cells and geometric yards, meant to impose order and atonement. But the Danville jail was no penitentiary. It was nothing more than a holding place for the accused. It was not meant to be a place of discipline or punishment. But perhaps after several months, it began to feel that way. Maybe they talked Biegler into loosening the iron locks. Maybe they bribed him. Or maybe they had been planning this all that winter.

On March 16, Biegler discovered it: Only the women and infants were there. Wiley and Micajah were gone.

In the jailer's accounts under March 19, Biegler scrawled a final expense: *Mending the wall in jail where the prisoners escaped.* Twelve shillings.[108]

CHAPTER 5

THE WICKEDNESS OF THE HEART

The Danville jail
Danville, Kentucky
April 1799

For Sally, locked into that small room, the days and nights blurred. Time passed. How much? She probably could not tell. On April 9, about three weeks after Wiley and Micajah had broken free, her belly began to tighten. Then it tightened more. When the pain became unbearable, the jailer brought a quart of whiskey. Finally, she delivered a little girl—Wiley's daughter.[1] *He led her over mountains and valleys so deep.*

The delivery underscored her abandonment. Childbirth, for most women, was a social time. Mothers and sisters visited to prepare for the baby's arrival. During labor, neighboring women were called to the mother's bedside to assist. They noshed on cakes and beer as labor progressed. "Most early American women literally gave birth in the arms or on the laps of their neighbors," writes one historian.[2] Sally had Susana and Betsy—sisters of a sort—and they surely helped her in her travail. But without her family and the usual bustle surrounding a child's birth, it must have felt very lonely.

After giving birth, most women had a "lying-in" period where they kept to bed for about a week, recovering and slowly taking up normal tasks before "return[ing] to the kitchen" (the eighteenth-century way of describing the end of a mother's recuperation).[3] But Sally would not be returning to the kitchen. She had mere days to recover physically before she had to appear in court.

She must have rued her fate. She was the daughter of an honorable man, a good girl, respectable. She had probably married Wiley for love. He was less respectable, his own past hazy. It was an aspirational marriage for him. But instead of Sally raising him up, Wiley had pulled her down. He fell into debt. He was sued. He gambled. He stole things. He drank. As his world fell apart, he took Sally with him. "Sally was thought a fine girl until married to Wiley," one man adjudged.[4] Now he had left her. Not two years after she married him, Sally was alone with a newborn, awaiting trial.

An eighteenth-century marriage was like a contract: The wife gave herself, her loyalty, her labor. In return, her husband was forever "responsible for her care." As a husband, Wiley Harp had failed spectacularly. He had broken every promise to protect her, to care for her, even—as husbands were obliged to do—to "house, feed, and clothe her."[5] (It is possible that the responsibility of providing for her even as his life spiraled had amplified Wiley's desperation.) Everything she might have imagined for herself, he had shattered.

But she was still his wife. She was still yoked to him. The question now for Sally, and for all the Harp women, was: What would that mean in court? All of Sally's alleged crimes had been committed by Wiley's side. Would she be seen as his accomplice, every bit as responsible for Thomas Langford's murder? Or was she more like a hostage, following along because she had no choice?

Was Sally Harp guilty? Could a wife in the eighteenth century even be thought of as such?

Only days after Sally gave birth, the district court in Kentucky took up that question. There would be an answer in the eyes of the law. In the eyes of history, it looks far less conclusive.

* * *

"I FELL IN love with a Knoxville girl, with dark and rolling eyes," the narrator sings in a once-popular Southern ballad. "I promised her I'd marry her, if me she'd ne'er deny."[6]

Sally Harp was memorable. Descriptions of her are surprisingly vivid. "Sally . . . was really pretty & delicate," one man recalled.[7] At the time of her trial, she was about twenty years old and lovely, "a woman of handsome features, genteel demeanor and, apparently, of delicate constitution," another wrote.[8] Susana and Betsy were seen—by some people, at least—as "coarse." But not Sally. She was remembered for her refinement and good looks, "a beautiful young woman, [who] had been well raised."[9]

Of the three Harp women, Sally Harp is best remembered. She breaks through the most brightly. But even Sally Harp is hard to gauge. It is difficult to tell how complicit she was in any of her husband's crimes. At times, Sally, Susana, and Betsy appear to have been loyal to Wiley and Micajah to the bitter end; at other times, they look hesitant, distant, and trapped. If taking their measure was a problem now facing Kentucky's courts, it's also a puzzle for anyone hoping to understand their actions.

The Harp wives have sometimes been cast as captives. "Alas, poor, lost and ruined girls!" moaned one writer.[10] Even their weddings, it's been implied, were involuntary. Long after the murders, one writer imagined that Wiley and Micajah had, in fact, abducted Sally and Susana and made them wives. It was perhaps appealing to think that Sally had been "ruthlessly stolen and borne off," spirited away from her family while "screaming and calling for help."[11] Or to paint Micajah "stealing and carrying off" Susana and leaving her relatives to search and search without the "least trace or trait of her."[12] But the truth is far less dramatic.

How Sally met Wiley and how they fell in love—if they fell in love—no one knows. Her maiden name was Rice. Perhaps Wiley had some previous association with her father, as John Rice seems to have sold Wiley his land. Perhaps he'd been Rice's tenant, or some kind of apprentice, and grown close to the man's daughter. How hopeful she must have felt on the day of her wedding, donning a pretty dress of ribbons and bright colors. There would have been singing and dancing, possibly guns fired and whiskey bottles passed.[13]

On that moment, her whole life turned. The same would have been true for any young girl. For good reason, many mountain songs—the tunes women hummed as they picked fruit and made soap and cured meat—were about courtship. They were about seduction. The plotlines all hinged on the choice of the right match. *Let's take a walk and view the meadows gay,* the suitor suggests in "The Knoxville Girl." *That we might have a little talk and plan our wedding day.*[14]

But once the fiddling faded and the wedding day was over, a woman's life dulled. She shrank into days of quiet duty. The ideal of the dutiful wife is captured in a tradition about Susannah Hart Shelby, the bride of Kentucky's first governor, who reportedly fashioned her own wedding gown from flax she had raised, pulled, spun, and woven herself—all to prove to her future husband that she would be a "helper and not a burden."[15] On the frontier, where the Appalachians bumped up against Indian country, life was grueling; it was pricked by hard times and war. Men wanted wives who would do what was expected, without complaint. They wanted helpmates: *Old Man, Old Man, I want your daughter,* went another old song. *To bake me bread and carry my water.*[16]

All three Harp women had no doubt carried plenty of water. Backcountry wives shouldered a lot of the toil, including what was elsewhere branded as men's work. In the mountains, it was not uncommon to find "delicate" women carting wood, yanking stumps from the ground, even slaughtering animals. Astonishing passersby who came from other parts of the country, hardy backwoods women would "knock down beef cattle with a felling ax, and then roll down their sleeves, remove their bloody aprons, tidy their hair, and invite their visitors to tea."[17]

But, always, the men ruled. Doing men's work did not make women equal. Far from it: Husbands, in Sally's world, were like little kings. "The historical myth that the frontier created a spirit of equality among the sexes could not be farther from the truth," writes historian David Hackett Fischer.[18] Even more starkly than in other parts of the United States, households in the backcountry were ruled—firmly—by men. "The man of the house was lord and ruler over all," one writer proclaims. His woman "seldom . . . spoke out."[19] She "was required to do his bidding quietly, cheerfully and without complaint."[20]

The rhythms of life for most women had not changed in generations. Sally Harp would have expected to live a life much like her own mother's—a life tethered to hearth and washtub and cradle. Her lot was to be a good wife and mother. It was to keep house. The typical wife did not know much about her husband's affairs outside the home. She didn't know how much money he had. She didn't know how much his things were worth. She didn't know about his debts or what was owed to him.[21] She cooked and baked and nursed and stitched and mothered. And obeyed.

Marriage swallowed a woman's identity. A wife had no being apart from her husband. When a woman took her wedding vows, she all but disappeared. "Her place in the world," as one historian writes, "was his place in the world."[22] That was true in American minds and also in American courts. In the eyes of the law, women were mere shadows, barely present. The legal construct that governed most women's lives was *coverture*—the notion that a wife's legal identity was entirely "covered" by her husband's. A married woman could not bring a lawsuit. She could not enter into a contract or even write a will. "The very being or legal existence of the woman is suspended during the marriage," jurist William Blackstone wrote.[23]

In Sally's lifetime, though, there were new calls for women's rights. "Yes, ye lordly, ye haughty sex, our souls are by nature *equal* to yours," wrote Judith Sargent Murray in her 1790 essay "On the Equality of the Sexes." There were even glimmers of change. Schooling became more available to girls. New female academies threw open their doors to well-to-do young women. "Let the ladies of [the] country be educated properly," the humanitarian Benjamin Rush proclaimed in 1787. Mothers, after all, had to raise good republican citizens.[24]

Marriage was changing, too. It is not easy to peek into the bedrooms and parlors of the eighteenth century and eavesdrop on whispers between husband and wife. But there are clues that marriages were becoming more balanced, more equal. Women began bearing fewer children: Those who were married after 1780 had smaller families, which, historians suppose, might mean that wives had more say in the matter.[25] Divorce, too, became slightly more common. Where legal separation was available, women sought it out. Tennessee passed its first divorce law in 1799, the very year of Sally's indictment. Had Sally Harp wanted to sue for divorce in 1799, she could have.[26]

"Wives owed fealty and obedience to their princes," writes one historian, but only "so long as those princes behaved as princes."[27] In reality, though, women had trouble shaking free of even the most troubled marriages. Their divorce petitions are sometimes pitiful litanies of "the most trying calamities." One woman in backcountry Virginia pled that she had been "denied the privileges of a dutiful wife" and "forced . . . with her infant in her arms from her bed and home," "compelled to throw herself and child upon the charity of the world." Her husband threatened to cut her throat. But even in circumstances like these, a divorce was not always granted.[28]

Mostly, for women, the Revolution's promises remained out of reach, as if atop a too-tall shelf.[29] Coverture was barely jostled by the Revolution. Kings were obsolete, but a woman was still a woman. Even Catharine Beecher, who founded the Hartford Female Seminary, thought so. "Heaven has appointed to one sex the superior, and to the other the subordinate station," she wrote in 1827.[30]

It's no surprise that Sally Harp is difficult to fathom. Appalachian women are notoriously hard to resurrect.[31] The sources are scant. Their lives are obscured by the "gendered codes" that for so long made them invisible to history. "Recognizing the historical agency of Appalachian women is not just . . . difficult," one scholar writes. "It's a heartache."[32] But one way into their lives is to listen to their songs. As women stitched and spun and quilted, they sang. "The mother is crooning over her work, some old ballad of an eerie sadness," one woman wrote, conjuring early Appalachia. Women kept alive these songs—"the ballads the family sang"—many of which were brought from Ireland or Scotland. Inside them are the echoes of "their feelings and needs," the refractions of many anonymous women.[33]

At the heart of many ballads lies a twisted menace: Violence abounds. Women die with grim, chilling frequency in Appalachian folk songs. Murder ballads turn, again and again, on young girls slain by lovers. The plot repeats: A suitor lures his victim away from home, then stabs or drowns her. ("One can't help but conjecture," one writer quips, "that if Appalachian women had only known how to swim, we'd have only half the murder ballads we do now.")[34] If you listen carefully, you begin to glean something of the threat lurking between the lines: A wrong choice, for a woman, could be deadly. Sally Harp must have felt this lesson keenly as she shivered in jail: Punishment came quick, when women were "too trusting."[35]

In "The Knoxville Girl," which begins as a sweet love song before turning sharply darker, the narrator kills his beloved. Before she dies, the victim falls to her knees. *Oh Lord, have mercy!* she cries. *Oh, Willie, dear, don't murder me here, I'm not prepared to die.* But he beats her till she's bloody. At the end, he tosses her in the river:

I took her by her long yellow hair, I dragged her round and round.
I dragged her to still waters deep that flows through Knoxville town.[36]

* * *

ONLY A FEW days after giving birth, Sally Harp went to court. The district court convened on April 15. The weather was warming, after a long winter. "*Fine growing weather,*" the *Kentucky Almanac* declared for the month of April. It predicted "light frosts" and "*cool mornings.*"[37]

Court day, in early Kentucky, was an event. Hundreds came. They packed the taverns surrounding the square. Danville had three watering holes: Barbee's, Gill's, and Grayson's, a fine place where the Political Club met, with plank floors, high mantels, and carved woodwork. When court was in session, these places crawled with men. People came from all over. They hauled in crops and livestock to be sold outside the courthouse. They gossiped. They drank and brawled. They brought their deeds to enter into record. Only a year or so earlier, Wiley—a new property owner—had been one of these men.[38]

But for a woman like Sally, walking into court in Danville would have been intimidating. She did not have far to go: The courthouse stood only a few feet from the jail where the Harps had spent the winter. It was a simple log structure. But it was capacious, perhaps even impressive, a place that had witnessed history. All ten of the conventions leading up to the drafting of the Kentucky constitution in 1792 had taken place within its walls. Sally wouldn't have known that. She could not have pictured the delegates crammed in by the dozens. But she would have felt the gravity of walking into a space so heavily masculine.[39]

The courtroom was noisy. Feet scuffling. Voices mumbling. People crowding in, the smell of bodies. Flies buzzing above heads as men waved them off. A shuffling mass of souls pressed up against the bar that separated the officers of the court—justices, lawyers, clerks—from the crowd. Everything was wooden: the planks of the floor, the bench, the bar. The men, too. They looked to the door with grave faces. The attorney general was there, staring at her. She would have been shackled. The jailer gripped her arm tightly.

"Oyez, oyez," the deputy sheriff called out.[40]

Sally, Susana, and Betsy were led in, accompanied by the jailer. They had spent months sleeping on a dirt floor. They were probably grimy, in tattered clothing. This was it: The moment of judgment was almost upon them.

All three—along with the absent Wiley and Micajah—had been indicted in the murder of Thomas Langford. They were to be tried separately: Susana first, then Betsy, then Sally. All three pleaded not guilty.

Were they? The real killer was not there. According to the indictments, Micajah was the one believed to have delivered the death blow to Langford. He had struck the man hard with a "piece of Iron," leaving a two-inch gash in Langford's right temple.[41] But how complicit were the Harp women? The jurymen had to wonder: Had these poor women recoiled at the actions of their husbands but obeyed and stood by as wives were supposed to do? Or had they helped plan the murder—perhaps by befriending Langford at Farris's tavern or luring him into their camp? Then, as now, it was hard to tell.

Almost certainly, the jurymen had never seen anything like it—a woman dragged up to the bar, accused of murder. Women killed far less often than men did.[42] And when they did kill, they hardly ever killed strangers. They killed babies they didn't want or husbands who came home drunk and beat them. They did not murder harmless travelers for money. That was unheard of. The dozens of women convicted of murder across the early republic are not well studied, but you can find them if you look. At least seventy-four went to the gallows for killing someone in the years 1776 to 1826.[43] Their stories are knotty tangles of malice and woe: Bits and pieces of what happened to them float through newspapers, crime literature, and trial records of the era, though some of the stories remain beyond reach, nothing more than a name and a date. Still, there's often enough to get a feel for who they were and what they did.

Their victims were often children. They killed other people's children whom they resented tending to. Or they killed their own. They stuffed poison into toddlers' mouths or beat them gravely.[44] They killed their unwanted babies, sometimes in ways that are achingly evocative of the trappings of femininity. When Hannah Pigen delivered a baby boy in 1785, she plucked a string of flax from a loom and tied it around the infant's throat. A few years later, Abiel Converse, an unmarried servant living in a little Massachusetts town, strangled her newborn son and then wound the body in a ball of fiber from the spinning wheel.[45]

These deaths took place inside the walls of unhappy homes. Husbands died, too, at the hands of their wives. In rural New York in 1798, Sylvia Wood blasted her husband with a shotgun when he tried to keep her from drinking.[46] In 1812, a New Jersey woman, Mary Cole, killed her cruel and meddling mother. Her husband found his wife cutting her mother's throat. "Mary, for God's sake what are you doing?" he asked. She replied: "She must be killed, for we can't live so any longer."[47] Only a few women out of dozens were accused of killing someone they did not know intimately.[48]

When you page through these cases, you don't find women who look or sound like Sally Harp or Susana or Betsy. What you find very often, instead, are women on the racial margins. Almost three-quarters of the women convicted nationally during this period were either Black or Native American. The vast majority of them were enslaved. They may not have done more of the murders, but they were more likely to be hauled before the bar and convicted. It is probably safe to say that the typical woman hanged for murder in the early republic was an enslaved Black woman who had killed either her own child, her master, or her master's child.[49]

It is a sad tale. Sifting through the records, you are immediately confronted with women choosing violence over the agonies of slavery. As you might imagine, sometimes these women acted out of passion or in self-defense, but others clearly planned their murders. Flora struck her master with a club when he tried to intervene in a quarrel between herself and his wife. (This may not have been as spur-of-the-moment as it appeared: "She had long owed him a spite," the widow testified.)[50] An enslaved woman in South Carolina bashed her sleeping mistress over the head, then cut her throat.[51] Two Virginia women, Daphne and Nelly, beat their overseer to death with sticks, rocks, and fists in 1793 after he whipped Nelly brutally.[52]

Just a few months after the Harp trials, in another part of Kentucky, an enslaved woman named Fanny was hanged. In June 1799, Fanny's mistress, Sarah Field, had accused her of stealing. "[W]hen Mr. Field comes home I will make him tie you up and give you one hundred lashes on your bare back," Sarah had said.[53] Fanny waited until later that night, slipped into Sarah's bedroom, and, in the dark, watched her mistress sleeping. She "stood by the bed side" next to the motionless Sarah, and then she struck. There was a violent struggle. Out of the corner of her eye, Fanny spotted a stocking. She grabbed it, drew it around Sarah's neck, and strangled her.[54]

All of these women died for their crimes. But placing Sally Harp beside them doesn't tell you much. She was nothing like them.

After the Harp women were arraigned, they were taken back to jail for several days before their trials began. As they were led out of court, they likely drew stares. Perhaps Sally Harp's appearance was an advantage—her very *difference* an advantage. A jury might readily believe that a slave would plot to strangle her mistress with a stocking, but a young, married white woman with a squirming babe in her arms? Would she do such a thing? Would she help lure a stranger to his death? You can almost sense the bafflement hanging over the court.

* * *

TWO DAYS LATER, the jailer brought the women back into court. The trials went curiously. Susana Harp was tried first.

The only record of what happened lies in an old court-order book. The edges of its pages were long ago eaten away by moisture and pricked with mold. They look like flinty shelves of shale. No testimony survives. All that is left is the barest of outlines sketched in faint, spindly script.

Susana Harp was a plain woman, perhaps a bit gangly and awkward. She was "rather tall," a sheriff remembered, but also "raw boned"—that is, wiry and gaunt. Around twenty-five years old, she was the eldest of the three Harp wives; Betsy and Sally were a few years younger. To the authorities, Susana may have looked like a mother hen or a leader among them. But there is little to suggest she was much more than a simple country girl who, as one Tennessean wrote, Micajah had "found living somewhere in the mountainous region of Sevier or Blount county."[55]

Although she must have worried, Susana had some reason to be hopeful. The courts in Kentucky were unpredictable. The gears of justice did not always turn smoothly, and they often favored the accused. Jurors were not painstakingly selected or screened. They were rounded up randomly by the sheriff. It was sometimes difficult to fill the jury box at all. Once jurors had been found, they were liable to be bribed—which was not unheard of. But even without bribes, Kentucky juries liked to free defendants. Whether this was because they sometimes related more to the accused than the prosecutors or because they were hesitant to send fellow Kentuckians off to be hanged is hard to say. But it was possible to get away with serious crimes, even murder.[56]

Standing before the bar to present the case against Susana was the attorney general of Kentucky, James Blair. He was a Virginian from an elite family who had come to Kentucky to better himself; he had not been satisfied with the money he was making as a lawyer and assemblyman in Virginia.[57] (He was likely disappointed quickly, as the attorney general post was a notoriously thankless circuit of travel and toil that eventually became famous for being more work than it paid for. Blair, unable to escape it though he tried, held the post for an interminable twenty-four years.)

Blair was everything the Harp men were not—a blueblood, upright, steeped in the law.[58] "Mr. Blair's moral rectitude is unexceptionable," a federal judge wrote about him in 1802, "& he is well respected."[59] As he paced the front of the courtroom, he must have seemed to the Harp women a serious foe.

The Harp women had lawyers.[60] But they may not have helped much, as most did not have a lot of training. It was not terribly hard to become a lawyer in early Kentucky. Many were self-taught. They simply read books, hung around court, absorbed what they could by working for other attorneys, and when they felt ready, tried to be admitted to the bar. All that stood between a man and a law license was a simple, sometimes cursory, examination by two judges.[61]

Lawyers were not well liked. They had grown fat and rich off of everyone's land woes, and as a profession, they were reviled as "blood-suckers, as pickpockets, as windbags, as smooth-tongued rogues."[62] They drew curses at the local taverns. If getting a law license was easy, lawyering—which required journeying long distances from courthouse to courthouse—was not, and some of Kentucky's lawyers were hardened characters who patronized pothouses and ran up debts. They lived transient lives and amused themselves by playing cards and gambling as they rode circuit. They kept Edmond Hoyle's card game rule books close at hand. "The card table was set out every night," one remembered. "There were *Gentlemen,* attending the Courts, who studied Hoyle, more than they did Blackstone."[63]

Blair presented the evidence to the jury.

He easily conjured Langford, the victim: an aspirational young Virginian visiting Kentucky with money in his pocket. The details of Langford's murder do suggest some amount of forethought and baiting. While the Harps likely met him unexpectedly, they charmed him intentionally at John Farris's tavern. One of them had noticed the spot where Langford's leggings had sprung a few loose threads, and Susana stepped in to mend them. "Susannah Roberts sewed it," Jane Farris testified, implying that Susana had knowingly drawn in the victim.[64]

Certainly, the Harp women had been with Langford. They had all left Farris's tavern together only a short spell before Langford's body was discovered, mangled and broken, a little farther up the Wilderness Road. But the most damning evidence of their involvement in his murder was the fact that when the Harps were caught in December, they'd had in their possession Langford's things, including his pocket book, his coats, his horse, even his shaving glass.[65] (According to tradition, one of the women was wearing his "drab great coat" when the Harps were captured, and another had some of his money "secreted" on her person.)[66]

The indictments put the murder weapon in Micajah's hand. But if the jury believed that the Harp women were there when Langford was slain, they could still be convicted of murder. "There are as many ways of killing," James Blair wrote a few years after prosecuting the Harp women, "as there are modes by which a man may die." Wounding. Poison. Lying in wait. Strangling. Suffocation. But one did not have to plunge a knife into another man's neck to be considered a killer. Doing anything that "clearly endangers another's life" and "occasions his death," Blair wrote, was also murder.[67]

More damningly, Blair did not believe Langford was their only victim. By this point, he had already concluded that the other dead man found along the Wilderness Road in February—in a flax shirt and buckskin breeches—had been slain by the Harps, too. Although the women were not charged for that murder, a note in the court records suggests he believed them responsible: He had ordered the sheriff to return to surviving family members the money and "personal goods" that belonged to Langford and the other man—now identified as James Clayton—found in possession of the Harps. (These things, the clerk jotted down, had been taken "at the time the said Lankford & Clayton were severally Murdered.")[68] If raised before the jury, this, too, was powerful evidence.

But as Susana stood nervously at the bar, her sex gave her some hidden advantages. Juries were notoriously reluctant to convict women of crimes, especially white women, and especially of felonies like murder. This had been true almost as far back as courts had existed. In medieval England, even women who actively murdered—brandishing swords and knives—were more often acquitted than men. Colonial American juries followed suit, acquitting women more often.[69] The pattern only deepened in the nineteenth century: "Favoritism toward women under the criminal law," writes journalist Ann Jones, "was the trade-off men made for stripping women of rights under the civil law."[70]

And there was another card to play. The wives had access to a legal defense that Wiley and Micajah themselves could not have used had they been present in court: coverture. Whatever other defense she offered, Susana Harp very likely would have made the argument that she was not guilty simply because she was a wife. If she had participated in Langford's murder, Micajah had made her do it.

How culpable a woman like Susana or Sally might be, in fact, was legally murky. Marriage made women invisible to the law, even when they broke it. Here was the other side of coverture: It protected women from prosecution for many crimes. Just as her civil identity was "covered" by her husband's, a woman's criminal acts often were, too. According to William Blackstone, if a wife committed a crime under the coercion of her husband—if he ordered her to do it—she was not responsible. In the eyes of the law, she might be blameless.

Under her husband's orders, a woman could not incur guilt. "Where there is no choice, there can be no act of the will," Blackstone explained. Crimes were not crimes if not committed willfully. There were many circumstances under common law in which will might be absent: If it was done by "misfortune or chance" or committed by a lunatic or a child, a wrong might not be willful. There were also cases of "compulsion and . . . necessity" that might push someone to act against their own judgment, as in relationships of subjection, like that of a sheriff acting on the king's orders. But the prime example of this, Blackstone wrote, was "matrimonial subjection"—a wife's to her husband.[71]

This rule applied even to some serious crimes. If a woman burgled a cellar with her husband, she was considered "not guilty of any crime."[72] If she robbed someone in the street with him, she might go free. In 1820, when a woman named Lavinia Fisher was convicted and hanged for committing highway robbery with her husband, many were shocked that she had been found guilty. "Where a man and his wife are tried for a robbery," a New York newspaper pointed out, "it seldom happens that both are convicted." Most people simply assumed the woman's crimes were done "under the orders and directions of men only."[73]

In theory, though, murder was supposed to be different. In a murder case, a woman could not simply plead that she had been coerced. Murder, Blackstone explained, was an act so terrible, so wrong—so "malum in se," or evil in itself—that it bent the laws of nature. It was a crime "of a deeper dye" from which no one could escape being punished.[74]

Although there is no transcript, it is possible to imagine what Susana might have said in court. At various turns in later conversations, the Harp wives seem to have begged off any responsibility for the murders. They implied that they were forced to go along. Once, Susana said, Micajah had forced her to wear the clothes of one of the victims: He "made her put on [a] hat & other articles." Later, when she was confronted by a relative of the victim, she had sheepishly handed him the hat and said, "This is your's." She then fell to her knees, begged for her life, and told him how she had been "compelled" to put it on.[75]

According to another account, Sally later told people that "she had married her husband without any knowledge of his real character." She had not seen any of it coming. "She was so much shocked at the first murder which they committed," she allegedly confessed, "that she attempted to escape from them, but was prevented." She made other attempts to get away, too, she said. If that is true, there is no evidence of it.[76] But it is very likely what she would have told the jury: I only participated in Langford's undoing because my husband forced my hand.

All three of the Harp women are ciphers. It's nearly impossible to tell what any of them were thinking. But in the end, they look a lot like the doomed women in eighteenth-century murder ballads who, like "perfect victims," never fight, never struggle, and never try to escape—even after "they learn what their lovers have in mind." Ever passive, they sometimes get on their knees and plead for their lives, but they never bolt. They never jump on a horse to ride away. Some don't even protest. "They say nothing before their deaths, staying ladylike and quiet . . . until the end."[77]

If Susana's lawyer blamed Micajah, it did not work. The case went to the jury, twelve men who needed to return a unanimous verdict. They deliberated. Then she stepped to the bar to learn her fate.

"The said Susannah Roberts is Guilty," the bailiff read.

She was ordered back to jail.[78]

* * *

THE FOLLOWING DAY, April 18, Betsy was tried. She faced a different jury, twelve new faces, who saw things rather differently.

It was the very same evidence, with the possible exception of Susana having stitched Langford's pants. But Betsy struck these jurymen, somehow, as less culpable.

"Elizabeth Walker is not Guilty of the felony whereof she stands Indicted," the jury found. The court announced that she was free to go without delay.[79]

It was a stunning twist. In one sense, Betsy should have been the guiltiest of them all. She was Micajah's second "wife"—but not officially, since they could not be legally married. ("Susan Harpe always professed to have been married to Micajah Harpe—but Betsey never did," someone recalled.)[80] She was the only one of them (including Wiley and Micajah) not to use the alias "Roberts." She was her own person. Shouldn't that have made her all the more guilty?

This second verdict—Betsy Walker's acquittal—turned out to be a windfall for all three women. A godsend. After spending a raw, icy winter at the mercy of the Danville jail's turnkey, Sally Harp was about to be given a great gift. Something about that split result—two juries, two different verdicts—spooked the attorney general. The very same day, he abandoned entirely the case against Sally Harp. To save Kentucky the expense of a trial that might lead to the same result as Betsy's, he would no longer seek to prosecute her. The state simply dropped the charges.[81]

In light of these staggering surprises, Susana petitioned for a new trial. She was granted one. But soon enough, the state abandoned her case, too. Blair directed the clerk to throw out her conviction. He would not prosecute her again.[82]

What was he thinking? Keeping the Harps warm and fed all winter had been expensive. Certainly he reasoned that it was not worthwhile to keep paying for Susana and her baby to sit in jail while awaiting the next district court meeting. He might also have feared another acquittal, a smear on his courtroom skills, perhaps. Or did some genuine hesitation creep in? He might have felt, sincerely, that it was unjust to convict one woman and acquit another on the very "same proof."[83]

One other thing seems to have weighed on his mind: The Harp women had defended one another. Each swore to the others' innocence. They were probably used to circling wagons. They did so, on occasion, even with their husbands. While on the run with Wiley and Micajah, Susana and Betsy later said, "many a night, the three women wd. go off by themselves & stay away."[84] They were protective of one another.

Rural women often leaned into sisterhood. They found "refuge" in "their fellow sisters who shared the same labors."[85] While the men in their lives gathered to "swap politics, stories, and drinks," women spent time with one another weaving, gossiping, or cooking. Surviving and finding comfort in the backcountry meant seeking others, and the Harp women, if faced with harsher circumstances, were no different.[86]

If the state tried Susana again, Blair knew, "the two other women" were very likely, once more, to produce evidence "operating in favor of the prisoner." So, as with Sally, he dropped the charges.

All three women escaped conviction. They were free.[87]

* * *

THE PEOPLE FELT badly for the Harp women. They took up a collection and gathered some things—"necessaries & an old mare." They helped them bundle up their babies. Then they packed them up and sent them on their way, back to their friends in Knoxville.[88]

Sally, Susana, and Betsy went free. The court considered them acquitted of any wrongdoing. One way to look at this is that they got away with murder. But another way to read it is that the courts in Kentucky understood a fundamental fact about their lives: that they were, in essence, owned by their husbands.

William Blackstone wrote that murder sprang from "the wickedness of the heart."[89] What he meant was that it was deliberate and willful. To kill in the heat of passion was manslaughter. But murder required malice aforethought, the product of a "bad heart." It is possible that Sally Harp heard this idea repeated in court. Nothing could have described her life better. The heart's wickedness was what had gotten her into trouble and her life nearly ruined. Sally Harp left no confession. She left no firsthand testimony at all. But there is a line in another woman's confession that makes a fitting epigraph for her: "Love, and its delusive promises are the causes of my untimely end."[90]

But it was not over yet. The Harp women left Danville, but they did not go south toward Knoxville. They had other plans. They hooked westward instead and found the Green River. They traded their horse for a canoe. At some point, they were spotted "paddl[ing] down stream like Ladies of the Lake." Then they, too, disappeared.[91]

CHAPTER 6

CANE

Russell's Creek
Green River country, Kentucky
April 1799

John Trabue was twelve, maybe thirteen. He was still a boy. But he was old enough to run errands for his father, to go to a neighbor's house and borrow seed for planting. That was his mission today. He may also have gone to the mill; he carried a sack of flour as he walked.

He had a little dog with him, scampering alongside. He knew the trail. He probably expected no trouble. It was early April—things were thawing and budding. The ground was muddy under his feet. The wilds of Kentucky could be loud: birds cawing, the grasses rustling. The creek waters were probably running high—gurgling loudly, not far off.

Maybe he didn't hear what was coming up behind him. Or maybe he did—realizing, with slow terror, that something, or someone, was following.

A little while later, the dog returned home. It had a gaping wound on the side of its head. Johnny was nowhere to be found.[1]

* * *

JOHNNY WENT MISSING about sixty miles west of Danville. The Trabue family lived in the Green River country, a vast and lonely expanse of southern Kentucky where the bottomlands were still mostly covered in cane. It was everywhere—giant tallgrass "as thick as a goose quill." It grew in wild, chunky thickets—"canebrakes"—that could swallow you whole. The stalks sometimes reached as high as thirty feet.[2]

The Trabue house overlooked Skinhouse Branch, a shallow brook that emptied into Caney Fork. It was a significant place. In one of their earliest forays into the region, Virginia men had built a hunting camp here. Skinhouse Branch took its name from the little shanty—or "skinhouse"—where they stored their pelts. In 1771, Indians captured two of the hunters while the rest were away. They pulled the bark off the skinhouse and left the skins to rot. RUINATION BY GOD, one of the surviving men carved into a beech tree nearby.[3]

But there was little trace of that now. It was a pleasant spot on a choice piece of land. Near where the Trabue house stood, a gentle knoll rose up from the creek. On sunny days, the warm wind stirred the grasses and the light would catch their blades, making them glint like the surface of the ocean. If you visit now, you can almost imagine Johnny sitting atop the hill, lounging in the grass. Or skipping stones in the brook.

Around the Trabue farm, the hills had just begun to sprout barns and smokehouses. The Green River country had only recently opened to settlement. It had once been Kentucky's military district, where Virginia sent its soldiers to claim their spoils. In 1795, looking to cash in on unclaimed lands, Kentucky opened it up to a wider array of migrants. The terms were alluring: Anyone who cleared two acres could have two hundred more, cheaply. Many rushed in.[4] The Trabues had arrived in 1796 as part of this rush, when Johnny was about nine years old.[5]

The land here, for the most part, was not much good. Although the Trabues settled in a historic spot with good prospects, others weren't so lucky. The farms were smaller than those in the Bluegrass, the richly fertile part of Kentucky that was settled first. The

Mount Gilead Baptist Church in Greensburg, Kentucky, near what was once the site of the Trabue home. Photo by the author.

people were humbler. Many were hardscrabble types with little more than a few pennies and hope. To some, this part of Kentucky looked like a dumping ground, filling with hordes of the poor. "Nothing but hunters, horse-thieves & savages," one politician wrote in 1796 about the people living south of the Green River.[6]

But the Trabues were not poor. Johnny lived in a well-off household. His father, a justice of the peace, was doing quite well. A stout and stern man with dark eyes, Daniel Trabue had made a successful life for himself by dint of his own hard work and by seizing the right opportunities. Johnny's father had lived a life many American men wanted, propelling himself out of hard circumstances following the Revolution into independence and respect.[7]

Born in the Virginia Piedmont the eighth of fifteen children, Daniel Trabue had known hardship as a child. He remembered the floods that swept away the tobacco warehouses in 1769 and the frosts that blackened the orchards in 1774. He remembered the first stirrings of the Revolution: men wearing hunting shirts emblazoned with LIBERTY, people forced to swear oaths, king's men getting roughed up. He remembered the hard times during the war when people were so desperate for salt, they cured their meat in hickory ashes. Or they dug up the floors of their smokehouses, hoping to sift out a few precious grains.[8]

He had fought in the Revolution himself after enlisting at sixteen. It was during the war, while serving under George Rogers Clark, when he first laid eyes on the wild grasses and twisted rivers of Kentucky. At Ruddell's Station in 1780, Trabue saw his own brother taken captive by Indians.[9] Remarkably, he was also at Yorktown for Cornwallis's surrender. The war was so central to Trabue's identity that he and his wife, Mary, were married on the Fourth of July in 1782. Their wedding guests startled when they felt the concussions of cannons fired in Richmond to celebrate independence.[10]

Daniel Trabue was an enterprising man. During the war, he had sold liquor to soldiers and made enough money to buy property. First, he moved onto his father's farm in Virginia and added thirty acres. Then he bought a gristmill nearby. From then on, the Trabues were often kissed by good fortune. They had a baby, a little boy named Robert. In 1785, they moved to Kentucky, toddler in tow. They went first to the Bluegrass, where Daniel built another mill and Mary gave birth to little Johnny. In time, they moved farther west and settled on Skinhouse Branch, where they were living when Johnny disappeared.[11]

Johnny's father was a man of faith. He had felt God's grace. Once, in a patch of woods, he had seen the light of heaven streaming down upon him. "I saw the great salvation of Jesus Christ," he wrote. "It is emposible to Describe it. It was unspeacable."[12] He was a founding member of one of the many little Baptist churches that came to define the Kentucky hills.[13] When Johnny went missing, he began to pray.

But it did no good.

* * *

A FEW DAYS after he went missing, Johnny Trabue's body was found. It was crumpled in a sinkhole by the creek. "The remains of the lad were found cut into pieces," the *Kentucky Gazette* reported.[14]

If there was an inquest, the records are lost. But locals concluded quickly that the Harps had killed the boy. "A report is in circulation," the *Gazette* informed its readers on April 18, that "the son of a Mr. Trabue, on Green river, has fallen victim to the murderers of Mr. Langford, since their escape from Danville jail." Perhaps they had been seen nearby. The following week, when a traveler reached Lexington—bearing details that are now lost—the newspaper confirmed the rumor: A "lad" had indeed been murdered "by the criminals who escaped from Danville jail."[15]

Almost certainly at some points during their spree, the Harps were blamed for murders they did not commit. It is easy to imagine, for instance, people in the Tennessee hills chalking up a stray incident or two—or even killings done by Cherokee or Shawnee men—as the work of the Harp brothers, once they became known as notorious killers. But that was not the case with Johnny Trabue's death. The rumors were true: Susana Harp admitted, much later, that Wiley had killed the boy—or at least that it had been his idea.[16] Why? What did they want with an innocent twelve-year-old boy?

There is no evidence that the Trabues knew the Harps. If they killed Johnny (which seems all but certain), the motive is murky. He was not like Thomas Langford, whose silver jangled seductively in his pocket. At most, Johnny carried a sack of meal. They did not need to kill him to get it.[17]

One wonders if they had been watching the property before Johnny left. Trabue's house likely gave him away as better-off. It was possible to read the landscape and the polished décor of a man's estate much as it was to read his dress. "A house in open view on the landscape was a continuing performance meant for the eyes of every passerby," writes one historian.[18] It's unlikely that the Trabues' house included the ornate flourishes that brightened gentry homes in more prosperous places—crisp blue or white paint or decorative pickets enclosing comely gardens. But the Trabues lived on a prized piece of land in a substantial house.[19] Johnny, though still young, was one of the most fortunate sons in this part of Kentucky.

There is an old folk ballad, once sung in the southern highlands, called "The Yorkshire Bite." It tells the tale of a farmer who sends his son to market. On the boy's journey home after selling his father's cow, he is approached by a highwayman. "I'll tell you in plain," says the robber: "It's your money I want, without any strife / If I don't get it, I'll end your sweet life."

But the highwayman is outwitted. The boy plunges his hands into his pockets, pulls his money out, and tosses it into the air—scattering it in "a high patch of weeds." When the thief slides off his horse to scoop it up, the boy turns the tables: He jumps into the marauder's saddle and rides off with his horse. "Come back, come back," the man roars. But the boy rides on, galloping off with the horse and the robber's riches.[20]

Johnny Trabue's death looks a little like "The Yorkshire Bite" turned upside down: The marauders win. When you see that, the whole picture begins to come into view. The Harps were writing a kind of topsy-turvy ballad, in which they—the losers—triumphed over society's winners. The worse punishing the better.

* * *

THE DEATH OF a young boy did not get much attention at first. No one knew, yet, to be afraid. Although the Harps were suspected, it would take time—and more bodies—for people to comprehend the menace they faced. For now, Kentucky's interest was elsewhere. The murder was lost in a heaving sea of conversation, most of which, in this moment, was about politics. In the spring of 1799, the state was in a froth: Its men were engaged in heated debate over who would rule going forward.

Kentucky was preparing to rewrite its constitution. Even by American standards, the original constitution was young; only seven years had passed since its writing. But many Kentuckians had long since grown dissatisfied with it. Even as they lobbed fire-breathing critiques at John Adams and his obnoxious Federalist oppressions, they turned their sights, too, on state government. To some, it seemed too aristocratic. It fell short of protecting common men.[21] By 1798, calls for a new constitutional convention had become angry and constant. Handbills flew, and newspapers swelled with a steady chant: CONVENTION, CONVENTION![22]

"Is not your constitution offensive & aristocratic?" one man asked in *Stewart's Kentucky Herald*. "Are you not imposed on by the rich?"[23]

"Act for yourselves; act like men," another snarled, ". . . [and] appal the patrons of *aristocracy*."[24]

Many of these calls came from the very part of Kentucky whose soil had recently opened up to swallow Johnny Trabue's body: the Green River country. Here, there were far fewer slave owners and far less wealth and power. Because the state had sold the Green River land off cheaply with little to be paid up front (it being, after all, mostly second-rate land), it was full of poorer farmers, scraping by. Some had a hard time paying at all.[25] But despite their pleas for "RELIEF," the Senate ignored and even rejected bills passed by the House that were intended to "alleviate the hard condition of the Green River settlers."[26] The settlers, in turn, felt that the state government had failed them.

Those calling to rewrite the constitution wanted more of a say in governing: They wanted direct elections. Under the original constitution, the governor and senators were chosen by electors, a stifling check on voters. Some wanted to do away with the senate—that bastion of aristocracy—entirely. "The division of the legislature into two chambers," wrote Henry Clay, a young lawyer, "has been founded upon the principle of two classes of men, whose interests were distinct . . . These distinctions not existing in America, the use of the senate has ceased."[27]

It made some men nervous. Well-heeled Kentuckians feared a mobbish takeover of government. They feared that the lower sort wanted to rewrite the constitution in order to grab at the wealth of their betters. Would they break up estates and free slaves, simply to pull down the "aristocracy"? Behind it all was pure greed, thought John Breckinridge, a Kentucky representative who boasted twenty thousand acres in land claims and dozens of slaves. "This is the Canker that preys upon you," he wrote. "This is what produces all your bellowings about conventions, conventions. This is what stirs up your envy, wounds your pride, and makes you cry out *aristocracy.*"[28]

The politics of the day were defined by the gulf between haves and have-nots. Elites painted the critics of the constitution as propertyless desperadoes—"Thieves, Robbers and beardless boys."[29] Was it their "sauntering in the streets" and "hanging around billiard tables" and "ill Luck at play" that made them hungry for a piece of their betters' wealth? Breckinridge wondered.[30] What they really wanted, some thought, was to "throw the state into confusion" in hopes that "in the general scuffle, those who are now at the bottom, will rise."[31]

By April 1799, all of this had risen to a fever pitch. It had long since become apparent to the state's political leaders that a majority of Kentuckians favored revising the constitution, and after a long battle in the legislature, a convention was called. Delegates were set to be chosen in May elections, about a month after John Trabue's death. As the Harps stalked the southern reaches of the state, sheriffs were steeling themselves to oversee the polling. Who was chosen to go to Frankfort to write the new constitution would decide: Would the state be for better men or for all men?

The Harp brothers' coming spree would play out against this backdrop, a refraction of Kentucky politics—indeed of American politics—in this period.[32] Wiley and Micajah may not have known much about what was unfolding in the halls of the Kentucky legislature. Certainly, they were not combing the newspapers each week. But the drama surrounding the Kentucky constitution is yet another key when placed alongside the murders—the one unlocking the other. The Harps were just the sort of men who Kentucky's gentry feared were coming for their share. And maybe that was the point.

"And where is the difference," John Breckinridge asked, "whether I am robbed of my horse by a highwayman, or of my Slave by a set of people called a Convention?"[33]

Yes, where is?

* * *

IT WAS DUSK, in late April, when Frederick Stump, Jr., went hunting. He had been plowing all day on his farm along the banks of Big Barren River. The sun was sinking behind the reeds. He had heard some wild turkeys going upriver to roost. Hoping to get a shot, he picked up his rifle and began walking along the water's edge.[34]

Stump, a young farmer, hailed from one of the best-known families in the region. He was veritable Tennessee royalty. His father had been one of the original settlers along the Cumberland, where he had built a little empire. The Stumps had an inn, several plantations, a throng of tenants, a mill, and a distillery, which had been burned by Cherokees in 1792 and which they rebuilt—bigger.[35]

From his father's home, Frederick had struck northward into Kentucky, where there was good pasturing land. He raised livestock.[36] He and his wife, Polly, settled on the banks of the Big Barren, where they kept a herd of cattle. They had three small children: two boys and a girl. Writers have sometimes cast Frederick Stump, Jr., as simple and poor—a "harmless, indolent shanty dweller, who owned a fiddle."[37] He was anything but. At just thirty years old, he had amassed quite an impressive amount of wealth in livestock—dozens of cattle, according to tax lists.[38]

Stump lived about seventy miles west of the Trabue house, even deeper into the bowels of the Green River country. His farm stood on the outer edges of a place called "the Barrens." It was a desolate stretch of grassland, perhaps sixty miles around. Visitors to Kentucky hardly ever failed to mention this quiet prairie haunt with its miles and miles of inscrutable, barren wastes. When André Michaux saw it, it reminded him of the plains of Illinois beyond Vincennes. In 1796, he passed through the area without seeing a house for thirty-seven miles—not a single soul.[39] Out here, even the slight rustling of a bird's wings was detectable. Stump paused, looked around. All he saw was grass—a shivering sea of cane.

The Barrens' appearance could shift—it depended on who was looking. Some saw great beauty: Hazel patches, partridges, and strawberries so thick underfoot that they stained horses' hooves. Wild vines with grapes as fat as those in French vineyards. And everywhere, "lush grass dotted with charming flowers."[40] Even the wildfires that struck the Barrens were "sublime, especially at night," wrote one inhabitant.[41] But to others, the grasses were suffocating. "Nothing can be more tiresome than the doleful uniformity of these immense meadows where there is nobody to be met with," Michaux complained.[42]

Stump walked the water's edge. He was not expecting to meet anyone, but as he walked, he noticed a small loop of smoke rising from the reeds. There was a fire burning at the riverside. Was it some new neighbor who had "pitched his tent there"? Stump made his way over to greet the fellow.

He saw two men—a bigger man with thick black hair and a slighter one with lighter, reddish hair. They were "camped in the cane."[43] There is little to suggest what happened next. If he talked to them or "picked up his fiddle and a gallon jug of whiskey" to welcome them—as one writer later imagined—he regretted it quickly.[44]

They cut his throat. They slashed open his body and filled it with stones.[45] Then they sank it in the river. Then they took his gun.[46]

Then they disappeared.

* * *

WITHIN A DAY or so, Stump's body was found. It was floating among the reeds, water lapping at limp limbs. Neighbors fished the body out of the river. They saw the yawning wound in his neck. The coroner's inquest noted that his belly had been "Riped open near 12 inches in length."[47]

Unable to make sense of the murder, the sheriff at first arrested two men who lived close to Stump's farm. "Some of his neighbors were suspected of the murder," the *Kentucky Gazette* reported, "and taken into custody."[48] On April 24, the two men—Charles Lucas and William Allen—were brought to the courthouse in Warren County to be examined. But after questioning them and interviewing several other witnesses, the court deemed they were not guilty of the murder. They were discharged.

"The Court dissolved," the clerk scrawled in his record book.[49]

* * *

MEANWHILE, MEN MUSTERED.

"The criminals confined in the Danville district jail, for the murder of Mr. Langford . . . have made their escape," the *Kentucky Ga-*

zette had announced on March 28, shortly after their jailbreak.[50] But the work of recapturing Wiley and Micajah began slowly.

It took some time for Kentucky to awaken, groggily, to the danger. When word had broken around Danville that the prisoners had escaped, some men considered rounding up dogs and pursuing them. But they decided against it. The cane was too thick, and they thought they had a "bad chance" of finding the fugitives. (Others may have suspected the Harps wouldn't get far: When the jailer reported them missing, he'd noted that "each had a case-hardened horse lock on their leg with an iron chain about three feet long.") New arrest warrants were, finally, drawn. "All sheriffs and constables are commanded to take and re-commit them," the *Gazette* publicized.[51] But this, too, went nowhere.

At first, the Harps were not grasped as a special threat, so no one rushed with much urgency to chase them. "What a pity it was," Daniel Trabue wrote, that the Harps had simply been allowed to ramble westward after breaking out of jail. Because of that, "These Murderers came nearly by my house" and "they got my son John."[52] In the coming months, Johnny's father would be one of the men most "active in haveing them hunted."[53] It was likely Daniel Trabue, mourning his son's murder, who pressured the governor of Kentucky to take more drastic steps.

Around the time Frederick Stump's body was pulled from the Big Barren, Governor James Garrard appealed to the public. On April 23, 1799, he offered a reward for the Harps' capture: "Whereas the ordinary methods of pursuit have been found ineffectual for apprehending and restoring to confinement the . . . fugitives," he announced, "I have judged it necessary to the safety and welfare of the community" to ask for the people's help.[54] Anyone who brought the Harps back to the jailer would be rewarded handsomely. Six hundred dollars for both men or three hundred for either one.

Garrard's proclamation conjures the Harps physically in ways that almost no other documents do:

"MACAIJAH HARP alias ROBERTS is about six feet high,—of a robust make, and is about 30 or 32 years of age," it reads. ". . . His hair is black and short, but comes very much down his forehead. He is built very straight and is full fleshed in the face When he went away he had on a striped nankeen coat, dark blue woollen stockings,—leggings of drab cloth, and trowsers of the same as the coat.

"WILEY HARP alias ROBERTS is very meagre in his face," it continued. He had short black hair, not as curly as his brother's. He looked older, "though really younger." His clothes were much the same as Micajah's, but over the "close bodied" nankeen, he also wore "a drab sur-tout coat."[55]

The clothing they wore may speak to their onetime aspirations to respectability—or, at least, the affectation of it. Micajah's matching coat and trousers sound very much like a suit, of sorts. To have a matching set—jacket and pants—was, as one historian of early American clothing told me, "pretty rare." Nankeen, a heavy cotton fabric that took its name from its origins in Nanking, China, was by 1799 not as prized and un-

ville diſtrict the ſaid MICAIJAH HARP alias ROBERTS, and a like reward of THREE HUNDRED DOLLARS for apprehending and delivering as aforeſaid the ſaid WILEY HARP alias ROBERTS, to be paid out of the public Treaſury agreeably to law.

In teſtimony whereof I have hereunto ſet my hand and have cauſed the ſeal of the Commonwealth to be affixed.

Done at Frankfort on the 22d day of April in the year of our Lord 1799, and of the Commonwealth the ſeventh.

James Garrard.

(L. S.) *BY THE GOVERNOR,*

HARRY TOULMIN, Secretary.

☞ *MACAIJAH HARP alias ROBERTS is about ſix feet high,—of a robuſt make, and is about 30 or 32 years of age. He has an ill-looking, down caſt countenance, and his hair is black and ſhort, but comes very much down his forehead. He is built very ſtraight and is full fleſhed in the face. When he went away he had on a ſtriped nankeen coat, dark blue woollen ſtockings,—leggings of drab cloth and trowſers of the ſame as the coat.*

WILEY HARP alias ROBERTS is very meagre in his face; has ſhort black hair, but not quite ſo curly as his brother's: he looks older, though really younger, and has likewiſe a down caſt countenance. He had on a coat of the ſame ſtuff as his brother's, and had a drab ſur-tout coat over the cloſe bodied one. His ſtockings were dark blue woollen ones, and his leggings of drab cloth.

Descriptions of Micajah and Wiley Harp "alias Roberts" were given in the Kentucky governor's proclamation, which appeared in the *Palladium* on May 9, 1799. Announcements of the Harps' escape and reward money ran alongside election returns in newspapers that spring. Image courtesy of Kentucky Digital Newspapers Program, University of Kentucky Libraries.

usual as it once had been (nor even, necessarily, imported), and a cotton suit was not "high end." But, still, the brothers' clothing seems to give away their desire to be well dressed, even to follow the era's fashions.[56]

All of Kentucky now knew who they were. For several weeks after this, with bounties on their backs, the Harps fell quiet. If there were other murders, they left no trace. Daniel Trabue later guessed that the Harps were secreted in a cabin on Canoe Creek near Red Banks, an extremely remote little hamlet out west on the Ohio. They "kept themselvs very private" and "hid their mony," he wrote. Lawmen went to look for the cabin, but they found nothing.[57]

Somewhere, the Harps hid. And they waited.

* * *

SUMMER CAME, TORRID and restless. Kentucky was a hothouse, in which political excitations grew like vines. Men bunched in taverns. They splayed newspapers over ale-splashed tables. They talked politics. They pored over election returns. They argued.

On the Fourth of July, a throng of six hundred gathered in the Bluegrass for a tremendous barbecue. Meats sizzled on the fires, spirits flowed liberally, and riflemen fired celebratory volleys. No fights broke out, and the papers praised the party's peacefulness. Twenty-one patriotic toasts were drunk, all later printed by the *Gazette:*

"May this day be remembered by all the sons of liberty, as long as the twilight of patriotism illuminates the atmosphere of the new world."

"May the rights of the American citizens dilate, and continue expanded as the wings of the eagle."

"May the right of suffrage be conducted in choosing administrators of government, so as to prevent the infringement of the rights of persons and property."

"The Vice-President and the patriotic minority in congress opposed to an alien and sedition bill."

"May freedom ever keep her pace until she free the human race."[58]

And on, and on.

Meanwhile, delegates struck out for the capital. Two months prior on Election Day that May, men tipsy and stuffed with treats had stumbled into courthouses across Kentucky and voted. Some brought with them an agreed-upon ticket of candidates. If there was going to be a convention, the conservatives figured, at least they could preselect a slate of names they approved of. All spring they had rallied behind particular men, conservative men, and it worked. By polling's end, it was clear that the conservatives had won the day: The delegates heading to Frankfort to draft a new constitution that summer would be the ones they had chosen.[59]

The delegates, by and large, were men of property. Almost all owned slaves. In 1792, the framers of the original Kentucky constitution had been farmers who simply returned to the plow. This lot was different—more propertied, more professional. Many of them were justices of the peace or lawyers.[60] Wealthy men heaved sighs of relief.[61]

The convention began on July 22, 1799, in Frankfort. The delegates packed themselves into the statehouse, where it was brutally hot. Quickly, it became apparent that few dramatic changes to the government were likely to be approved.

A few delegates stood up and suggested radical things, like abolishing the senate. What was the use of such a body, in a society without nobility? one man asked. There were, after all, no lords and no commoners in a republic—there were only men. Wasn't that right? "We are capable, or are not capable of self Govt," another delegate insisted.[62]

But as the votes proceeded, not much changed. There was not going to be a revolution favoring common men. Despite the furor that had preceded the calling of the convention, it ended with a whimper. The delegates made almost no major changes.[63] On the morning of August 17, the delegates approved the new constitution. Only one man actively objected.[64]

The beardless boys had been prevented from throwing the government into chaos and grabbing up property. "Nothing but a sacred observance of the laws," John Breckinridge wrote in 1798, "can ultimately insure to an Individual success, or a good name. It is disregard of these that produces robbers on highways, and despots on Thrones. So it is with Governments."[65]

On the very day the convention began, the Harp murders resumed.

* * *

AS THE DOG days descended on the Appalachians, the Harps began a nightmarish fit of killing. Once they resurfaced, they ratcheted up the tempo. Interrupted, once, when Ballenger apprehended them, and then again when the governor papered Kentucky with inky descriptions of their profiles, the two brothers reappeared with their minds fixed on taking lives. It was as if something snapped—or something had been decided. The lid came off.

They moved at a furious pace: At least thirteen deaths over the next month would be identified as Wiley and Micajah's doing. Every day or two, someone stumbled onto a body. Two or three were shot "in cold blood, by the fires where they had encamped."[66] Near the Kentucky line, a couple of corpses were found in a cabin, rotting. The killers had reportedly used an axe to "split the heads of both open."[67] Two more men, returning from a salt lick, were "waylaid" by the Harps. One of them was shot in the head from behind, according to later accounts. The other tried to run, but the killers caught up and bashed him over the head with his own gun.[68]

They moved briskly across territory. Even as the delegates

climbed into coaches, rattling toward Kentucky's convention, the Harps were crossing the state, too. But not toward Frankfort. They were headed south, back to Tennessee. People soon saw them near Knoxville. On July 25, they were spotted—"two men, supposed to be the Harps, that were in the Danville jail, were seen to cross the Clinch river, at Davidson's ferry."[69] After a long and bloody stint in the canebrakes of southern Kentucky, they had come home.

Soon, the dead began turning up near Wiley's land. Late July brought a crop of bodies, blooming in the heat. The first to be discovered, on July 25, was Isaac Coffee, the son of one of Wiley's neighbors. He might have been chasing cattle beyond Black Oak Ridge. His killers filched his gun and shoes, then "left his body where they killed him." He was found on Beaver Creek—Wiley's old haunts.[70]

The very same day, another body was found. Outside Knoxville, perhaps bobbing in the Clinch River, lay William Ballard, a respectable citizen (mistaken by the Harps, it was later suggested, for a peace officer). His body had been slashed open, filled with stones, and sunk in a stream.[71] About three miles south of Knoxville, around the same time, another man—named Hardin—was found dead, floating limply in the Holston River. He, too, was "ripped open and stones put in his belly."[72]

Yet another died near Knoxville that July—a farmer named Hezekiah Bradbury. The circumstances of his death are hazy: He simply disappeared, abruptly, from the record in 1799. But Knoxville men counted him among the Harps' victims. He had been murdered, the deputy sheriff's son later said, on a road leading away from Beaver Creek, his body splayed out on a "large ridge, which has ever since borne the name of Bradbury's ridge."[73]

The details of some of these murders are lost. Examining the bodies of Isaac Coffee and William Ballard, juries of inquest declared them murdered by "persons unknown." No trials followed. No evidence proves directly that the Harps committed the crimes. But at the time, everyone believed they had. "From strong circumstances," the *Knoxville Gazette* reported, "it is believed that these horrid deeds were committed by two brothers of the name of Harps."[74] Strong circumstances do point to the Harps. Not only did this cluster of murders occur in the vicinity of Wiley's old neighborhood—where his former neighbors well remembered him and his various feuds and disagreements—but at least some of the bodies were slashed open and filled with stones, a move which was becoming something of a gruesome signature.

Why did they return to Tennessee? Under the gun in Kentucky, they needed to keep moving. They might have been looking for safe harbor with old friends or relations. (It was rumored that they were seeking refuge with Sally Harp's father, John Rice.)[75] What touched it off is obscure, but this manic outburst of violence near Knoxville seems more frantic, more frenzied. It is possible they had begun to feel desperate or that they had less to lose. But there was also another reason to return home: They came to settle old scores.

Those in Knoxville saw their return as vengeful. One man, Hugh Dunlap, feared they were looking for him. Dunlap was a justice of the peace. He knew everything about their crooked past. He knew they had stolen livestock from their neighbors and then sold the meat to a Knoxville butcher. He knew Wiley had skipped out on lawsuits. By his own account, he had tried to arrest the Harps "on several occasions." They had threatened him. He believed they had come back for him, to take revenge, only to kill another man by mistake. "They killed Bullard under the impression it was me," he wrote.[76]

While visiting "home," they might have sought other forms of revenge, too. Although no one said so at the time, some of their targets smack of anger over the Cherokee border debacle. On the outskirts of Knoxville, around this time, a barn went up in flames—an arson that was later attributed to the Harps. The torched stables belonged to

David Henley, agent of the War Department. Henley was, in many ways, the face of the federal government in Knoxville. Locals saw him as embodying John Adams's orders, the villain behind the expulsions from Cherokee country. ("All the orders from government were forwarded through me," he wrote, and "I bore the brunt.") Dunlap, too, had once carried "Colonel Butler's proclamation"—the announcement ordering people off of Cherokee land—"to the frontiers."[77]

Something profound—and novel—was now under way. No longer could anyone count the dead on one hand—or even two. The murders came so quick that when men sat down, years later, to recount them, they began to blur. "How many others they slaughtered, in cold blood," one wrote, "no one can tell." Even Daniel Trabue, deeply tormented by his own son's death, had trouble keeping track. When he tried to tabulate the victims in his own narrative, he failed to identify all the dead. In his mind, they swam together. They "killed one or two more men going Down Barren River," he wrote, vaguely. "I Don't Recolect their names."[78]

The Harps left, in their wake, ripples of terror. At first, these were small shock waves around each body. But then they radiated farther outward. Early Appalachia's flimsy web of roads and streams offered, at best, rudimentary communication. But bad news traveled fast. Whenever some pilgrim shuffled into a country store or tavern and blurted out news of a murder, newspaper printers went to work, feverishly inking type: "We are informed by a gentleman who arrived here . . . from Danville . . . ," they would report, or "A gentleman just arrived . . . from Nashville, confirms . . ."[79]

After finding their neighbor slain and encountering a witness, two Kentucky men traveled forty miles, on foot, to alert a justice of the peace. (That person just happened to be none other than Daniel Trabue, still reeling from Johnny's death.) He took their statement carefully. "I rote [it] Down, and I swore them to it," he said. Then he gathered neighbors, warned them, and chose two to ride as messengers—one to the west and one to the governor's office in Frankfort. "Derected the men to go as fast as they could and spread the knews as they went."[80] His affidavit was printed in many newspapers, first in Kentucky but later in places as far away as New York, New Jersey, and Pennsylvania.

It is striking how quickly news about the Harps sometimes appeared in the newspapers. John Bradford, publisher of the *Kentucky Gazette*, kept a small office in Lexington, where he sometimes wrote, according to one account, "by the flickering light of a buffalo tallow candle" or "a bear grease lamp." He printed the *Gazette* weekly, squeezing out its pages on an old press that his brother had dragged all the way from Pittsburgh in 1787. He often had to "dig into his own pocket" to buy paper.[81] But on a number of occasions, he was able to print stories about the Harps—sometimes covering events dozens of miles away—within a week of something occurring. He knew when Ballenger captured them. He reported Johnny Trabue's murder. He even knew within days of Frederick Stump's murder that Stump's neighbors had been accused—despite the Barrens being in a distant prairie nowhere near Lexington.[82]

What appeared in the newspapers was not always strictly accurate. No reporters yet existed to rush to the scene of a crime. Printers did not go hunting for stories. They expected the news to arrive conveniently at their doorsteps, "as spices were delivered to the grocer or bolts of cloth to the tailor," and they printed whatever drifted in, by letter or by rumor.[83] But printers also had ways of gathering and sharing that were surprisingly effective. They regularly traded content over long distances. Both Bradford and George Roulstone, who published the *Knoxville Gazette*, kept a network of private post riders to distribute their newspapers over dozens of miles.[84] Their ability to collect distant clues—and put pieces together—far outpaced law enforcement at the time.

Unevenly, in fits and starts, people began to know the Harps' names. About four or five hundred readers subscribed to the *Kentucky Gazette* by 1799, and countless others read it in taverns, or heard it recited, each week, when the latest copy reached their little hamlet.[85] But newspapers were likely not the way most people first heard about the Harps. Tongues were wagging, much more than the papers could capture. When one man wandered into a drinking hole in Danville, Kentucky, that summer, he found that the Harps and "their multiplied cruelties . . . was familiar to everyone about the tavern."[86]

"They soon acquired a dreadful celebrity," one man wrote.[87] As weeks slipped by, and the brothers were not caught, alarm set in. People, at last, began to grasp that something unusual was happening. The Harps' "bloody work," wrote one Tennessean, "alarmed and terrified . . . the whole country." Women were afraid to stray out of doors. Children were warned not to wander too far. Men clutched their guns a little more tightly. "Every man carried his fire arms, his dirk or his butcher knife about him," one recalled.[88] Panic swept Kentucky. "The whole state got in a Great uprore," Daniel Trabue wrote. "The people was afraid to opin their Doors."[89]

When business necessitated a venture out into Kentucky's quiet byways, some men braced themselves for a possible encounter with the killers. Crossing the Green River country that summer, one tried to swallow his dread. "I had repeatedly heard of the dreadful outrages committed by the Harps . . . in the neighborhood," he wrote. "It was said . . . wherever in their rambles they met a man alone, he was sure to fall a victim." Before setting off, he stuffed a pocket pistol into his trousers. If he should meet the Harps and "find escape impossible," he reasoned, then he could at least shoot one of them.[90]

As fear spread, the pace of death quickened. A new phase of the spree was under way—one that would not end until the Harps were stopped for good. It was more furious, but a sort of smirking trickery was also involved. They were enjoying themselves. They sneered at those who failed to capture them. Sometimes they even pretended to be peace officers or posse members, looking for the dreaded Harps—a cruel play on the fact that it was terribly difficult, in the American backwoods, to tell men apart. It was hard to get a read on who a man was—a criminal or a lawman. They were playing a grand joke, getting the last laugh.

* * *

ONE OF THE riddles of the Harp murders is this: How did they choose their victims? Why *these* people? The victims were varied—younger men, older men, people they knew, people they didn't. Some of the victims seem to have been chosen spontaneously—in a moment of aloneness on the road, where they were weak and relatively defenseless. "The thickly settled portions of the country they purposely evaded," wrote one early observer, "and plundered the solitary cabin, or waylaid the unsuspecting traveler."[91] Some were robbed. Others were not. You begin to think you see patterns. But no one equation solves them all.

It becomes necessary to think about the murders in a wider frame. Folktales have framed the Harps as wildly indiscriminate killers: "They murdered every defenceless being who fell in their way," claimed one writer, "without distinction of age, sex, or colour."[92] But that is not quite true. Mostly, the Harps killed men, and boys. They sometimes killed prominent men or their sons. Many of those who fell victim to Wiley and Micajah Harp were men who had done well in the post-Revolutionary years—justices of the peace, men of property, Continental Army veterans. But no single murder unlocks the pattern. Only by seeing all of them, together, can you grasp the murders' meaning: The Harps were on a rampage. They were taking back from other men what they felt had been taken from them.[93]

Rampage killing, almost always, is about revenge.[94] It isn't about savoring violence. It isn't about any of the perverse, sadistic pleasures that we associate with modern serial killers. It isn't usually about worldly or material things to be gained once the victims are dead. The gains are mostly psychological: It is about having the last word, about vengeance against those who have caused the killer's unhappiness. Others must be made to suffer "as he has in the past," criminologist James Alan Fox writes of the typical offender.[95]

Sometimes this means killing strangers, if the killer feels wronged by all of society. Or men sometimes murder whoever is available, in lieu of those they blame most for their troubles. But rampage killers also kill people they know, people who tend to represent the killer's grievances.[96] The Harps' spree looks a lot like this: They killed strangers, yes, but they also killed people they knew. They killed men who had prospered while they had suffered. They targeted those who looked like agents of their misfortune: a young gentleman flush with money, and a justice of the peace who'd once tried to have them arrested.

It is nearly impossible, even now, to predict who will go on a murderous rampage. But criminologists, studying this kind of mass violence, can see patterns when they look at cases in retrospect. Like Wiley and Micajah, modern rampage killers often have a "history of failures."[97] Their lives, typically, have been "filled to overflowing" with disappointments, frustrations, and anger.[98] They want people to take notice. Seizing attention—and sending convulsions of fear through all of society—is part of the calculus.[99] But mostly, they want to get even. They want to "settle an account with the uncaring world."[100]

The Harps are perhaps the first of their kind in American history. Labeling them or classifying them is less important than understanding them as the faint beginnings of a certain species of violence still plaguing American society, in which "angry and desperate young men"—those who have expected great things for themselves but who "feel that life is becoming overwhelming" and "blame others"—lash out in a way meant to "bring them glory and a halo of power and evil."[101]

There is one final chilling characteristic of rampage killers: They don't care whether they live. Most do not expect to survive; they presume, at some point, they will die. (Some, in fact, are hoping to die.) The ending matters little. "Their revenge has been taken; their point has been made," as one writer puts it. Once they have acted out, sticking around to face battles in court, or to fend off punishments, holds no interest. The object, in the end, is simply to "leave a black mark on the pages of history."[102]

* * *

ON JULY 29, two brothers named Robert and James Brassel were walking along a quiet road outside of Knoxville. They may have been hunting bees. The wildflowers were blooming, and it was a good time to look for hives.

Bee hunting was a delicate game of patience and observation. The object was to find a hive full of honey. But first, you had to find a bee or two to lead you there. You could locate a quiet patch of flowers and wait. Or you could attract them. Bee hunters sometimes carried buckwheat flowers, whose perfume was very seductive to bees. Even more effective, though, was to heat a bit of honeycomb by placing it on a hot rock. Its scent was irresistible to bees. "The treacherous incense rising among the trees," one Kentuckian described, ". . . [would attract] the unsuspecting little insect, if any should be near." They would come, one by one.[103]

Then you watched closely: Each bee "sucked its fill," then rose, circled, and flew off in a straight line—a "beeline." Once you saw several bees flying off on a particular course, you had a clue as to where the hive could be found. Off you went to find the tree that housed it. To get the hive, bee hunters would sometimes fell the tree, which was risky, as all could be lost—"the honey-comb mashed and scattered on the ground, and while a quart or two was hastily gathered up, its enraged and courageous little owners would be as busily occupied in punishing the plunderers."

The fun, in a bee hunt, was discovery. "The pleasure is in the finding, and not the taking—in the anticipation, much more than the possession," one hunter wrote.[104]

The Brassels did not realize that they, too, were being watched and followed. But as they were walking, two men came up behind them.

"Jentlemen, what is the knews?" one of the strangers asked.[105]

Robert Brassel looked them over. Both were wearing short sailor's coats, "very dirty," and greatcoats—gray. Both carried guns, one with a reddish stock and the other black with a silver star.[106]

"The most I've heard of," Robert answered, "[is] the Harpes going through the country, killing people, robbing & stealing." The two men nodded. Robert continued: "I suppose you heard about the Murder of Ballard and Coffey."[107]

Who did they think "had Done the mischief"? the men asked.

"It was thought it was the Harps," one of the Brassels replied.[108]

Well, aren't you afraid of encountering the Harps? asked one of the men.

No, said James. Not here. They wouldn't be likely to travel so unfrequented a road.[109]

The four men continued talking, exchanging news. One of them wondered aloud: What would be done to the Harps if they were ever captured? What do you do with men of that sort?

Robert Brassel chuckled. "Why, drown them, hang them, or shoot them," he said.[110]

Maybe then, looking up into the eyes of the two strangers, he caught something worrisome. The smaller man's demeanor changed.

His eyes turned stony. Now he shifted the conversation. He said he was part of a posse that had been sent "in persuete" of the murderers. He looked at both Brassels. Then he said he believed they were the Harps and ordered them to surrender.[111]

"You are the men that has Done this Murder," he said to the Brassels. "We have more men behind a coming, and you must stop until they come up." The Brassels, baffled, agreed.[112]

The big man took James's gun. He set it against a tree. Then he took out a piece of twine.

"Hold your hand[s] together while I tye you," he said to James.

At this, Robert froze. "Don't be tyed," he said to James.

The smaller man looked at him coldly.

"Dam you," he said. "I will kill you in a minuet if you Resist."[113]

Robert Brassel understood, now, what was happening. He lunged toward James's gun, leaning against the tree. But he could not grab it. So he ran.

Wiley aimed at him as he bolted.

Robert Brassel went to find help. He zigzagged frantically through the woods as he ran, so he would not be followed. But by the time he had mustered a search party to try to save his brother's life, it was too late. James Brassel's body was found "Dreadfully Buchered," "much beaten, and his throat cut."[114]

CHAPTER 7

THE PURSUIT

Deer Creek
Henderson County, Kentucky
August 1799

The evening of August 20, 1799, was hot and dark, under a faint quarter moon. Mary Stegall, a young wife and mother, was alone, nursing her four-month-old son. Her husband was away. Night sounds pricked through the walls of the house—the chittering of crickets and the clicking of katydids, thousands of them packed into the hazel as the air cooled and the damp gathered in the grasses. Mary listened. Then she heard something unexpected: shuffling feet, outside, and a knock at the door.[1]

The Stegalls lived in a solitary cabin. It stood in far western Kentucky close to where the Green River dead-ended in the Ohio. The county, Henderson, was brand-new. Surveyors were arriving, dragging chains. Squatters, meanwhile, were already digging in their heels. Entrenched along the steep red banks of the Ohio River, they defended their bluff-side shacks and groggeries and demanded to be paid off by the newcomers who came marching in with paper claims. No one had bothered until recently to ask who had legal rights.[2]

This was the outer edge of the United States. Across the river lay unorganized federal lands. The Stegalls' chosen home was within the bounds of Kentucky, but it felt very distant from the Bluegrass. Even as the rest of the state buzzed about the convention in 1799, Henderson barely batted an eye. "I hear your town & Neighborhood are deeply engaged in politics," one of its residents wrote to a Lexington friend in April. "Not so here . . . we Care Very little."[3]

The Stegalls did not have many close neighbors, but they may have been accustomed to visitors. Their house was not far off the road to Robertson's Lick, which drew a steady march of men gathering salt, mostly local comers and goers.[4] But even strangers were entitled to ask for a bit of hospitality when they needed it. That was the custom of the country.

Mary opened the door. Standing there on her porch were two men and three women, with babies. They asked if she might be so kind as to let them stay.

Mary hesitated.

My husband is not at home, she told them. *And I already have a boarder. There's no room here.*

This was true: Asleep in the loft was a man named William Love. He had been out all day under the summer sun, surveying land. Mary had given him the upper room for lodging. She was "not in a situation to take travellers," she informed them.[5]

But they insisted. It was late. They would put up with any fare, they said—whatever small bit of food and comfort she was prepared to offer them. So Mary relented. She said she would try to find space for the women downstairs with her. The two men would have to share the loft, above, with Love.[6]

Out here in western Kentucky, in the lowlands of the Pond River valley—where the countryside was punctuated by bunched low grasses and the sandy whorls of the salt licks, and where the Stegall family had staked out a little plot on the muddy edge of Deer Creek—this was where it all began to lurch toward the end.

* * *

HOW HAD THEY arrived here? In a mad dash. It had been less than a month since the Knoxville murders. In that time, they had covered an astounding three hundred miles. By the time they stood on Mary Stegall's doorstep, the Harps had nearly reached the Ohio River and the unorganized territory beyond. What drew them to Henderson County? Were there other scores to settle? Or were they simply running?

Running, certainly. Outside of Knoxville, men had given chase. When several victims' bodies were found near town, Tennessee governor John Sevier, not knowing what else to do (and concluding, evidently, that East Tennessee's feeble web of local sheriffs would no longer suffice), called up the only police force available to him—militiamen. He directed Captain Arthur Crozier to raise ten men in his company and "make immediate and deligent search after the murderers." The governor gave Crozier's company nearly unlimited license: "You will take *every necessary measure* to have the perpetrators apprehended," he ordered. Four days later, he gave the nod to another search party, this time naming the Harps as suspects.[7]

But the fervor fizzled. Men fanned into the hills in furious little cavalries, but they found nothing. Meanwhile, the people of Knoxville offered a reward. "Upwards of four hundred and fifty Dollars," chirped the *Knoxville Gazette*, "have been subscribed by the citizens of Knoxville . . . to any person or persons, who will apprehend and commit to the jail of Knox county, the above mentioned Harps."[8] The newspaper tallied: All told, the reward money had topped two thousand dollars. But a king's ransom could not do the trick. No one since Ballenger had come close to apprehending them. By the time this announcement appeared, the Harp brothers were long gone.

Once more, they had crossed deep into Kentucky. The rampage continued. They lit the byways with a fiery wrath. In Stockton's Valley, a beautiful little oasis bursting with wildflowers at the foot of Poplar Mountain, another man disappeared. John Tully was a humble teamster who drove wagonloads of goods to market. He did not own much—he had two hundred acres, two horses, no slaves, and eight children. (Mercifully, the Kentucky legislature later excused Tully's "desolate" widow, Christiana, from paying off his debts, saddled as she was with all of those little ones.)[9]

Some have imagined that the Harps were acquainted with Tully, even that he had ferried messages for them. But the circumstances are more suggestive of a chance encounter, some unlucky meeting on the highway. After he vanished—"strangly lost," as Daniel Trabue put it—men went looking. Searchers found his body near the road, "hid by a log." He had possibly been shot and robbed of his horse and some money.[10]

Two more bodies surfaced in August. The victims were a man named Graves and his young son, who was perhaps between twelve and fourteen. They had just moved to a spot near Marrowbone Creek and were "making a crop at a new place" so that the rest of the family could follow. "Those villains who broke the Danville jail, (the HARPS)," reported the *Palladium*, "have added two more murders to their black catalogue of crimes." The bodies were tossed into a brush fence. No one found them for days, until the smell disclosed their decay.[11]

The Harps kept moving. You can almost follow them in print, as the newspapers reported where they were allegedly spotted: Beaver Creek. Davidson's ferry. Wolf River. Cumberland Mountains. Price's settlement. Stockton's Valley. Marrowbone Creek. If you plot the murders, you can see them moving through territory, due northwest. "They were seen the 2d of this instant on Marrowbone, a north branch of the Cumberland river," the *Palladium* informed its readers that August. "We are happy to hear they are closely pursued."[12] But they were not closely pursued.

There had been efforts all along to capture the Harps. Arrest warrants had been drawn up. Men had scrambled to their horses. Extravagant rewards had been dangled. But nothing worked. Nothing stopped them. The Harps were a novel threat, and eighteenth-century law enforcement was not equipped to deal with men who skipped county lines and kept on killing. After their escape from the Danville jail, Kentucky had ordered all its sheriffs and constables—"every of you in your respective counties, towns and precincts"—to "make diligent search" for the fugitives.[13] But no coordination existed among sheriffs or counties or even governors of different states. The problem itself was not unthinkable: In 1793, the United States had passed a law requiring each state to arrest and deliver "fugitives from justice" (and, significantly, escaped slaves) to any state from which they had fled. But it made no prescription for how that might happen.[14]

Pursuing the Harps was an improvisational game of rounding up men and knocking on doors, scouring highways, talking to roadside travelers, and finding witnesses who had spotted them. "These murderers were seen by several people, riding the road towards Stockton's valley," a justice of the peace wrote in early August.[15] Outside Knoxville, Captain Crozier's men allegedly "came very near overtaking them," as one man remembered it. But the Harps slipped away, into the caverns.[16] Another group—gathered by Robert Brassel after his brother's murder—apparently crossed paths with the Harps near the scene of that crime, but they lost their stomachs for confronting the killers and silently let them pass by.[17]

One of the driving questions in the Harps' story—the question that consumes you as you piece it together—is: Why? Why did they commit all of these murders? Why so many bodies? There are several ways to answer that question, but the simplest one is this: They kept killing, in part, because they could. Because no one stopped them.

Micajah worried about being caught. At times, he tremored. "He fancied the ground continually trembled beneath his feet," Susana confided to a friend, much later. Sometime during their spree, he told Wiley that they needed to stop. He said they needed to quit killing and "go to some other backwoods country—if they did not, he feared they wd. be detected & killed."[18]

Wiley flew into a rage. He called his brother a coward. *If you ever talk that way again,* he said, *I'll shoot you.*[19]

* * *

THE STEGALLS' LOFT could only be reached from outside. Mary pointed Wiley and Micajah to the entrance. They climbed the ladder that rested against the side of the house and crawled into the loft.[20] It was hot. The air smelled of damp wood and sweat. But it was a place to lay their heads. What else they imagined might happen that night is a bit of a mystery.

The Harps had not turned up at the Stegall house accidentally. They meant to be there. They had been looking for it. Four days earlier, on August 16, the Harp women had called at a house on Highland Creek to "inquire the way" to the Stegall cabin. They wanted to collect on a debt. Susana had a promissory note for one dollar, collectible from Mary's husband, Moses Stegall. It had been passed on to her—because debt was currency—by someone who lived nearby, and she wanted the money.[21]

Because of what later befell the Stegall house, some writers have assumed the Harps knew the family. Were they acquainted? Did they have some sort of relationship with Mary's husband? Were they looking for safe quarter among friends—a place to shelter and hide? (Or perhaps to mete out some special vengeance?) A promissory note is not necessarily evidence of a previous acquaintance. Such things passed promiscuously among parties, and it was fair game to visit the last person who had vowed to pay so you could translate their promise into real money. But the note itself may speak to connections the Harps had in the neighborhood.

The West was a small world. Counting the miles—or running your fingers over a map—is deceiving. To immerse yourself in the

Harps' world is to be confronted, repeatedly, with the startling intimacy that was sometimes shared by men across dozens and dozens of miles, their lives intersecting in strange ways. Many of the people the Harps met along the way had led lives that were geographic echoes of their own—beginning on the border of North Carolina or Virginia, drifting into Tennessee, landing in Kentucky.

It is very possible that the Harps knew people in the neighborhood. There is some evidence they had lived—or hidden—for a time on Canoe Creek, which splintered off from the Ohio only twenty miles or so west from the Stegall house. Some thought the Harps had spent time there, perhaps during their lull in the spring of 1799. "They had built a cabin," one man suggested. Although that seems unlikely, they may have rented or squatted in one. Had they slipped away there while they waited for Kentucky authorities to give up the chase?[22]

Inside the loft, they found Mary's boarder, William Love, asleep. Love's presence was an unwelcome twist. He was an odd bedfellow for the brothers Harp. "A man of fine character, & good acquirements," as one relative put it.[23]

William Love was a stark contrast to the two brothers. "Handsome made" with a "prepossessing" appearance, he belonged to a prominent family, and in 1799, he was building up his estate. With his wife, Esther, and six children, he had just recently moved to Caney Creek, where they were busily assembling a respectable household—filling it with feather beds, tea accoutrements, and six slaves, all trappings of the good life.[24]

Almost certainly, he had spent that day—August 20—trudging through the tallgrasses and the mucky flats of Henderson, making notes about metes and bounds. Among other things, Love was a surveyor, one of an army of men who were feverishly conjuring the county out of notched blackjack oaks and crooks in creeks, turning the unorganized west into a spiderweb of properties. Love's son later confirmed that his father was "on a tour of surveying" when he stopped to spend the night at the Stegall house. It was just a convenient place to stay.[25]

To duck into a stranger's home was the solace and privilege of those wandering the American West. Taverns were few, out here, but people were welcoming. "I have entered freely the meanest habitations," one traveler wrote. "When I approached the door of the rudest hut, I was invited to enter." Families readily found a seat for a traveler or offered up a plateful of turnip greens, "however homely their fare might be." Claiming a bed in an unfamiliar house, far from home, was for most men a great comfort.[26]

To understand this is also to grasp the unique terror the Harps were sowing in this society. Western folks were accustomed to being terrified of Indians. The pricking fear of an approaching war party of Shawnees or Miamis or Cherokees, appearing from nowhere, had been bred into them for generations already. But they were not predisposed to be fearful or suspicious of white strangers to whom they opened their doors. There was, among neighbors, and even among strangers, an element of unspoken trust, which the Harps were slowly but insidiously eroding, even as they took advantage of it.

Most of what happened at the Stegall house that night will probably never be known. One of the more fanciful traditions—which appeared almost immediately in the newspapers, perhaps based on what was later said by the Harp women or Micajah himself—is that Love was a restless sleeper. He snored. He twitched. Disturbed by Love's tossing and turning (or possibly because of his own anxious tremors), Micajah Harp alit with rage. He woke Mary Stegall, screaming that she was a "damn'd bitch" for "put[ting] them in bed with a man who had fits."[27]

That could have happened. But there was something else about Love that might have tipped things over into chaos: He was not just a surveyor. He was also a lawman. He was a recently minted justice of the peace for Livingston County and had presided over sessions there as recently as late July, barely a month earlier.[28] Did he suspect them? Did some type of scuffle break out? Love was a physically imposing man, six feet tall and well-built. At thirty-nine years old, he was "in the prime of life and manhood."[29] He would have put up a fight.

If the Harps did know the Stegalls, and if they had gone there looking for refuge, then Mary's ushering them into bed with a peace officer would have seemed like a serious betrayal. Had she failed to warn them that they would be spending the night just a few feet away from a man who might try to arrest them?

Whatever took place that evening, it became a night of horrors. Mary's fate—which would only become clear later—suggests some type of personal grudge or venomous anger, as if, perhaps, they thought her guilty of wronging them.

They left in a hurry. But first, they ransacked the house. At least one account—from one of the first peace officers to investigate and visit the scene of the crime—suggests that Susana, Betsy, and Sally participated in the plundering: They pilfered "clothing, provisions, knives and forks, soap, and some other articles," including William Love's hat.[30] (Susana later claimed that Micajah had forced her to wear some of Mary Stegall's things against her will.)[31] Then they took Love's horse, piling loot across its back.

After gathering their things, they shut the Stegalls' dogs in the house and lit it on fire. As the flames climbed the walls, the dogs began to howl.

"I reckon the dogs begin to smell hell," one of them said, according to what one of Love's relatives later heard.[32]

* * *

THE NEXT DAY, a man named John Pyles was riding back from Robertson's Lick. As he passed the Stegall farm, he saw the spot where the house had stood. It had burned to the ground. Nothing was left but "smoking ruins." He galloped straight to the house of Silas McBee, a justice of the peace, and told him: Stegall's place was in ashes. McBee thought he was joking.

If you don't believe me, Pyles said, *go see for yourself.*[33]

They later found the bodies, burned badly. Mary Stegall, William Love, and the Stegalls' infant, James. Love may have been murdered with an axe, perhaps one that was kept in the loft. Despite the damage from the fire, it was obvious how Mary Stegall died. She had been stabbed, several times. Three case knives were plunged deep into her body. One was "buried so deep" that its handle did not burn, though the fire had consumed the house entirely.[34]

McBee, stunned, began to contemplate what to do next.

* * *

WHERE YOU DIE, if you are murdered, matters a lot. That is still true in America, but it was truer in the eighteenth century. The United States is a wobbly, uneven patchwork of criminal jurisdictions, none quite the same. The origins of that crazy quilt lie with the Revolutionary settlement. Sovereignty—in the investigation, pursuit, and prosecution of crime—is still breathtakingly local, precisely because that is what the founders designed. Certain rights—like the right to a trial by jury and due process, generally—exist as guardrails.[35] But town by town, county by county, state by state, idiosyncrasies reign.[36]

It's hard to say whether the Harps understood this. But they did take advantage of it. They rampaged across dozens of counties and hundreds of miles. Clues about the murders—where they have survived at all—are scattered in a rambling archipelago of county courthouses and provincial repositories. When the law got too close, they kept moving. Every time they moved, they sucked in a new set of local characters—sheriffs, coroners, justices of the peace. *The people.*

There were no police in the eighteenth century. There were only other men, deputed (usually by a governor) or elected to keep order. The face of law enforcement, in most places, was the county sheriff. He was sometimes assisted by a deputy or constables, who were lesser peace officers. All of these men were ordinary citizens fulfilling a civic duty. They were generally paid very little or nothing at all. Constables often resented their responsibilities, likely as they were to get punched while serving a subpoena or spat on by the local drunk. "You must not mind the trouble," wrote Nicholas Boone in *The Constables Pocket-Book,* "but consider the Publick Interest."[37]

In fact, the "Publick" were the police. Criminal justice, in the early republic, was done by the people. Law enforcement did not yet belong solely to the government. All men were expected to assist constables and sheriffs in the capturing of criminals.[38] When a crime happened, locals would raise a "hue and cry" to hunt down the offenders. Eighteenth-century magistrates could also muster a "posse comitatus," or a group of "able-bodied white men of the community," to aid the sheriff in capturing criminals.[39]

Some of this was inherited from English tradition. The word "sheriff" derives from "shire-reeve," an office dating to perhaps the year 700. In each English shire, one man—the shire-reeve—upheld the law on behalf of the king. The raising up of neighborhood men to capture outlaws was another practice with English roots.[40] But American peacekeeping parted with English precedent in some ways, particularly after the American Revolution. Sheriffs no longer worked for the king—but they did not work for the president, either. The popular character of law enforcement intensified.

Diffuse policing protected against tyranny. The men who designed the United States government in 1787 were deeply leery of putting too much force into any one man's hands. "Authoritative police institutions seemed inherently at odds with liberty," writes historian Adam Malka.[41] Inheriting British political prejudices,

Americans had long believed that men with great power were prone to abusing it, if unchecked. "Considering what sort of a creature man is," read one popular political tract, "it is scarce possible to put him under too many restraints, when he is possessed of great power."[42]

They had seen what could happen when kings used force against their own subjects. The war itself had begun as something of a police action, with redcoats cracking down on unruly Americans. Coming out of the Revolution, Americans feared tyrannical government. They feared professional armies that might be used not against foreign enemies but against citizens themselves. "A standing army is one of the greatest mischiefs that can possibly happen," James Madison told Virginians in 1788.[43] Any permanent armed body "should be watched with a jealous Eye," agreed Samuel Adams.[44] Better to let other citizens do the policing.[45]

They left the question of how to the states. The Tenth Amendment spelled this out: Any powers not delegated to the United States were "reserved for the States respectively, or to the people," it read. The task of keeping peace and order, and prosecuting most crimes, stayed with the states—that is, with local people.[46]

The Kentucky Resolutions that fall had defended this very point. When Congress passed the Sedition Act in 1798, it had created whole new categories of "crimes against the United States." Kentuckians balked. The Constitution gave the federal government the power to punish a few crimes—treason, counterfeiting, piracy and felonies on the high seas, violations of the law of nations. But nothing else—"no other crimes whatever." The power to "create, define, and punish such other crimes," Kentucky objected, "is reserved . . . to the respective states, each within its own Territory."[47]

Part of the reason the Harps' rampage has remained such a shadowy, illegible episode is that it drew no major law enforcement response. Even after dozens of deaths in at least two states, the federal government did not get involved. Why would it? Nothing in surviving records suggests that President John Adams (or any other federal official in his administration) was even aware of the murders. In the end, the stubbornly local character of most law enforcement not only allowed the Harps' spree to last longer than it might have, it also somewhat obscured the nature of what they were doing.

You can see some of the odd asymmetries in law enforcement if you set the Harps alongside another episode that occurred in 1799. When Congress passed a direct tax on property (to pay for the "half war" with France), a small rebellion broke out in Pennsylvania. Outside Philadelphia in the heavily German counties surrounding the city, protest boiled over. The people here—much like those in Tennessee—had had trouble establishing secure claims to property in the post-Revolutionary years. Many had "faced foreclosure and eviction."[48] They were in no mood for new taxes. When taxmen arrived in late 1798, people refused to pay. Some had signed associations, vowing to resist the law. Women threw hot water in the faces of the assessors. Six assessors resigned.[49]

A central character, in this resistance, was John Fries. Fries was, in many ways, an unlikely rebel. In 1799, he was nearing fifty. With him, always, was his constant companion, a little black dog named Whiskey. A small and spare man with barely any education (though he could read and write), Fries made his living as a vendue crier, barking out prices at public auctions, where bits of men's property were sold off to satisfy debts. It was an occupation that gave him intimate knowledge of the region's people and their financial woes.[50]

Fries held meetings in his house and told people to resist the new taxes. He saw the situation through the eyes of someone who had once protested Britain's taxes, and he imagined his indebted neighbors as the victims of a powerful monied class. "All those people who were Tories in the Last War mean to be the leaders," he told a crowd of men. "They mean to get us quite under, they mean to make us

Slaves!"[51] As assessors gave up and the tax became a farce, a U.S. Marshal arrived and began arresting people, confining them at the Sun Inn, a roomy public house in Bethlehem, Pennsylvania. On March 7, 1799, a group of resisters—led by John Fries—stormed the inn and freed all the prisoners. Fries, it appeared, had won.

It was hardly an insurrection.[52] Fries and the other tax resisters did not intend to provoke war with the United States. They simply saw themselves as protesting an unjust law. But John Adams marshaled every bit of existing federal law enforcement to bring the hammer down on Fries. The administration declared Fries's actions "treason" and announced that the president would use military force to suppress the insurgency. "Government should shew its arm stretched out, and ready to correct or punish," the secretary of war wrote to Adams.[53] Troops were raised. They gathered in Philadelphia and began marching on April 4.[54]

Fries was at an auction, bell in hand, when the troops arrived to arrest him. At the sight of the soldiers, the crowd stirred wildly. People ran. Fries leapt down from the cider barrel on which he had been standing and fled on foot. In the confusion, the commanding officer lost sight of him. For a while, Fries eluded the searchers. He hid on a nearby farm in a quiet meadow. But eventually, they found him. He had crouched down in a patch of briars. His little dog, Whiskey, gave away his hiding spot.[55]

All of this unfolded while the Harps wasted away in the Danville jail that spring. Fries was arrested at almost the same moment that Wiley and Micajah escaped. John Fries and Wiley Harp were part of the same social fabric—a restless republic of disaffected and insolvent men. Men wracked by debt. But the Harps broke no federal laws. Murder, unlike treason, was not a federal crime. They did not raise the ire of the government. Had they, the Harps' spree might have been recognized for what it was: rebellion.

The rebel John Fries ultimately knew mercy. Convicted of treason and sentenced to death, he spent his last month in the Philadelphia prison, praying. A minister gave him a small Bible, "with which to console his hours of confinement." In his final hours, he inscribed it for his children. But just before he was to be hanged, John Adams pardoned him. Spared from the gallows, Fries went home. He returned to auctioneering and lived out the rest of his life in Milford Township. The little Bible given to him in prison—which he kept as a somber reminder of his trials—passed quietly into his children's possession, when he died in 1818.[56]

The end, for the Harps, was very different. There was no massive manhunt. No federal marshals were sent to arrest the fugitives. John Adams raised no troops. Justice came, instead, in the wilds of western Kentucky, at the hands of a man they had wronged very badly: Mary Stegall's husband, Moses.

* * *

STEGALL WENT JUST up the road to Robertson's Lick to raise the men. There was a saltworks there—a gathering place—where he knew he could find men to ride with him.[57]

The Lick was a busy spot. Salt licks were natural salt springs where mineral-filled water bubbled up to the surface. (They were called "licks" because buffalo and other animals were often found licking the salty clay.) In Kentucky, they were like little beehives—people flitting in and out, carrying in firewood, carrying out pails of salt. Robertson's Lick was not as big as some of the other saltworks, where hundreds of slaves worked the kettles and fashioned piles of salt for sale as far away as Nashville. But here, too, men were drawing up buckets of water from wells to be boiled over great troughs of fire. They were chopping wood for the furnaces and tending the kettles or bartering for a bit of salt to take home. If you wanted to preserve meat—if you wanted to eat—you had to have salt.[58]

No one knows for sure how Moses Stegall learned of the murders of his wife and child. As Silas McBee remembered it, he was the one who broke the news to Stegall, and, of course, it "affected him deeply."[59] "Mr. Stegall returned in the morning," a local informant told one newspaper, and after "finding his wife and child murdered, went . . . in pursuit of the murderers."[60]

Moses Stegall is a difficult character to sketch. He had lived a life not unlike the Harps' before the murders—somewhat humble and unremarkable. Like the Harps, he was almost certainly from North Carolina, possibly the son of a loyalist. He had also lived, for a time, in Knox County, Tennessee. While there, he served in the militia and ranged the frontiers during the Cherokee wars of the early 1790s. In 1794, he rode with James White's mounted infantry, protecting the fringes of eastern Tennessee.[61]

There were dark chapters in his past, too. "Steigal bore a bad character," one man wrote.[62] In Knoxville, he'd had run-ins with the law. Once, he was found guilty of assault and battery. Twice, he was tried for horse stealing. In both cases, he seems to have been acquitted, but the second jury found him guilty of trespass and fined him ten dollars. Soon after that, he disappears from the records in Tennessee. Nothing suggests that he paid the fine. Instead, he left.[63] He went to Kentucky. By 1797, he was in Christian County, deep in the Green River country, where he turned up on a tax list for the first time: "Stagler, Moses." He had no family listed. No slaves. Just himself and two horses.[64] There is no record of him purchasing any land, nor any of him getting married (though, clearly, Mary had come into his life somehow in Kentucky).

He seemed an odd figure to act as the arm of the law. But now, after the deaths of Mary and baby James, he took justice into his own hands. He gathered a posse. They were men he knew, all of whom lived nearby: John Leeper, Matthew Christian, Neville Lind-

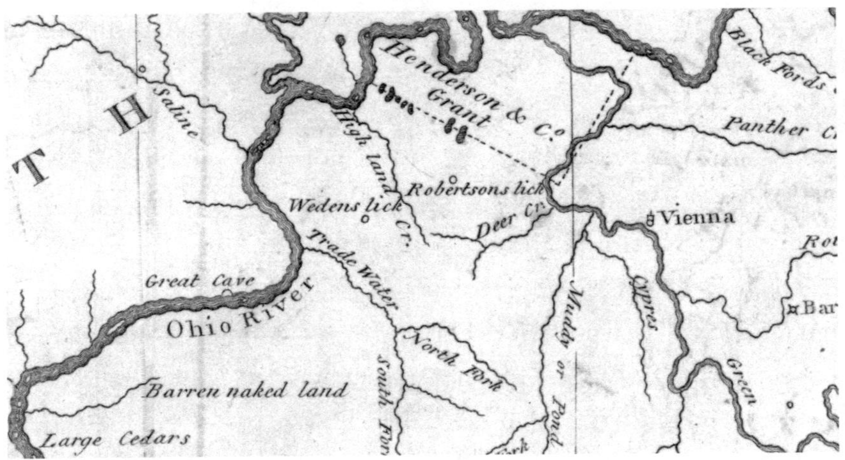

This portion of a map is from "Kentucky, Reduced From Elihu Barker's Large Map" (circa 1795). Robertson's Lick, where Moses Stegall gathered men for his posse, is at the center. The Stegall house was on Deer Creek, just to the south. Courtesy of Tennessee State Library and Archives.

sey. They were joined soon enough by three more: James Tompkins, William Grisson, and justice of the peace Silas McBee, whose presence gave the posse an added air of legitimacy. Seven, all told.[65]

The posse was a woozy blend of vengeance and law. To this day, western Kentuckians sometimes imagine that it was a mob of grizzled locals who finally gathered to stop the Harps.[66] But this was not quite a mob—it was, in fact, legal. Though Stegall has often gotten credit, it was McBee who suggested gathering the posse, which meant that they could claim to be acting at the direction of a peace officer.[67] Because the government did not wholly own law enforcement, it was forced to rely on the people to help—even if that included those seeking revenge.

In the heat of the moment, no one found fault with the idea of deputizing victims to act as police. After the cluster of murders in Knoxville weeks earlier, Tennessee's governor had allowed the *father* of one of the victims to raise six men and pursue the Harps, and he would later give the okay to William Love's brother, a Tennessean, as well. Armed with the governor's imprimatur, Chesley Coffee's Tennessee posse was promised all manner of assistance from "all other officers of the State, both civil and Military." Anyone who gave aid, a judge later decreed, was to be paid out of the state treasury.[68]

Stegall's posse knew who they were looking for—they knew the Harps were responsible—though it is not completely clear how. Poking around the ruins of the Stegall house, they "discovered *tracks*"—from horses? five sets of footsteps?—"which convinced them full well that the Harps were the authors of the mischief."[69] Perhaps Stegall did, in fact, know the Harps. Perhaps he recognized them by their descriptions. (They had by now become somewhat notorious.) It is even possible, as some writers later intimated, that he had had some sort of illicit business relationship with them, rustling horses into nearby territories or smuggling stolen goods. Or it could be as simple as this: His neighbor, Isham Sellers, told him that he'd sent the rough-looking family to the Stegall house with a promissory note to collect on.

The posse set out looking for the Harps on August 25, five days after the Stegall house burned.

* * *

IT IS POSSIBLE that Micajah Harp foresaw his own death. On the morning of the day he died, he awoke early. He "roused the others" and told them he could not sleep. Then he "cursed the ground" for the noises he heard and "the constant trembling he felt." The shaking—it was getting worse. He knew. He felt it: Men were coming after him. On August 26, 1799, Micajah Harp faced his fate.[70]

The showdown was destined to become legend. Years later, several of the men in Stegall's posse told the story of the final pursuit. John Leeper related it to relatives and neighbors. Decades later, Silas McBee, old and portly, narrated it in person to Lyman Draper, one of the first historians of the West. Draper found his way to Pontotoc, Mississippi, the tangled southern jungle where McBee kept his home in the 1840s, and interviewed him. "His memory is yet retentive," Draper marveled. Much of what is known about the Harps, even now, comes from McBee's own recollections.[71]

McBee had his own reasons for wanting the Harps hunted down. He seems to have been in their crosshairs. As a justice of the peace and "distinguished as one of the most enterprising and worthy citizens, [with] a handsome property," as one account later put it, he was a likely target.[72] (Nothing suggests he had a personal relationship with the Harps, though he had also rambled west from the Carolinas into East Tennessee and had even fought, at fifteen, at the Battle of Kings Mountain, where, it has been suggested, men in the Harp family had fought as loyalists. McBee fought on the patriot side. He had even gazed upon British major Patrick Ferguson's dead body. "I counted nine bullet holes," he later said.)[73]

On the same night the Harps had called on Mary Stegall—August 20—there was a disturbance in the McBees' yard. It was earlier in the evening, perhaps around twilight. As night fell, McBee's wife, Catherine, heard the dogs barking. Silas had already gone to bed, and Catherine and her sister were awake, talking. Their hushed chatter was interrupted suddenly when the dogs—big hunting dogs—roused to life in the yard. Both women went to the window and peered outside. The dogs were in an "uproar." Mrs. McBee thought she saw two men. She did not open the door. Although nothing came of it, some concluded from this mysterious visitation that the Harps had intended to target McBee, too, as he was "the only Justice of the Peace for many miles around."[74]

On the first day of searching, the posse found nothing. Tracking involved some intuition, guessing where fugitives might hide. Searchers had to know what signs to read in the landscape: moccasin prints, horse manure, disturbed vegetation. But especially horse tracks.[75] When the Harps were eventually discovered, they had with them eight horses—a difficult thing to hide.[76]

It is a commonplace in histories of American law enforcement to say that one of the earliest forms of policing—particularly in the South—was the slave patrol. Little gangs of local men, usually drawn from militia rolls, slave patrols evolved as a way to keep order where there were significant numbers of enslaved people. Trawling the countryside, patrollers searched cabins for stolen goods and trotted the roads of their districts at night. They interrogated enslaved men and women who were caught without passes. They broke up congregations of enslaved revelers on Whitsuntide and Christmas. And they combed the woods, helping to capture runaways.[77]

But the pursuit of the Harps is suggestive of how other traditions also contributed to early American approaches to law enforcement. In the West, a different practice shaped the efforts to capture fugitives: scouting. This was a military technique in which little flocks of men—sometimes only in twos or threes—patrolled the borderlands to defend against Native people. In Kentucky, this was not a distant memory. As late as 1795, Kentuckians were still flooding the governor's office with petitions begging him to send scouts to protect their frontiers.[78] When the governor of Tennessee called up small posses of militiamen to chase the Harps, he was reacting as he might have in the face of an Indigenous threat.

Some of Stegall's posse members had served as scouts patrolling eastern Tennessee to anticipate Cherokee attacks. Some had ranged the mountain country of Kentucky for the same reason. They "had proved full well their daring intrepidity in many a gallant Indian fight and border foray, when it was emphatically 'every man to his man, and each to his tree,'" as Lyman Draper romanticized. In the way they approached the flight of the Harps, even in the way they talked about their task—they "took a short scout to see if they could discover any signs of the murderers, still prowling about"—they drew on methods used by scouts and spies.[79]

They picked up a trail where the horses had disturbed the shrubbery and followed it for a few miles. In places, there was confusion—the tracks forked, rejoined. In one spot, it looked as if "the outlaws had . . . dispersed a large drove of buffaloes," in hopes of "so tramping down and tangling the wild grass and shrubbery" that they could not be traced. But it did not work: The men found the path again. But the first day of searching ended empty-handed. When night fell, they camped on the western shore of the Pond River; overnight, a "smart hash of rain" fell.[80]

On the second day, they woke early. Orange streams of sunlight were just breaking over the hills as they mounted their horses. They forded the river and picked up the trail. It was still morning when they discovered a cave of sorts with obvious signs of a camp. Beneath a shelf of rock at the edge of a ridge, they found a little shelter, about fifteen feet wide. The men dismounted. They took their guns. Then they crept, slowly, toward the entrance.[81]

Inside was a woman, alone. She stared at them, stone-faced. It was Sally Harp.

She might have stayed behind to protect the babies; one account suggested she was hiding with her daughter when discovered.[82] What was she thinking in this moment? Did she feel fear? Or relief? Perhaps she had known all along that this meeting was bound to happen; in some small corner of her mind, there must have been a sense of inevitability about it. Did she think about returning to a jail room—about what she had done in the past year?

Where are the others? they demanded.

She told them that Micajah had just been there, a few moments ago. He'd taken Susana and Betsy and two horses and "darted off in great haste."[83] She said nothing about Wiley.

I'll kill you instantly if you don't give us correct information about where they went, Silas McBee threatened.

Sally moved toward the edge of the cave. She pointed in the direction of Micajah's flight.[84]

The posse mounted their horses to give chase. They took Sally with them.

* * *

ABOUT TWO MILES from the camp, they spotted him. He was on a horse—probably William Love's. Betsy and Susana were with him. Stegall's men shouted at him: *Stop*.

Micajah paused, looked. Then he broke off, galloping on his horse. He left the women behind.

Four of Stegall's posse gave chase.[85] They fired shots.

The final moments of the chase were chaotic—and desperate. They rode after Micajah for nine miles, deep into the Pond River bottoms. The pursuers shouted at him to surrender. At one point, Micajah asked them to dismount so he could comfortably give himself up. But then he veered and took off. It did not last long, though. In a half mile, they had closed the gap again.[86]

John Leeper, who had the fleetest horse, broke out ahead of the other pursuers. He followed Micajah closely, firing at him. Finally, a small victory: One of the posse's shots hit Micajah in the leg. It might have injured the horse he was riding as well. His pace eased. Leeper rode faster, closer. Eventually, he was within earshot.

Go back, or I'll kill you, Micajah screamed.

Then one of us, Leeper shouted back, "must die."[87]

Leeper gained on him. He raised his gun and took a shot.

Micajah was struck, again. This time, it was catastrophic. The bullet hit him in the back, tearing through his spine. He paled and then slumped. He dropped his gun. His horse slowed.

Leeper caught up. He was a big man and very strong: "a large, heavy framed man, 6ft, 210 lbs, & a very noted hunter & woodsman," one acquaintance remembered.[88] He was prepared for a fight. But when he reached Micajah, the outlaw's horse was walking "leisurely," one posse member related, "and Harpe's wonted daring and bravery seemed to have forsaken him." Leeper approached. He pulled Micajah from his horse.[89]

Micajah did not die immediately. He lay in the grass, blood pouring out beneath him. He asked for water; Leeper fetched some. The two were alone for several minutes. Later, in court, Leeper recounted Micajah Harp's last words. He said that Micajah had asked for Susana, his wife. He wanted to tell her where he had hidden some money, in saddlebags buried along the banks of the Pond River. (If this was true, the money was never found.) He said he wished she would "do better in the future" and that "the whole of them would do better in the future."[90]

As he lay bleeding, Micajah confessed to many of the murders. "Prior to the death of Harp," the newspapers reported, "he confessed that he, aided by his brother, had committed murders to the number of 27." One of them was the Johnson murder, the very first.[91] Another was Frederick Stump. Some of the other victims became clear later, as the men went through the plunder that the Harps had with them: Isaac Coffee's gun, which was returned to his family. William Love's horse. (It did not live long after the chase.)

It was in this moment, as Micajah languished in the grass, that John Leeper collected some of the only real testimony about what lay behind the rampage. Leeper asked what had pushed him to commit so many murders. Micajah replied that he had been "badly treated."[92] He offered no other specifics. (According to a sheriff who talked to them later, the Harp women alleged that some injustice had happened in Knoxville, that the brothers had been accused of something "when they were innocent.")[93] Micajah simply told Leeper that he "had . . . become disgusted with mankind."[94]

The two brothers had made a pact. They "declared war against all mankind," Micajah said—according to what Leeper and the Harp wives later shared—and "agreed with each other, to destroy as many persons as they could."[95] The rampage, in other words, was planned. Micajah knew how it would end: "He knew, at the time they commenced the perpetration of these bloody deeds, that he must die, some day . . . but he determined to risk the consequences, and slay as many as he could, before the sword of justice should overtake him."[96]

Twenty-seven bodies. Nine months. Hundreds of miles. And here it was. The spree was not a frantic set of impulsive acts. There was nothing accidental about it. It was calculated, and it was not, in the end, primarily about robbery or any other material motives. It sprang from a place of grievance and alienation—a need to visit pain on others as comeuppance for his own bad treatment. It is a remarkable confession—a precious, if incomplete, glimpse into Micajah's thinking.

There is something chillingly modern about it. Confessing murderers in the eighteenth century did not sound like this. When they stood before the scaffold and reflected on their crimes, those convicted usually spoke of a kind of reverse pilgrim's progress in which little sins—petty theft, card playing—had led, inexorably, to bigger ones. Often coached by clergymen, the condemned tried to draw moral lessons from their own lives, to inspire hearers to take stock of their own transgressions. Or they talked about earthier motives, like resentment toward a drunken wife who spent too much money. None announced they were at war with mankind.

It must have sounded exotic to Leeper. It would not be entirely legible to succeeding generations, either. It is startling how Micajah's words have been overlooked, skidded over, by almost all those telling this story. Partly, this is because the confession was, for a while, lost. Some of what Micajah said was not uncovered until years afterward, when Lyman Draper collected new testimony about Micajah's final moments. But one senses, too, a kind of resistance to Micajah's own explanation of the murders. Even Draper left it out of the story he published. (He wrote, instead, that the brothers were "prompted seemingly by an insatiable thirst for their fellow's blood.")[97]

It is almost as if Micajah was speaking a language that no one could quite understand. His contemporaries can perhaps be forgiven for missing the gravity of what he was saying. Or for not recognizing it. They could not see all that we see; they did not know of the Harps' past misfortunes. But even more, they had not seen anything like it. No one had. The Harps were engaged in a confoundingly novel project in violence, for its time. It was a statement, in blood, that could only have come with the advent of the new American republic, with all of its soaring ideals and its bruising disappointments. The Harps were inaugurating something. They were, in fact, speaking a new language, dumbfounding their peers.

But, read by the light of the twenty-first century, there is something lurking in Micajah Harp's words that is uncanny and recognizable. Like other mass killers who would follow, he saw himself as taking revenge "for some perceived slight, whether real or imagined"—waging war on society. He was having the last word. He wanted to leave a black mark on the pages of American history.[98]

Micajah asked Leeper not to kill him. He begged to be brought to justice rather than be put to "instant death."[99]

You have nothing to fear from me, Leeper reportedly told him. *But Stegall is close behind, and he probably cannot be restrained.*[100]

Soon enough, the rest of the search party reached the patch of grass where Micajah lay dying. He was curled onto his right side, weak and unable to rise, "rapidly ebbing his life away." As one of them remembered it, they gave Micajah a few moments "for prayer and preparation for another world." He was not interested. He cared nothing for appeals to heaven.

Stegall, then, drew his gun. He mentioned the murder of his wife and child. Then he shot Micajah in the chest, killing him.[101]

Then Stegall took out a knife and cut off Micajah Harp's head.

* * *

NO ONE HAS ever disputed that the Harp murders were profound. But most have stumbled in trying to make sense of them. Writing in the 1920s, Otto Rothert called the murders "unmeaning and unprovoked," like a fire that sparked mysteriously and then just consumed everything in its path.[102] But the murders were not meaningless. They were a kind of protest.

Murder is a public crime, an act against society. That idea predates the United States. It even predates the English colonies. "Morth," the Old English root of "murder," means "secret." In early England, "morth-works"—secret wrongs—were righted simply by giving restitution to the victims. But somewhere in the mists of medieval England, possibly under Edward the Confessor, a sense emerged that murder was such a profoundly terrible act that it did not simply wrong the victim and his survivors. It was a wrong committed against the state itself.[103]

Ever since, common law has distinguished between "private wrongs"—civil injuries—and "public wrongs"—crimes. In his widely read *Commentaries on the Laws of England*, William Blackstone explained the difference: Civil injuries infringe the rights of certain individuals but not everyone. But some wrongs—like robbery or murder—are public, because "besides the injury done to individuals, they strike at the very being of society."[104]

Among all crimes, murder has long been viewed as the most noxious. Even before the Harps tore through Tennessee and Kentucky,

Americans had begun to think differently about some other crimes. Stealing a horse: Did that really merit hanging? The American Revolution had spurred critiques of capital punishment, as people began to wonder whether public hangings were an outgrowth of tyranny. Violent spectacles of death might be fit for kings, some argued, but they were not fit for a republic. Was "the punishment of *death* . . . really just or useful in a well-governed state?" Cesare Beccaria asked in an essay read by countless Americans. "What *right*, I ask, have men to cut the throats of their fellow-creatures?"[105] By the 1790s, American states were striking the death penalty from their lawbooks.

They thought instead of reforming people. They began to build penitentiaries—places where men and women could go to be penitent, to recover their goodness. In 1790, the Walnut Street jail in Philadelphia was transformed into the first state penitentiary, with sixteen cells. By 1798, Kentucky was building one, too. It was under construction in Frankfort that summer.[106] Meanwhile, only a few months before Thomas Langford's murder, Kentucky revised its criminal code to include vastly fewer capital crimes. Before 1798, there were 160 crimes punishable by death. Afterward, there was only one: murder.[107]

Murder was different. None of the reforms of the era, in fact, extended to the crime of murder. Some writers did suggest that capital punishment should be abolished for every crime, even murder. "If society can be secured from violence, by confining the murderer," wrote the Philadelphia physician and humanitarian Benjamin Rush, it should do so. "In confinement, he may be reformed" (or, at least, "restrained").[108] But in every state in the nation in 1799, murder remained punishable by death. Murderers were arch outlaws—people so far outside of society, so irredeemable, that they must be banished from life itself.

If anything, attitudes toward murderers were darkening. Even as opinions about other crimes softened, the feeling that those who killed were somehow *different*—alien, even—was hardening in the late eighteenth century. For much of early modern history, murderers had been viewed as ordinary sinners. All men were depraved; all sinned. Since all were stained by original sin, the surprise was "not that one sinner had committed [murder]," one historian writes, "but that everyone else in the community had not."[109] But that view was shifting. Belief in everyone's innate depravity was beginning to crumble. Murderers, in the public imagination, were becoming monsters. Enlightenment views of human nature were more hopeful and bright, which made it far more complicated to explain men's most hideous behaviors. When murder couldn't be explained, as it often couldn't, Americans fell on a new theory: Murderers were aberrant. Monstrous.[110]

In 1787, the Political Club of Danville, Kentucky, considered this question: "Ought capital punishment to be inflicted for any other crime than that of murder and treason?" Members answered no. But no one quibbled about inflicting it for murder.[111]

Murder was its own kind of treason.[112] An affront to the state itself. An affront to the people, as it tore at the very foundations of society. That was how it stood in American law and in American minds, and that is how best to understand Wiley and Micajah Harp. American society—with all its promises—had not worked for them. The markets, the government, even their own choices as free men, had failed them. It mattered to no one else whether or not Wiley kept his land. Or if he was sued. Or if the sheriff came and seized everything. So in 1798, he decided to step out of society and levy his own little war on its people. He knew he would lose his property, his livelihood, perhaps even his life. So he began to prey on others'.

Murder, in the end, is social protest. The ultimate, final declaration of one's opposition to society. The most profound. And it wasn't over yet.

* * *

THE THREE HARP women were taken first to the jail in Henderson County, an abandoned blockhouse on the lip of the Ohio River. The sheriff had fitted it with a new door and lock only a few weeks earlier. Susana, Betsy, and Sally were, reportedly, the first to be jailed there.[113] They must have had their children with them (though the babies are not mentioned). Six men guarded them. On September 4, they appeared before the Henderson County court, accused of being "parties in the murder of Mary Stegall, James Stegall an infant and William Love," as well as arson and larceny. The court found probable cause to believe them guilty of these felonies, so they were sent to be tried in the Logan County District Court.[114]

They left September 6 in the custody of the Henderson sheriff and five other men. On September 28, after traveling ninety-five miles (for which trouble the accompanying sheriff eventually collected $71.25), they were deposited into the care of the Logan County sheriff, William Stewart.[115] He was to keep them under close watch until the trial. Stewart was an odd, colorful character. A historian who met him in the 1830s called him "the fright of little girls, and the admiration of mischievous boys."[116] But he took care of the Harp women. When they became "dirty & lousy" in jail, he brought new clothing and soap and "had them & the children cleaned up." He brought spinning wheels to keep them busy.[117]

In October, he brought them to court. For the second time in a year, all three faced murder charges. All three, once more, were acquitted. Presumably, these jurymen also had difficulties seeing them as culpable (though several of the posse members who captured the Harp women testified that items belonging to the Stegalls—including such tender trappings of home as two rose blankets, perhaps knitted by Mary herself—were found in their possession).[118]

Tradition has it that Moses Stegall was waiting outside the courthouse prepared to "mete out justice . . . as the court failed to do it." But Stewart brought them safely back to jail to wait.

Later, under cover of night, they were taken several miles away and set free. Stewart left them somewhere "among the Knobs."[119] He watched them slip into the darkness, into anonymity.

* * *

FOR A LONG time after Micajah Harp died, a certain story circulated about his death: It was rumored that he was killed by his own gunpowder. The tale went like this: Before arriving at the Stegall house, the Harps had turned up on the doorstep of James Tompkins. Having no idea who they were, Tompkins fed them a meal. As they ate, Tompkins complained that he had no gunpowder; Micajah, in turn, shared some of his own. With "affected generosity," he poured it into a saucer and handed it to his host.

Tompkins later joined the posse that captured Micajah. In the final pursuit, John Leeper had allegedly borrowed Tompkins's gun, newly filled with Micajah's gunpowder, and when he shot Micajah through the back, it was that powder that sent the ball through his spine. "By a most singular providence," one Kentucky historian wrote, "Big Harpe was mortally wounded by his own powder."[120] Which is to say, the story ended just as it should: Micajah Harp's actions were his own undoing. Poetic justice was served.

But the truth was more complicated. The legitimacy of Micajah Harp's death was questionable. His "execution" had happened without due process, despite his asking to be brought to trial. And it had been done to avenge Stegall's murdered family members, which looked, to some, like a very personal sort of vengeance.[121] Undoubtedly, as the news spread, Kentuckians exhaled with relief. "We are happy in having it in our power to announce to our readers the apprehension and death of Micaijah Harp," one newspaper crowed in the fall of 1799.[122] But some evidence hints at discomfort with Stegall's actions.

The Kentucky legislature did eventually pay out a reward to Stegall's posse.[123] In December 1799, it passed an act to do so and attempted to paper over any question regarding the death of Micajah Harp. There was no doubt, of course, that "Micaijah Harpe, a notorious offender" had committed "the most unheard of murders"—acts unconscionable. The legislature, though, also felt pressed to note the unfortunate fact that the "sundry good citizens" who had pursued the outlaw "were, while in the attempt to apprehend him, reduced to the necessity of slaying him." That phrasing—"reduced to the necessity"—implied some more hesitation and justifiability than had actually gone into the killing.[124]

But if Kentucky officials wanted to remove "all doubt as to the right of these men," others were not reassured.[125] Some of the posse members never shook the ghost of Micajah Harp. John Leeper fell under some suspicion of having known the Harps previously and harboring some personal grudge against them. Early accounts of this episode sometimes included overwrought defenses of Leeper's character: He was a "humane man, easy, slow-spoken, and not quickly excited, but a thorough soldier when roused," James Hall wrote years later. "Leeper was as honest as any man that ever lived, brave and truthful," one of his neighbors attested. Although some accounts suggest he was "celebrated as the capturer of the famous outlaw, Big Harpe," another claims that in 1807, he died "friendless," his character viewed by some as suspect.[126]

Stegall, too, fell under reproach. His slaying of Micajah Harp did not go unquestioned. Rumors swirled that Micajah had been alive and able to talk, although wounded, when Stegall "stepped forward and deliberately cut off his head." Was this to keep him from revealing some "lawlessness" in which Stegall himself had taken part? "It used to be said," one man recalled, that "the reason why Steigal had hurried when he came up to cut off Harpe's head, was, the company before his arrival had got some confessions from Harpe, & Steigal was afraid but he shd. be implicated—& wanted him out of the way." Some even suggested that Stegall had left home on purpose that night in August to allow the Harps to kill his family.[127] The accusations lobbed at him betray a wider squeamishness about revenge killing in the name of law and order.

It's a myth that people in the West reveled in their lawlessness. They did not. Most people wanted order. They wanted the law. They wanted protections against their neighbors. They wanted to be able to walk into a courthouse, to arbitrate disputes. They wanted jails and sheriffs, and where those things did not exist, they demanded them.[128] Vigilantism, historically, has flourished in places where the power of the law was faint. It has mostly reared its head where courts and "other institutions of the law" were "either unavailable or unreliable."[129] That certainly describes Kentucky in 1799. But it was slowly becoming less true.

There were courts. There were lawmen. Multiple juries had sat in judgment of the Harp women. As the shadow of the law haltingly overspread parts of Kentucky, there may have been an increasing discomfort with the kind of eye-for-an-eye justice that Moses Stegall represented. Histories of popular justice are often written as if vigilantes enjoyed broad support, and indeed they often did. (A bit of verse in a Georgia newspaper published in 1794 proclaimed: "*Lynch's Law, ought still to be in vogue / It will rid the town of every cursed rogue.*")[130] But in the hesitations around Micajah Harp's death, we may be witnessing, in real time, an evolution in attitudes.

Stegall's later life was no happier. A few years later, he helped a friend elope to Illinois with a young girl and, ironically, fell victim to the same brand of retribution he himself had practiced. He was shot to death by the girl's father and brothers.[131]

Micajah Harp's body was left in the woods. The posse placed his severed head in the crook of a tree at a crossroads about twenty miles from the town of Henderson. "The skull and jaw-bone remained there for many years," one writer attested, "after all else had been decomposed and mingled with the dust." The oak itself was still standing in 1874. You could see the letters "H.H." carved into its trunk. They stood for "Harp's Head," which became the name for this "wild and lonely spot."[132]

* * *

WILEY HARP DISAPPEARED. He was allegedly spotted, near Knoxville, in June 1800. "Harpe, who escaped, is returned to this state, and has been seen not very far from Clinch river, by some persons who recognized him," the *Kentucky Gazette* reported.[133]

But he was not seen again afterward.

MISSISSIPPI

I keep my Horse; I keep my Whore;
I take no Rents; yet am not poor;
I travel all the Land about,
And yet was born to ne'er a Foot.

—"The Highwayman," from *The Widow* (1652)

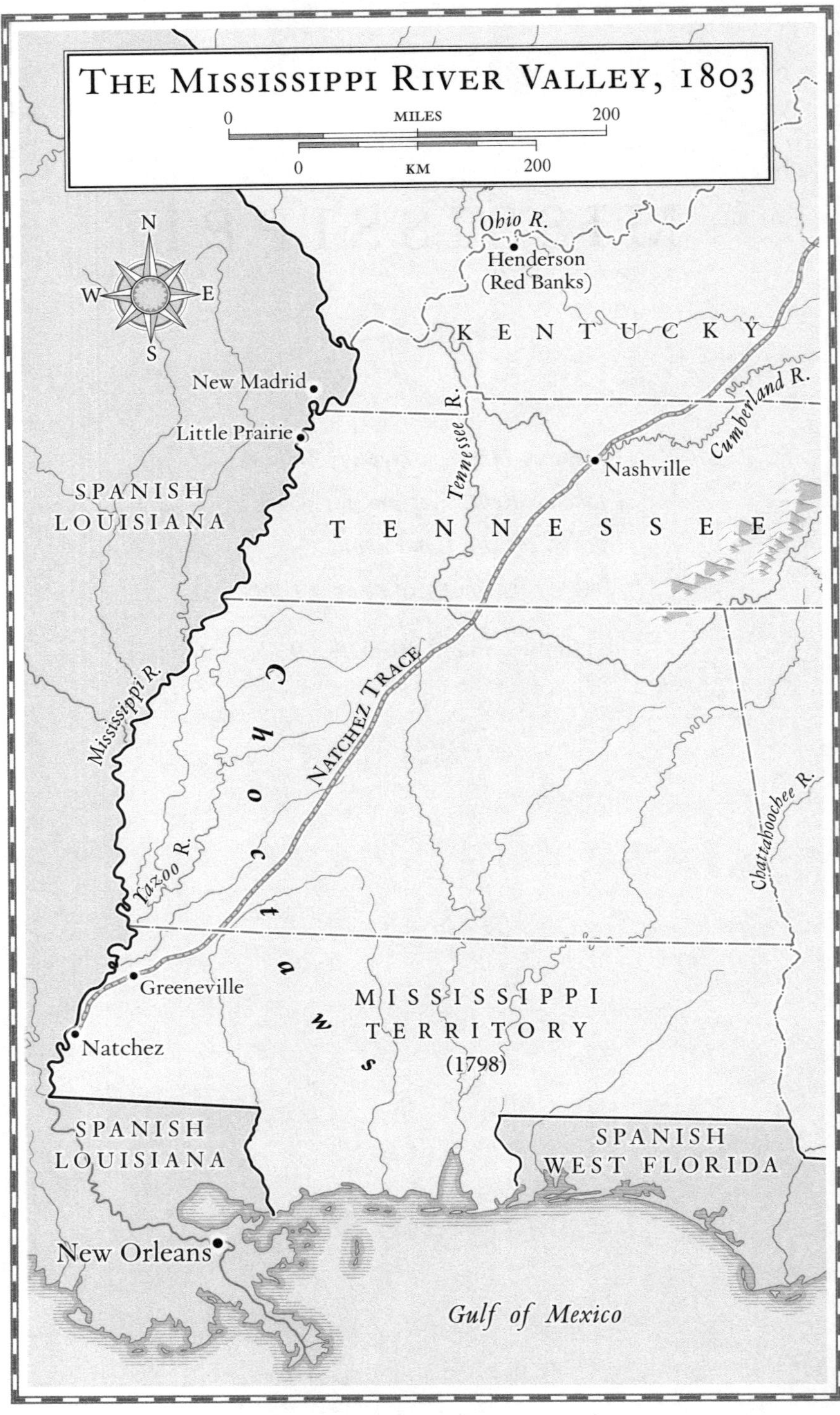

The Mississippi River Valley, 1803
0
MILES
200
0
KM
200
N
W
E
S
Ohio R.
Henderson
(Red Banks)
KENTUCKY
New Madrid
Little Prairie
Cumberland R.
Tennessee R.
Nashville
SPANISH
LOUISIANA
TENNESSEE
Choctaws
NATCHEZ TRACE
Mississippi R.
Yazoo R.
Chattahoochee R.
Greeneville
Natchez
MISSISSIPPI
TERRITORY
(1798)
SPANISH
LOUISIANA
SPANISH
WEST FLORIDA
New Orleans
Gulf of Mexico

CHAPTER 8

THE TRACE

The Mississippi River
Border of New Spain and the United States
Spring 1801

Sometime in the spring of 1801, Colonel Joshua Baker, a Kentucky merchant, loaded several flatboats with horses and goods and pushed off the banks of the Ohio. He was off, on the long journey that Kentucky men often made to bring their goods to market: down the Ohio, into the wide and mighty Mississippi, to New Orleans, then back.

For many Americans, this was becoming customary. Much of what was tilled, gathered, or slaughtered in western Pennsylvania, Ohio, Tennessee, and Kentucky eventually emptied down the Mississippi into Spanish New Orleans. Thousands of barrels of whiskey, cider, flour, pork, beef, and apples went down the river that spring. The port of New Orleans was the doorstep to global trade.

First, the float downriver, for hundreds of miles. What a sight the Mississippi must have been. Thronged with rafts bringing people and things. Barges, huge and lumbering; scows and skiffs; keelboats with pointed prows and covered cabins. And flatboats, with their giant oars sticking out of the water like antennae. Baker had men with him to help man the boats. Flatboats were sturdy and easy to manage, but you had to be vigilant. You had to watch for whirlpools, eddies, boils, and sucks. The river was high and swift in spring, but there were always unknown threats waiting beneath the surface. An upturned tree hidden just below the waterline could easily snare a boat.[1]

The river was alive with people and song. Baker passed others also making pilgrimages to market or new lands. They crammed onto flatboats with all they had: sheep, dogs, and chickens, and spinning wheels and looms, roped on top. They brought turnips and coffee and dried mutton to eat along the way. On the east bank, Choctaws would come among the boatmen to sell turkey, venison, and pumpkins. Meals were shared with others. "We have but one general dish for soup & for meat," one traveler wrote. "Out of this all take their piece of meat" or "each takes his tin cup of salt meat soup."[2]

At night, many lashed their boats together and congregated on the shore. They drank, sang songs, fiddled. Crewmen serenaded the camps, belting out ballads about "bold young fellers" and "ladies gay": *Here's to those that has old clothes, / And never a wife to mend 'em,* went one tune.[3] Lucky travelers might encounter a character like Old Pap, a fiddler who would "sing the live-long night" accompanied by his companion, a violin named Katy. When they weren't singing, boatmen passed the time playing cards or telling "marvellous tales" while slinging back corn whiskey.[4] It could take weeks, even months, to descend the river, depending on how high its waters were running.

At the end of it lay New Orleans. It was a walled city, though the fortifications were crumbling. Along its riverside ran a great levee. The levee was built to keep the floodwaters out, but it doubled as a pretty promenade; it was planted, pleasantly, with orange trees. White houses faced the river, sheltering the well-off people inside as they supped on lavish meals of stewed meats, fish, crabs, and coffee before retiring for an afternoon siesta.[5]

There was so much wealth in New Orleans. Perched at the delta, the port drew all that glittered in the world, from all reaches of the

A flatboat floating downriver in the nineteenth century. Engraving by Alfred Waud, circa 1855–1890. Courtesy of the Historic New Orleans Collection (accession no. 1977.137.18.685).

earth. Dazzling, exotic things, all captured in tariff schedules: Taffeta, hazelnuts, chickpeas. "Silk lace of all types." Mahogany. Tortoiseshell. Gold and silver brocade. Chocolate, plain or with sugar and cinnamon. Glass shades for candles, velvet ribbon, elephant tusks, pickled cabbage. Mother-of-pearl. Cured buffalo meat. Rugs, ebony, wool. Wooden bidets.[6]

And slaves. Men in New Orleans measured their wealth in slaves. Unlike in Tennessee, where men paid for land in horses, here, they took one another's measure in bound labor. "The local manner of calculating wealth is very singular," a visitor wrote. "It is said such a man is worth ten negroes a year, and another one hundred; and it is understood to a dollar how much the income amounts [to]." The waters around New Orleans were infested with alligators, and the French planters told their slaves that the creatures had a "predilection for negro flesh." Most slaves didn't swim.[7]

Baker arrived in midsummer, when the air was heavy and stagnant. New Orleans could be squalid in the heat. Garbage clogged gutters, meat went rotten, books mildewed. Yellow fever flowered. The mosquitoes were ferocious.[8] There are no records describing how long Baker's party stayed in town or where they went. But Kentucky boatmen were known to venture into the seedier parts of town—beyond the respectable brick houses that lined the waterfront, past the markets and produce stands, to the swamplands, where snake-filled shanties housed illicit cabarets and billiard rooms.[9]

Baker sold his goods, then headed homeward. The custom among Kentucky men, having sold their produce, was to break up and sell their flatboats as lumber and then journey home over land. It was easier than battling the current, going upstream. The usual route was the Natchez Trace, a five-hundred-mile gravelly path that reached from Natchez on the eastern bank of the Mississippi, through Choctaw and Chickasaw country, all the way to Nashville.[10]

The trouble happened soon after Baker and his crew started up the Trace. It was August, stifling hot. The path was dusty, their throats dry. The horses needed a drink. They stopped at Twelve Mile Creek, about 150 miles north of New Orleans, to wash and refresh themselves. As soon as they knelt at the water, the men appeared.

There were four of them, their faces all blacked. They brandished arms. That's what Baker saw as he turned: several men with guns. He paled and froze, kneeling at the creek. Then he stood and called out—*what do you want?*—but he surely knew. He knew that instant what was going to happen. One of the packhorses, spooked, ran into the woods. With it went all of the gold and silver it had been carrying.

They stole everything else.[11]

"We are informed, that on the 4th of August," the *Kentucky Gazette* reported weeks later, "Colonel Joshua Baker, a Mr. William Baker, and a Mr. Rogers, of Natchez, were robbed of their horses, travelling utensils, and about 2300 dollars cash." Baker's men had tried to pursue the "villains," the newspaper added, but with no luck. Still, someone in Baker's party had, in fact, recognized one of the robbers. "One of them who was described by Col. Baker," noted the *Gazette*, "formerly resided at the Red Banks."[12]

This might have come to nothing. But the next year, inconceivably, Baker was nearly robbed again, this time on the Mississippi itself. He was able to fight off the men who tried to board his boat, but he had reached a breaking point—he had had enough.

* * *

THE FINAL SCENES of the Harp saga took place in the Mississippi River valley. By 1801, Micajah Harp had been dead for years. His skull was moldering in the crook of a tree in Kentucky, hundreds of miles away. Sally Harp had slinked back into anonymity. Susana was, by some accounts, living on a chicken farm. Wiley had disappeared. To all observers, the spree seemed long over. But its postscript unfolded on the Mississippi's shores.

Only the faintest tendrils of American influence had touched this world surrounding New Orleans. It was not yet the Cotton Kingdom. Slaves had only begun to trickle downriver from the upper South; Eli Whitney had invented the cotton gin less than a decade earlier, in 1793. At the river's mouth, you were more likely to see stalks of sugarcane than fields of cotton. In autumn, the season for sugar refining, the furnaces along the riverbank burned around the clock, "belching clouds" of sweet smoke.[13] Things mostly went down the river, not up. Not until 1811 would a steamboat appear, chugging against the current. Many more decades would pass before Mark Twain pictured Huckleberry Finn swearing a loyalty oath to Tom Sawyer's gang, itself a figment plucked from "pirate books, and robber books."[14]

The Mississippi River was not only a lively conveyor belt of people and things, it was also the western border of the United States. On its eastern side, in 1801, were American shores. On the west was Spanish Louisiana. Once the French colony of "La Louisiane," Louisiana was a giant, sprawling claim of territory, mostly untouched by Europeans and still in the hands of the Osages and Lakotas and Hidatsas and other tribes who peopled it. (Some of whom Lewis and Clark would meet a few years later when the United States acquired it.) As the nineteenth century dawned, Louisiana was about to undergo a whiplash-inducing series of changing hands, so quick, as the novelist William Faulkner later wrote, "as to resemble the limber flicking of the magician's one hand before the other holding the deck of inconstant cards: the Frenchman for a moment, then the Spaniard for perhaps two, then the Frenchman . . . for that one last second, half-breath."[15]

In the Mississippi borderlands lived a dense tangle of different peoples, a tumult of faiths and foods and tongues. Hugging the river's shores were Caddo horse rustlers and rich Spanish planters and even migrant Cherokees drifting onto Arkansas shores. Many were French, the remnants of Louisiana's long history as a French colony. To elites, they looked feral. In 1803, one of Napoleon's ministers breakfasted at the Sancier plantation near New Orleans, where the wife served him steaming pots of café au lait and the husband regaled him with tales of how he had descended from the first French settlers of Mobile. The official was not impressed by their attempts to prove pedigree. "They were half-wild," he wrote in his journal.[16]

Among the valley's characters were a handful of venturesome Americans, mostly living in little clots on the east bank in the fledgling province of Mississippi Territory—a small patch of the United States so new that its statesmen had barely had time to scrape together a code of laws. Still under federal supervision, Mississippi was not yet a state; in 1801, most of what later became the state of Mississippi still belonged to the Choctaws.

It was here, in Mississippi Territory, that some few stray Americans huddled and governed in rude little buildings whose walls, their descendants would remember, many years later, "had held someone who might have been Wiley Harpe."[17]

* * *

IN NOVEMBER 1801, about three months after the Baker robbery, a new governor sailed into the statehouse in Natchez, Mississippi.[18] He was tall and handsome, "with a typical American complexion," "a kind face," and "deliberate speech" (as a French diplomat later described him).[19] Already possibly the youngest person ever to have been seated in Congress, he was the sort of young politician who was making a name for himself, rocketing to renown in the expanding early republic by rushing into the offices and opportunities created by the opening of western lands—even if it meant moving to less savory places, like the stifling, remote wilds of Mississippi Territory.

William Charles Cole Claiborne was plucky and self-made. He came from a humble family. He had grown up in Virginia listening to his father, a proud Revolutionary soldier, spin yarns about the war and its "atrocities." According to family lore, his father imparted Claiborne's "invincible attachment to free government." But his father also lost all the family money. At fifteen, "a poor and almost friendless boy," possessed of nothing more than his good looks, Claiborne left home. He went to New York, where he made improbably important political acquaintances and landed on his feet.[20]

Claiborne was just twenty-six years old in 1801 when Thomas Jefferson appointed him governor of Mississippi Territory. It was an important post—the president's eyes and ears into the Spanish frontier—and Claiborne was more or less "young and untried." But Jefferson knew him well. As a teenager, Claiborne had worked as a clerk in Congress. He had studied law in books loaned to him by Jefferson and John Adams and at the College of William and Mary. Then he had gone west to Tennessee, where he was serving as a congressman—a strong Democratic Republican—when Jefferson tapped him to govern.[21]

Claiborne worried about law and order.[22] As he settled into his muggy new office, it was one of his first pieces of business. In early 1802, he was spooked by a report of river pirates prowling the Mississippi. He was disturbed not only by their presence but by the conundrum of how to capture and punish them. The river, after all, was shared as a border between Spanish and American lands. Under Pinckney's Treaty—an agreement brokered in 1795 after years of territorial disputes—the official border between New Spain and the United States lay in the very middle of the riverbed. But people blissfully crossed it, daily. Whose jurisdiction was it? Claiborne wrote to the officer at Chickasaw Bluffs, an American fort on the river, and ordered the soldiers there to "arrest those Pirates and Felons, if . . . found upon the American soil."[23] But "Pirates and Felons" could easily skip out of American territory. Claiborne knew he would need Spanish cooperation as well.

He wrote to the governor of Louisiana, Juan Manuel de Salcedo. "Sir," he opened, "I take the liberty to acquaint your Excellency, with a daring Robbery which has lately been committed upon some Citizens of the United States, who were descending the River Mississippi." He didn't know who had done this "act of Piracy." He didn't know whether the offenders were Spanish subjects. But it seemed, he wrote, "that the offence was committed . . . within the Jurisdiction of Spain." He wanted Salcedo's help in apprehending the pirates and keeping the Mississippi open for safe passage.[24]

Free navigation of the Mississippi was at the heart of the Jeffersonian project. It was deeply important, not only for those living in Mississippi Territory, but for all Americans. The economies of much of the western United States depended on the Mississippi—on being able to reach Natchez or New Orleans. In fact, in the Republican vision for America, the very political economy of the republic hinged on free access to foreign markets. In an agrarian nation, farmers needed to be able to sell their surplus. "Since the 1780s," writes historian Drew R. McCoy, "most Americans had regarded free navigation of the Mississippi River and the right of deposit at New Orleans as essential to the national interest."[25]

In his letter to Salcedo, Claiborne tried to put the threat in global terms. "The safety of the Western Commerce" mattered to both the United States and Spain, Claiborne implored. "If prompt and decisive Efforts should not be made to detect, & punish those recent offenders," other crimes would follow—and the free trade of both Spanish subjects and American citizens alike would suffer.[26]

Salcedo responded coolly.

"It is truly impossible to determine, whether the delinquents are Spanish or Americans," he wrote. "I see no reason why it ought to be more particularly charged to my Nation." For every six or seven Spanish boats on the river, Salcedo pointed out, "there passes two hundred American Flats & Barges."

American fugitives hid in Louisiana, and it annoyed Salcedo. "Vagabonds without number . . . who have fled from, or who do not, or cannot return to the United States" slipped across the river, melted into the woods, and vanished, he acknowledged. But he had very little interest in tangling with them.[27]

Salcedo promised, weakly, to try to capture the pirates. He probably did not do much afterward. He was not much interested in helping the United States. A brigadier general hardened by years of service in the Spanish military, who regularly raged at members of the cabildo (New Orleans's city council), he was unlikely to warm to Claiborne's overtures.[28]

But only two months later, Claiborne received word of an attempted robbery on the Mississippi—the second Baker incident. As it was later described, men "attempted in a hostile manner to board the Boat of Colo: Joshua Baker," but they were driven off "by Colo: Baker's, making a shew of arms."[29] On reaching Natchez, a furious Baker reported it to the governor. Claiborne took the matter to heart.

* * *

BAKER THOUGHT HE knew who was responsible for these robberies. It was the unnamed man, identified after the first incident, who had once "resided at the Red Banks"—that is, in Kentucky. (It is possible that Baker, a Kentuckian, had once known him personally.) In 1802, he was already somewhat notorious in certain places. In time, his gang's escapades would become the stuff of folklore. "His depredations became the talk of the whole Western country," John James Audubon wrote in the 1840s.[30] His name was Samuel Mason.

Mason had a colorful and twisted past. By 1802, he had lived a long life of thievery and violence. Born about 1739 in western Virginia, he had bounced from Pennsylvania to the western edges of Kentucky Territory to the humid lands of Natchez country. Earlier in life, he had been a Revolutionary soldier, though not a very good one. In 1777, he led fourteen men straight into a Shawnee ambush. They all died; he survived.

For a time after the war, Mason lived well. In Pennsylvania, he served as a county judge. He hoarded land, hundreds of acres, and owned four slaves. But he fell into debt. The sheriff came and seized his farm. Without settling any debts, he fled the state. After that, he turned, resolutely, to a life of cheating and stealing. In Kentucky, travelers who visited him disappeared. His neighbors' horses and slaves vanished. When authorities took notice, he left.[31]

In 1798, Mason alighted on a marshy fork of Bayou Pierre in Mississippi Territory, the better to prey on river commerce. (He was apparently still living in the vicinity of Bayou Pierre when Joshua Baker was robbed not very far up the Trace from Mason's house.)[32] Along with his own sons, Mason seems to have collected a number of other men who aided in his exploits. The produce and spoils of western farmers, floating down the Mississippi in ever increasing numbers, were simply too tempting. Mason's men took to poaching these goods. They also robbed unlucky farmers as they returned home to Kentucky or Tennessee, trudging overland with bags of silver and gold heaped on the backs of their packhorses and banknotes stuffed into their pockets.

Mason's men sometimes pretended they were interested in buying goods before demanding them at gunpoint. "They hailed us from the shore, telling us they wished to purchase some rifles," one boatman recalled. When the flatboat ignored them, the men jumped into pirogues and "commenced the pursuit."[33] When Mason lived on the Natchez Trace, he stalked the public house up the road. Once, he came in just after three Kentucky traders had arrived. "I noticed him as he passed the saddlebags of the travelers," the innkeeper remembered. "He managed to give each of them a push with his foot as if to feel their weight." Satisfied that they were stuffed with specie, "he bade me good day, and rode off." The next day, riding away, the same travelers whose bags he had sized up were confronted by men with blackened faces and robbed.[34]

Some of his robberies became legendary. Near Gum Springs in Choctaw Nation, Mason's men confronted a bunch of Kentucky boatmen who were getting ready to camp for the night. Frightened, the Kentuckians ran off in all directions, some of them half-dressed. The next morning, when the post rider came upon the empty campsite and blew his bugle, they staggered out from their hiding places. Taking up knives and clubs, the victims vowed to pursue Mason's gang and "attack them . . . knocking down right and left" with cudgels. But about two miles into their pursuit, Mason appeared with guns drawn. "Go back or I'll kill every last one of you," he hissed.[35]

Mason was a nasty character. While in Red Banks, Kentucky, where his career of petty piracy probably began, he learned to duck the law. He had allegedly beaten a constable to death. Other stories wafted behind him like smoke. In the late 1790s, a traveler passing by Mason's house vanished into thin air. One of Mason's slaves later confessed to someone that she had helped him drag a body into the Cumberland River. Apparently, he had wanted to keep the man's valises, "in which were plenty of money."[36]

All of this sounds a bit romantic. But it isn't surprising that robberies had begun popping up along the Mississippi. Highwaymen thrive on emerging markets. They prey on vulnerable and unprotected routes of exchange.[37] The steady parade of flatboats gliding downriver were easy targets. As the volume of river commerce grew (it was relatively new and still peaking in these years), so did theft.[38] How much is hard to say—Mason's very notoriety suggests he was somewhat unusual—but there is no doubt it was happening. However much river pirates were later romanticized, Mason's men were real.[39]

Mason never stayed in one place for long. His piracy depended in large part on the fact that the Mississippi was something of a hazy borderland. New Orleans, a Spanish port, lay at the nexus of many different territories and interests—Spain, the Choctaws, the Chickasaws, and the United States. Mason took advantage of these weak and blurred jurisdictions. He counted on them. When he feared the law would find him in any one place, he simply hopscotched to another.

But once Mason was fingered by Baker, he became a target for territorial governor William Claiborne. "While these Sons of Rapine and Murder are permitted to Rove at large," Claiborne wrote angrily, "we may expect daily to hear of *outrages* upon the Lives &

properties of our fellow Citizens." He asked a militia officer to round up some volunteers and seek out Mason.[40]

But almost a year passed as the sons of rapine continued to rove freely. Even as Claiborne wrote, Mason was already on the move, headed across the river and preparing to perch in a place where he believed the arm of American law could never touch him.

* * *

NEW MADRID IN 1803 was a muddy outpost in Upper Louisiana. It lay on the west bank of the Mississippi, about five hundred miles north of New Orleans. It was situated on a pretty, fertile plain, but it was also swampy, and when the river flooded, it occasionally carried away whole buildings. Around the turn of the century, the "government-house" simply tumbled into the Mississippi and was washed away. Its people were fairly humble, from a mix of ethnic backgrounds. Thomas Ashe, an Irish traveler who passed through in 1806, found them unimpressive. He called them "the dregs of Kentucky, France and Spain."[41]

On January 11, 1803, a French villager shuffled into court in New Madrid. It was a court day, when Louisianan provincial officials would be meeting to hear cases, and he had something to tell them. An acquaintance of his who was on his way downriver with a load of salt pork had seen some suspicious men at Little Prairie, about thirty miles below New Madrid. He had passed with his cargo, unmolested. But something had bothered him.[42]

Others around Little Prairie, it turned out, had also noticed some odd characters nearby. Little Prairie was an even smaller place, a cluster of houses in the remote Spanish district of New Madrid. Newcomers did not go unnoticed. A strange new family had just appeared there, taking up residence in an empty house, and they made the neighbors nervous. One man who lived at Little Prairie told the New Madrid court that these strangers seemed to be well armed.

They guarded their house very carefully. He did not believe they were ordinary, unremarkable Spanish subjects. He thought they might be some of Samuel Mason's men, perhaps even Mason himself.

How the people of Little Prairie even knew of Samuel Mason is a mystery. That they knew to suspect him in 1803 speaks to the improbable small-world quality of the Mississippi borderlands. In Natchez, in Red Banks, in Frankfort, in New Orleans, and in Nashville, people met, recognized each other, found they had crossed paths earlier. But, too, the rumor that Mason had come to Little Prairie suggests further involvement between the two governors, Salcedo and Claiborne. Perhaps Salcedo had acted on Claiborne's information after all, at the very least forwarding notice to his district posts. One of the villagers was somehow aware that "the Governor of Natchez [Claiborne] had put the militia after them," looking for Mason and his henchmen.[43]

The commandant at New Madrid, Henri Peyroux de la Coudrèniere, took this clue very seriously. The very next day, January 12, 1803, he ordered a small force of men to go to Little Prairie. He sent two militia officers (one of whom was also "commissioner of police"), an interpreter, and a number of soldiers. They rode to the house where Mason had allegedly taken up residence. When they got there, they found several horses saddled and heaped with baggage, as if everyone was poised to flee. They also found seven thousand dollars in banknotes. Inside the house were Samuel Mason, several of his sons, and his daughter-in-law. With him, too, was a man who called himself "John Setton."

All were arrested. Then they were taken to New Madrid. Peyroux, following Spanish precedent, would do some preliminary investigation. If he found sufficient evidence of their criminality, he would send the prisoners to Salcedo, the governor-general, for a further trial.[44] Meanwhile, he kept them under lock and key. (He contracted, quickly, with a blacksmith for "irons" and "handcuffs.")[45]

Contemporary accounts as well as historians give the impression that getting justice in Spanish Louisiana could be difficult. First, judgments could be summary. Districts were ruled by military commandants—Peyroux, in this case—who had total authority in civil disputes. But judicial power resided mostly with the governor. The governor-general of Louisiana, Salcedo, was both a military commander and a civilian leader, and as both "head of the police" and supreme judge, he had at his command several battalions of militia to keep order. He heard cases and dispensed judgments with no possibility of appeal. There was no judicial branch of the government. In New Orleans, there were not even lawyers, excepting those who held government office.[46] At least one resident of New Orleans, James Pitot, thought the governor was far too minutely involved in the "details of police administration." All justice flowed through Salcedo.[47]

With Salcedo controlling everything, the system was hopelessly inefficient. Pitot also thought that policing in Louisiana was scandalously lax. In his view, New Orleans was out of control. "The patrols in town are so poorly organized that nighttime burglaries in the warehouses are frequent," he complained. (Pitot, a merchant, knew something about this.) He knew of murders among "vagrants." Gambling halls catered to thieves, some of them slaves, who filched goods from their masters and fenced "the household pilferage" by making bets. "The government is aware of and permits all of that; and woe unto the minor official who would want to stop it," Pitot lamented. "The governor general reserves to himself alone the right to decide."[48] It was a system that could be both fumbling and harsh.

That is not quite the impression one gets from reading the record of the Mason hearings. Peyroux, the highest official in New Madrid, interrogated Setton and the Masons for ten days.[49] He was scrupulously careful. He asked everything he could think to ask.

What was Mason's intent in coming to Little Prairie? Where had all these banknotes come from? If the prisoners had lived lives of such innocence, why could they not produce any neighbors or acquaintances to vouch for them? But mostly he asked about the Baker robbery, among other incidents. Over and over, he asked what Mason, Setton, and the others knew and whether they had been involved.

Mason was cocky. In his interview, he first tried to argue that "he had never do[ne] any thing wrong on the Spanish's Side." He assumed Spanish authorities would care little about what he had done on American soil, let alone in Choctaw country. But he was wrong. Mason, stunned by this, changed strategies. He began to say that he knew who had robbed Baker—and several other traders—on "the other side," and that he could "prove that [it] was not him."[50] When pressed, Mason named a wild, endless bunch of characters who, he heard, had been involved in these robberies.

But most of all, he tried to pin the crimes on one of the men who had been captured with him: John Setton.

* * *

SETTON SAT DOWN to be interviewed next. He swore, before God, to tell the truth. He was a thin, shifty man, by turns both terse and expansive. Often in the transcript, his answers sound cool and detached. But in other moments, he comes across as nervous, overeager.

He first gave a different name, an alias. He said his name was Taylor. But soon he confessed to being John Setton. Mason had tried to sandbag Setton. He blamed him for everything. But Setton was no criminal mastermind, he claimed. When the interrogators asked why he didn't give his real name, he offered a simple answer: Mason had told him to lie.[51]

Setton puzzled Peyroux. He seemed odd, a sphinx. His very presence—the only one of the prisoners captured at Little Prairie who was not related to Samuel Mason by blood or marriage—was strange. His biography, too, was strange. He told the interrogators that he was an Irishman, a Catholic by faith, and that he had arrived in America in 1797. He said he was an army deserter. He said he had worked as a sawyer and a carpenter. He said he had hunted for furs on the White River. He said he had served the Spanish king at Nogales. He said he had been in prison. Finally, he said he had met Mason's sons somewhere in Choctaw country and they had "invited him to go and steal horses on the coaste of the Natchez."[52] If even half of that was true, it is not difficult to understand why Setton might have drifted, for good, into Mason's circle. He appeared to have lived a rather shiftless life.

But Setton also comes across in his testimony as something of a hostage. He told stories of how Mason had tied him up, held him at knifepoint. He said the Mason family had taken his money and his clothing. He claimed that Mason had tried to make him go to a justice of the peace, under duress, and "confess" to the Baker robbery so the Masons themselves would finally be cleared of suspicion. He said the Masons had "kept him as a prisoner" and that "he has never been able to escape till to day."[53] And maybe some of that was true, too. It was plausible enough that Mason would have kept Setton in his pocket to take the blame if necessary.

If Mason had hoped for that outcome, it was not what happened. Setton sold him out completely. On the second day, he sat before Peyroux and answered questions:

What were you all doing in New Madrid? Peyroux asked.

Mason wanted to escape the law, Setton said.

And what were your intentions?

No other intention but to rejoin my family in the United States, Setton said. He wanted to earn enough money to buy clothes and then go back downriver, he said.[54]

Do you know where Mason has hidden other stolen goods? Peyroux asked.

No, Setton declared. *They hide them from me, too.*[55]

And where had all the banknotes come from?

Well, I don't know, Setton answered. But Mason was known to be a rogue and a thief. He had been doing it for forty years, at least, he said. And when he was drunk, Setton added, Mason liked to crow about his exploits. Setton had heard the Masons talking about the robberies they planned to commit and about how they would pawn the goods afterward, "without any body could say a word about it." Mason had associates in Kentucky and Tennessee who stole horses and slaves and all kinds of loot, Setton said. Mason had even stolen horses from the guests at his own daughter's wedding, Setton divulged, galloping toward a climax. And, yes, Setton added finally, the Masons had robbed Baker, too.[56]

Peyroux, no doubt on the edge of his seat, paused. Then he asked: *Has Mason ever asked* you *to rob or kill?*

Yes, Setton said. *Mason asked me to steal horses, to beat a flatboat owner to death, to plunder the boat, and then burn it.*[57]

Setton was clever. The others had tried pointing the finger at him; he turned things around as if he was the only one offering the truth. He gave some of the only straight answers in the interrogation, and he must have appeared believable. Peyroux began to imagine using John Setton as a state's witness against the others. But it was a dangerous game the authorities were playing, to trust Setton, a man with a confounding story and a shadowy identity.

It's hard to know precisely how Peyroux saw Setton. He might have seemed relatively harmless, a down-on-his-luck petty thief. For years, Mason had been collecting aimless drifters, "wild, carousing & reckless" men who came into his orbit and never quite left.[58] In Setton's telling, at least, Mason seemed to have held him almost in captivity. Perhaps he came across as somewhat pathetic, a simple patsy. Or perhaps Mason knew something about Setton's identity that gave him a bit of leverage over Setton, something that Peyroux did not yet suspect.

It was for good reason that Peyroux could not quite get a handle on Setton: He was not really John Setton. "John Setton" was an alias. His real name, the evidence suggests, was Wiley Harp.

* * *

BOTH AMERICAN AND Spanish authorities had begun to suspect this, at least as early as 1802. William Claiborne wrote that Samuel Mason and "a Man by the name of Harp" were said to be the ones who had tried to board Baker's boat that year. (Claiborne knew something about Wiley Harp; he had been a Tennessee congressman during the murders.) To Claiborne, Wiley Harp was by some measures the worse of the two. "The crimes of Harp, are many and great," he wrote, "and in point of Baseness, Mason is *nearly* as celebrated."[59]

By 1802, Wiley Harp had been missing for years. There had been a few alleged sightings near his old haunts. Some thought they had spied him in Tennessee in September 1799, not long after Micajah's death. "Sir, I am informed by Travelers that there was a footman seen . . . in the Mountains," one wrote to the Tennessee governor. He looked like "the young Harp that is yet alive." Hearing this and seeking vengeance, William Love's brother took ten armed men to hunt down Wiley Harp wherever he was "harboured or concealed."[60] But nothing came of it.

Wiley vanished. No one had spotted him for years. He disappeared as if into air. What he may have been doing all that time, it appears, was refashioning himself into "John Setton."

That Wiley could have fallen in with Mason is plausible. Mason had once lived in Red Banks, only a short distance from where the final pursuit of the Harps had taken place in western Kentucky. One of Mason's perches had been Cave-in-Rock, a hideout near the mouth of the Ohio; the Harps were also said to have hidden there at times. With his brother dead and his wife in jail, Wiley had had nowhere to go and no one to turn to. He was a wanted man. Is it unreasonable to think he might have looked to the Masons as a proximate family and a way, perhaps, to make money—even if illegally?[61]

There is no doubt that Setton looked like Wiley. "Sutton was a man who very well answered the description of Little Harpe," one man attested.[62] (This alternate spelling of Setton's name occasionally appeared.) Another, studying Setton's profile, consulted the Kentucky governor's 1799 proclamation, issued when the Harps were on the run. "The description of . . . Harpe so well corresponded with Sutton's appearance" that he could hardly believe it.[63] But Setton's resemblance to Wiley went beyond his general looks. Various physical marks, including "a mold on his neck," a deformed toe, and, allegedly, a scar on his chest that dated to a knife fight in Knoxville, would later be mentioned as evidence of his true identity.[64]

Interrogating him in New Madrid, Henri Peyroux asked Setton forthrightly: Did he know a man named Harp?

Setton, unfazed, replied: Why, yes, he'd known someone in the Cumberland country by that name. But that person had been killed. (He added, without emotion, that he knew the man had had a brother. But "he did not see him and do not know where he is.")[65]

Peyroux must have grown frustrated. All of them deflected, misled, obfuscated. They talked in circles. Much of the testimony taken in New Madrid in January 1803 has a kind of looping, aimless feel. You can sense how Mason, in particular, had made a life of evasion. Even his stories wander and go nowhere. But Henri Peyroux decided, nonetheless, that he had collected enough evidence to send the prisoners to New Orleans to be tried before Governor Salcedo.

He sent them downriver to the highest court in Spanish Louisiana.[66] He does not appear to have suspected yet that he had Wiley Harp in custody.

No trial record survives, but Salcedo in New Orleans likely heard the same vague, meandering testimony that Mason's crew had offered in New Madrid. He, too, was irritated by the "continued infamous contradictory accusations" they lobbed at one another.[67]

Salcedo, though, doubted his ability to sit in judgment. These were American citizens whose crimes had occurred on American soil. He listened to the case, then decided to send them back into the United States.[68] In March 1803, all of the prisoners were loaded onto a boat bound for Mississippi Territory. "No crime could be charged upon them as being committed in the Spanish Government," *The Western Spy* reported, so "the Governor General ordered them to be taken to Natchez, and delivered to our Government."[69] Mason and his sons had repeatedly pleaded with Peyroux not to "deliver them to the American Government."[70] But now they were, it appeared, headed for just such a fate.

On the way, though, things went sideways. Off the banks of Pointe Coupée, the boat's mast broke. When some of the crew went ashore to gather wood for its repair, Mason and the others broke free. They took up guns and began firing. In the fray, Mason was hit by a bullet. But he rallied quickly. "Mason fell and rose, fell and rose again," according to one account, and was able to drive the guards off the boat. Eventually, he abandoned the boat altogether and disappeared into the Louisiana woods.[71]

All of the prisoners, including Setton, escaped.

CHAPTER 9

THE TWO FACES OF JOHN SETTON

The mouth of the Mississippi River
Near New Orleans
Spring 1803

The Mississippi River, as every boatman knew, was not tame. It was not delicate. It was furious. In some places, it was roiling and muddy. You couldn't drink its water without letting it sit in jars overnight so all the dirt sank to the bottom. Along with everything else, the river was ever changing. Its waters constantly overran and reshaped its banks. "The river chews away and deepens its banks on one side," one man wrote, "while it forms and builds them up on the other . . . In this way it enlarges its delta each year, a little at a time."[1]

Trying to divine what happened to Wiley Harp at the end of his life is sometimes like diving for oysters beneath muddy, bubbly waters. It is hard to know what to grab on to; a lot is clouded, obscured. Even the scenery changes before your eyes. In the balmy spring of 1803, Louisiana—once a French colony, now Spanish—was about to change hands again, twice. The picture was shifting, even as Mason and the other prisoners broke free.

Mason's men prized the borderlands for their very cloudiness. They had ended up here, in the reedy, scrubby Mississippi valley, because it was a good place to hide. No one was quite sure where jurisdictions began or ended. The bayous and inlets of the river itself offered a tempting warren of watery nooks into which they could slip. Officials passed off responsibility like hot potatoes. (Notwithstanding the fact that his prisoners had escaped as he tried to foist them back into American custody, Juan Manuel de Salcedo nonetheless wanted Mississippi Territory to foot the bill for his taking care of them temporarily.)[2] The fringes of the United States were a playground for criminals.

But in 1803, all of that began to shift, ever so slightly. Tentatively, the American federal government began to make motions to extend its reach and take control. After years of declining to get its hands dirty in criminal justice, it began to make some faltering moves to maintain order in the borderlands. It is tempting to paint this as a moment in which the might of the federal government came riding in to save the day. But the truth is a bit more complicated.

* * *

EVEN AS MASON and his men waded ashore in Louisiana in the spring of 1803, shaking off their captors, President Thomas Jefferson was awaiting news from Europe about the very territory into which they now absconded. As warmth crept in over the new Federal City on the Potomac and spring melted into summer, he waited.

It feels fitting, somehow, that Jefferson would preside over these last shadowy and indistinct moments in the pursuit of Wiley Harp. He himself was cagey, oblique. Jefferson, famously, was a man of contradictions. Shy, soft-spoken, almost embarrassed by public speaking, he was also thoroughly political—a viper. He kept notes on his enemies, jotting down gossip in code. He was calculating, even sneaky. Even for historians, it can be hard to pin him down. If all the other presidents could be painted in a "few broad strokes," the historian Henry Adams wrote, "Jefferson could be painted only touch by touch, with a fine pencil, and the perfection of the likeness depended, upon the shifting and uncertain flicker of its semi-transparent shadows."[3]

He had ridden into the presidency in a wild ride of an election. John Adams had known he was unlikely to win reelection in 1800. ("An Election is approaching which will Sett Us at Liberty from these uncomfortable Journeys," he wrote to Abigail in 1799.)[4] Some of his own party had turned on him; Alexander Hamilton penned a long screed, dissecting Adams's "disgusting egotism."[5] What Adams did not expect was to be bested by both Republican candidates, Thomas Jefferson and Aaron Burr, who tied, each with seventy-three electoral votes, sailing past Adams's sixty-five. It took thirty-six ballots over five days, during which Washington City was buried in snowdrifts, to break the tie: Jefferson prevailed.[6]

Jefferson had endured the Federalist presidencies as a trial to be suffered, patiently. "A little patience, and we shall see the reign of witches pass over, their spells dissolve," he had written to a Republican friend in 1798.[7] He called his own election the "Revolution of 1800," the sun breaking on a new America. On the day he was inaugurated in 1801, he wore plain clothes, with no sword fastened to his hip and no powder in his hair. Instead of riding in a carriage, he simply marched on foot from Conrad and McCunn's boardinghouse to the Capitol building. (John Adams, embittered, did not attend. He had already left for Massachusetts.)[8]

His calling card was small government. True to his word, Jefferson shrank almost everything. He cut the size of the federal army down by a third, the navy to a mere handful of ships. He dropped federal taxes. ("Take your choice, then, between Adams, war, and beggary, and Jefferson, peace, and competency!" a political booster had written during the election.)[9] Shrinking the executive branch, he sent people packing from Washington City. "We are hunting out and abolishing multitudes of useless offices," he wrote, celebrating, in 1801.[10] But Thomas Jefferson also did things as president that were big and bold and belied his professed philosophies. In that category, no other sleight of hand quite rivals the improbable magic he worked on Louisiana.

Louisiana was very much on Jefferson's mind. Almost from the time he took the oath of office, he thought about it—looming to the west, cramping the United States, and threatening commerce. Thousands of his people relied on the river, heaping flatboats high and putting themselves at the mercy of whoever controlled New Orleans. He was determined to exert better control over the region. As long as it was ruled by the Spanish, he worried little; the Spanish were mostly "feeble," quiet. But in 1801, Jefferson learned that Spain—under pressure, its coffers drained after years of warfare—had secretly ceded Louisiana back to the French. Now he began to worry.[11]

France, under Napoleon Bonaparte, was in a belligerent posture. After seizing power in 1799 (not long after Wiley Harp's escape and disappearance), Napoleon had turned France into the world's most fearsome military power, invading various places around the Mediterranean and flexing the muscle of his country's "military arm." He openly mused about reviving France's American empire, making Louisiana a jewel in its global crown. "I think it material at once to let him see that we are not of the powers who will receive his orders," Jefferson wrote in 1805 after years of witnessing Napoleon's antics.[12] To have such a bellicose ruler as a next-door neighbor was, to say the least, alarming.

But what most frightened Jefferson was the thought of Napoleon holding the keys to New Orleans. "There is on the globe one single spot, the possessor of which is our . . . enemy," Jefferson wrote. "It is New Orleans." For the French to control New Orleans, the doorway to the world for much of the western United States, would almost certainly mean war. "France, placing herself in that door," Jefferson wrote, "assumes to us the attitude of defiance."[13] So he took action:

He sent orders to Robert Livingston, the American minister to France, to try to purchase New Orleans and the Floridas.

Jefferson's timing was impossibly lucky: Napoleon's American dreams were flagging in strong headwinds even as the offer to buy New Orleans arrived. He had sent an expedition of twenty-five thousand men—led by his own brother-in-law, Charles Leclerc—to crush a slave rebellion (the ongoing Haitian Revolution) in Saint-Domingue. It was ending in "disastrous failure": Leclerc was already dead, and the others were being chewed up in gruesome fighting against island rebels or dying of malaria. Napoleon could be impulsive. His mood was shifting. What happened next, one historian writes, had "nothing to do with Jefferson's diplomatic maneuverings and everything to do with the shifting European context and the unpredictable Napoleonic character."[14]

Napoleon thought about the offer. He thought about the value of the colony. "Louisiana is still in her infancy," one of his advisers told him. "The country is scarcely at all inhabited; you have not fifty soldiers there. Where are your means of sending garrisons thither?" Moreover, the British wanted it; they might simply invade and take it. "I already consider the colony as entirely lost," Napoleon told his councilors in early April.[15]

On April 30, 1803, he sold the entire colony to the United States. At almost the very same moment authorities began to offer rewards for "SAMUEL MASON and his associates," the news broke in American newspapers that the United States had purchased Louisiana. The first reports, in early July, have a tone of blank astonishment. LOUISIANA CEDED TO THE U. STATES, read a shocked headline in the *Columbian Courier.* THE THING IS FIXED.[16] A New York paper announced breathlessly: "The French government [has] *ceded* to *the United States* the *province of Louisiana*."[17]

Conquest without war: It was a thing unheard of. Without a soldier lifting his gun, Jefferson had doubled the size of the United

States. And for a mere fifteen million dollars! "You have bought Louisiana for a Song," Horatio Gates gasped. Plaudits rolled in, bathing Jefferson in exuberant praise. "All the western Hemisphere rejoices in the Joyfull news," Andrew Jackson gushed to the president in August. With only a dollop of flattery, John Breckinridge reportedly called the Louisiana Purchase "the most Brilliant thing ever achieved."[18]

It was not without controversy. For a man who prided himself on limiting government, purchasing Louisiana was a shocking expansion of executive—and federal—power. It seemed to stride gleefully beyond the bounds of the Constitution, a document that Jefferson had heretofore insisted on reading strictly to the letter. Nowhere did the Constitution grant presidents the power to acquire foreign territory. "There is a difficulty in this acquisition," Jefferson admitted: It was a "thing beyond the constitution." Jefferson himself believed an amendment was necessary to stitch Louisiana to America's side.[19]

In the end, it wasn't. Congress was called into special session, and Jefferson decided to keep his mouth shut about his own misgivings. "The less is said about any constitutional difficulty, the better," he wrote. "It will be desireable for Congress to do what is necessary, *in silence*."[20] It did. Within a few days, the Senate—packed with men of Jefferson's party—approved the purchase, as if merely ratifying a treaty. The thing was fixed.

* * *

AS NEWS OF the Louisiana Purchase was breaking in newspapers that July, William Claiborne, the plucky young governor of Mississippi Territory, circulated a proclamation offering a reward for the capture of the Mason fugitives. "*Five hundred dollars*," it barked, "for apprehending SAMUEL MASON and his associates." It framed their crimes in national language: They were wanted for "commit[ing] unparralled outrages upon the property and persons of the citizen[s] of the United States." It ran in newspapers as far away as Baltimore.[21]

Then something extraordinary happened: The president followed up with his own proclamation. "By order of the President of the United States," it, too, offered a reward for the capture of the "evil minded persons" harrying the Trace.[22] It was not unusual for a governor or a sheriff in this era to enlist public help in bringing criminals to justice. But almost no crime in 1803 had yet turned the heads of federal officials. This may be the very first bounty ever offered by the United States, a distant ancestor of the "Wanted" posters that would later paper the post offices and saloons of the American West or, even later, the FBI's Most Wanted list. But there was no Federal Bureau of Investigation in 1803, nor would there be for a very long time. (It was founded a century later in 1908.)[23]

In 1803, there was hardly any federal policing at all. The president had at his service federal marshals who made arrests and served subpoenas for federal courts.[24] But with so few federal crimes on the books, they were not yet the gunslinging lawmen of romanticized Westerns. Criminal justice was patently not the purview of the federal government. Although the Constitution appeared to allow Congress to pass criminal laws, it largely didn't. It created no federal prisons; in fact, it directed the states to build prisons for holding those accused of federal crimes.[25]

But in the Mississippi borderlands during the Jefferson years, you can see something a bit different happening—more confused, more indistinct. Law enforcement here was weak, and it was driven by provincial and territorial officials making it up as they went along. But because Mississippi was a territory, not yet a state, any crisis was more likely to draw federal attention. Although he remained behind the scenes, Thomas Jefferson's fingerprints are all over the final efforts to catch Mason and his men.

The president was moved by reports of several more robberies. Not far from Bayou Pierre in July 1803, another party of boatmen was attacked and robbed. "The loss sustained is computed at between four and five thousand dollars," the *Western Spy* reported.[26] Among those trying to keep order, despair set in. "These pirates had practically blockaded the navigation of the river," one man wrote that spring.[27] Nor was the Natchez Trace tranquil: 1803 saw a burst of roadside attacks. Several governors begged for federal help in keeping the road safe. "The present Road is . . . an object of fear," Claiborne pled.[28]

Jefferson was listening. "The dangers on the road to Natchez are really serious," he told Henry Dearborn, the secretary of war. He imagined setting up a cavalry, a mounted patrol that could be constantly "scouring the road and hovering about the caravans of passengers." Or perhaps the United States could hire Choctaws as police since the Trace ran in a jagged course through their territory? The president also raised the idea of offering dazzling rewards for the apprehension of criminals.[29]

"The President of the United States is desirous of affording every aid in his power," Dearborn wrote on July 18.[30] At Jefferson's suggestion, the federal government now floated a reward for the snatching up of Mason or anyone else responsible for mayhem along the Mississippi trade routes: four hundred dollars. "The President has . . . thought it advisable," wrote Dearborn, to pay handsomely "any citizen or Indian" who captured the "banditti" or gave information leading to their capture and conviction.[31] This news was widely reprinted in the papers. Many took comfort. "We trust," one newspaper chirped, "the measures about to be taken by the General government, will be an end to the depredations of this gang of robbers."[32]

Meanwhile, Samuel Mason lurked in the piney woods. Shadows came and went. He looked over his shoulder. He might have heard, with a chill, of Jefferson's purchase of Louisiana. Gone, then, went some of his hope of escaping American authorities. He surely heard about the bounty on his head—the reward money now totaling almost a thousand dollars.[33] Maybe he found it flattering. Maybe he even joked about it at fireside. Maybe John Setton was there, listening.

* * *

SOMETIME THAT FALL, two men arrived in Greeneville, Mississippi, a little township north of Natchez. They were carrying a severed head. They claimed it was Samuel Mason's, and they wanted the reward money.

Governor William Claiborne exhaled, briefly. Relieved to be nearing the end of his struggle to secure the Mississippi against this inveterate pirate, he was eager to pay. But once more, something odd happened. Two men by the name of Winters happened to be in town, too, and caught sight of Mason's killers. They "immediately recognized them as companions of Mason in the robbery of their father."[34]

Elisha Winters had been robbed on the Mississippi's east bank. On the eastern shore, there was a bend in the river where the Yazoo spilled into it. Boatmen knew the place; nearby was a large willow beach, wispy branches tickling the water. It was a tricky spot. Keep close to the right shore, warned *The Navigator*, a popular boatman's guide, to avoid being pulled into eddies.[35]

Near here, Winters's flatboat had been looted. Several men rushed the boat. Though Winters and his sons had tried to resist, the thieves got away with "a considerable sum of money."[36] They did notice, however, a few distinctive things about the bandits—including, according to one account, the "peculiar blaze" on the face of one of their horses.[37] When the men rode into town on the same horse and demanded reward money for having killed Samuel Mason, the blaze gave them away.

The Winterses reported this, and the two men tried to flee but were taken into custody. "The men who robbed Mr. Elisha Winters," the *Kentucky Gazette* reported, "have been taken and committed to jail."[38] One of the culprits was a man named James May, an alleged associate of Mason's.

The other was John Setton.

* * *

IN THE FOLKLORE surrounding this episode, all the villains get their just deserts. Mason dies at the hands of disloyal fellow thieves. The killers themselves are revealed as Mason's men. Wiley Harp is captured. Not all of this is quite so clear in official records.[39] But the tales that survived in Southern memory all end with a satisfying justice. No questions. No loose ends.

The ending is almost too good to be true. Later generations of storytellers rehearsed it with relish. "Harpe took an opportunity," one wrote breezily in the 1820s, "when the rest of his companions were absent, to slay Meason, and putting his head in a bag, carried it to Natchez, and claimed the reward. The claim was admitted; the head of Meason was recognized; but so also was the face of Harpe, who was arrested."[40] This is so delicious, and so perfect, that it feels fantastical. It is impossible not to wonder whether it has gathered some layers, over many years of telling, like Mississippi silt.

Of all the parts of the Harp saga, the recapture of John Setton is among the murkiest. A lot of what happened in the Mississippi borderlands between 1801 and 1804—even when it seems like it must be the stuff of tall tales and folklore—is borne out by contemporary documents. Flatboats were robbed by Samuel Mason and his men. The culprits were captured in New Madrid and then, incredibly, escaped en route to American custody. The president himself pushed for them to be brought to justice. Elisha Winters lost his cargo, apparently to Setton and May. (Winters would later testify against them in court.) All these things are verifiable in contemporary sources. But the precise details of how Setton was taken back into custody—and the tale about Mason's head being offered for the reward—are much murkier. How was Setton caught? What exactly led to his rearrest? Did he really carry *Mason's* head to the authorities? Not much tells us that.

Almost all the Mississippi court records that once held the answers are lost. I went to Mississippi looking for them. I combed the state archives in Jackson. Then I drove south, hugging the old Natchez Trace. If any vestige of John Setton had survived, I figured, maybe it was stashed in a closet, or a drawer, at one of the courthouses in the old Jefferson District, where he was captured. In Claiborne County, I pulled brittle file papers from a wall of long-forgotten verdicts. But he wasn't there. At the Jefferson County courthouse in Fayette, a man named Speedy, wearing striped prison fatigues, helped me pull old record books from their high perches, where they were stacked haphazardly in a storage room. But when I opened them, my hopes dissolved: Nothing inside dated before the late 1800s.

The ghosts are strong in Mississippi. Across the street from the courthouse in Fayette stands a little green, where a charming walkway beckons toward an old monument to Confederate soldiers. Not far upriver is the site of the plantation where Jefferson Davis lived with his wife, Varina, in the years before the Civil War. History permeates everything, like an overhanging fog. But mostly, it's not on paper. In Fayette, I met an older Black man named Andrew Jackson, everyone's agreed-upon local authority on matters of the past. When I asked him how to find out more about local history, he said, "Not in books. In signs." I later found out that there had been a fire at the Jefferson County courthouse on March 19, 1901, and in the confusion that followed, the Setton and May documents had disappeared.

All of this makes it very difficult to confirm what exact series of events led to Setton's capture or to verify the story about Mason's death. But there is one piece of intriguing secondhand evidence. I found it in an unprocessed box of papers kept by Otto Rothert, who researched the Harps in the 1910s and later left his notes to the Filson Historical Society in Kentucky. In a 1917 letter to Rothert, a man named Jeff Truly penned what he claimed was a faithful relation of the final stages of the Setton and May caper, based on what he had seen in the court records before they were lost or destroyed. Truly was a judge who had presided over the circuit court where the records were kept before the fire. So there are reasons to think his account is reliable.[41]

Truly's letter confirms quite a lot of the traditional belief surrounding Setton's capture—even down to the severed head. Setton and May surfaced in Greeneville, he wrote, "bringing with them a man's head in a sack and presenting [it] as that of Mason, the robber." They wanted the reward. Court messengers were sent to the territorial capital to fetch a warrant for the weighty sum of two thousand dollars to be paid out, Truly explained. But while Setton and May were in town, Elisha Winters and his sons recognized them—or, at least, their horse. It is Truly who provided the detail that Winters knew the thieves by "the blazed face horse" that one of them had ridden. Based on this, the letter concluded, Setton and May "were taken into custody."[42]

This is not perfect evidence. As Truly himself admitted, he wrote his account "from memory."[43] Assuming he had actually seen the relevant court records, by the time he wrote this letter, they had nevertheless been lost for years—more than a decade. Still, it is the closest we may ever get to placing this piece of the puzzle.

There are a few things the letter does not resolve. For instance: Was Mason really dead? Was the head truly his? "It does not appear that the identity of the man whose head was produced was ever judicially determined," Truly wrote. (According to "local tradition," he noted, Mason's wife had vouched for the claimants that the head was, in fact, her husband's. Some other evidence, though, indicates she protested that it was not: "Many fully identified the head by certain marks thereon, except his wife who as positively denied it," wrote a Mississippi local many years later.)[44] But Setton and May must have convinced the court that "it was that of the notorious bandit," Truly deduced. Otherwise, runners would not have been sent to the capital for reward money.[45]

Nor does Truly's letter give even a glint of illumination to the most knotty—and the most frustrating—mystery: Who was John Setton?

* * *

SETTON AND MAY came to trial in January 1804. They were charged with robbing the Winters family and brought to court in Greeneville, the little hamlet closest to where they were captured. Each was given his own separate trial. The courthouse was drafty. Its chill in winter became infamous: One of the presiding judges died in 1805, allegedly after catching a cold while sitting on the bench.[46]

Three judges squinted at the accused as they were led in. All appointed by presidents, the men of the court nonetheless had varying degrees of preparation in law. David Ker had been a professor at the University of North Carolina before making the unlikely leap in Mississippi Territory to sheriff and then territorial judge. Peter Bruin seems never to have studied law, though he had served in the judiciary under Spanish authority. He was "a Man of Good Education and good Sense, and when Sober, Upright in his Judgements," a colleague wrote. But unfortunately, he had an "unhappy propensity To drinking."[47]

The third judge, Thomas Rodney, was a veteran and onetime member of the Continental Congress who had lost everything and gone to debtors' prison in the 1790s, only to see his fortunes take a wild upturn with Jefferson's election. In 1803, after purchasing Louisiana, Jefferson sent Rodney into the borderlands to sort out the confusion of Spanish and American land grants and graced him with a judgeship. He had been in Mississippi Territory for only a month before Setton's trial.[48]

But the most consequential man in the room—the man poised to prosecute the case against Setton and May—was the attorney general of Mississippi Territory, George Poindexter. It is worth dwelling on him momentarily, if only because he was responsible for shaping the charges and the trial itself. Poindexter was a wild character. He was handsome, with dark hair, and acute, concerned blue eyes. He was a drinker, a gambler, and often depressed. Rash, "abnormally suspicious," and "savagely jealous," he was also a brawler who was frequently in fistfights. "He was never without a quarrel on

An engraving on paper of George Poindexter (1808) by Charles Balthazar Julien Févret de Saint-Mémin. National Portrait Gallery, Smithsonian Institution; gift of Mr. and Mrs. Paul Mellon.

his hands," a biographer writes, "and for the settlement of these he used the courts, his fists, his cane, his riding crop, his pistols, and his superb vocabulary of invective." He was twenty-four years old.[49]

Poindexter's task in prosecuting was not easy. It was an impossibly complicated case. Although Setton and May had been fingered by eyewitnesses (and the Winters family was on hand to testify), the outcome of the trial was by no means certain. Beneath the surface, the case was a nightmarish morass of legal uncertainties. It exposed holes in the American judiciary that had not, as of 1804, been papered over by law. But in the end, these were brushed aside in brash improvisations. Although the evidence is fragmentary (comprised mostly of clues in letters written by Judge Thomas Rodney), Setton's trial looks very much like an awkward but brazen lurch toward federal power in the region.

The basic facts were simple enough. Setton and May were accused of robbing Elisha Winters. "Mr. Elisha Winters . . . was robbed on his voyage up the Mississippi," a newspaper had reported. "We understand they took from him his cargo, and about 400 dollars in cash."[50] There was no doubt that this was robbery. And Winters and one of his sons stood by in court ready to swear by oath that Setton and May were the very rogues who had ransacked their flatboat.

But there was a stumbling block: The robbery had occurred in Choctaw Nation, outside the bounds of Mississippi Territory. The exact location is hazy, but it had occurred on the banks of the Mississippi while Winters's flatboat was docked "in the Indian country above the Yazoo."[51] An oblong reserve of tens of millions of acres just north of Mississippi Territory, Choctaw Nation ran right up to the river's edge. Much of the river's east bank belonged to the tribe. Mississippi Territory's northern border lay where the Yazoo spilled into the Mississippi, where the willows danced and the swans gathered. Stopped during his voyage downriver, Winters was outside of it when the robbery happened.

Every boatman brushed elbows with Choctaw men and women. Choctaw Nation was not some exotic, unfamiliar territory. It lay at the very center of trans-Appalachian commerce, in the eye of the storm. Descending the river, a boatman glided past dozens of miles of their shoreline on the left. Returning northward overland, he traversed the nation over dusty pathways that wound by Choctaw farms and shacks and chicken coops. Choctaws operated rest stands along the Natchez Trace, where you could buy food or hitch horses.[52]

They were a formidable presence, deep in the belly of the United States. One of Jefferson's cabinet members thought the Choctaws were "the most powerful Nation of Indians within the limits of the United States." And they were: They were not just surrounded by the United States, they were a part of it. The Choctaw homelands had a peculiar status unique to Indians: Although it was a sovereign territory, Choctaw Nation—legally, at least—lay within the borders of the United States.[53] It was reserved for the Choctaws, much as reservations are today. But it was also American: The Choctaws had signed treaties with the federal government acknowledging their land to be "under the protection of the United States of America."[54]

But though it was considered part of the United States, the Choctaw coastline where Winters was robbed lay *outside* of Mississippi Territory. They did not overlap. This presented a problem. As Poindexter himself admitted, the robbery had happened in "the tract of Country assigned to the Choctaw nation . . . by treaty."[55] By any man's measure, Mississippi Territory's laws against robbery did not apply here. They dead-ended at the Yazoo. Could Mississippi try the accused?

Poindexter arrived at a clever—and daring—solution. To sidestep the toothlessness of Mississippi law in this case, he blithely assumed the power of the federal government instead. He charged Setton and May under United States laws against piracy.

Poindexter stood and read the charges. What statute had the two thieves violated? The only real candidate was a law passed by Congress in 1790, which is what he must have recited in court: "If any person or persons shall commit upon the high seas, or in any river, haven, basin or bay, out of the jurisdiction of any particular state, murder or robbery . . . every such offender shall be deemed, taken and adjudged to be a pirate and a felon." The punishment for such crimes if convicted? Death.[56]

Setton and May's lawyers balked. This was preposterous: Not only had the robbery taken place outside of Mississippi's boundaries, but the territorial court, in their opinion, had no federal standing. Nothing qualified Poindexter to prosecute federal crimes! They lobbied the court to throw out the case. How could it be legitimate to try the defendants for piracy when the superior court of Mississippi did not even have jurisdiction? "That question was discussed at great length," one man later wrote. Before even a peep of evidence had been heard, the courtroom exploded into vigorous argument.[57]

Any confident ruling, everyone knew, was something of a fairy tale. In claiming federal powers, Poindexter was brashly wading into very murky waters. What precisely, as Judge Thomas Rodney put it, was the "relation of this Territory to the U.S."?[58] The relationship between the territorial courts and federal law was blurry at best. "Were the territorial courts United States courts? If they were, which of them enjoyed federal jurisdiction, and to what extent?" pondered one legal historian, more than a century later. ". . . For that matter, were the territories part of the United States?"[59] None of this, in 1804, was settled law.

In some sense, Poindexter's decision to apply federal law was not a stretch. Territorial government was, at base, federal. American territories were little crucibles, under the oversight of the federal government until they were ready for statehood. Mississippi's governor and judges were all federal appointees. Was it unreasonable, then, to argue that its courts were an extension of the federal judiciary? On the other hand, Poindexter himself had not been appointed by the president; he'd been chosen by Claiborne, the governor. Mississippi had no United States attorneys, no federal marshals. Nowhere had anyone said explicitly that its courts could try men for federal crimes.

The defense lawyers pressed the court to toss out the case. It almost worked. One of the territorial judges sided with them. But the two others—Thomas Rodney and Peter Bruin—overruled him. They decided the case could move forward as if the territorial court were simply an arm of the federal court system.

Rodney, in particular, was adamant. He had no qualms. "At the Trial of Masons Men," he later wrote, "I gave it as my opinion that this Superior Court of this Territory is Subordinate to the Supreme Court of the United States." It could, therefore, try men for federal crimes. No act of Congress was required to extend federal jurisdiction to the territorial courts, he scoffed; "they Constitutionally possess it."[60]

But, as would later become clear, the United States Congress was not so sure. A few weeks after the trials, Rodney was annoyed to hear that some congressmen objected to his ruling. "I have read in the papers that Congress seems to think differently on this Subject," he wrote testily.[61] When word of the Setton and May trials rippled into Washington, it sparked serious debate. A congressional committee was tasked with looking into the issue. In March 1804, the committee found that the territorial courts did, indeed, have federal jurisdiction. Nevertheless, a year later, in March 1805, still nervous, Congress passed a law granting it to the superior courts of the territories. Setton and May, lowly river rats, quietly pulled the reach of federal law over the American territories, like a blanket.[62]

But first, they learned their fates in that drafty courthouse in Greeneville.

"A daring banditti, headed by one Mason," Poindexter would have told the jury (as a congressional report would later summarize), had "infested the wilderness road . . . and the river Mississippi." For years, this gang of thieves "committed vast depredations both upon the persons & property of individuals, and were the terror of all travelling through the wilderness."[63]

Setton and May were two of these brigands, he said. "Thes[e] persons are notoriously confederates of Masons junto," he argued, just as he had written to the governor two weeks prior.[64]

The Winters family testified. They gave crucial evidence. Poindexter later confirmed that without their appearance in court, there would have been no hope of convicting.[65]

The trials of Setton and May lasted nine days. Both men were found guilty and sentenced to hang.

* * *

ON FEBRUARY 8, 1804, in a barren field in Mississippi Territory, John Setton faced his fate. Four days earlier, he had been convicted of piracy and felony. That was, in fact, the least of what he had done. His past crimes were many and varied, and the law had finally caught up to him. Now he stood in a meadow outside Greeneville, the wind kicking up dust in his face as he stared at a rude gallows.

A crowd likely gathered around him. Execution day was public, for all to see. People brought liquor and children and took in the ghoulish spectacle, as if they were at the races. Some watched soberly, contemplating their own lives. To make an example of the condemned was, after all, the point. The sheriff read his death warrant. In his hands was a cap, ready to pull over the prisoner's face before the hanging. Swallows dipped down overhead. It was over, or nearly so. He had finally lost.[66]

By the time hanging day arrived for John Setton, Louisiana had joined the republic. Jefferson chose William Charles Cole Claiborne to receive it ceremonially from France on December 20, 1803, in New Orleans. It was an unseasonably warm day. Even the French prefect, Pierre Clément de Laussat, ceding control to the Americans, felt upbeat. "The day was beautiful and the temperature as balmy as a day in May," he wrote. "Lovely ladies and city dandies graced all the balconies." City Hall teemed with beautiful women. That night, there were balls: toasting, celebration, and dancing.[67] At Jefferson's request, Claiborne soon left his post as governor of Mississippi to become the governor of the new Territory of Orleans.

The Louisiana Purchase aided in the final unmasking of John Setton. To ensure a peaceful transfer of the territory, Jefferson sent troops to the delta. Some of them recognized Setton. One of the soldiers was Captain Frederick Stump, the father of one of the Harps' victims. When he arrived in Natchez to "aid in taking possession of Louisiana," Stump was summoned to peer into the prison room where John Setton was being held. "Stump," recalled one of his descendants years later, "said he believed that Sutton was really [Wiley] Harpe."[68] Another soldier from Knoxville, who was present at Setton's execution, also identified him as Harp.[69]

Almost all of the contemporary accounts agree: Setton, really, was Wiley Harp. He "calls himself John Sutton," a writer explained in the *Kentucky Gazette*, "but was proved to be the villain who was known by the name of little or red headed Harp . . . who committed so many acts of cruelty in Kentucky."[70] Newspapers from Frankfort to Philadelphia and as far away as Albany and Hartford printed reports that identified the convicted man as "John Sutton, (alias Harpe)."[71] Placards were put up at Natchez landing announcing that "it was believed Wiley Harpe was taken" and that any Kentucky boatmen who had known him were invited to "examine the prisoner." Five claimed to recognize him.[72] Even George Poindexter, the wily prosecutor, believed he had tried Wiley Harp. "Harp was recognized," he later swore. "He was identified by several marks."[73]

You sense, in the moment, a thirst for that ending—a kind of desperate, eager belief in Wiley Harp's death. No one wanted to live in a world in which a man might be able to get away with such horrible acts. Whatever suspensions of disbelief—whatever contortions of probability—were necessary to stitch back together a sense of safety and justice, they would be done. Even as Setton neared the gallows, people wanted to believe that this was, in fact, the end. They yearned to believe that everything the Harps represented—the chaos, the lawlessness, the violence, the rage, even the treason—was over. It had been vanquished.

But there were a few who wondered. Some other men belonging to the Tennessee companies that were stationed in Natchez—including some who had lived on Beaver Creek, Wiley's old neighborhood—went to visit Setton before his death. They looked him dead in the eyes. Then they all said, "He was not Harpe."[74]

Setton, himself, denied it to the moment of his death. Even as he faced the noose, he "denied being Harpe, said he knew nothing of him; that his real name was John McDowell Sutton."[75]

He climbed the ladder. He mumbled a garbled confession, naming a few accomplices. Then he swung by his neck.

* * *

ALL THE REMNANTS of John Setton are now gone.

His burial place is a mystery. After his execution, according to one account, his head was placed on a pole along the Natchez Trace, a little outside of Greeneville. If that's true, the spot was never marked.

Nor can you visit the gallows field where he breathed his last. Old Greeneville is now overgrown, buried under a riot of briars—a ghost town. In 1825, the county seat was moved to Fayette. Greeneville, in turn, quickly withered and "declined": "The houses decayed or were moved away," one man wrote. Around the turn of the twentieth century, one of its few remaining buildings went up in flames. "Now only a blackened chimney in a cultivated field is all that is left."[76]

Who swung from the gallows on February 8, 1804, we may never know for sure. But perhaps that's fitting. How many, in life, had looked into this man's eyes, unsure of what they were seeing? In the end, the tidy justice of Setton's tale was a bit like the fragile, inchoate power of Jefferson's federal government. It was a thing that was powerful because people chose to believe in it, however uncertain.

EPILOGUE

THE ASHES OF THE GRAVE

Big Rockcastle River
Near the Cumberland Gap
February 1805

As wintry gales whistled through the mountains in 1805, three Shaker missionaries made their way through the Kentucky wilderness. They were on a long journey, far from home. Wild waves of religious enthusiasm were rising up in the West, sometimes marked by strange bodily outbursts and convulsions. ("They laugh, they sing, they dance," and all "involuntarily," one newspaper reported.) The Shaker travelers were hoping to witness some of this explosive revivalism with their own eyes.[1]

But along the way, they witnessed something else.

As they crossed the "high ridges," "deep gullies," and "uninhabitable [sand] & rocks" near Big Rockcastle River, they heard about the murder of Thomas Langford six years earlier "by two men by the name of Harp." They learned from those living nearby that Langford's memory was etched into the landscape itself. "We were told that we might see the spot where he was killed," Issachar Bates wrote.[2]

They went. On the bark of a tree near the riverbank was a crude little memorial. Bates was stunned at its simplicity—its shocking understatement. "I expected to see some horrid expression," he wrote, perhaps a long exegesis capturing the full horrors of murder. But when he stepped closer to the tree, he saw that there were just two words written there: LANKFORDS DEFEAT.[3]

"My soul and my flesh shuddered," Bates wrote. The moment brought him to his knees. He was overcome with "horrid feelings," he later confessed to his journal. "I was suddenly panic struck," doubting his mission. But then, a heavenly voice came to him, the same voice he had heard in his "conviction," and told him: "You are in the work of God and you must not flinch." Almost as suddenly, Bates felt renewed. His terror dissolved.

"I put on the whole armor of God and set my face as flint against earth and hell," he wrote. The long walk continued.[4]

For years, even after they were dead, the Harps shook people to their foundations.

* * *

THE HARP WOMEN all went on to live unremarkable lives. All quietly slipped free of the name "Harp." But they did not go far. Four years after Micajah's death, Betsy was still living in Logan County, Kentucky, where the sheriff had deposited her in 1799. In 1803, she married a "simple-hearted Dutchman" named John Hufstutter. She and her husband lived as tenants on a farm outside of Russellville, in the shadow of the courthouse where she had been tried for the Stegall murders. They raised chickens.[5]

Susana joined her. She moved into a cabin on the same plantation and, as one man remembered it, took up weaving. Toddling behind her was her daughter, Micajah's child, a spirited little girl named Lovey. The girl could not have remembered her father. But she grew up playing with her half brother, Joe, also Micajah's child, whom Betsy and her husband raised. No one who was asked about Susana in later years recalled her remarrying. But according to the Logan County marriage records, "Susanna Roberts" wed Richard Butler in 1807. Almost certainly, this is our Susana.[6]

People knew who they were. Their past was not hidden, not completely. William Calhoun Love, whose father had been killed by the

Harps, knew where Betsy lived. He kept track of her, making note that she had married and on which road she lived. "In 1818 I took breakfast near her house as I was on my way to Frankfort," he wrote.[7] Nor did Susana keep her identity secret, at least not from her neighbors. Many of the details about the Harp spree have survived because she told them stories about it.

Susana and her daughter had a hard go of it. "None of the young ladies in the neighborhood would be seen associating with the daughter of Big Harpe," one man remembered. Lovey was vexed. "Lovey grew up to womanhood—very pretty," with her father's black hair, he said. But she also had "a dark & sometimes bad, devilish eye," perhaps also inherited from Micajah. "Her temper was bad at school—always pouting & angry." She was disliked. "Had Lovey Harpe, with her beautiful form & naturally pretty appearance, been properly brought up under other circumstances," he thought, "she wd. not only have been a belle, but really a fine woman." In time, Lovey and her mother moved elsewhere, perhaps—as several accounts suggest—because they were driven out of the neighborhood.[8]

Sally Harp fared better. Multiple accounts agree: After she was acquitted in Logan County, her father came and retrieved "his prodigal daughter" and took her home. "She was restored to the society of her kindred and friends," one Tennessean wrote.[9] Court records confirm that by 1803 she was back in Tennessee, living near (or in) her father's house. Around then, she accused neighbors of "words spoken to her damage" and sued for a whopping one thousand dollars in damages. The lawsuit was later dropped, but it may speak to her attempts to restore her reputation. Although the files don't reveal precisely what was said, one imagines "Sally Rice alias Sally Harpe" (as she is identified in court documents) might have been touchy about references to her past.[10]

In time, things brightened. Sally, too, found a husband. She "married a highly respectable man, and raised a large family," filling her house with children. Sally's little ones grew up to be "much esteemed for honesty, sobriety, and industry," according to one man's recollection.[11] Sally may have been more careful about cloaking her past as Wiley Harp's widow. Her second husband's last name is unknown. When those who knew it were asked in the nineteenth century, they would not tell out of respect for the family.[12]

William Stewart, the eccentric sheriff who had taken care of the Harp women in 1799, thought he spied Sally and her brood twenty years later. At a ferry crossing on the Ohio River, he stumbled into the family. "He did not recognize them, but thought he knew them, particularly Sally, who eyed him closely & after a little went in side, sat down & with her face in her hands had a weeping spell," he related. Only later, when he remembered the "old gentleman called Rice," did he realize who it was.[13]

Ominously, there is no mention of Sally Harp's daughter—Wiley's child—after 1799. In a story repeated again and again, tradition strongly suggests that one of the Harp children was killed in infancy by Micajah himself. (Several authors have him stating, before death, that this one was the only murder he regretted.) But in every version, the murdered child is identified as Micajah's own—a detail that, in itself, calls into question the trustworthiness of the tradition, since both his son and his daughter appear to have lived into adulthood.[14] No contemporary record confirms the story.

Stewart, the sheriff, later implied that Sally's baby was alive at the end of the spree. As the posse closed in, he said, she had sought to protect the little girl. "The wife of Little Harpe," he told a Kentucky writer, "took her child off to the branch, where she had seen a projecting, shelving rock, under which she placed it, and laid down at its outer side, determined to remain and die with her child."[15] Perhaps that was what she was doing when Stegall's men found her. Either way, the child's fate is obscure. She disappears from the record.

* * *

ON A FRIGID January day in 1800, the thing that had haunted Wiley finally came to pass: The deputy sheriff rolled up to the little house on Beaver Creek, his cart wheels biting into the snow, and seized Wiley Harp's property to settle his debt. In court, the Harps' creditor, Joseph Carnes, had at last been awarded the $222 owed to him by the Harps.[16] To "render unto Carnes his debt," the sheriff's deputy—a man named Henry Breazeale, whose son would go on to write one of the earliest printed accounts of the Harp murders—put up Wiley's land for public auction. A man named Jesse Parker bought it, all one hundred acres. He kept it for the next forty-two years, almost to the eve of the Civil War.[17]

Sheriffs were still busy as bees, summoning, seizing, evicting. Almost none of the men who created Tennessee's nightmare of fraudulent land claims ever faced comeuppance. After Andrew Jackson brought the forgeries into the light, investigators were sent into the records looking for suspect warrants. They found mountains of them: About 700,000 acres, they estimated, had been assigned fraudulently, the duplicitous riches accruing to only a handful of men. Unimaginable numbers of land sales descended from these counterfeit origins. The sad souls living on these parcels, in many cases, were entirely unaware that their claims rested on such rotten ground.[18]

Particular men were named as perpetrators, but only some faced consequences. North Carolina's secretary of state, James Glasgow (whose name would forever be attached to the frauds, much as his signature adorned the dummy warrants), resigned in disgrace and fled the state. Others sidestepped prosecution. When he heard he was implicated, the grand speculator and merchant Thomas Blount pretended surprise, even indignation. "It is false as Hell," he wrote about the charge.[19] Tried in July 1800, the Blount brothers were acquitted. (It helped that the prosecutor was a personal friend of theirs.)[20] Most of the other accused men refused to return to North Carolina to have their cases tried. The notorious William Tyrell, land jobber extraordinaire, eluded authorities. At one point, he sent one of his slaves to break into the secretary of state's office and steal the evidence. (The enslaved man was caught and hanged.)[21]

One of the most flagrant offenders was Andrew Jackson's brother-in-law, Stockley Donelson. He, too, avoided prosecution. But he was haunted for the rest of his life by the frauds he had committed. "My mind is rackd and distress[ed] to a great degree," he wrote in 1800. "My fears is that I might be arrested in vexatious Suits."[22] Vexatious suits did, in time, all but ruin him. North Carolina never punished him (it couldn't, as he remained safely beyond reach in Tennessee), but angry land owners—whose claims overlapped with his hundreds of thousands of acres—did. He was sued repeatedly. He died in 1805, in heavy debt.[23] Jackson, who had unwittingly revealed the "rascality" of his own brother-in-law, claimed not to regret it.[24]

Meanwhile, the outer edge of Cherokee Nation was gnawed and pecked at by the United States. In the summer of 1798, Bloody Fellow had rebuffed John Adams's treaty men. "We will not sell a foot of land," he said. He pointed to a barge on the Tennessee River. Not for a boatful of dollars would they sell, he told them.[25] But they came back. They always came back. Cherokees began to seethe when they were pressured for concessions. "I expect you will think we have a right to say yes or no as answers," Doublehead snapped, once, to American negotiators.[26] But Cherokee resistance did not last. When treaty commissioners returned in the fall of 1798 (too late for the Harps), they wrested ninety thousand acres from the Cherokees. Five thousand dollars in cash and an annual payment of one thousand dollars would flow into Cherokee coffers, in exchange for the contested acres.[27] This arrangement would last but a few years before new treaties—for more land—needed brokering.

Rapacious Tennesseans kept helping themselves to Cherokee lands. "I know I must die by the hands of these men," Doublehead told one of Adams's negotiators, gesturing at his American neighbors. "But it will be in contending for my right."[28] Still, his will eventually cracked. After years of fending off the greedy pleas of treaty men, Doublehead himself began to yield to bribes and special persuasions. (A treaty he signed in 1805 contained a secret article reserving a little parcel near the mouth of the Clinch River—coincidentally, very nearby Sally Harp's father's house—for himself.) He was half right about his fate: He did not die at the hands of Tennesseans, but he did die because of them. In 1807, a man named Bone Polisher said to Doublehead, "You have betrayed our people . . . you have sold our hunting grounds." Doublehead shot him. He was, in turn, killed by Bone Polisher's friends and kin.[29]

* * *

MEANWHILE, THE STRAINS and pains of the late eighteenth century sent people, by the thousands, into churches. The unchurched masses found God. In the years after the Harp spree, massive revivals swept the backcountry. People fell to their knees, writhed on the ground, shook, had visions. In August 1801, twenty thousand thronged to a camp meeting at Cane Ridge in Bourbon County, Kentucky. Carts clogged the byways, horses filled the hills. By the glow of five hundred candles and lanterns, they prayed through the night. At the Turtle Creek meetinghouse a month later, a crimson rain fell, "which many believe[d] to be blood."[30]

Bursts and trickles of religious fervor had been bubbling up for years, swirled up in little eddies by the same itinerant preachers who had strutted confidently into East Tennessee only to proclaim it the devil's favorite resort. Such circuit riders were a common enough sight by 1799 that the Harps reportedly aped them. ("They intended to personate *methodist preachers*," one man later supposed.)[31]

But in the years after the rampage, the awakening quickened dramatically. Some of the same distresses that sent the Harp brothers into the highways of Kentucky likely sent others into camp meetings and church pews. All of the dislocations of the republic's uneasy early years—so many on the move, isolated, indebted, reeling from political convulsions—stoked Americans' appetites for God's comforts. "The Great Revival" salved the "social uneasiness" that stalked them at every turn.[32]

Some of those who had been touched by the Harps' escapades were swept up in the revivals. Around the turn of the nineteenth century, Methodist ministers visited Joseph Ballenger, the sometime deputy who had once pulled off a near-miraculous capture of the Harps. They called at his house, the same place where the Harps had been kept under guard in 1799. Ballenger was primed for the message. He "expressed considerable anxiety" to form a circuit—a cluster of churches served by one minister. They assented. "Bal-

"Camp-meeting." Drawn by Hugh Bridport; Kennedy & Lucas Lithography, circa 1829. Courtesy of the Library of Congress.

linger's house was to be the nucleus," one recorded.[33] Daniel Trabue, whose son was murdered by the Harps, helped to found the Russell's Creek Baptist Church, a place in which he eased his grief. For its congregants, one historian supposes, Johnny's death was likely a "catalyst to set men to pondering the ways of the devil as well as the mysteries of God."[34]

In 1802, the Reverend Jacob Young, a Methodist, wandered into a cabin filled with people. "Many of them had neither hats nor bonnets on their heads, nor shoes on their feet," he wrote. He read a hymn and began singing. Suddenly a man caught his eye, "a very large man, with strongly-marked features"—a high forehead, bulging eyes, unkempt hair. "He wore no hat; his collar was open, and his breast bare; there was neither shoe nor moccasin on his feet." The man stared, unfriendly, at Young, who met his gaze dead on. He preached and prayed as he always did. Before long, the man had tears streaming down his cheeks.

After he left, Young could not get "the big man" out of his mind. Who was he? Young heard later that he was Micajah Harp's brother-in-law—presumably Susana's or Betsy's brother.[35]

Methodist preachers liked to use the Harps' infamy to coax hearers into God's warm embrace. Reverend Young relished the idea that he could lure a Harp into the church—even the brother-in-law of "the infamous robber, Micajah Harp," as he boasted. He congratulated himself on winning over a profligate, lost soul. "No doubt they had been together in many a bloody affray," he guessed. (This was hopeful conjecture; there is no evidence that any men other than Wiley and Micajah took part in their bloody affrays.) Even this man could become a Christian and "respectable" having found the gospel![36]

Methodism could save Harps; it also saved men from the Harps. A Methodist minister named William Lambeth, who had trudged into Tennessee seeking converts in 1798, purportedly once met

Wiley Harp. Years later, he liked to tell the story: One night, asleep in the woods, he awoke to see the shadow of a man "creeping toward him." The man grabbed his arm. *What do you want?* Lambeth asked. "I want all your money and must have your horse," the man said. "Or I will kill you." He rifled Lambeth's Bible. But when he heard Lambeth was a preacher, he let him go. He allowed the minister, quaking in his boots, to keep his horse and his money—not to mention his life.[37]

Lambeth told this story for "many years afterward." He wove it into a sermon. The punch line was clear: God's protection was powerful, even in the face of such a ruthless character as one of the Harps. Did his congregants doubt the man was one of the brutal brothers? Helpfully, the would-be robber had told Lambeth his identity: "My name is William Harpe," he allegedly had said. (From Lambeth, too, came one of the slivers of evidence that Wiley had a loyalist background. After spotting George Washington's name in a book Lambeth was carrying, Wiley sniffed: "That is a brave and good man, but a mighty rebel against the king.")[38]

Whether or not Lambeth had truly brushed elbows with Wiley Harp is anyone's guess. But the Methodists grasped the rhetorical power of the murders. They sensed that what they were offering to their hearers was an antidote of sorts to the chaos and disorder that the Harps represented. Whatever had created these two monsters, everyone needed to be inoculated against it. One could spiral and drown, tugged under by the dislocations of the age, or one could be lifted up, jubilant, by the word of the Lord. It was a potent cure. Westerners joined the church by the thousands, yanking along children, cousins, siblings, anyone they could find.

The families of the Harp victims, meanwhile, went on with their lives. Some reaped only more unhappiness. Esther Calhoun Love, the widow of the Stegalls' boarder, William, remarried. But her new husband drank and mistreated her. "She could not bear to have such an example set before her children," her eldest son wrote. She left her husband after only eighteen months, and in 1844, she died alone. Her gravestone in Piney Fork, Kentucky, faded and bitten with lichen, suggests how she never really got over the murder of her first husband. MY HUSBAND WM. LOVE WAS KILLED BY THE HARPS AUG. 1799, it reads. BLESSED ARE THE DEAD WHICH DIE IN THE LORD.[39]

* * *

SLOWLY, THE HARPS became ghosts. Memory dimmed, turning them into "vanishing avatars" of an earlier time, when vulgar backwoodsmen had prowled the early West. Steamboats came, churning up the rivers where "the gutted rock-weighted bones of . . . Mason's murderees," as William Faulkner wrote, "tumbled gently to the motion of the paddle-wheels." Old log jails and courthouses, which according to legend had once "held someone who might have been Wiley Harpe," rotted and crumbled away.[40]

For a time, they knew real fame. The story of the Harps knocked around Appalachia for years. Riding into Cherokee country in the fall of 1799 (shortly after Micajah's death), Moravian missionaries "often heard" about the robber band that had so recently menaced the region. "Two brothers, Harp by name, have killed many persons in the western district," they were told by a Kentuckian. (The more fanciful parts of the legend took root early: The Harps were said to have "ended the life of about one hundred persons.") *Why had they done this?* the missionaries wondered. "Not for the sake of robbery or of revenge," came the answer, "but for the pure love of murder."[41]

The first real printed account of the murders appeared in the 1820s. It was inspired when James Hall, a Philadelphian with a hankering to see the West, boarded a keelboat and floated down the Ohio. The humble, sun-bronzed people he met along the river's shores told him fantastical tales of two brothers who had once killed and pillaged their way across the West. He could hardly believe his ears, but he drank it all in. In 1823, he married a girl from Henderson County, Kentucky, whose people surely knew all about the Harps. They hailed from the place where all the final spasms of the spree occurred.[42]

Hall penned two long accounts of the Harp murders, both published in *The Port Folio,* a magazine his brother edited. By the time they saw daylight in print, the unpleasant aftershocks of the American Revolution had largely been forgotten. An "Era of Good Feelings" had begun. Some of *The Port Folio*'s readers, removed from the pockets and places where Harp lore had remained garishly fresh, objected. When one wrote a complaining letter calling the story hogwash, Hall slapped down the skeptics by providing testimonials from several parties, including an affirmation from George Poindexter, the fiery attorney general who had once stared down John Setton in a Mississippi courtroom.

Their stars rose. Others chimed in, trying their hands at the Harps' tale. J.W.M. Breazeale, whose father had been deputy sheriff of Knox County (he was, in fact, the very lawman who had auctioned off Wiley's property in 1800), composed his version, drawing on Knoxville knowledge. The Harps got top billing in his history of early Tennessee.[43] More writers caught the fever as the nineteenth century wore on. An oddball named T. Marshall Smith, a cousin of the illustrious Supreme Court justice John Marshall, made the Harps the stars of his *Legends of the War of Independence and of the Earlier Settlements in the West*, a sort of wild compendium of Southern folklore.[44] It's a very odd book, rambling and fanciful. But it was Smith who suggested they came from a loyalist family—"Scotch Tories" bent on ruthless rapine—and whom later writers parroted again and again in conjuring the Harps.

Around 1840, one of the first historians of the trans-Appalachian West, Lyman Draper, took a shine to the Harps. Draper is perhaps most responsible for preserving and collecting evidence about the murders. He was close enough on their heels to harvest memories from living people. He collected dozens of oral histories and interviews from people who knew the Harps or had lived through their episodes. He wrote letters to Harp acquaintances, begging for their recollections. He filled notebooks.

From his own frosty northern climes, Draper traveled to the humid wilds of Pontotoc, Mississippi, where he met Silas McBee, one of the posse members who had chased the Harps across western Kentucky. They talked and talked. They rode horses together. ("Though his weight cannot be less than two hundred and fifty [pounds]," Draper wrote about the aging McBee, "he can nevertheless . . . mount his steed and ride for hours.") McBee vetted everything Draper wrote. "It is to Silas McBee that the reader is indebted," Draper confessed.[45] Draper's visit, it turned out, was just in time. McBee died only two years later at the age of eighty. But Draper's "A Sketch of the Harpes: An Episode in Western History," a magazine piece that McBee proofread for accuracy, had by then preserved the story.[46]

But then their stars flickered and fell. Union armies tore through the South in the 1860s, destroying the places where documents lived. Courthouses burned down or succumbed to floodwaters. People forgot. Appalachia was eventually branded as aberrant, backward, by Americans who fancied themselves soldiers of progress, and many lost interest in recovering its history. Echoes of the Harp legend, liberated from its origins, turned up in the novels of Mark Twain, who pictured Huckleberry Finn joining Tom Sawyer's band of robber boys. It surfaced in episodes of *Gunsmoke* during the mid-twentieth century's faddish obsession with Westerns. But mostly it withered away.

The last to publish a serious, deeply researched book about the Harps was Otto Rothert, an eccentric thinker who had more of a mind for fossils and botany than for business. His mother, Franziska, "saw he was too full of abstractions to turn a shrewd deal," a newspaper carped. The son of German immigrants, Rothert graduated from the University of Notre Dame but could not seem to find his way forward. When his father died, he inherited 2,700 acres of "wild topography" in Muhlenberg County, Kentucky. (Otto hoped there might be coal or oil beneath it; perhaps his father had, too.) It had on it an old log house, which Rothert fell in love with, remodeled, and dubbed "Forest Retreat." It was not far from where Micajah Harp had been slain.[47]

In 1924, Rothert published *The Outlaws of Cave-in-Rock*, a roundup of early American piracy and brigandry that also included a deeply researched retelling of the Harp murders. It was not a great success. As the motion picture industry dawned, he tried to convince people that the Harps should be in the movies. But no one listened. "There is not sufficient love interest or sufficient sympathy for any of the characters to make this book an available picture subject," one producer pronounced. "So much work would have to be done" to flesh out the story, he thought, that it was hardly worth it.[48]

Wiley and Micajah slipped from view. They faded away. Resurrecting them has never been an easy thing. It has only been made more difficult by the ravages of time. To spend years fitting together the little shards of their lives—and countless hours in the company of the clues they left behind—does not immunize you against the feeling that they are still somehow, stubbornly, unknowable. There is no intimacy with the Harps. As one early historian wrote about the American Revolution: "Much, perhaps, remains to be known . . . but much is irrevocably covered by the ashes of the grave."[49]

* * *

AND YET THE Harp brothers haunt the republic still.

They are the revenants of the Revolutionary past, dragging its chains into the present. The American Revolution gave rise to a new kind of society: Common people felt promised new liberties, new possibilities. With these changes came a new "release of energy," "a flowering of individualism, a magnificent display of economic and artistic virtuosity." But the Revolution was not only freeing; it also sent men spiraling into a fearful new world of competition and aloneness. They came to know "the sorrows of rootlessness."[50] Migrating into new places, breaking family bonds and traditions. Entering markets, newly speculative and punishing. Scrambling to do a little better than one's neighbors. In raising men's aspirations, the founding also created an imprint—a watermark—on American society that remains with us.

Popular memory of the Harps stripped a lot of the truth from their story, pushing them outside the mainstream of American history. But there is no more quintessentially American tale. The founders gave Americans a beautifully aspirational ideal—the promise that all men are created equal and all are entitled to "life, liberty, and the pursuit of happiness." Never has a nation been built upon a loftier sentiment. But as long as that sentiment stands, there will always be those who fall short. There will always be those who fail in their pursuits. America will always have losers.

Some of them become violent. Despite their internet reputation, the Harps don't quite make sense as serial killers—those cold, patient predators who wait long periods between murders. They don't fit comfortably alongside a figure like H. H. Holmes, who lured young female victims to their deaths in the shadow of the 1893 World's Fair. They look a lot more like modern mass killers who undertake murderous rampages in the hope that "people may now stand up and take notice."[51] Often triggered by some failure the killer has weathered, this sort of killing is about taking back power—taking revenge. Others need to feel the pain, too, just as the killer has.[52]

Many clues to unlocking the Harp murders have been hiding in plain sight for years. Almost since the eighteenth century, people knew that Wiley and Micajah had felt slighted. They felt wronged. As one early writer put it, Micajah had confessed the spree was done "in retaliation for some fancied injury."[53] He told John Leeper he had become "disgusted with mankind" and that he and his brother had "declared war" on their fellow citizens. All of these declarations are hallmarks of rampage killing. The Harps were reclaiming power from a world that had taken it away from them. The spree was a rebellion of sorts—the revolt of young men who felt pushed out of America's social and economic order.

Musing through the folktales of old Mississippi, William Faulkner traced the extinction of men like Wiley Harp. He saw the figure of the boorish American settler—"the pioneer, the tall man, roaring with Protestant scripture and boiled whiskey"—becoming obsolete, disappearing. He imagined him vanishing, extinguished by history, as he was "dragged out of what remained of his secret wilderness haunts . . . into the towns to his formal apotheosis in a courtroom and then a gallows or the limb of a tree."[54] But he was wrong. There has been no apotheosis. There has been no vanishing.

The Harps are still with us. They seem so distant, separated from us by fathoms and fathoms of the past. But in their story lies a key—a kind of cipher for decoding why some Americans choose violence. They are an origins story, the first stone, as it were, laid more than two hundred years ago. As early as the founding, young American men, alienated from the nation and its values, began declaring their disaffection—their total disengagement from America's social and political experiment—with violence. Even now, even in some of the murderous outbursts that mar our twenty-first-century news cycles, Wiley Harp lives.

ACKNOWLEDGMENTS

I AM NOT sure I can fully capture the cast of characters who made this book possible. Recovering this story required the help of many others who showed me, in various ways, how to fit the pieces together. I have incurred more debts than I can count.

I could not have written this book without the support of several fellowships and grants. In the early stages, an AAS-NEH long-term fellowship allowed me to conduct research at the (incomparable) American Antiquarian Society. Several critical chunks of the book came into focus while I was there. Ashley Cataldo, Vincent Golden, and Elizabeth Watts Pope all provided important research advice, and Nan Wolverton was a gracious host. Meanwhile, my stellar cohort of fellows and affiliated scholars also helped greatly: Steve Bullock, Samantha Harvey, Reeve Huston, Roberto Saba, and Adrian Weimer, thank you. Peter Onuf, whom I first met at AAS, gave his thoughts on several pieces of the book in ways that challenged and bolstered me. Many thanks to the National Endowment for the Humanities and the AAS.

I am also deeply grateful to the American Council of Learned Societies, which awarded me a yearlong Frederick Burkhardt Fellowship—a gift of precious time to think and write. The book I've written is in large part owed to support from the ACLS. During that fellowship year, I also had the good fortune of being hosted as a resident fellow at the University of Connecticut Humanities Institute, which proved a very rewarding intellectual home. The generosity of Michael Lynch and Alexis Boylan and my conversations with the stellar faculty and fellows at UConn, including Nina Dayton, Lynne Tirrell, Ellen Litman, Aimee Loiselle, and others, made my time at UCHI especially productive.

A short-term fellowship at the Filson Historical Society in Louisville, Kentucky, proved a windfall of research material. Patrick Lewis and his expert team warmly welcomed me, and I am deeply grateful for their support. Special thanks to Kelly Hyberger, who, one spring day in 2022, brought me several dusty boxes of uncatalogued documents that I had long ago written off as lost. (Their contents appear throughout this book.) Many of my other discoveries are owed to the luxury of funding from Wellesley College that allowed me to visit widely scattered archival collections—and to comb through the evidence in many far-flung places in Tennessee, Kentucky, North Carolina, Wisconsin, and Mississippi.

The John Carter Brown Library and the C.V. Starr Center for the Study of the American Experience each hosted me for several months as the JCB–Hodson Trust Fellow. One of the more delightful experiences I had writing this book was the summer I spent in Chestertown, Maryland, affiliated with Washington College's Starr Center. While there, I finished a first draft of the book. I am especially grateful to Adam Goodheart and Molly Streit for making me feel so at home.

As I moved forward, many archivists and librarians lit the way. At the Knox County Archives, Phillip Smith first unearthed several critical documents for me and later entertained many questions. And over the years, Eric Head has provided invaluable research help, support, and friendship. (Thank you, Eric, too, for helping me locate Wiley's land.) I am also indebted to the many others who tirelessly answered my questions, sent digital files, and pointed me in new directions—especially those at the Tennessee State Library and Archives, the Calvin M. McClung Historical Collection at the Knox County Public Library, the Kentucky Department for Libraries and Archives, the Kentucky Historical Society, the University of Kentucky (especially the Special Collections Research Center), the Wisconsin Historical Society, the John Carter Brown Library, Western Kentucky University Special Collections, the North Carolina State Archives, and the Mississippi Department of Archives and History.

Many fellow historians and mentors read sections of this book as I drafted and completed it. Deepest thanks, especially, to Gregory Ablavsky, Jessica Choppin-Roney, Christopher Clark, Jonathan Gienapp, Patrick Griffin, Kate Jewell, Adam Malka, Bruce Mann, Megan Kate Nelson, Peter Onuf, Ryan Quintana, Kristofer Ray, Randolph Roth, and Bruce Stewart, all of whom read substantial portions of the manuscript, lent their expertise, and shaped my thinking. Brendan McConville listened to me talk about this book over months and years, and entertained my ideas with utmost patience. I am also thankful for the various members of Book Squad, who made crucial suggestions about my writing: Joe Adelman, Liz Covart, Caitlin DeAngelis, Sara Georgini, Reed Gochberg, Kevin Levin, Chris Parsons, and Karin Wulf. Others who shared tips, fielded queries, and generously sent me in the right directions include Douglas Winiarski, Christina Snyder, Gail Miller, Laura Edwards, Kate Haulman, and Richard Bailey.

I shared many of the ideas in this book in various talks, workshops, and other events. Several chapters benefited extensively from conversations I had as part of SHEAR's Second Book Writers Workshop, in sessions led, respectively, by Tamara Thornton, Ashli White, and Michael Witgen. In those workshops, Michael Blaakman, Mark Boonshoft, Kelly Kennington, and Jessica Lepler all contributed important insights. I am also grateful to audiences and conference participants at Boston College, the Columbia University Early American History Seminar, the Massachusetts Historical Society, the McNeil Center for Early American Studies, the Mahindra Humanities Center at Harvard University, the Museum of the American Revolution, and several SHEAR conferences, as well as those who commented on the work I presented, including Eliga Gould, Jason Opal, and April Hatfield. I am especially grateful to Ken Miller, who invited me to speak at Washington College in 2019.

I am lucky that some very talented people shaped the book through the publishing process. Katherine Flynn saw the promise in this story years ago and brought both light and ballast along the way. Katherine, your support made this book possible. Molly Turpin, my talented (and patient) editor, shaped the book in ways that made it immeasurably better: Molly, thank you. I am also grateful to Maddie Caldwell and Monica Brown at Random House, who steered the book through some of its final phases.

I am most grateful to the many friends and fellow travelers who sustained me through the ups and downs of this project, all of whom have added not only to the story in these pages but to my life generally: Andrew Lancaster, Mike Smith, Kristen Smith, Daniel Ezra Johnson, Megan Kate Nelson, Kate Jewell, Ryan Quintana, Jess Roney, Reeve Huston, Brendan McConville, Phil Mead, Brenna Greer, Steve Marini, Sean Harvey, Drew Lipman, thank you for everything. My "better angels"—Luiza deCamargo, Carrie Weinstein, and Wera von Wulfen—kept me afloat when I hit the doldrums. Loving thanks, too, to Cliff and Dorene Grandjean, and Morgen and Ben, and Jim and Dorian O'Neill, for their love and support. And finally, there is Sarah Schuetze. Although it was far too short, I am grateful for the time I got to count her as part of my life, and I hope that wherever she is, she's looking over me.

This book is for my family. They have been wonderful and patient as I gave myself to this book in ways that were not always easy. Laura, Carey, and Zack, you are the greatest gifts of my life, the sparkling stars in my night sky. This is for you.

NOTES

Prologue: The Shaving Glass

1. Jane Farris deposition, January 4, 1799, transcription, in folder labeled "Pages 1 to 16 Stanford Notes," Otto Rothert Papers, unprocessed, Filson Historical Society, Louisville, Ky.
2. *The Kentucky Almanac, for the Year of Our Lord 1798* (Lexington: J. Bradford, 1797).
3. James Hall, *Letters from the West; Containing Sketches of Scenery, Manners, and Customs; and Anecdotes Connected with the First Settlements of the Western Sections of the United States* (1828; repr., Gainesville: Scholars' Facsimiles & Reprints, 1967), 266 ("Boon's Trace"); Interview with Jane Stevenson, Lyman Draper Manuscripts Collection, CC series, vol. 13, 135, Wisconsin Historical Society, Madison (hereafter cited as Draper Manuscripts, WHS). For a sense of the West in the era of the American Revolution, see Patrick Griffin, *American Leviathan: Empire, Nation, and Revolutionary Frontier* (New York: Hill and Wang, 2007).
4. Isaac Weld, *Travels Through the States of North America, and the Provinces of Upper and Lower Canada, During the Years 1795, 1796, and 1797*, 2nd ed., 2 vols. (London: John Stockdale, 1799), 1:236.
5. Jane Farris deposition, Filson Historical Society.
6. J.W.M. Breazeale, *Life as It Is; Or, Matters and Things in General: Containing, Amongst Other Things, Historical Sketches of the Exploration and First Settlement of the State of Tennessee* (1842; repr., Knoxville: University of Tennessee Press, 2009), 137.
7. Major William Stewart recollections, Draper Manuscripts, WHS, 30S, 188 ("tallest class"); "Winchester May 22," *Claypoole's American Daily Advertiser*, May 30, 1799 ("full-fleshed").
8. "Mercer County," *Palladium* (Kentucky), March 21, 1799, clipping, Draper Manuscripts, WHS, 1Q, 34 ("light made"); Major William Stewart recollections, 30S, 188 ("under common size").
9. Hall, *Letters from the West*, 267.
10. Hall, *Letters from the West*, 266; Breazeale, *Life as It Is*, 140; Richard H. Collins, *Collins' Historical Sketches of Kentucky: History of Kentucky*, 2 vols. (1847; repr., Covington, Ky.: Collins, 1874), 2:345.
11. George P. Garrison, "A Memorandum of M. Austin's Journey from the Lead Mines in the County of Wythe in the State of Virginia to the Lead

Mines in the Province of Louisiana West of the Mississippi, 1796–1797," *American Historical Review* 5, no. 3 (1900): 525.

12. Collins, *Collins' Historical Sketches*, 2:348.
13. Craig Thompson Friend, "Work & Be Rich: Economy and Culture on the Bluegrass Farm," in *The Buzzel About Kentuck: Settling the Promised Land*, ed. Friend (Lexington: University Press of Kentucky, 1999), 133.
14. *A Letter from George Nicholas, of Kentucky, to His Friend, in Virginia* (Lexington, 1798), 40.
15. Jane Farris deposition, Filson Historical Society.
16. Jane Farris deposition, Filson Historical Society.
17. "The Harpes (from James Givens)," Draper Manuscripts, WHS, 29S, 133.
18. "Lexington, January 9," clipping, Draper Manuscripts, WHS, 1Q, 33.

Introduction: "The Backwoodsmen"

1. Daniel Aaron, *Cincinnati, Queen City of the West, 1819–1838* (Columbus: Ohio State University Press, 1992), 15, 24–25 (steamboats); Richard C. Wade, *The Urban Frontier: The Rise of Western Cities, 1790–1830* (Cambridge: Harvard University Press, 1959); Steven J. Ross, *Workers on the Edge: Work, Leisure, and Politics in Industrializing Cincinnati, 1788–1890* (New York: Columbia University Press, 1985); Fifth Census of the United States, 1830, microfilm publication M19, 201 rolls, Records of the Bureau of the Census, Record Group (hereafter cited as RG) 29, National Archives, Washington, D.C.
2. On *The Port Folio*'s history and readership, see William C. Dowling, *Literary Federalism in the Age of Jefferson: Joseph Dennie and The Port Folio, 1801–1812* (Columbia: University of South Carolina Press, 1999); Catherine O'Donnell Kaplan, *Men of Letters in the Early Republic: Cultivating Forums of Citizenship* (Chapel Hill: Omohundro Institute and the University of North Carolina Press, 2008); Linda K. Kerber and Walter John Morris, "Politics and Literature: The Adams Family and the Port Folio," *William and Mary Quarterly* 23, no. 3 (1966): 450–476 (quote on p. 450); and Laura Rigal, *The American Manufactory: Art, Labor, and the World of Things in the Early Republic* (Princeton University Press, 1998), 117.
3. The image of the material world of *The Port Folio*'s genteel readers is drawn from Richard L. Bushman, *The Refinement of America: Persons, Houses, Cities* (New York: Vintage Books, 1992), especially 238–279, and Jack Larkin, "From 'Country Mediocrity' to 'Rural Improvement': Transforming the Slovenly Countryside in Central Massachusetts, 1775–1840," in *Everyday Life in the Early Republic*, ed. Catherine E. Hutchins (Winterthur, Del.: Henry Francis du Pont Winterthur Museum, 1994), 175–200.
4. "The Backwoodsmen," *Port Folio*, April 1824, 271. Hall was not identified as the piece's author, though his authorship of the magazine's "Letters from the West" series was revealed later.
5. "The Backwoodsmen," 271.

6. "The Backwoodsmen," 271.
7. "The Backwoodsmen," 271.
8. "From the Cincinnati Literary Gazette," repr. in "The Story of the Harps," *Port Folio,* August 1825, 122–123.
9. W. H. Venable, *Beginnings of Literary Culture in the Ohio Valley, Historical and Biographical Sketches* (Cincinnati: Robert Clarke, 1891), 365–366.
10. Hall, *Letters from the West,* 112.
11. Venable, *Beginnings of Literary Culture in the Ohio Valley,* 365.
12. Hall, *Letters from the West,* 111–112.
13. Elliott J. Gorn, " 'Gouge and Bite, Pull Hair and Scratch': The Social Significance of Fighting in the Southern Backcountry," *American Historical Review* 90, no. 1 (1985): 24.
14. "The Backwoodsmen," 271, 273.
15. "The Story of the Harps," 120, 124.
16. "The Story of the Harps," 123.
17. "The Story of the Harps," 123.
18. "The KNOXVILLE GAZETTE, Wednesday *Evening, August* 7," *Knoxville Gazette,* August 7, 1799.
19. Breazeale, *Life as It Is,* 138.
20. "Winchester May 22," *Claypoole's American Daily Advertiser,* May 30, 1799 ("robust," "downcast"); Collins, *Collins' Historical Sketches,* 2:345.
21. Lyman C. Draper, "A Sketch of the Harpes: An Episode in Western History," *Western Literary and Historical Magazine* 1, no. 9 (1842): 164.
22. "By the Governor, a Proclamation," April 22, 1799, repr. in Otto A. Rothert, *The Outlaws of Cave-in-Rock* (Cleveland: Arthur H. Clark, 1924), 89; "Winchester May 22," *Claypoole's American Daily Advertiser,* May 30, 1799.
23. Herman Melville, *The Confidence-Man: His Masquerade* (1857; repr., New York: Hendricks House, 1954), 2.
24. William Faulkner, *Requiem for a Nun* (New York: Random House, 1951), 16.
25. Breazeale, *Life as It Is,* 136.
26. Hall, *Letters from the West,* 265.
27. Richard Maxwell Brown, "Historical Patterns of American Violence," in *Violence in America: Historical and Comparative Perspectives,* eds. Hugh Davis Graham and Ted Robert Gurr, rev. ed. (Sage Publications, 1979), 29.
28. Eric H. Monkkonen, *Murder in New York City* (Berkeley: University of California Press, 2001), 157.
29. *The Last Confession & Dying Words of Conrad Englehart* (1807), 4.
30. Robin W. Winks, ed., *The Historian as Detective: Essays on Evidence* (New York: Harper & Row, 1969), 497–498.
31. Thomas Paine, *Letter Addressed to the Abbe Raynal on the Affairs of North-America* (Philadelphia, 1782), 49–50.
32. Hall, *Letters from the West,* 112–113.
33. Quotes from the newspaper are all taken from Harlow Giles Unger, *The Last Founding Father: James Monroe and a Nation's Call to Greatness* (Philadelphia: Da Capo Press, 2009), 270.

34. Quoted in "Cincinnati: Saturday, May 28, 1825," *Cincinnati Literary Gazette*, May 28, 1825, 174 (in the context of the Harps controversy).
35. Breazeale, *Life as It Is*, 136–137.

1: Liberty and Property

1. Mary U. Rothrock, *The French Broad-Holston Country: A History of Knox County, Tennessee* (Knoxville: East Tennessee Historical Society, 1946), 52–53; T. W. Humes, *The Half-Century of Knoxville* (Knoxville, 1852), 60–61.
2. James Weir's description of early Knoxville, repr. in Otto Arthur Rothert, *A History of Muhlenberg County* (Louisville, 1913), 56.
3. Robert M. Coates, *The Outlaw Years: The History of the Land Pirates of the Natchez Trace* (New York: Literary Guild of America, 1930), 27.
4. Simon P. Newman, "Principles or Men? George Washington and the Political Culture of National Leadership, 1776–1801," *Journal of the Early Republic* 12, no. 4 (1992): 483 (flowers), 494 (church bells). On the atmosphere of the Constitutional Convention, see, for introductions, Richard Beeman, *Plain, Honest Men: The Making of the American Constitution* (New York: Random House, 2009), and Carol Berkin, *A Brilliant Solution: Inventing the American Constitution* (Boston: Mariner, 2003).
5. John Adams to Abigail Adams, March 5, 1797, in Sara Martin et al., eds., *The Adams Papers: Adams Family Correspondence*, vol. 12, *March 1797–April 1798* (Cambridge: Harvard University Press, 2015), 9 (hereafter cited as *AFC*).
6. Thomas Jefferson to James Madison, January 8, 1797, in Ralph Adams Brown, *The Presidency of John Adams* (University Press of Kansas, 1975), 22.
7. Major William Stewart recollections, 188 (blue eyes, light hair, "handsome"); John L. Ballenger to Lyman Draper, Frankfort, Ky., January 11, 1845, Draper Manuscripts, WHS, 12C, 46 (sandy hair, "pleasant agreeable"). Descriptions of Wiley's appearance vary somewhat; some described his hair as light or "sandy," others as "dark," while a few saw him as a redhead.
8. Major William Stewart recollections, 188, 190; Breazeale, *Life as It Is*, 137 ("gentleman").
9. Willie Harp and Sarah Rice marriage bond, Knox County, Tenn., June 1, 1797, in Knox County Archives, Knoxville, Tenn. (hereafter cited as KCA).
10. John Rice to Wiley Harp deed, August 4, 1797, in Knox County Warranty Deed Book C1V2, 161–162, KCA; "The Journal of John Sevier," August 4, 1797, originally published in *Tennessee Historical Magazine*, 1919–1920, vols. 5–6, https://penelope.uchicago.edu/Thayer/E/Gazetteer/Places/America/United_States/Tennessee/_Texts/THM/5/3/Sevier_Journal/1797*.html (rain).
11. Charles H. Faulkner, *Massacre at Cavett's Station: Frontier Tennessee During the Cherokee Wars* (Knoxville: University of Tennessee Press, 2013); quotes are from John P. Brown, *Old Frontiers: The Story of the Cherokee Indians from*

Earliest Times to the Date of Their Removal to the West, 1838 (Kingsport, Tenn.: Southern Publishers, 1938), 392.

12. William G. McLoughlin, *Cherokee Renascence in the New Republic* (Princeton University Press, 1986), 19–20 ("fire and slaughter," "shot, hacked"); Brown, *Old Frontiers*, 388 (Doublehead).
13. John Sevier to the Secretary of War, July 20, 1796, Governor John Sevier Papers, Box 1, Folder 2, Tennessee State Library and Archives, Nashville, Tenn. (hereafter cited as TSLA).
14. Cynthia Cumfer, *Separate Peoples, One Land: The Minds of Cherokees, Blacks, and Whites on the Tennessee Frontier* (Chapel Hill: University of North Carolina Press, 2007), 93. Cumfer notes that Tennessee's population increased from 77,262 in 1795 to 105,602 in 1800.
15. *Vermont Repository*, November 1795, from a letter dated Knoxville, July 1795, in Samuel Cole Williams, *Early Travels in the Tennessee Country, 1540–1800* (Johnson City, Tenn.: Watauga Press, 1928), 430.
16. Charles H. Faulkner, "'Here Are Frame Houses and Brick Chimneys': Knoxville, Tennessee, in the Late Eighteenth Century," in *The Southern Colonial Backcountry: Interdisciplinary Perspectives on Frontier Communities*, eds. David Colin Crass et al. (Knoxville: University of Tennessee Press, 1998), 137–161; King & Crozier advertisement, quoted in Rothrock, *The French Broad-Holston Country*, 74; "Report of the Journey of the Brethren Abraham Steiner and Frederick C. de Schweinitz to the Cherokees and the Cumberland Settlements (1799)," in Williams, *Early Travels in the Tennessee Country*, 454–455.
17. "Thomas Dillon's Account (1796)," in Williams, *Early Travels in the Tennessee Country*, 360.
18. James Weir's description of early Knoxville, repr. in Rothert, *A History of Muhlenberg County*, 56–57.
19. *The Constitution of the State of Tennessee* (Knoxville, 1796), 10.
20. Daniel Smith, *A Short Description of the State of Tennessee* (Philadelphia, 1796), 5.
21. The probate records referenced here can be found in *Knox County Tennessee Estate Book, Volume 1, 1792 to 1811*, KCA. Kearns's record is on p. 35; Roseberry's is on p. 26.
22. William Blount to John Gray Blount, Knoxville, November 7, 1797, in William H. Masterson, ed., *The John Gray Blount Papers*, vol. 3, *1796–1802* (Raleigh: State Department of Archives and History, 1965), 178.
23. Charles William Janson, *The Stranger in America* (London, 1807), 304–305.
24. On the pursuit of land as fundamental to masculinity in this region and period, see especially Stephen Aron, *How the West Was Lost: The Transformation of Kentucky from Daniel Boone to Henry Clay* (Baltimore: Johns Hopkins University Press, 1999), 58; Jack P. Greene, "Independence, Improvement, and Authority: Toward a Framework for Understanding the Histories of the Southern Backcountry During the Era of the American Revolution,"

in *An Uncivil War: The Southern Backcountry During the American Revolution*, eds. Ronald Hoffman et al. (Charlottesville: University of Virginia Press, 1985), 3–36; Richard Bushman, "'This New Man': Dependence and Independence, 1776," in *Uprooted Americans: Essays to Honor Oscar Handlin*, ed. Bushman (Boston: Little, Brown, 1979), 79–96.

25. Breazeale, *Life as It Is*, 137.
26. I have yet to find any baptismal records for the two brothers, but a number of contemporary sources indicate that they were born about this time. A Frankfort, Kentucky, *Palladium* report estimated Micajah Roberts, in 1799, to have been "about thirty five years of age," and Wiley "a little older." But most descriptions suggest they were a few years younger than this. See "Mercer County," *Palladium*, March 21, 1799, clipping, Draper Manuscripts, WHS, 1Q, 34.
27. Collins, *Collins' Historical Sketches*, 2:345; Chester Raymond Young, ed., *Westward into Kentucky: The Narrative of Daniel Trabue* (1981; repr., Lexington: University Press of Kentucky, 2004), 146.
28. Harry L. Watson, *An Independent People: The Way We Lived in North Carolina, 1770–1820* (Chapel Hill: University of North Carolina Press, 1983), 5.
29. Worth S. Ray, *Colonial Granville County and Its People: Loose Leaves from the Lost Tribes of North Carolina* (1945; repr., Baltimore: Genealogical Publishing, 1965), 215 (Thomas and John Harp marriages), 297 (tax lists).
30. T. Marshall Smith, *Legends of the War of Independence and of the Earlier Settlements in the West* (Louisville: J. F. Brennan, 1855), 22; Hall, *Letters from the West*, 265.
31. "Harp" is likely a Scottish name, derived from (and sometimes rendered as) "Earp." See Smith, *Legends of the War of Independence*, 23, where the author identifies the Harps as Scottish. On Scottish migrants to Granville, see Nannie M. Tilley, "The Settlement of Granville County," *North Carolina Historical Review* 11, no. 1 (1934): 18.
32. Between 1763 and 1775, more than forty thousand Scots immigrated to America. See Bernard Bailyn, *The Peopling of British North America: An Introduction* (New York: Knopf, 1986), 9.
33. J.F.D. Smyth, *A Tour in the United States of America*, 3 vols. (London, 1784), 1:104.
34. See, for instance, Alvaretta K. Register, *State Census of North Carolina, 1784–1787* (1973; repr., Baltimore: Genealogical Publishing, 2001), 53 (John Harp); Granville County Tax List, 1782, Epping Forest District, https://digital.ncdcr.gov/Documents/Detail/tax-lists-granville-county-1782/288740?item=288855 and "List of Taxes for Granville County for the Year 1785," https://digital.ncdcr.gov/Documents/Detail/tax-lists-granville-county-1785/349652?item=349655, both in North Carolina Digital Collections, Tax Lists and Records; and John Harp land grant, 240 acres on Long Creek, September 24, 1779, in *North Carolina, U.S., Land Grant Files, 1693–1960* [database online], ancestry.com, original at North Carolina State Archives, Raleigh, N.C.

35. Hugh Talmage Lefler and Albert Ray Newsome, *North Carolina: The History of a Southern State* (Chapel Hill: University of North Carolina Press, 1963), 84–85, 113–114 (houses, tobacco); John S. Ezell, ed., *The New Democracy in America: Travels of Francisco de Miranda in the United States, 1783–84* (Norman: University of Oklahoma Press, 1963), 9 (frogs' music).
36. On childhood in early America, see Steven Mintz, *Huck's Raft: A History of American Childhood* (Cambridge: Harvard University Press, 2004); Constance B. Schulz, "Children and Childhood in the Eighteenth Century," in *American Childhood: A Research Guide and Historical Handbook*, eds. Joseph M. Hawes and N. Ray Hiner (Westport, Conn.: Greenwood Press, 1985), 57–109; Daniel Blake Smith, "Autonomy and Affection: Parents and Children in Eighteenth-Century Chesapeake Families," in *Growing Up in America: Children in Historical Perspective*, eds. N. Ray Hiner and Joseph M. Hawes (Urbana: University of Illinois Press, 1985), 45–58.
37. M. L. Weems, *The Life of George Washington* (Philadelphia, 1800), 9.
38. On colonists' relationship to the king in the years prior to the American Revolution, see especially Brendan McConville, *The King's Three Faces: The Rise and Fall of Royal America, 1688–1776* (Chapel Hill: Omohundro Institute and University of North Carolina Press, 2006).
39. Benjamin Franklin to William Strahan, July 5, 1775, in William B. Willcox, ed., *The Papers of Benjamin Franklin, Volume 22: March 23, 1775, through October 27, 1776* (New Haven and London: Yale University Press, 1982), 85.
40. Young, *Westward into Kentucky*, 42.
41. See especially Jeffrey J. Crow, "Liberty Men and Loyalists: Disorder and Disaffection in the North Carolina Backcountry," in *An Uncivil War*, eds. Hoffman et al., 125–178, and that edited collection generally; Larry E. Tise and Jeffrey J. Crow, eds., *The Southern Experience in the American Revolution* (Chapel Hill: University of North Carolina Press, 1978); Wayne E. Lee, *Crowds and Soldiers in Revolutionary North Carolina: The Culture of Violence in Riot and War* (Gainesville: University Press of Florida, 2001); John S. Pancake, *The Destructive War: The British Campaign in the Carolinas, 1780–1782* (Tuscaloosa: University of Alabama Press, 1985); and Russell F. Weigley, *The Partisan War: The South Carolina Campaign of 1780–1782* (Columbia: University of South Carolina Press, 1975).
42. Quoted in Lee, *Crowds and Soldiers*, 138.
43. Robert O. DeMond, *The Loyalists in North Carolina During the Revolution* (Durham: Duke University Press, 1940), 117.
44. Adelaide L. Fries, ed., *Records of the Moravians in North Carolina*, vol. 4, *1780–1783* (Raleigh, 1930), 1822–1823.
45. Fries, *Records of the Moravians in North Carolina*, 4:1777.
46. Dr. A. L. Hammond, "Revolutionary Incidents—No. 7: The Battle of Cedar Springs," *Charleston Courier*, January 1859, clipping, Draper Manuscripts, WHS, 1DD, 92.
47. Ensign Robert Campbell's account in Robert M. Dunkerly, *The Battle of Kings Mountain: Eyewitness Accounts* (Charleston: Arcadia, 2007), 22.

48. William H. Masterson, *William Blount* (Baton Rouge: Louisiana State University Press, 1954), 28.
49. Five percent of Virginia's soldiers were, in fact, boys—fourteen or fifteen years old. Mintz, *Huck's Raft*, 61–63; M. M. Quaife, ed., "Documents: A Boy Soldier Under Washington: The Memoir of Daniel Granger," *Mississippi Valley Historical Review* 16, no. 4 (1930): 538–560.
50. Rothert, *The Outlaws of Cave-in-Rock*, 60 ("under the British"); Coates, *The Outlaw Years*, 24 ("tried to turn").
51. T. Marshall Smith, who wrote about the Harps in the nineteenth century, called the family "Scotch Tories." He seems to have inaugurated the tradition of intimating that their father—and perhaps even Wiley and Micajah themselves—had been present with loyalist militia at the Battle of Kings Mountain in 1780. Modern historians have repeated this story countless times, as if it were verifiable truth. But there is no corroborating evidence, and no one seems to have put these traditions onto paper before Smith. See Smith, *Legends of the War of Independence*, 318–323.
52. McLoughlin, *Cherokee Renascence in the New Republic*, 20; Rennard Strickland, *Fire and the Spirits: Cherokee Law from Clan to Court* (Norman: University of Oklahoma Press, 1975), 49.
53. William Henry Perrin, ed., *County of Christian, Kentucky: Historical and Biographical* (Chicago and Louisville: F. A. Battey, 1884), 170.
54. Katherine Grandjean, "Pockets Full of Ashes: The Lingering Embers of the Revolutionary War in the South," Special Issue: A New Kind of American Revolution, *Early American Studies* 23, no. 1 (2025): 93–116.
55. Deed of Conveyance Book (1792–1805), 108, KCA. I am grateful to Phillip Smith for finding this record for me.
56. Breazeale, *Life as It Is*, 137.
57. Greene, "Independence, Improvement, and Authority" (quote on p. 12); also see Jonathan Levy, "The Mortgage Worked the Hardest: The Fate of Landed Independence in Nineteenth-Century America," and the other essays in *Capitalism Takes Command: The Social Transformation of Nineteenth-Century America*, eds. Michael Zakim and Gary J. Kornblith (University of Chicago Press, 2012).
58. William Blackstone, *Commentaries on the Laws of England in Four Books*, vol. 2 (1766), 2.
59. Michael A. Blaakman, *Speculation Nation: Land Mania in the Revolutionary American Republic* (Philadelphia: University of Pennsylvania Press, 2023) (observer quote on p. 5).
60. Blaakman, *Speculation Nation*, 2. Land speculation had been a part of American history well before this. But, Blaakman notes, "land speculation in the 1780s and 1790s was a chapter apart, defined by its entanglement with revolutionary ideas, politics, and state formation" (2). In this post-Revolutionary moment, a "tremendous wave" of speculation engulfed the West (1).
61. Aron, *How the West Was Lost*, 60. In other parts of the early republic, the

federal government was able to superimpose more order over the process of western land distribution. But not here. Well before Tennessee existed, North Carolina had promised away much of its territory. When North Carolina ceded its western territory to the federal government in 1789, it was essentially too late to put any oversight in place. Under the terms of the cession, the rights of land purchasers and Revolutionary soldiers whose claims descended from North Carolina were very carefully protected. Should any former soldier be unable to find land within the territory set aside by North Carolina for military grants, he was allowed to claim land elsewhere. What this meant on the ground was that there was precious little unreserved land left in North Carolina's cession—the future Tennessee. So the United States government opened no public land office in the southwest. None of these parcels were entered in an orderly grid-like pattern. It was largely willy-nilly, often illegal and fraudulent. And the overlapping jurisdictions of Cherokee country, North Carolina, and Tennessee led to utter confusion and chaos. See especially Daniel Dovenbarger, "Land Registration in Early Middle Tennessee: Laws and Practice" (master's thesis, Vanderbilt University, 1981); Gale Williams Bamman, "This Land Is Our Land! Tennessee's Disputes with North Carolina," *Genealogical Journal* 24, no. 3 (1996); and Stanley John Folmsbee, "Sectionalism and Internal Improvements in Tennessee, 1796–1845" (PhD diss., University of Pennsylvania), repr. of East Tennessee Historical Society, Special Studies in Tennessee History, no. 1 (Philadelphia, 1939), 21.

62. Dovenbarger, "Land Registration in Early Middle Tennessee," especially chap. 2.
63. Willie Blount to John Gray and Thomas Blount, May 26, 1800, in *The John Gray Blount Papers*, 3:386–388. One example: In 1793, Willie Blount obtained and filled in dozens of blank warrants, not to deceive or defraud anyone, he later said, but because he was told the originals had disappeared. Stockley Donelson, Andrew Jackson's brother-in-law, assured him that the original warrants had been with Donelson's father "and that his father was killed by the Indians and probably had the warrants with him." Blount admitted: "I never saw the originals."
64. Michail Rogers to John Gray Blount, December 24, 1787, in Alice Barnwell Keith, ed., *The John Gray Blount Papers*, vol. 1, *1764–1789* (Raleigh: State Department of Archives and History, 1952), 364.
65. Daniel M. Friedenberg, *Life, Liberty, and the Pursuit of Land: The Plunder of Early America* (Buffalo: Prometheus Books, 1992), 177–185.
66. By the 1790s, a few great speculators—North Carolina elites, mostly—owned much of eastern Tennessee. In the years 1790 to 1810, almost 70 percent of private land in Tennessee—or 266,201 acres—was held by absentees. In fact, absentee landholders owned three-quarters of southern Appalachia, according to county tax lists. Wilma A. Dunaway, *The First American Frontier: Transition to Capitalism in Southern Appalachia, 1700–1860* (Chapel Hill: University of North Carolina Press, 1996), 56–57, 62.

67. Andrew Jackson, "Statement Regarding Land Frauds," December 6, 1797, in *The Papers of Andrew Jackson, Volume 1, 1770–1803*, eds. Sam B. Smith and Harriet Chappell Owsley (Knoxville: University of Tennessee Press, 1980), 157; Russell S. Koonts, " 'An Angel Has Fallen!': The Glasgow Land Frauds and the Emergence of the North Carolina Supreme Court," *North Carolina Historical Review* 72, no. 3 (1995): 310.
68. See Kristofer Ray, *Middle Tennessee, 1775–1825: Progress and Popular Democracy on the Southwestern Frontier* (Knoxville: University of Tennessee Press, 2007), 95–96 (quote on p. 95).
69. See Bamman, "This Land Is Our Land!"
70. *The Lover's Almanac, No. 1.* (Fredericksburg, Va.: T. Green for M. L. Weems, 1798).
71. Micajah Harp and Susana Roberts marriage bond, Blount County, Tenn., September 5, 1797.
72. "From Walter McCormick," Draper Manuscripts, WHS, 15CC, 225–226.
73. Breazeale, *Life as It Is*, 138; "Andre Michaux's Travels (1793–1796)," in Williams, *Early Travels in the Tennessee Country*, 338.

2: Unrest

1. This description is based on William Smith Shaw to Abigail Adams, December 16, 1798, in *AFC*, 13:309.
2. Edward Lawler, Jr., "The President's House in Philadelphia: The Rediscovery of a Lost Landmark," *Pennsylvania Magazine of History and Biography* 126, no. 1 (2002): 5–95. George Washington to Tobias Lear, September 5, 1790 (quote on p. 23).
3. Adams's note, December 1, 1797, agreeing to host the delegation at his house, and John Sevier to Andrew Jackson, January 8, 1798, in Governor John Sevier Papers, Box 1, Folder 5, TSLA.
4. Alexander Hamilton to George Washington, May 5, 1789, in Joanne B. Freeman, ed., *The Essential Hamilton: Letters & Other Writings* (New York: Library of America, 2017), 165. In fact, Hamilton thought only senators should be allowed to meet individually with the president, not members of the House of Representatives.
5. On Jackson's life, particularly the early years, see especially Robert V. Remini, *Andrew Jackson and the Course of American Empire 1767–1821* (New York: Harper & Row, 1977); the quote is from Peter Cozzens, *A Brutal Reckoning: Andrew Jackson, the Creek Indians, and the Epic War for the American South* (New York: Knopf, 2023), 156.
6. Cozzens, *A Brutal Reckoning*, 158–159.
7. Remini, *Andrew Jackson and the Course of American Empire*, 93. A wider sense of the tensions between the Southwest Territory (later Tennessee) and the federal government with regard to Native peoples can be gleaned from Masterson, *William Blount*, especially chaps. 9–11.

8. Andrew Jackson, "To the Cherokee Tribe of Indians East of the Mississippi" [circular], March 16, 1835.
9. The President's First Annual Message to Congress, December 8, 1829, in Camilla Townsend, ed., *American Indian History: A Documentary Reader* (New York: Wiley-Blackwell, 2009), 107.
10. William L. Anderson, ed., *Cherokee Removal: Before and After* (Athens: University of Georgia Press, 1991); Theda Perdue and Michael D. Green, *The Cherokee Nation and the Trail of Tears* (New York: Viking Penguin, 2007); Theda Perdue and Michael D. Green, *The Cherokee Removal: A Brief History with Documents* (Boston: Bedford Books, 1995); Adam J. Pratt, *Toward Cherokee Removal: Land, Violence, and the White Man's Chance* (Athens: University of Georgia Press, 2020); Gregory D. Smithers, *The Cherokee Diaspora: An Indigenous History of Migration, Resettlement, and Identity* (New Haven: Yale University Press, 2015). For a recent history of Indian removal across tribes, see Claudio Saunt, *Unworthy Republic: The Dispossession of Native Americans and the Road to Indian Territory* (New York: W. W. Norton, 2020).
11. John Sevier to Andrew Jackson, January 8, 1798, in Governor John Sevier Papers, Box 1, Folder 5, TSLA.
12. Alexander Hamilton, "Letter from Alexander Hamilton, Concerning the Public Conduct and Character of John Adams, Esq. President of the United States, October 24, 1800," in Joanne B. Freeman, ed., *Alexander Hamilton: Writings* (New York: Library of America, 2001), 941.
13. John Adams to Abigail Adams, December 25, 1798, in *AFC*, 13:323.
14. On John Adams's life and presidency, I have benefited especially from Brown, *The Presidency of John Adams;* Lindsay M. Chervinsky, *Making the Presidency: John Adams and the Precedents That Forged the Republic* (New York: Oxford University Press, 2024); John Ferling, *John Adams: A Life* (Knoxville: University of Tennessee Press, 1992); Woody Holton, *Abigail Adams* (New York: Free Press, 2009); and David McCullough, *John Adams* (New York: Simon & Schuster, 2001).
15. John Adams to Abigail Adams, March 22, 1797, in *AFC*, 12:44.
16. Abigail Adams to Mary Smith Cranch, May 24, 1797, in *AFC*, 12:125.
17. Abigail Adams to Mary Smith Cranch, July 21, 1797, in *AFC*, 12:211.
18. Abigail Adams to Mary Smith Cranch, May 24, 1797, in *AFC*, 12:124–125.
19. Abigail Adams to Mary Smith Cranch, June 23, 1797, in *AFC*, 12:172.
20. On tensions with France and the XYZ Affair, see Carol Berkin, *A Sovereign People: The Crises of the 1790s and the Birth of American Nationalism* (New York: Basic Books, 2017), 151–200.
21. "Speech to Both Houses of Congress," in *The Works of John Adams, Second President of the United States: With a Life of the Author, Notes and Illustrations, by His Grandson Charles Francis Adams*, vol. 9 (Boston: Little, Brown, 1854), 114.
22. James Monroe to Thomas Jefferson, May 4, 1798, in Barbara B. Oberg et al., eds., *The Papers of Thomas Jefferson*, vol. 30, *1 January 1798 to 31 January 1799* (Princeton University Press, 2003), 329 (hereafter cited as *TPTJ*).

23. Abigail Adams to John Adams, December 23, 1798, in *AFC*, 13:319.
24. Quoted in Robert H. Churchill, "Popular Nullification, Fries' Rebellion, and the Waning of Radical Republicanism, 1798–1801," *Pennsylvania History* 67, no. 1 (2000): 110.
25. Paul Douglas Newman, *Fries's Rebellion: The Enduring Struggle for the American Revolution* (Philadelphia: University of Pennsylvania Press, 2004).
26. Lindsay M. Chervinsky, *The Cabinet: George Washington and the Creation of an American Institution* (Cambridge: Harvard University Press, 2020), 185, 219–220; Donald H. Stewart, *The Opposition Press of the Federalist Period* (Albany: State University of New York Press, 1969), 7–9.
27. *The Works of John Adams*, 291 ("war measure"); Thomas Jefferson to James Madison, June 7, 1798, in *TPTJ*, 30:393 ("so palpably"). On the Alien and Sedition Acts, see Terri Diane Halperin, *The Alien and Sedition Acts of 1798: Testing the Constitution* (Baltimore: Johns Hopkins University Press, 2016), and James Morton Smith, *Freedom's Fetters: The Alien and Sedition Laws and American Civil Liberties* (Ithaca: Cornell University Press, 1956).
28. *The Works of John Adams*, 291.
29. Emphasis mine. Joanne B. Freeman, "Explaining the Unexplainable: The Cultural Context of the Sedition Act," in *The Democratic Experiment: New Directions in American Political History*, eds. Julian Zelizer, Meg Jacobs, and William Novak (Princeton University Press, 2003), 32; Berkin, *A Sovereign People*, 227; Halperin, *The Alien and Sedition Acts*, 94–95; Smith, *Freedom's Fetters*, 270–274. On the ultimate failure of the Sedition Act (Republican newspapers exploded in numbers in its wake), see Jeffrey L. Pasley, *The Tyranny of Printers: Newspaper Politics in the Early American Republic* (Charlottesville: University of Virginia Press, 2001), chap. 5.
30. Abigail Adams to Mary Smith Cranch, July 6, 1797, in *AFC*, 12:192.
31. This episode does appear in other works, briefly, mostly in those touching on Cherokee history or federal Indian policy. See Gregory Ablavsky, *Federal Ground: Governing Property and Violence in the First U.S. Territories* (New York: Oxford University Press, 2021), 212–221; Cumfer, *Separate Peoples, One Land*, 91–93; Cumfer, "Local Origins of National Indian Policy: Cherokee and Tennessean Ideas About Sovereignty and Nationhood, 1790–1811," *Journal of the Early Republic* 23, no. 1 (2003): 21–46; Merritt B. Pound, *Benjamin Hawkins, Indian Agent* (Athens: University of Georgia Press, 1951), 118–137; and Francis Paul Prucha, *American Indian Policy in the Formative Years: The Indian Trade and Intercourse Acts, 1790–1834* (Cambridge: Harvard University Press, 1962), 139–187 (especially 150–155). For a broader view of the Federalist presidents' efforts to keep order in this era, see David Andrew Nichols, *Red Gentlemen and White Savages: Indians, Federalists, and the Search for Order on the American Frontier* (Charlottesville: University of Virginia Press, 2008).
32. On the custom among backcountry women of hanging their coats and bedgowns on wooden pegs as a way of decorating the walls of their cabins, see David Hackett Fischer, *Albion's Seed: Four British Folkways in America* (New York: Oxford University Press, 1989), 732.

33. C. Daniel Crews and Richard W. Starbuck, eds., *Records of the Moravians Among the Cherokees*, vol. 1, *Early Contact and the Establishment of the First Mission, 1752–1802* (Tahlequah, Okla.: Cherokee National Press, 2010), 136.
34. William G. McLoughlin, *Cherokees and Missionaries, 1789–1839* (New Haven: Yale University Press, 1984), especially 14, 30 (population estimates, towns). On Cherokee history, particularly in this era, see also McLoughlin, *Cherokee Renascence in the New Republic;* Anderson, *Cherokee Removal: Before and After;* Tyler Boulware, *Deconstructing the Cherokee Nation: Town, Region, and Nation Among Eighteenth-Century Cherokees* (Gainesville: University Press of Florida, 2011); Cumfer, *Separate Peoples, One Land;* Smithers, *The Cherokee Diaspora;* and Kristofer Ray, *Cherokee Power: Imperial and Indigenous Geopolitics in the Trans-Appalachian West, 1670–1774* (Norman: University of Oklahoma Press, 2023).
35. McLoughlin, *Cherokees and Missionaries*, 30.
36. Quoted in Matthew C. Ward, *Making the Frontier Man: Violence, White Manhood, and Authority in the Early Western Backcountry* (University of Pittsburgh Press, 2023), 7.
37. McLoughlin, *Cherokee Renascence in the New Republic*, 3–6; see also Gregory A. Waselkov, ed., *Native American Log Cabins in the Southeast* (Knoxville: University of Tennessee Press, 2019).
38. Crews and Starbuck, *Records of the Moravians Among the Cherokees*, 1:216.
39. Crews and Starbuck, *Records of the Moravians Among the Cherokees*, 1:262–263, 287–288; C. Daniel Crews and Richard W. Starbuck, eds., *Records of the Moravians Among the Cherokees*, vol. 2, *Beginnings of the Mission and Establishment of the School, 1802–1805* (Tahlequah, Okla.: Cherokee National Press, 2010), 428, 779.
40. Colin G. Calloway, *White People, Indians, and Highlanders: Tribal Peoples and Colonial Encounters in Scotland and America* (New York: Oxford University Press, 2008), especially chap. 6; McLoughlin, *Cherokee Renascence in the New Republic*, 43; Reginald Horsman, *Expansion and American Indian Policy, 1783–1812* (Lansing: Michigan State University Press, 1967).
41. "Thomas Dillon's Account (1796)," in Williams, *Early Travels in the Tennessee Country*, 360.
42. "Francis Baily's Tour (1797)," in Williams, *Early Travels in the Tennessee Country*, 429.
43. W. S. Lovely to Return J. Meigs, November 23, 1808, quoted in McLoughlin, *Cherokee Renascence in the New Republic*, 146. On Rogers running the ferry over the Clinch River, see Pound, *Benjamin Hawkins*, 127–129, and *The Collected Works of Benjamin Hawkins, 1796–1810*, ed. Thomas Foster (Tuscaloosa: University of Alabama Press, 2003), 161.
44. Hawkins, quoted in Wilma A. Dunaway, *Women, Work, and Family in the Antebellum Mountain South* (Cambridge University Press, 2008), 69. The Trade and Intercourse Act of 1796 stipulated: "No . . . person, shall be permitted to reside at any of the towns, or hunting-camps, of any of the Indian tribes as a trader, without a license under the hand and seal

of the superintendent of the department, or of such other person as the President of the United States shall authorize to grant licenses." See James McHenry to George Washington, July 12, 1796, in David R. Hoth and William M. Ferraro, eds., *The Papers of George Washington*, vol. 20, *1 April–21 September 1796* (Charlottesville: University of Virginia Press, 2019), 426.

45. Much later, in the nineteenth century, one author intimated that the Harps had extensive ties to Cherokee country. Although his account is fanciful and sensationalistic—primarily aimed at explaining the brothers as "savage"—it may be rooted in some distant truths about their proximity to Cherokee life. See Smith, *Legends of the War of Independence*, especially 319–323.
46. David Andrew Nichols, *Engines of Diplomacy: Indian Trading Factories and the Negotiation of American Empire* (Chapel Hill: University of North Carolina Press, 2016) (quotes on p. 1).
47. James McHenry to John Sevier, June 20, 1796, accessed at Papers of the War Department 1784–1800, https://wardepartmentpapers.org/s/home/item/54008.
48. George Washington to Timothy Pickering, July 1, 1796, in Hoth and Ferraro, *The Papers of George Washington*, vol. 20, 1 April–21 September 1796, 349.
49. Reeve Huston, "Land Conflict and Land Policy in the United States, 1785–1841," in *The World of the Revolutionary American Republic: Land, Labor, and the Conflict for a Continent*, ed. Andrew Shankman (New York: Routledge, 2014), 324–325. For other instances of the federal government removing illegal settlers from Indian land, see, for example, Michael D. Green, *The Politics of Indian Removal: Creek Government and Society in Crisis* (Lincoln: University of Nebraska Press, 1982), 29–36, and Claudio Saunt, *A New Order of Things: Property, Power, and the Transformation of the Creek Indians, 1733–1816* (Cambridge University Press, 1999), 67–110.
50. James McHenry to George Washington, February 25, 1797, in Adrina Garbooshian-Huggins, ed., *The Papers of George Washington*, vol. 21, *22 September 1796–3 March 1797* (Charlottesville: University of Virginia Press, 2020), 770, fn. 5 (five hundred families, "daily increasing").
51. Dunaway, *Women, Work, and Family*, 66.
52. Prucha, *American Indian Policy in the Formative Years*, 145.
53. James McHenry to John Sevier, June 20, 1796.
54. James McHenry to John Sevier, June 20, 1796.
55. See especially Colin G. Calloway, *The Victory with No Name: The Native American Defeat of the First American Army* (New York: Oxford University Press, 2015); and Calloway, *The Indian World of George Washington: The First President, the First Americans, and the Birth of the Nation* (New York: Oxford University Press, 2018), especially 378–396 (colonel quote on pp. 391–392).
56. James H. Merrell, "Declarations of Independence: Indian-White Relations in the New Nation," in *The American Revolution: Its Character and Limits*, ed. Jack P. Greene (New York University Press, 1987), 201.
57. On this shift, see especially Merrell, "Declarations of Independence,"

197–223; also Reginald Horsman, "The Indian Policy of an 'Empire for Liberty,'" in *Native Americans and the Early Republic*, eds. Frederick E. Hoxie, Ronald Hoffman, and Peter J. Albert (Charlottesville: University of Virginia Press, 1999), 37–61; and for an expansive view of policy toward Native peoples as it evolved in the early nation, Horsman, *Expansion and American Indian Policy*.

58. Horsman, *Expansion and American Indian Policy*, 59–63.
59. Masterson, *William Blount*, 298–323 (quote on p. 313).
60. Not all of these people were squatters. Some apparently had legal claims from North Carolina that dated to the early 1780s when the state had opened a land office to get rid of its war debt. Many "citizens of the State, holding certificates for services performed, or supplies furnished, during the war, when they saw no prospect of being paid any other way . . . made entries of land on the Western waters." Some moved onto their land. Others held on to their warrants, waiting for a peaceful time to survey. But in 1791, in a treaty with the Cherokees, the United States had, in essence, returned the land to the Indians. Thousands of settlers were left, marooned, inside Cherokee boundaries. See *American State Papers: Documents, Legislative and Executive, of the Congress of the United States: Indian Affairs* (Washington: Gales and Seaton, 1832), 623–626.
61. Pound, *Benjamin Hawkins*, 118–137.
62. Pound, *Benjamin Hawkins*, 123 ("No indulgence"), 125 ("holy pack," "brutes," liar).
63. Benjamin Hawkins to Eliza Trist, November 25, 1797, in *The Collected Works of Benjamin Hawkins*, 254. Emphasis mine.
64. Brown, *Old Frontiers*, 197.
65. Brown, *Old Frontiers*, 447.
66. My thinking and description here are informed heavily by the discussion of the Cherokees' relationship to the federal government in Cumfer, *Separate Peoples, One Land*, 78–84, which is also (on p. 82) where the quote about Washington can be found.
67. "To John Adams from James McHenry, 8 August 1797," *Founders Online*, National Archives, https://founders.archives.gov/documents/Adams/99-02-02-2074. Under the Trade and Intercourse Act passed in May 1796, the president was authorized to remove illegal settlers—using "military force"—from Indian lands. See "An Act to Regulate Trade and Intercourse with the Indian Tribes, and to Preserve Peace on the Frontiers," sec. 5, p. 470, and Prucha, *American Indian Policy in the Formative Years*, 145.
68. Quoted in J.G.M. Ramsey, *The Annals of Tennessee to the End of the Eighteenth Century* (Philadelphia: Lippincott, Grambo, 1853), 679.
69. Thomas Butler to Samuel Hodgdon, February 18, 1798, accessed at Papers of the War Department 1784–1800, https://wardepartmentpapers.org/s/home/item/61227.
70. Willie Blount to John Gray Blount, November 7, 1797, in *The John Gray Blount Papers*, 3:176.

71. James McHenry to John Sevier, April 20, 1797, accessed at Papers of the War Department 1784–1800, https://wardepartmentpapers.org/s/home/item/57256.
72. Masterson, *William Blount*, 329.
73. "Francis Baily's Tour (1797)," in Williams, *Early Travels in the Tennessee Country*, 429–430; *American State Papers*, 628.
74. Quoted in Ramsey, *The Annals of Tennessee*, 680.
75. Inez E. Burns, *History of Blount County Tennessee: From War Trail to Landing Strip, 1795–1955* (Nashville, 1957), 35–36 (2,500 to 3,000 people).
76. John Sevier to Andrew Jackson, November 19, 1797, in *The Papers of Andrew Jackson*, 154.
77. "Francis Baily's Tour (1797)," in Williams, *Early Travels in the Tennessee Country*, 429–430.
78. "The Journal of John Sevier," October 29, 1797, https://penelope.uchicago.edu/Thayer/E/Gazetteer/Places/America/United_States/Tennessee/_Texts/THM/5/3/Sevier_Journal/1797*.html.
79. Several testaments prove that John Rice lived on the waters of the Tennessee River. The location where he was living can be further pinpointed by looking at a petition to the Tennessee General Assembly that he signed with neighbors in 1799: "39-2-1799 Residents living in Knox Co. below the mouth of Turkey Creek or north of Clinch petition that Knox County may be divided and that a new county be formed so as to contain land lying between the Holston and Clinch Rivers above South West Point and part of the land lying north of Clinch." See "Petition to the General Assembly of Tennessee for the Division of Knox County," July 15, 1799, in Mable Harvey Thornton, *Pioneers of Roane County, Tennessee, 1801–1830* (Rockwood, Tenn., 1965), xiv–xvi.
80. John Rice's name, along with Wiley's, appears on one of the 1798 passports identifying the expelled settlers. See "Pass port to enter the Cherokee Nation," for Willie Harp, Lewis Brimm, John Rice, John Preston, and James Gallaway, April 23, 1798, Governor John Sevier Papers, Box 5, Folder 4, TSLA. On the passports and their role in the crisis, see Burns, *History of Blount County Tennessee*, 35–36, 290.
81. On marriage portions in the backcountry, see Fischer, *Albion's Seed*, 673–674.
82. Nathaniel J. Sheidley, "Unruly Men: Indians, Settlers, and the Ethos of Frontier Patriarchy in the Upper Tennessee Watershed, 1763–1815" (PhD diss., Princeton University, 1999), 91–92.
83. Sheidley, "Unruly Men," 91–92; David Crockett, *Narrative of the Life of David Crockett, of the State of Tennessee* (Philadelphia: E. L. Carey and A. Hart, 1834), 67.
84. Credit to Jessica Lepler, who said it to me in July 2023, for this insight.
85. "Copy of a letter from Judge Campbell to the members of Congress from the state of Tennessee, dated January 16, 1798," *Knoxville Gazette*, February 2, 1798.

86. "Francis Baily's Tour (1797)," in Williams, *Early Travels in the Tennessee Country*, 429.
87. Brown, *Old Frontiers*, 187.
88. Remini, *Andrew Jackson and the Course of American Empire*, 117–124.
89. Brown, *Old Frontiers*, 198; Governor Martin to Colonel John Sevier, February 11, 1784, in Walter Clark, ed., *The State Records of North Carolina*, vol. 17, *1781–'85* (Goldsboro, N.C.: Nash Brothers, 1899), 15; "A Talk Delivered by the Old Tassel," in Clark, 175.
90. John Sevier to the inhabitants settled on the Indian lands, August 20, 1797, Governor John Sevier Papers, Box 1, Folder 4, TSLA.
91. "Pass port to enter the Cherokee Nation," for Willie Harp, Lewis Brimm, John Rice, John Preston, and James Gallaway, April 23, 1798, Governor John Sevier Papers, Box 4, Folder 5, TSLA.
92. "Francis Baily's Tour (1797)," in Williams, *Early Travels in the Tennessee Country*, 428.
93. Aron, *How the West Was Lost*, 102–103.
94. The previous governor had occasionally granted passports for the retrieval of horses from inside Cherokee Nation; see William G. McLoughlin, "Cherokee Anomie, 1794–1809: New Roles for Red Men, Red Women, and Black Slaves," in *Uprooted Americans*, 154.
95. Thornton, *Pioneers of Roane County, Tennessee, 1801–1830*, xvi.
96. There is no proof, but the timing is suggestive: Wiley bought his land in the summer of 1797, just before federal troops were about to arrive. He proved the deed in open court as the deadline to remove was passing.
97. Lt. Col. Thomas Butler to Capt. William Preston, April 25, 1798, Preston Family Papers: Joyes Collection (1780–1956), Box 1, Folder 7, Filson Historical Society, Louisville, Ky.
98. "Lexington, April 18, 1798," *Kentucky Gazette*, April 18, 1798.
99. "Knoxville, July 17," *Kentucky Gazette*, August 8, 1798.
100. "The Harpes—from Col. Sevier," Draper Manuscripts, WHS, 30S, 306.
101. Hall, *Letters from the West*, 271–272.
102. "The Harpes—from Col. Sevier," 306.

3: The Quarter Race

1. Hermann Bokum, *The Tennessee Hand-Book and Immigrant's Guide* (Philadelphia: J. B. Lippincott, 1868), 8–9.
2. McLoughlin, *Cherokee Renascence in the New Republic*, 55; Crews and Starbuck, *Records of the Moravians Among the Cherokees*, 1:116. For wider views of Native peoples' relationship to horses in this era, see also Tyler Boulware, "'Skillful Jockies' and 'Good Sadlers': Native Americans and Horses in the Southeastern Borderlands," in *Borderland Narratives: Negotiation and Accommodation in North America's Contested Spaces, 1500–1850*, eds. Andrew K. Frank and A. Glenn Crothers (Gainesville: University Press of Florida, 2017),

68–95, and James Taylor Carson, "Horses and the Economy and Culture of the Choctaw Indians, 1690–1840," *Ethnohistory* 42, no. 3 (1995): 495–513.

3. David Henley to James McHenry, June 5, 1799, accessed at Papers of the War Department, 1784–1800, https://wardepartmentpapers.org/s/home/item/68475.
4. David Henley to James McHenry, June 5, 1799.
5. David Henley to Charles Hicks, May 29, 1799, accessed at Papers of the War Department, 1784–1800, https://wardepartmentpapers.org/s/home/item/68278.
6. Return J. Meigs to Henry Dearborn, December 19, 1807, quoted in McLoughlin, *Cherokee Renascence in the New Republic*, 55–56.
7. One man who died in 1792 had almost no earthly possessions—only a bed, a few pots, a plow, and a shaving knife. But he nonetheless had "six head of horses, eighteen head of black cattle, seven head of sheep, [and] thirteen head of hogs." Strapped for cash, even the richest Tennessee men—like Stockley Donelson, Andrew Jackson's wild brother-in-law, a greedy hoarder of (mostly fraudulent) speculative land claims—could be found paying "in good horses." Knox County Book of Record, 83. Calvin M. McClung Historical Collection, Knox County Public Library.
8. Return J. Meigs to Henry Dearborn, December 19, 1807, 55–56.
9. "The Harpes—& Their Murders," Rutledge, Tenn., August 31, 1844, Draper Manuscripts, WHS, 32S, 250 ("carried the mail"); *American State Papers: Documents, Legislative and Executive, of the Congress of the United States: Selected and edited under the authority of Congress: Finance* (Washington: Gales and Seaton, 1832), 1:542 (Teele rides express); August 1, 1797, entry in Indian Department Expense Book, Knoxville, 1797–98, Microfilm 83, TSLA (Teele carries message).
10. Breazeale, *Life as It Is*, 138.
11. Breazeale, *Life as It Is*, 137.
12. *The Virginia & North Carolina Almanack and Annual Register for the Year 1800* (Petersburg, Va.: George Douglas, 1799), 28.
13. *The Kentucky Almanac, for the Year of Our Lord 1798*.
14. George Morgan Chinn, *Kentucky Settlement and Statehood 1750–1800* (Frankfort: Kentucky Historical Society, 1975), 342; for a more detailed description of hog slaughtering, see John B. Rehder, *Appalachian Folkways* (Baltimore: Johns Hopkins University Press, 2004), 214–216.
15. On smokehouses, see Rehder, *Appalachian Folkways*, 129–130.
16. Journal of Thomas Underwood, Draper Manuscripts, WHS, 16U, 54–55.
17. John A. Chapman, *History of Edgefield County from the Earliest Settlements to 1897* (Newberry, S.C.: Elbert H. Aull, 1897), 158–159.
18. Quoted in Gordon S. Wood, *The Radicalism of the American Revolution* (New York: Vintage, 1991), 308.
19. A copy of the note survives in the KCA. See Joseph Carnes v. Micajah Harpe case file (1797), docket no. 1069/1106, Knox County Court of Pleas and Quarter Sessions Files, Box 2, KCA. Promissory notes were like

IOUs—paper promises to deliver borrowed dollars or other goods at some future date. They passed like currency in the specie-starved counties of the early nation. To be obligated to pay out the debt of a promissory note within two weeks was unusual. More typically, they came due within three months to a year. This one may have represented the renewal of an old debt, money that had previously been borrowed from Carnes or from someone else who had signed over the debt to Carnes. "In many cases, sympathetic creditors would renew the notes they were holding at the end of the term for another three to twelve months, allowing debtors another chance to raise the money to pay the note," explains Walter Johnson in *River of Dark Dreams: Slavery and Empire in the Cotton Kingdom* (Cambridge: Harvard University Press, 2013), 44–45. Perhaps Carnes was less sympathetic in December 1797 or more economically pressed than he or an original creditor had once been. On promissory notes, also see Bruce H. Mann, *Republic of Debtors: Bankruptcy in the Age of American Independence* (Cambridge: Harvard University Press, 2002), 11–14.

20. Thomas Jefferson to Nicholas Lewis, December 19, 1786, in Julian P. Boyd et al., eds., *TPTJ*, vol. 10, *22 June to 31 December 1786* (Princeton University Press, 1954), 640. On Jefferson and debt (and for this quote), see Herbert E. Sloan, *Principle and Interest: Thomas Jefferson and the Problem of Debt* (New York: Oxford University Press, 1995), especially 13–49.
21. On debt in the eighteenth century and early republic, see especially Mann, *Republic of Debtors*. Also see Peter J. Coleman, *Debtors and Creditors in America: Insolvency, Imprisonment for Debt, and Bankruptcy, 1607–1900* (Madison: State Historical Society of Wisconsin, 1974); Tom Cutterham, " 'A Very Promising Appearance': Credit, Honor, and Deception in the Emerging Market for American Debt, 1784–92," *William and Mary Quarterly* 75, no. 4 (2018): 623–650; Jennifer J. Baker, *Securing the Commonwealth: Debt, Speculation, and Writing in the Making of Early America* (Baltimore: Johns Hopkins University Press, 2005); and Robert E. Wright, *One Nation Under Debt: Hamilton, Jefferson, and the History of What We Owe* (New York: McGraw-Hill, 2008).
22. See *The John Gray Blount Papers*, 3:xiii–xvi, for the Blount brothers' experience. The Blounts speculated in tens of thousands of acres of Tennessee land, but they were forever cash-strapped and nearly ruined by the economic upheavals of the late 1790s.
23. Mann, *Republic of Debtors*, especially 4.
24. The literature on the transition to capitalism and capitalistic behavior in the Revolutionary era is extremely vast. But I have benefited from reading studies that describe the shift in rural places like East Tennessee in concert with those that paint with broader brushstrokes the evolution in Americans' economic ideals and thinking in this period. See, for instance, Christopher Clark, *The Roots of Rural Capitalism: Western Massachusetts, 1780–1860* (Ithaca: Cornell University Press, 1990); Winifred Barr Rothenberg, *From Market-Places to a Market Economy: The Transformation of Rural Mas-*

sachusetts, 1750–1850 (University of Chicago Press, 1992); Joyce Appleby, *The Relentless Revolution: A History of Capitalism* (New York: W. W. Norton, 2010); Emma Hart, *Trading Spaces: The Colonial Marketplace and the Foundations of American Capitalism* (University of Chicago Press, 2019); James A. Henretta, *The Origins of American Capitalism: Collected Essays* (Boston: Northeastern University Press, 1991); Allan Kulikoff, *The Agrarian Origins of American Capitalism* (Charlottesville: University of Virginia Press, 1992); John Lauritz Larson, *The Market Revolution in America: Liberty, Ambition, and the Eclipse of the Common Good* (New York: Cambridge University Press, 2010); Jonathan Levy, *Freaks of Fortune: The Emerging World of Capitalism and Risk in America* (Cambridge: Harvard University Press, 2012); Charles Sellers, *The Market Revolution: Jacksonian America, 1815–1846* (New York: Oxford University Press, 1991); Melvyn Stokes and Stephen Conway, eds., *The Market Revolution in America: Social, Political, and Religious Expressions, 1800–1880* (Charlottesville: University of Virginia Press, 1996); and Gordon S. Wood, "The Enemy Is Us: Democratic Capitalism in the Early Republic," *Journal of the Early Republic* 16, no. 2 (1996): 293–308.

25. Richard S. Chew, "Certain Victims of an International Contagion: The Panic of 1797 and the Hard Times of the Late 1790s in Baltimore," *Journal of the Early Republic* 25, no. 4 (2005): 565–613 (quote on p. 567).
26. Thomas Paine to Thomas Jefferson, April 1, 1797, in Barbara B. Oberg et al., eds., *TPTJ*, vol. 29, *1 March 1796 to 31 December 1797* (Princeton University Press, 2002), 340–341.
27. Brown, *The Presidency of John Adams*, 22.
28. Mann, *Republic of Debtors*, 19, 28–29, 201, and passim. On Morris, see also Ryan K. Smith, *Robert Morris's Folly: The Architectural and Financial Failures of an American Founder* (New Haven: Yale University Press, 2014).
29. Mann, *Republic of Debtors*, 192–193.
30. On the damage radiating outward from speculators' failures, see Mann, *Republic of Debtors*, 191–193. For the impact of the credit contraction on wheat markets and other mercantile businesses, see Chew, "Certain Victims of an International Contagion," 582–586. Also see *The John Gray Blount Papers*, 3:xiii–xvi, for the Blount brothers' travails.
31. William Tyrell v. Joseph Carnes case file (1797), docket no. 692/678, Knox County Court of Pleas and Quarter Sessions Files, Box 1C, KCA; Abraham Swaggerty v. Joseph Carnes case file (1797), docket no. 615/547, Knox County Court of Pleas and Quarter Sessions Files, Box 1C, KCA; John Chisolm v. Joseph Carnes case file (1798), docket no. 712/644, Knox County Court of Pleas and Quarter Sessions Files, Box 1C, KCA.
32. In early 1798, Carnes himself promised to pay another man $325, an obligation he apparently ducked. It was later complained that he "hath removed or is about to remove himself" from Knox County and "absconds or conceals himself [so] that the Ordinary process of law cannot be served upon him." See Benjamin White v. Joseph Kearns case files (1798), docket

nos. 781/780 and 782/781, Box 1C, and 908/946, Box 1D, Knox County Court of Pleas and Quarter Sessions Files, KCA. For the Lyons Creek sales, see JC to John Cameron, October 31, 1797, in Knox County Deeds, Book C2 (vol. 1), 158, and JC to Martha McMully et al., October 17, 1797, in Knox County Deeds, Book F (vol. 1), 285.

33. Joseph Carnes v. Micajah Harp case file (1799), docket no. 985/869, Knox County Court of Pleas and Quarter Sessions Files, Box 1D, KCA.
34. Willard M. Oliver, *The Birth of the FBI: Teddy Roosevelt, the Secret Service, and the Fight over America's Premier Law Enforcement Agency* (Lanham, Md.: Rowman & Littlefield, 2019), 15.
35. Mann, *Republic of Debtors,* 24–30.
36. On the history of debtors' prisons, see, for example, Coleman, *Debtors and Creditors in America;* Robert A. Feer, "Imprisonment for Debt in Massachusetts before 1800," *Mississippi Valley Historical Review* 48, no. 2 (1961): 252–269; Mann, *Republic of Debtors,* chap. 3; Alexander Wakelam, *Credit and Debt in Eighteenth-Century England: An Economic History of Debtors' Prisons* (New York: Routledge, 2021).
37. *Narrative of the Life, and Dying Speech, of John Ryer* (Danbury, Conn., 1793), 6–7 and passim.
38. *The Last Speech and Confession of John Ryer* (1793).
39. Young, *Westward into Kentucky,* 146 ("Daring looking"); Major William Stewart recollections, 188 ("sunken"); "The Harpes (from James Givens)," 137 ("vacant look").
40. George Herridon and Mrs. Herridon recollections, relaying a description from a "Mrs. Burnett," 188.
41. Breazeale, *Life as It Is,* 137.
42. "The Journal of John Sevier," June 1798, https://penelope.uchicago.edu/Thayer/E/Gazetteer/Places/America/United_States/Tennessee/_Texts/THM/5/3/Sevier_Journal/1798*.html (June rains).
43. Joseph Carnes v. Micajah Harp case file (1799).
44. Quote is from Philip Vickers Fithian, *Journal and Letters of Philip Vickers Fithian, 1773–1774: A Plantation Tutor of the Old Dominion,* ed. Hunter Dickinson Farish (Colonial Williamsburg, 1943), 240–241.
45. Janson, *The Stranger in America,* 301–303; Weld, *Travels Through the States of North America,* 1:192; Gorn, "'Gouge and Bite, Pull Hair and Scratch,'" 18–43.
46. William B. Allen, *A History of Kentucky, Embracing Gleanings, Reminiscences, Antiquities, Natural Curiosities, Statistics, and Biographical Sketches* (Louisville: Bradley & Gilbert, 1872), 393–394.
47. Margaret Burr DesChamps, "Early Days in the Cumberland Country," *Tennessee Historical Quarterly* 6, no. 3 (1947): 227.
48. These counts are for the years 1793 through 1804 in Hamilton District Superior Court. See vol. 3 of the Superior Court Hamilton District Minute Book, KCA.

49. Quote is from Edward L. Ayers, *Vengeance and Justice: Crime and Punishment in the 19th Century American South* (New York: Oxford University Press, 1984), 22.
50. I am wading here into a long-standing debate over the roots of violence in early America and the Old Southwest particularly. For some sense of the contours of this debate, see Bruce E. Stewart, ed., *Blood in the Hills: A History of Violence in Appalachia* (Lexington: University Press of Kentucky, 2012); Randolph Roth, *American Homicide* (Cambridge: Harvard University Press, 2009); Richard Slotkin, *Regeneration Through Violence: The Mythology of the American Frontier, 1600–1860* (Middletown, Conn.: Wesleyan University Press, 1973); Patrick Griffin et al., eds., *Between Sovereignty and Anarchy: The Politics of Violence in the American Revolutionary Era* (Charlottesville: University of Virginia Press, 2015); Michael A. Bellesiles, ed., *Lethal Imagination: Violence and Brutality in American History* (New York University Press, 1999); Richard Maxwell Brown, *No Duty to Retreat: Violence and Values in American History and Society* (Norman: University of Oklahoma Press, 1991); David T. Courtwright, *Violent Land: Single Men and Social Disorder from the Frontier to the Inner City* (Cambridge: Harvard University Press, 1996); and Christine Daniels and Michael V. Kennedy, *Over the Threshold: Intimate Violence in Early America* (New York: Routledge, 1999). One of the very few writers to link the precariousness of the early West to its violence is Matthew C. Ward in *Making the Frontier Man.*
51. On the creation of the mythology of violent Appalachia, see Allen W. Batteau, *The Invention of Appalachia* (Tucson: University of Arizona Press, 1990); Anthony Harkins, *Hillbilly: A Cultural History of an American Icon* (New York: Oxford University Press, 2004); David C. Hsiung, *Two Worlds in the Tennessee Mountains: Exploring the Origins of Appalachian Stereotypes* (Lexington: University Press of Kentucky, 1997); Bruce E. Stewart, " 'These Big-Boned, Semi-Barbarian People': Moonshining and the Myth of Violent Appalachia, 1870–1900," in Stewart, *Blood in the Hills*, 180–206; and Altina L. Waller, "Feuding in Appalachia: Evolution of a Cultural Stereotype," in *Appalachia in the Making: The Mountain South in the Nineteenth Century*, eds. Mary Beth Pudup et al. (Chapel Hill: University of North Carolina Press, 1995). Quotes ("hot-blooded," "high-tempered") are from John C. Campbell, *The Southern Highlander and His Homeland* (New York: Russell Sage Foundation, 1921), 118.
52. Edwin E. White, *Highland Heritage: The Southern Mountains and the Nation* (New York: Friendship Press, 1937), 83.
53. Horace Kephart, *Our Southern Highlanders* (New York: Outing, 1913), 151.
54. Historians now mostly discount these theories of peculiarity. Almost always when violence has afflicted the southern highlands, as historian Bruce E. Stewart writes, it has been "a reflection and result of deeper tensions within the fabric of all American society." For revisionist scholars pushing back on some of the stereotypes of violent Appalachia and rooting their analyses in more specific historical circumstances, see Dwight B.

Billings, Gurney Norman, and Katherine Ledford, eds., *Back Talk from Appalachia: Confronting Stereotypes* (Lexington: University Press of Kentucky, 2000); Stephen L. Fisher, ed., *Fighting Back in Appalachia: Traditions of Resistance and Change* (Philadelphia: Temple University Press, 1993); Stewart, *Blood in the Hills;* and Altina L. Waller, *Feud: Hatfields, McCoys, and Social Change in Appalachia, 1860–1900* (Chapel Hill: University of North Carolina Press, 1988). Quote is from Stewart, *Blood in the Hills,* ix.

55. On cabins as "an expression of the insecurity of life," see Daniel Blake Smith, " 'This Idea in Heaven': Image and Reality on the Kentucky Frontier," in Friend, *The Buzzel About Kentuck,* 92–93.
56. Lawrence M. Friedman, *Crime and Punishment in American History* (New York: Basic Books, 1993), 176.
57. Herding cultures, in fact, are especially likely to drift into honor culture and violence because theft and raiding tend to be endemic and men are always in peril of losing all of their wealth. See Richard E. Nisbett and Dov Cohen, *Culture of Honor: The Psychology of Violence in the South* (Boulder: Westview Press, 1996).
58. Micajah Harp v. Joseph Roberts case file (1798), docket no. 901/923, Knox County Court of Pleas and Quarter Sessions Files, Box 1D, KCA.
59. According to a tradition that circulated later, Micajah once complained that he "had once been put in jail in Knoxville, Tenn., upon suspicion of crime," when he was, in fact, innocent. Allegedly, he nursed that grudge for quite some time. That story may be a slightly garbled version of this episode: an unlawful arrest. See Collins, *Collins' Historical Sketches,* 2:351.
60. Mann, *Republic of Debtors,* 29. Christopher Clark notes, too, that rural people sometimes "contested the conduct of the debt process itself," including with false imprisonment charges. See Clark, *Roots of Rural Capitalism,* 125.
61. Micajah Harp v. Joseph Roberts case file (1798).
62. The interview, from an 1813 edition of the *Gallatin Examiner* (Tennessee), is reprinted in J.F.H. Claiborne, *Mississippi, as a Province, Territory, and State, with Biographical Notices of Eminent Citizens* (Jackson, Miss.: Power & Barksdale, 1880), 226–227; John L. Swaney's recollections can also be found in Josephus Guild, *Old Times in Tennessee, with Historical, Personal, and Political Scraps and Sketches* (Nashville: Tavel, Eastman & Howell, 1878), 99.
63. Alexis de Tocqueville, *Democracy in America,* vol. 1, 4th ed. (New York: J. & H. G. Langley, 1841), 461.
64. Alexis de Tocqueville and Phillips Bradley, *Democracy in America,* vol. 2 (New York: Vintage Books, 1945), 165.
65. Philip Alexander Bruce, *Social Life of Virginia in the Seventeenth Century,* 2nd ed. (Lynchburg, Va.: J. B. Bell, 1927), 199–215 (quote on p. 199). Racing spread early on to North Carolina, too—particularly in the Halifax district, very close to the Harp family hearth. John Hervey, *Racing in America: 1665–1865,* 2 vols. (New York: Scribner Press, 1944), 1:59 (fallow fields); 1:156 (Halifax district as "one of the strongholds of the quarter-horse").

66. Katherine C. Mooney, *Race Horse Men: How Slavery and Freedom Were Made at the Race Track* (Cambridge: Harvard University Press, 2014), 4.
67. On racing and racetracks, also see Gary A. O'Dell, "At the Starting Post: Racing Venues and the Origins of Thoroughbred Racing in Kentucky, 1783–1865," *Register of the Kentucky Historical Society* 116, no. 1 (2018): 29–78; Lara Otis, "Washington's Lost Racetracks: Horse Racing from the 1760s to the 1930s," *Washington History* 24, no. 2 (2012): 136–154; and Randy J. Sparks, "Gentleman's Sport: Horse Racing in Antebellum Charleston," *South Carolina Historical Magazine* 93, no. 1 (1992): 15–30. On the evolution of "sporting culture," including horse racing, in the colonial and early national periods, see Kenneth Cohen, *They Will Have Their Game: Sporting Culture and the Making of the Early American Republic* (Ithaca: Cornell University Press, 2017).
68. Hervey, *Racing in America*, 1:225–228; *Kentucky Gazette* advertisement, 1789, quoted in Hervey, 1:227.
69. Michael L. Cook, *Lincoln County, Kentucky, Records*, vol. 2 (Evansville, Ind.: Cook Publications, 1987), 36–37; John M. Findlay, *People of Chance: Gambling in American Society from Jamestown to Las Vegas* (New York: Oxford University Press, 1986), 37; and Laura D. S. Harrell, "Horse Racing in the Old Natchez District," *Journal of Mississippi History* 13, no. 3 (1951): 123–124.
70. Rhys Isaac, *The Transformation of Virginia, 1740–1790* (Chapel Hill: University of North Carolina Press, 1982), 99.
71. Findlay, *People of Chance*, 37.
72. Findlay, *People of Chance*, 37–43; Harrell, "Horse Racing in the Old Natchez District," 124.
73. Charles Cotton, *The Compleat Gamester* (London, 1674), 1.
74. Cotton, *The Compleat Gamester*, 19.
75. He probably raced the horse himself—that was customary. Swaney's account isn't clear, but that had been the custom since racing's origins in colonial Virginia. See O'Dell, "At the Starting Post," 29–32.
76. Guild, *Old Times in Tennessee*, 99. Claiborne, *Mississippi, as a Province, Territory, and State*, 227.
77. Daniel A. Cohen, *Pillars of Salt, Monuments of Grace: New England Crime Literature and the Origins of American Popular Culture, 1674–1860* (New York: Oxford University Press, 1993); David D. Hall, *Worlds of Wonder, Days of Judgment: Popular Religious Belief in Early New England* (New York: Knopf, 1989); Karen Halttunen, *Murder Most Foul: The Killer and the American Gothic Imagination* (Cambridge: Harvard University Press, 1998); Daniel E. Williams, " 'Behold a Tragic Scene Strangely Changed into a Theater of Mercy': The Structure and Significance of Criminal Conversion Narratives in Early New England," *American Quarterly* 38, no. 5 (1986): 827–847.
78. *A Brief Narrative of the Life and Confession of Barnett Davenport* (Hartford, Conn., 1780), 7.
79. *The Confession, &c. of Thomas Mount, Who Was Executed at Little-Rest, in the State of Rhode-Island* (New Haven, 1791), 17.

80. Breazeale, *Life as It Is*, 127–128 (caves), 138 ("They stole").
81. For one example of a horse thief's punishment, see *History of Tennessee from the Earliest Time to the Present* (Chicago and Nashville: Goodspeed, 1887), 816.
82. Thomas Ashe quoted in Katherine E. Ledford, " 'A Possession, or an Absence of Ears': The Shape of Violence in Travel Narratives About the Mountain South, 1779–1835," in Stewart, *Blood in the Hills*, 139.
83. The timing of this murder is difficult to pinpoint exactly. But both J.W.M. Breazeale, whose father was a deputy sheriff in Knox County, and John Swaney, who witnessed Wiley's lost bet, place it before the Harps left Tennessee. Swaney's account places it very soon after the race; Breazeale places it after the incident with Teele's horses. By deduction, it must have been in the late fall of 1798. See Breazeale, *Life as It Is*, 139; Guild, *Old Times in Tennessee*, 99.
84. "The Harpes—from Col. Sevier," 307.
85. Guild, *Old Times in Tennessee*, 99 ("robbed"); "The Harpes—from Col. Sevier," 307 ("taken into the woods"); Guild, *Old Times in Tennessee*, 99 (after the race).
86. Breazeale, *Life as It Is*, 139 ("ripped . . . open"); "The Harpes—from Col. Sevier," 307.

4: *No Want of Hells*

1. Interview with Gen. Thomas Love, Draper Manuscripts, WHS, 30S, 115.
2. David Irby deposition, January 4, 1799, transcription, in folder labeled "Pages 1 to 16 Stanford Notes," Otto Rothert Papers, unprocessed, Filson Historical Society, Louisville, Ky.; Rothert, *The Outlaws of Cave-in-Rock*, 73–74.
3. Craig Thompson Friend, *Kentucke's Frontiers* (Bloomington: Indiana University Press, 2010), 176–177, 216.
4. Malcolm J. Rohrbough, *Trans-Appalachian Frontier: People, Societies, and Institutions, 1775–1850*, 3rd ed. (Bloomington: Indiana University Press, 2008), 65 (set prices for taverns).
5. Quoted in Robert L. Kincaid, *The Wilderness Road* (Indianapolis: Bobbs-Merrill, 1947), 191.
6. On the Wilderness Road, see Henry Addington Bruce, *Daniel Boone and the Wilderness Road* (New York: Macmillan, 1910); Archer Butler Hulbert, *Boone's Wilderness Road* (Cleveland: A. H. Clark, 1903); Kincaid, *The Wilderness Road;* William Allen Pusey, *The Wilderness Road to Kentucky* (New York: George H. Doran, 1921); and Thomas Speed, *The Wilderness Road, a Description of the Routes of Travel by Which the Pioneers and Early Settlers First Came to Kentucky* (Louisville: J. P. Morton, 1886).
7. Quoted in Kincaid, *The Wilderness Road*, 202.
8. Rev. Jacob Young, *Autobiography of a Pioneer; Or, the Nativity, Experience, Travels, and Ministerial Labors of Rev. Jacob Young* (Cincinnati: L. Swormstedt & A. Poe, 1857), 109, 111–112.

9. Kincaid, *The Wilderness Road*, 203–204.
10. Quoted in Kincaid, *The Wilderness Road*, 202.
11. Garrison, "A Memorandum of M. Austin's Journey," 525.
12. Aron, *How the West Was Lost*, 84–85; also see John Mack Faragher, *Daniel Boone: The Life and Legend of an American Pioneer* (New York: Holt, 1992), especially 235–263.
13. Quoted in Friend, *Kentucke's Frontiers*, 163.
14. "The number of men who were able to become the fabled patriarchs of booster lore was vanishingly small," writes historian Honor Sachs. On the struggles of men in early Kentucky, see especially Sachs, *Home Rule: Households, Manhood, and National Expansion on the Eighteenth-Century Kentucky Frontier* (New Haven: Yale University Press, 2015), especially chaps. 2–3 (quote on p. 72), and Fredrika Johanna Teute, "Land, Liberty, and Labor in the Post-Revolutionary Era: Kentucky as the Promised Land" (PhD diss., Johns Hopkins University, 1988).
15. Harry Toulmin, *A Description of Kentucky, in North America* (London, 1792), 73 (black, vermillion soil, limestone); on the "southernization" of Kentucky, its development of a plantation economy, and the growth of slavery, see Friend, *Kentucke's Frontiers*, 214–229.
16. Friend, "Work & Be Rich," 125–151. By 1800, Friend notes, less than half of landholders owned even thirty acres. Less than half of households, in fact, owned any land at all. On the illusory nature of independent land-holding in Kentucky during these years, see also Stephen Aron, "Pioneers and Profiteers: Land Speculation and the Homestead Ethic in Frontier Kentucky," *Western Historical Quarterly* 23, no. 2 (1992): 179–198; Neal O. Hammon, "Settlers, Land Jobbers, and Outlyers: A Quantitative Analysis of Land Acquisition on the Kentucky Frontier," *Register of the Kentucky Historical Society* 84, no. 3 (1986): 241–262; Thomas D. Clark, *Agrarian Kentucky* (Lexington: University Press of Kentucky, 1977), 6–10; Patricia Watlington, *The Partisan Spirit: Kentucky Politics, 1779–1792* (New York: Atheneum, 1972), 11–34; Teute, "Land, Liberty, and Labor"; and Sachs, *Home Rule.* Quote is from Garrison, "A Memorandum of M. Austin's Journey," 526.
17. William Elsey Connelley and E. M. Coulter, *History of Kentucky*, 5 vols. (Chicago: American Historical Society, 1922), 1:399.
18. Lewis Collins, *Historical Sketches of Kentucky* (1847), 54.
19. John Breckinridge to James Monroe, August 12, 1798, Monroe Papers, New York Public Library.
20. James Morton Smith, "The Grass Roots Origins of the Kentucky Resolutions," *William and Mary Quarterly* 27, no. 2 (1970): 221–245.
21. Ethelbert Dudley Warfield, *The Kentucky Resolutions of 1798* (New York: G. P. Putnam's Sons, 1887), 41–42.
22. On the famed Kentucky Resolutions, see especially Douglas Bradburn, "A Clamor in the Public Mind: Opposition to the Alien and Sedition Acts," *William and Mary Quarterly* 65, no. 3 (2008): 565–600; Smith, "The Grass Roots Origins of the Kentucky Resolutions"; Warfield, *The Kentucky Reso-*

lutions; William J. Watkins, *Reclaiming the American Revolution: The Kentucky and Virginia Resolutions and Their Legacy* (New York: Palgrave Macmillan, 2004).

23. The word "nullification" does not appear in the text. Thomas Jefferson, who would later be revealed as the document's author, had originally written "a nullification of the act is a rightful remedy." John Breckinridge, who brought the Resolutions before the legislature, excised that. But the idea and spirit of nullification remains in the text. See Watkins, *Reclaiming the American Revolution,* 67–75. The full texts of the Kentucky Resolutions of 1798 and 1799, as well as Jefferson's draft, can be found in Watkins, 165–177.
24. *Palladium,* December 4, 1798, quoted in Stewart, *The Opposition Press of the Federalist Period,* 363–364.
25. Farris's payroll record appears in U.S. Compiled Service Records, Post-Revolutionary War Volunteer Soldiers, 1784–1811 [database online], Provo, Utah: Ancestry.com Operations, 2011. He appears frequently in the early Lincoln County court records. For his assault and battery cases and his fine for selling liquor without a license at the races, see Cook, *Lincoln County, Kentucky, Records,* 2:36, 38.
26. On early American taverns and public houses, see Kym S. Rice, *Early American Taverns: For the Entertainment of Friends and Strangers* (Chicago: Regnery Gateway, 1983); Sharon V. Salinger, *Taverns and Drinking in Early America* (Baltimore: Johns Hopkins University Press, 2002); and Peter Thompson, *Rum Punch and Revolution: Taverngoing and Public Life in Eighteenth-Century Philadelphia* (Philadelphia: University of Pennsylvania Press, 1998).
27. Thompson, *Rum Punch and Revolution,* 3.
28. Quoted in Rice, *Early American Taverns,* 88.
29. "Richmond, January 22," *Georgia Gazette,* February 14, 1799.
30. Hall, *Letters from the West,* 266–267.
31. Jane Farris deposition, Filson Historical Society; Rothert, *The Outlaws of Cave-in-Rock,* 75–76.
32. On the emergence of the confidence man as a specter in middle-class American minds, see Karen Halttunen, *Confidence Men and Painted Women: A Study of Middle-Class Culture in America, 1830–1870* (New Haven: Yale University Press, 1982) (quote on p. xv). Tricksters and prevaricators of various sorts had popped up in earlier times but not regularly. See, for instance, Steven C. Bullock, "A Mumper Among the Gentle: Tom Bell, Colonial Confidence Man," *William and Mary Quarterly* 55, no. 2 (1998): 231–258.
33. I owe this assessment to Peter Onuf, who said as much about the nineteenth century, generally, in conversation at the American Antiquarian Society in 2018.
34. A portrait of this blurry, deceptive, money-mad world, circa the 1830s, can be found in Joshua D. Rothman, *Flush Times and Fever Dreams: A Story of Capitalism and Slavery in the Age of Jackson* (Athens: University of Georgia Press, 2012).

35. See, for example, Draper, "A Sketch of the Harpes," 168 (preachers), 169 (accusing other men of their crimes).
36. Jane Farris deposition, Filson Historical Society; Rothert, *The Outlaws of Cave-in-Rock*, 75.
37. Jane Farris deposition, Filson Historical Society; Rothert, *The Outlaws of Cave-in-Rock*, 75; Interview with Gen. Thomas Love, Draper Manuscripts, WHS, 30S, 115.
38. Hall, *Letters from the West*, 267.
39. "Hartford, September 12. Murder and Robbery!" *Georgia Gazette*, October 13, 1796.
40. "From a Philadelphia Paper," *Weekly Museum* (New York), August 25, 1792.
41. "Rutland, June 14, 1806," *Rutland Herald* (Vermont), June 14, 1806; *Report of the Trial of Dominic Daley and James Halligan for the Murder of Marcus Lyon* (Northampton, Mass.: S. & E. Butler, 1806).
42. Instances of men committing murder in the early republic are legion. To find patterns among them, I tried to identify all of the white men executed for murder between about 1776 and 1810. I used several established databases and anthologies of legal executions in American history to find them. Then I combed newspapers, crime literature, trial records, local histories, scholarly works, and whatever else I could find to learn about the circumstances of each case. Obviously, I have missed some—those that did not come to trial or men who were acquitted, which is potentially a very substantial number. But I have collected dozens and dozens of examples, enough to see recurring patterns.
43. Randolph Roth found that homicide rates rose nearly everywhere in the Revolutionary era, though they began to fall in the North and the mountain South as the republic got on surer footing in the early nineteenth century. (They did not decline in the backcountry, he notes based on his research on Ohio and Georgia, until after the War of 1812.) They remained higher in the lower South. Personal communication with Roth, December 14, 2024. For his discussion of these trends, see Roth, *American Homicide*, 145–249.
44. Roth, *American Homicide*, especially "The Causes of Homicide Among Unrelated Adults" in the Introduction, 16–26.
45. Stephen Mix Mitchell, *A Narrative of the Life of William Beadle* (Hartford, Conn., 1783), 8–9. Scholarly treatments of the Beadle case are few, but see Christopher Grasso, "Deist Monster: On Religious Common Sense in the Wake of the American Revolution," *Journal of American History* 95, no. 1 (2008): 43–68; Halttunen, *Murder Most Foul*, 51–56, 128–139; and Steven Wilf, *Law's Imagined Republic: Popular Politics and Criminal Justice in Revolutionary America* (Cambridge University Press, 2010), 124–137.
46. *A Poem, Occasioned by the Most Shocking and Cruel Murder* (Boston, 1782).
47. John Marsh, *The Great Sin and Danger of Striving with God; A Sermon Preached at Wethersfield, December 13, 1782* (Hartford, Conn., 1783), 31–32.

48. See Wilf, *Law's Imagined Republic*, 126, 129; Mitchell, *A Narrative of the Life of William Beadle*, 6.
49. Wilf, *Law's Imagined Republic*, 131.
50. "Extracts from Mr. Beadles Letters," in *The Literary Diary of Ezra Stiles*, ed. Franklin Bowditch Dexter, 3 vols. (New York: Charles Scribner's Sons, 1901), 3:53 ("Continental Trash"); Mitchell, *A Narrative of the Life of William Beadle*, 6.
51. Mitchell, *A Narrative of the Life of William Beadle*, 7.
52. Mitchell, *A Narrative of the Life of William Beadle*, 7. Contemporaries understood this to be part of his motive. William Beadle chose murder and suicide, a Connecticut minister thought, "rather than live in a style below what he vainly imagined became a person of his consequence." Marsh, *The Great Sin and Danger*, 27.
53. These cases are not a comprehensive list of all murders by white men during these years. They are limited to the white men listed in the Espy database of legal executions in American history, supplemented by several other anthologies of executions: Daniel Allen Hearn, *Legal Executions in New Jersey: A Comprehensive Registry, 1691–1963* (Jefferson, N.C.: McFarland, 2005); Hearn, *Legal Executions in New York State: A Comprehensive Reference, 1639–1963* (Jefferson, N.C.: McFarland, 1997); Hearn, *Legal Executions in New England: A Comprehensive Reference, 1623–1960* (Jefferson, N.C.: McFarland, 2008); and Lewis L. Laska, *Legal Executions in Tennessee: A Comprehensive Registry, 1782–2009* (Jefferson, N.C.: McFarland, 2011). I have excluded entirely those listed in Espy about whom I could find no details at all regarding their murders or motives. The qualitative evidence in this chapter ranges far beyond these sixty-three cases to include many others who do not appear in Espy, since they were not tried, died by suicide, were acquitted, or for other reasons were not captured by anthologists. Espy can be found at "Executions in the U.S., 1608–2002: The Espy File," https://deathpenaltyinfo.org/executions/executions-overview/executions-in-the-u-s-1608-2002-the-espy-file.
54. The best exegesis of these new social ideals is Wood, *The Radicalism of the American Revolution*. But on changing understandings of citizenship, especially as centered on propertied independence, also see, for instance, Richard L. Bushman, *King and People in Provincial Massachusetts* (Chapel Hill: University of North Carolina Press, 1985); Greene, "Independence, Improvement, and Authority," 3–36; Drew R. McCoy, *The Elusive Republic: Political Economy in Jeffersonian America* (Chapel Hill: University of North Carolina Press, 1980), 48–75; and Alfred F. Young, *The Shoemaker and the Tea Party: Memory and the American Revolution* (Boston: Beacon Press, 1999). Iredell's quote can be found in Watson, *An Independent People*, 81.
55. Lefler and Newsome, *North Carolina: The History of a Southern State*, 106–107, 113.
56. Young, *The Shoemaker and the Tea Party*, 3–4.

57. Thomas Paine, *Common Sense* (1776; repr., New York: Penguin Books, 1982), 76.
58. Gordon S. Wood, *The American Revolution: A History* (New York: Modern Library, 2002), 99.
59. E. Anthony Rotundo, *American Manhood: Transformations in Masculinity from the Revolution to the Modern Era* (New York: Basic Books, 1993), 3. On masculinity and the shifting ideals of manhood in early America, see also Toby Ditz, "The New Men's History and the Peculiar Absence of Gendered Power: Some Remedies from Early American Gender History," *Gender and History* 16 (April 2004): 1–35; Thomas A. Foster, ed., *New Men: Manliness in Early America* (New York: New York University Press, 2011); Lorri Glover, *Southern Sons: Becoming Men in the New Nation* (Baltimore: Johns Hopkins University Press, 2007); Michael S. Kimmel, *Manhood in America: A Cultural History* (New York: Free Press, 1996); Dana D. Nelson, *National Manhood: Capitalist Citizenship and the Imagined Fraternity of White Men* (Durham: Duke University Press, 1998); Sachs, *Home Rule;* and Ward, *Making the Frontier Man.*
60. Larson, *The Market Revolution in America*, 8, 141, and passim. Scholarship on the emergence of capitalism in American history is extensive and unwieldy. But for introductions, see also Joyce Appleby, *Inheriting the Revolution: The First Generation of Americans* (Cambridge: Harvard University Press, 2000); Jackson Lears, *Something for Nothing: Luck in America* (New York: Viking, 2003); Levy, *Freaks of Fortune;* Scott A. Sandage, *Born Losers: A History of Failure in America* (Cambridge: Harvard University Press, 2005); and Wood, "The Enemy Is Us," 293–308.
61. Daniel Webster to Mr. Fuller, August 29, 1802, in Fletcher Webster, ed., *The Private Correspondence of Daniel Webster*, 2 vols. (Boston: Little, Brown, 1857), 1:121.
62. One exception, with regard to familicide only, is Daniel A. Cohen, "Homicidal Compulsion and the Conditions of Freedom: The Social and Psychological Origins of Familicide in America's Early Republic," *Journal of Social History* 28, no. 4 (1995): 725–764. Wood gestures at connections, very briefly, in *The Radicalism of the American Revolution*, 306–307. Roth connects the rising tides of American murder to falling faith in the social hierarchy; see *American Homicide*, 23–25.
63. "Elizabethtown, May 11," *Pennsylvania Mercury and Universal Advertiser*, May 14, 1791.
64. Hearn, *Legal Executions in New Jersey*, 62–63.
65. "Domestic," *Star* (Raleigh, N.C.), July 6, 1809.
66. Hearn, *Legal Executions in New Jersey*, 60.
67. *A Full and Particular Narrative of the Life, Character and Conduct of John Banks* (New York, 1807), 12–14.
68. *An Analysis or Outline, of the Life and Character of Josiah Burnham* (Hanover, N.H., 1806), 5–6.

69. *Narrative of the Life, Last Dying Speech and Confession of John Young* (New York, 1797), 7.
70. This kind of murder was all but unheard of in the colonial period—there are virtually no recorded instances of it until the early national period, which saw a number of cases. After 1850, instances of familicide appear to have fallen, though they have become more common again in modern times. For an analysis that links these family murders with societal change in the early republic, see Cohen, "Homicidal Compulsion." Cohen suggests that freedom, revolution, and the "expansion of individual autonomy in the early republic" came with "significant psychic cost" (727). He posits that economic instability, religious liberty, and geographic mobility were very socially destabilizing.
71. "American Intelligence. Baltimore, May 10," *Columbian Herald* (Charleston), June 10, 1785.
72. "Elizabeth-Town, December 5. Horrid Murder!," *Maryland Herald and Hager's-Town Weekly Advertiser*, December 5, 1799; "Baltimore, December 7. *A most unnatural murder*," *Virginia Argus*, December 13, 1799; "Domestic Intelligence," *Stewart's Kentucky Herald*, January 14, 1800.
73. "Horrible MURDER Near Clarksburg Vir.," *Federal Gazette* (Baltimore), November 18, 1805; *Murder—Horrible Murder!!* (Morgantown, 1805).
74. Quoted in Kate Manne, *Down Girl: The Logic of Misogyny* (New York: Oxford University Press, 2018), 125; see 121–128 for her discussion of family annihilators. See also Catharine Skipp, "Inside the Mind of Family Annihilators," *Newsweek*, February 10, 2010.
75. On Werner, see "Domestic Intelligence," *Stewart's Kentucky Herald*, January 14, 1800. A narrative of the Purrinton murders can be found in *Horrid Massacre!! Sketches of the Life of Captain James Purrinton* (Augusta, Maine, 1806) (quotes on pp. 3–4). The Purrinton murders are also covered in Laurel Thatcher Ulrich, *A Midwife's Tale: The Life of Martha Ballard, Based on Her Diary, 1785–1812* (New York: Knopf, 1991), chap. 9.
76. Steven F. Messner and Richard Rosenfeld, *Crime and the American Dream* (Belmont, Calif.: Wadsworth, 1994), 6.
77. For sociological and criminological theories connecting the American ethos with criminal and deviant behavior, see especially Robert K. Merton, "Social Structure and Anomie," *American Sociological Review* 3, no. 5 (1938): 672–682, and Messner and Rosenfeld, *Crime and the American Dream*. Merton notes: Closed channels to prosperity alone do not necessarily inspire criminal deviance or violence. "A high frequency of deviate behavior is not generated simply by 'lack of opportunity' . . . A comparatively rigidified class structure, a feudalistic or caste order, may limit such opportunities far beyond the point which obtains in our society today." It is the perception (and reality) of unavailable channels to success *coupled* with "unrelieved ambition" and expectation that is problematic (quote on p. 680).

78. "Extracts from Mr. Beadles Letters," 3:53.
79. *Palladium* clipping, January 2, 1799, Draper Manuscripts, WHS, 1Q, 33; Hall, *Letters from the West*, 267–268.
80. C. S. Morehead and Mason Brown, *A Digest of the Statute Laws of Kentucky*, 2 vols. (Frankfort, Ky., 1834), 1:462.
81. "To the Constable," August 1811, folder labeled "Inquests" in "Commonwealth Cases, 1808–1818," Western Kentucky University Special Collections.
82. Commonwealth v. Micajah Roberts, A1998–199, Lincoln County Circuit Court, Ordinary Case File No. 1134, Kentucky Department for Libraries and Archives, Frankfort, Ky. (hereafter cited as KDLA).
83. *Palladium* clipping, January 2, 1799, Draper Manuscripts, WHS, 1Q, 33; Hall, *Letters from the West*, 268.
84. "Lexington, January 8," *Stewart's Kentucky Herald*, January 8, 1799.
85. Bettie Cummings Cook, *Lincoln County, Kentucky, Records*, vol. 3 (Evansville, Ind.: Cook Publications, 1990), 209.
86. John Farris and David Irby depositions, January 4, 1799, transcriptions, in folder labeled "Pages 1 to 16 Stanford Notes," Otto Rothert Papers, unprocessed, Filson Historical Society, Louisville, Ky.; Rothert, *The Outlaws of Cave-in-Rock*, 74–75.
87. "Richmond, January 22," *Georgia Gazette*, February 14, 1799.
88. Joseph Ballenger deposition, January 4, 1799, transcription, in folder labeled "Pages 1 to 16 Stanford Notes," Otto Rothert Papers, unprocessed, Filson Historical Society, Louisville, Ky.; Rothert, *The Outlaws of Cave-in-Rock*, 73.
89. "Lexington, January 8," *Stewart's Kentucky Herald*, January 8, 1799.
90. Young, *Autobiography of a Pioneer*, 110 ("gentleman"); Collins, *Collins' Historical Sketches*, 2:351 ("Devil Jo"); Cook, *Lincoln County, Kentucky, Records*, vol. 1, 40 (marriage bond); Hattie M. Scott, "The Logan Family of Lincoln County, Kentucky," *Register of Kentucky State Historical Society*, 30, no. 91 (1932): 173–178.
91. May Wilson McBee, *The Natchez Court Records, 1767–1805: Abstracts of Early Records* (Ann Arbor: Edward Brothers, 1953), 79, 84–85, 147–148.
92. Toulmin, *A Description of Kentucky, in North America*, 73.
93. Joseph Ballenger deposition, Filson Historical Society; "The Harpes. (from James Givens)," Draper Manuscripts, WHS, 29S, 134.
94. Major William Stewart recollections, Draper Manuscripts, WHS, 30S, 191 (not dreaming of detection); also "The Harpes. (from James Givens)," Draper Manuscripts, WHS, 29S, 134 (eating at camp).
95. Joseph Ballenger deposition, Filson Historical Society; "Richmond, January 22," *Georgia Gazette*, February 14, 1799; Rothert, *The Outlaws of Cave-in-Rock*, 73.
96. Garrison, "A Memorandum of M. Austin's Journey," 526.
97. Sheriff's accounts reproduced in Rothert, *The Outlaws of Cave-in-Rock*, 76–77.

98. John L. Ballenger to Lyman Draper, Draper Manuscripts, WHS, 12C, doc. 46.
99. Rothert, *The Outlaws of Cave-in-Rock*, 72; Commonwealth v. Micajah Roberts, KDLA.
100. Jane Farris deposition, Filson Historical Society.
101. Rothert, *The Outlaws of Cave-in-Rock*, 76.
102. "The Harpes. (from James Givens)," Draper Manuscripts, WHS, 29S, 135.
103. A replica of this first jail now stands on the town green in Danville, Kentucky.
104. Rothert, *The Outlaws of Cave-in-Rock*, 77–78.
105. John Sevier to Robert Houston, April 7, 1797, Governor John Sevier Papers, Box 1, Folder 5, TSLA.
106. *Palladium* clipping, Draper Manuscripts, WHS, 1Q, 33–34. This may be the peddler named "Peyton" whose murder J.W.M. Breazeale attributed to the Harps later on. See Breazeale, *Life as It Is*, 139–140.
107. Rothert, *The Outlaws of Cave-in-Rock*, 79.
108. Rothert, *The Outlaws of Cave-in-Rock*, 78.

5: The Wickedness of the Heart

1. Biegler's expenses in Rothert, *The Outlaws of Cave-in-Rock*, 80.
2. Ulrich, *A Midwife's Tale*, 185. Also see Mary Beth Norton, *Liberty's Daughters: The Revolutionary Experience of American Women, 1750–1800* (Boston: Little, Brown, 1980), 78, and "Travail" in Laurel Thatcher Ulrich, *Good Wives: Image and Reality in the Lives of Women in Northern New England, 1650–1750* (New York: Vintage Books, 1982), 126–145. On childbirth in American history generally, see Richard W. Wertz and Dorothy C. Wertz, *Lying-In: A History of Childbirth in America* (New York: Free Press, 1977).
3. Ulrich, *A Midwife's Tale*, 188–193 (quote on p. 189).
4. Maj. William Stewart recollections, Draper Manuscripts, WHS, 30S, 190. This comment came from a sheriff who encountered Sally in 1799.
5. Hendrik Hartog, *Man and Wife in America: A History* (Cambridge: Harvard University Press, 2000), 122, 156.
6. "The Knoxville Girl," *A Treasury of Southern Folklore: Stories, Ballads, Traditions, and Folkways of the People of the South*, ed. B. A. Botkin (New York: Crown, 1949), 737.
7. Maj. William Stewart recollections, Draper Manuscripts, WHS, 30S, 188.
8. Breazeale, *Life as It Is*, 150.
9. Collins, *Collins' Historical Sketches*, 2:351.
10. Smith, *Legends of the War of Independence*, 323.
11. Smith, *Legends of the War of Independence*, 217.
12. Smith, *Legends of the War of Independence*, 179–180. The abduction of brides has some folk history among Scottish and backcountry people, though it was more symbolic and ritualized by the late eighteenth century. Smith's descriptions may hint at more ceremonial marriage practices of mock bridal abductions. See Fischer, *Albion's Seed*, 669–671.

13. On backcountry wedding customs, see Fischer, *Albion's Seed*, 669–675.
14. "The Knoxville Girl," 737.
15. Mary Florence Taney, *Kentucky Pioneer Women: Columbian Poems and Prose Sketches* (Cincinnati: Robert Clarke, 1893), 68.
16. "Sourwood Mountain," quoted in Rus Dowda, " 'He Took Her by Her Golden Curls and Throwed Her Round and Round': Appalachian Women in the 19th Century and Their Image in the Murder Ballads of the Time" (master's thesis, Berea College, 1978), 3.
17. Fischer, *Albion's Seed*, 676 (quote); Emma Bell Miles, *The Spirit of the Mountains* (New York: J. Pott, 1905), 21. Also see Dunaway, *Women, Work, and Family*, especially 142–143.
18. Fischer, *Albion's Seed*, 677.
19. Dowda, " 'He Took Her by Her Golden Curls,' " 4.
20. Fischer, *Albion's Seed*, 677.
21. Norton makes this claim based on loyalist wives' experiences in *Liberty's Daughters*, 5–6. Though, for a description of how it was possible to be "dependent . . . without being either servile or helpless" and how women sometimes acted as "deputy husbands," especially in their spouses' absence, see Ulrich, *Good Wives*, 36–50.
22. Hartog, *Man and Wife in America*, 100.
23. Blackstone, *Commentaries on the Laws of England*, 1:430.
24. Judith Sargent Murray, "On the Equality of the Sexes," *Massachusetts Magazine* (Boston, 1790), 134; Benjamin Rush, "Thoughts upon Female Education" (Boston, 1787), 19. On republican motherhood, see especially Linda K. Kerber, *Women of the Republic: Intellect and Ideology in Revolutionary America* (Chapel Hill: University of North Carolina Press, 1980).
25. See especially Nancy F. Cott, *The Bonds of Womanhood: 'Woman's Sphere' in New England, 1780–1835* (New Haven: Yale University Press, 1977); Nancy F. Cott, *Public Vows: A History of Marriage and the Nation* (Cambridge: Harvard University Press, 2000); and Susan E. Klepp, *Revolutionary Conceptions: Women, Fertility, and Family Limitation in America, 1760–1820* (Chapel Hill: University of North Carolina Press, 2009). In the backcountry, these trends were likely heavily curbed by a strong commitment to traditional gender roles. See Fischer, *Albion's Seed*, 677.
26. Lawrence B. Goodheart, Neil Hanks, and Elizabeth Johnson, " 'An Act for the Relief of Females': Divorce and the Changing Legal Status of Women in Tennessee, 1796–1860, Part I," *Tennessee Historical Quarterly* 44, no. 3 (1985): 318–339.
27. Hartog, *Man and Wife in America*, 156, 122.
28. "Cox, Margaret, Petition for Divorce," Greenbrier County, Va., December 3, 1823, Legislative Petition Digital Collection, Library of Virginia, Richmond, repr. in Connie Park Rice and Marie Tedesco, eds., *Women of the Mountain South: Identity, Work, and Activism* (Athens: Ohio University Press, 2015). Victoria E. Bynum finds that the North Carolina Supreme Court "routinely denied legal separations and divorces to women trapped

in abusive, degrading marriages." See Bynum, *Unruly Women: The Politics of Social and Sexual Control in the Old South* (Chapel Hill: University of North Carolina Press, 1992), 2.

29. As many scholars have shown, the early republic was a time of both hopeful tumult and retrenchment—even contraction—surrounding women's rights. Despite growing calls for women's rights and education, the fiery rhetoric of revolution did little to expand women's political and legal roles. Where doors opened, as Rosemarie Zagarri and others have shown, they often later closed. The literature on women and the Revolution is vast. But see, for introductions, Norton, *Liberty's Daughters;* Kerber, *Women of the Republic;* Zagarri, *Revolutionary Backlash: Women and Politics in the Early American Republic* (Philadelphia: University of Pennsylvania Press, 2007); Jill Lepore, *Book of Ages: The Life and Opinions of Jane Franklin* (New York: Knopf, 2013); Barbara B. Oberg, ed., *Women in the American Revolution: Gender, Politics, and the Domestic World* (Charlottesville: University of Virginia Press, 2019); Mary Beth Norton, *Founding Mothers and Fathers: Gendered Power and the Forming of American Society* (New York: Knopf, 1996); Carol Berkin, *Revolutionary Mothers: Women in the Struggle for America's Independence* (New York: Knopf, 2005); Klepp, *Revolutionary Conceptions;* Margaret A. Nash, *Women's Education in the United States, 1780–1840* (New York: Palgrave Macmillan, 2005); Lucia McMahon, *Mere Equals: The Paradox of Educated Women in the Early American Republic* (Ithaca: Cornell University Press, 2012); and Ulrich, *A Midwife's Tale.*
30. Quoted in Nash, *Women's Education in the United States,* 1.
31. For some sense of this problem and for attempts to understand Appalachian women's history, see, for example, Mary K. Anglin, "Lives on the Margin: Rediscovering the Women of Antebellum North Carolina," in Pudup et al., *Appalachia in the Making,* 185–209; June Langford Berkley, "Telling the Untold Stories," in *Beyond Hill and Hollow: Original Readings in Appalachian Women's Studies,* ed. Elizabeth S. D. Engelhardt (Athens: Ohio University Press, 2004), 232–250; and, especially, Barbara Ellen Smith, " 'Beyond the Mountains': The Paradox of Women's Place in Appalachian History," *NWSA Journal* 11, no. 3 (1999): 1–17.
32. Smith, " 'Beyond the Mountains,' " 3. Smith suggests looking past "orthodox sources of data and fields of action to locate women's history-making" and using oral history and "family legend," as well as mining "jokes, 'old wives' tales,' and fugitive actions," rather than "records of conventional history" (1, 9).
33. Miles, *The Spirit of the Mountains,* 30 ("The mother"); Dowda, " 'He Took Her by Her Golden Curls,' " 5 ("the ballads," "their feelings").
34. Dowda, " 'He Took Her by Her Golden Curls,' " 6.
35. Dowda, " 'He Took Her by Her Golden Curls,' " 10.
36. "The Knoxville Girl," 738.
37. *The Kentucky Almanac, for the Year of Our Lord 1799* (Lexington: J. Bradford, 1798).

38. The best study of the rituals and meanings of court day in this period, particularly for this region, is A. G. Roeber, "Authority, Law, and Custom: The Rituals of Court Day in Tidewater Virginia, 1720 to 1750," *William and Mary Quarterly* 37, no. 1 (1980): 29–52. Also see Robert M. Ireland, *The County Courts in Antebellum Kentucky* (Lexington: University Press of Kentucky, 1972). On Danville, Kentucky, specifically, see Calvin Morgan Fackler, *Early Days in Danville* (Louisville, 1941), 25–29.
39. On women at the courthouse and the experience of walking into an early American court as a woman, see Cornelia Hughes Dayton, *Women Before the Bar: Gender, Law, and Society in Connecticut, 1639–1789* (Chapel Hill: University of North Carolina Press, 1995), especially 16–17.
40. On the "archaic bidding" that the undersheriff or deputy called out to open court, see Roeber, "Authority, Law, and Custom," 35.
41. Commonwealth v. Micajah Roberts, KDLA.
42. Even in intimate or family homicides, the killer was almost always a man, the victim more often a woman. See Roth, *American Homicide,* 108–109.
43. The two principal datasets I used to identify these women are the Espy file of legal executions in American history and Hearn's printed anthologies of executions in various American states. For Espy, see "Executions in the U.S., 1608–2002: The Espy File," https://deathpenaltyinfo.org/executions/executions-overview/executions-in-the-u-s-1608-2002-the-espy-file.
44. Some of these deaths were deliberate and some resulted from cruel mistreatment, as in the case of Barbara Stillwell, who was hired to care for the three-year-old son of loyalist parents as they fled New York City when the British evacuated in 1783. Hearn, *Legal Executions in New York State,* 24; "New-York. February 5," *Independent Gazette; Or, the New York Journal Revisited,* February 5, 1784.
45. Hearn, *Legal Executions in New England,* 169; "Springfield, July 26," *Connecticut Courant,* August 1, 1785 (Hannah Pigen), and Hearn, *Legal Executions in New England,* 174; "Northampton, July 23," *Hampshire Gazette,* July 23, 1788 (Abiel Converse).
46. Hearn, *Legal Executions in New York State,* 29; Pomroy Jones, *Annals and Recollections of Oneida County* (Rome, N.Y., 1851), 42–43.
47. *A Genuine Sketch of the Trial of Mary Cole* (New Jersey, 1812), 4–5, 12.
48. With an accomplice, one woman murdered a Spanish seaman in South Carolina by stabbing him in the throat and chest with scissors. Another woman, Ann Connolly, was part of a "gang of thieves" who shot a merchant on Charleston's Meeting Street in 1788. Connolly was tried with eight associates, mostly men; she had given them powder and shot and "advis[ed] them to go out and rob." But these stories are anomalous and few. David V. Baker, *Women and Capital Punishment in the United States: An Analytical History* (Jefferson, N.C.: McFarland, 2016), 114; "Charleston, (S.C.), March 13," *New York Packet,* March 25, 1788; "Charleston, June 7, 1788," *City Gazette and Daily Advertiser* (Charleston, S.C.), June 7, 1788.

49. No one has looked closely at the stories of women executed in the early republic. But these findings fit broadly with what other scholars have contended across other periods of American history: Black women have been overrepresented both in the carceral system and among those whom the state punished by death. "Black women's overrepresentation in prison has a long history rooted in the tangled dynamics of race, gender, enslavement, and the law," write Kali N. Gross and Cheryl D. Hicks. In the sweeping study *Women and Capital Punishment in the United States*, Baker finds, similarly, that "poor and marginalized bonded servants and slaves typify most women executed historically." By his count, an astonishing 79 percent of female executions between the 1760s and the 1890s were of Black women. Baker points out that this pattern has endured into the present. "One of the most enduring features of capital justice in the United States," he writes, "is that the social attributes of women executed in more modern eras correspond closely to women executed in earlier periods in the history of American capital justice." See Baker, *Women and Capital Punishment*, 1, 41, and passim. For more discussion of the roots of this pattern, see Gross and Hicks, "Introduction—Gendering the Carceral State: African American Women, History, and the Criminal Justice System," *Journal of African American History* 100, no. 3 (2015): 359.
50. Frederick County (Va.) Coroners' Inquisitions, 1779–1927, Frederick County Court Records, Library of Virginia, Richmond, accessed August 22, 2019, https://ead.lib.virginia.edu/vivaxtf/view?docId=lva/vi03354.xml.
51. "Crimes and Casualties," *New Hampshire Observer*, March 21, 1825.
52. Baker, *Women and Capital Punishment*, 111.
53. *Sundry Letters and Petitions Addressed to His Excellency James Garrard, Esq. Governor of Kentucky; Relative to the Case of Henry Field* (1799), 11.
54. *Sundry Letters and Petitions*, 11.
55. Maj. William Stewart recollections, Draper Manuscripts, WHS, 30S, 187; Breazeale, *Life as It Is*, 137.
56. The sense that serious crimes often went unpunished was one of the reasons the state was revising its criminal law code even as the Harp women were being tried: Perhaps juries would convict more frequently if the punishments were more proportional to the crimes. See Robert M. Ireland, "Law and Disorder in Nineteenth-Century Kentucky," *Vanderbilt Law Review* 32, no. 1 (1979): 281–299, and Nancy J. King, "The Origins of Felony Jury Sentencing in the United States," *Chicago-Kent Law Review* 78, no. 3 (2003): 937–993.
57. Adolph Paul Gratiot, "Criminal Justice on the Kentucky Frontier" (PhD diss., University of Pennsylvania, 1952), 122.
58. A few years after prosecuting the Harp women, Blair helped to draft *A Review of the Criminal Law of the Commonwealth of Kentucky*. He wrote the section on murder.

59. Harry Innes to Thomas Jefferson, December 13, 1802, in Barbara B. Oberg et al., eds., *TPTJ*, vol. 39, *13 November 1802 to 3 March 1803* (Princeton University Press, 2012), 148.
60. Under the Kentucky constitution, they were guaranteed counsel. Gratiot, "Criminal Justice on the Kentucky Frontier," 232.
61. Gratiot, "Criminal Justice on the Kentucky Frontier," 108–109, 117–120.
62. John Bach McMaster, *A History of the People of the United States: From the Revolution to the Civil War*, 5 vols. (New York: D. Appleton, 1884), 1; quoted in Charles Warren, *A History of the American Bar* (Boston: Little, Brown, 1911), 216.
63. Gratiot, "Criminal Justice on the Kentucky Frontier," 123–124. This portrait of early Kentucky lawyering is informed heavily by the memoirs of Micah Taul, a lawyer and representative in early Kentucky. See "Memoirs of Micah Taul," *Register of Kentucky State Historical Society* 27, no. 79 (1929): 343–380 (quote on pp. 366–367). Also see "Memoirs of Micah Taul (Continued)," *Register of Kentucky State Historical Society* 27, no. 80 (1929): 494–517, and "Memoirs of Micah Taul (Concluded)," *Register of Kentucky State Historical Society* 27, no. 81 (1929): 601–627.
64. Jane Farris deposition, Filson Historical Society; Rothert, *The Outlaws of Cave-in-Rock*, 75.
65. Jane Farris, John Farris, David Irby, Thomas Welsh, and Joseph Ballenger depositions, January 4, 1799, transcriptions, in folder labeled "Pages 1 to 16 Stanford Notes," Otto Rothert Papers, unprocessed, Filson Historical Society, Louisville, Ky. Ballenger's deposition gives the detail about the pocket book with Langford's name in it.
66. "The Harpes (from James Givens)," 134.
67. Harry Toulmin and James Blair, *A Review of the Criminal Law of the Commonwealth of Kentucky*, 3 vols. (1804–1806), 1:4.
68. "Lincoln District Court Danville Order Book 1796–1800," 346, KDLA.
69. Roger Lane, *Murder in America: A History* (Columbus: Ohio State University Press, 1997), 26, 56, and passim.
70. Ann Jones, *Women Who Kill* (New York: Feminist Press, 2009), 120–122 (quote on p. 122).
71. Blackstone, *Commentaries on the Laws of England*, 4:21–29.
72. Blackstone, *Commentaries on the Laws of England*, 4:28.
73. "Execution," *Charleston Courier*, republished from the New York *National Advocate*, March 25, 1820.
74. Blackstone, *Commentaries on the Laws of England*, 4:28–29.
75. George Herridon and Mrs. Herridon recollections, Draper Manuscripts, WHS, 30S, 184.
76. Hall, *Letters from the West*, 280.
77. Dowda, "'He Took Her by Her Golden Curls,'" 7–8.
78. "Lincoln District Court Danville Order Book 1796–1800," 321, KDLA.
79. "Lincoln District Court Danville Order Book 1796–1800," 327, KDLA.
80. George Herridon and Mrs. Herridon recollections, 186.

81. "Lincoln District Court Danville Order Book 1796–1800," 328–329, KDLA.
82. "Lincoln District Court Danville Order Book 1796–1800," 329–331, KDLA.
83. "Lincoln District Court Danville Order Book 1796–1800," 330–331, KDLA.
84. George Herridon and Mrs. Herridon recollections, 185.
85. Milton Ready, "Forgotten Sisters: Mountain Women in the South," *Journal of the Appalachian Studies Association* 3 (1991): 63.
86. Ready, "Forgotten Sisters," 64.
87. "Lincoln District Court Danville Order Book 1796–1800," 330–331, KDLA.
88. George Herridon and Mrs. Herridon recollections, 183.
89. Blackstone, *Commentaries on the Laws of England,* 4:190, 199–200.
90. "Domestic. Harrisburg, Nov. 5," *Mercantile Advertiser* (New York), November 11, 1799. On Clark's case, see "Carlisle, June 14," *Carey's United States Recorder* (Philadelphia, Pennsylvania), June 23, 1798; "Carlisle, June 20," *Boston Gazette, and Weekly Republican Journal,* July 16, 1798.
91. George Herridon and Mrs. Herridon recollections, 184.

6: Cane

1. "Lexington, April 18," *Kentucky Gazette,* April 18, 1799; "Lexington, April 25," *Kentucky Gazette,* April 25, 1799; "From Esqr. James Leeper of Henry Co.—Tennessee," Draper Manuscripts, WHS, 30S, 122–123. Leeper knew the Trabue family well, including Johnny's brother, Robert. The details about the dog's wound and that Johnny was borrowing seed come from him.
2. This draws from "Andre Michaux's Travels (1793–1796)," in Williams, *Early Travels in the Tennessee Country,* 339–340.
3. Young, *Westward into Kentucky,* 8.
4. Friend, *Kentucke's Frontiers,* 187. In 1795, the Kentucky legislature passed a land act offering buyers up to two hundred acres (at thirty cents an acre) for every two they cleared as long as they had settled by January 1, 1796. The state extended the deadline several times.
5. Young, *Westward into Kentucky,* 9–10.
6. Friend, *Kentucke's Frontiers,* 213.
7. An extremely thorough biography of Daniel Trabue can be found in Chester Raymond Young's introduction to his narrative, Young, *Westward into Kentucky,* 1–34.
8. Young, *Westward into Kentucky,* 41–43.
9. Young, *Westward into Kentucky,* 5–6, 41–43, 79–94.
10. Young, *Westward into Kentucky,* 124.
11. Young, *Westward into Kentucky,* 5–10.
12. Young, *Westward into Kentucky,* 132.
13. Young links the founding of this church to the Harps' terrorizing the region. See the introduction in Young, *Westward into Kentucky,* 10.
14. "Lexington, April 18," *Kentucky Gazette,* April 18, 1799; "Lexington, April 25," *Kentucky Gazette,* April 25, 1799 (quote).

15. "Lexington, April 18," *Kentucky Gazette*, April 18, 1799; "Lexington, April 25," *Kentucky Gazette*, April 25, 1799.
16. George Herridon and Mrs. Herridon recollections, Draper Manuscripts, WHS, 30S, 184: "Susan said it was Little Harpe who was the cause of young Trabue's death." Several others closely involved in the case, including Joseph Ballenger's son and James Leeper, also indicated that the Harps had killed Johnny Trabue—which strongly suggests that the fugitives later admitted to the murder.
17. "They killed young Trabue, a boy who was riding on a bag of Meal, which they wanted," Joseph Ballenger's son later attested. John L. Ballenger to Lyman Draper, Draper Manuscripts, WHS, 12C, doc. 46.
18. Bushman, *The Refinement of America*, 257.
19. Bushman, *The Refinement of America*, 134–137. A simple fence setting the yard apart from the house would have marked it as different, in important ways, from the "much larger number of ordinary log and frame houses" populating the countryside, where barnyard animals could amble up just as freely as people.
20. Mellinger E. Henry, "Still More Ballads and Folk-Songs from the Southern Highlands," *Journal of American Folklore* 45, no. 175 (1932): 30–31. Also known as "The Highwayman Outwitted," this song circulated in West Virginia, Tennessee, and other places. This version is North Carolinian.
21. Neither the governor nor senators were popularly elected. Nothing prevented county court justices from also serving in the legislature, where they could simply make new laws inoculating themselves against the critiques of local people.
22. On the clamor surrounding and the framing of the Kentucky constitution of 1799, I am heavily indebted to Joan Wells Coward, *Kentucky in the New Republic: The Process of Constitution Making* (Lexington: University Press of Kentucky, 1979), especially 97–161; Lowell H. Harrison, "John Breckinridge and the Kentucky Constitution of 1799," *Register of the Kentucky Historical Society* 57, no. 3 (1959): 209–233; and Connelley and Coulter, *History of Kentucky*, 1:390–402.
23. "A Voter," *Stewart's Kentucky Herald*, April 17, 1798, quoted in John Breckinridge, "To the Voter," Breckinridge Family Papers, series 1, vol. 16, Manuscript Division, Library of Congress, Washington, D.C.
24. Gracchus, "Shall There Be a Convention?," quoted in Humphrey Marshall, *The History of Kentucky*, vol. 2, *Exhibiting an Account of the Modern Discovery; Settlement; Progressive Improvement; Civil and Military* (Frankfort, 1824), 249.
25. Their struggles began to bleed into politics as the Green River counties elected men to the state legislature who pressed, rabidly, for "RELIEF." Those in power resented the Green River men muscling in on politics, demanding things. "The whole southern section of the state were united in expecting indulgences," one wrote bitterly. Marshall, *The History of Kentucky*, 2:179.
26. Connelley and Coulter, *History of Kentucky*, 1:391.

27. Scaevola [Henry Clay], "To the Electors of Fayette," *Kentucky Gazette*, April 25, 1798.
28. Breckinridge, "To the Voter," Breckinridge Family Papers.
29. Quoted in Coward, *Kentucky in the New Republic*, 119.
30. Breckinridge, "To the Voter," Breckinridge Family Papers.
31. "At a Meeting of a Large Number of the Farmers and Planters of the County of Fayette, at the Big Spring," April 28, 1798 (Lexington, 1798).
32. A good sense of the reorientation of American politics in this period pitting common men against the aristocracy can be found in Wood, *The Radicalism of the American Revolution*, 271–286.
33. Breckinridge, "To the Voter," Breckinridge Family Papers.
34. Col. John Stump recollections, Draper Manuscripts, WHS, 31S, 55; Young, *Westward into Kentucky*, 147. These details came from Stump's brother, John.
35. Harriette Simpson Arnow, *Flowering of the Cumberland* (Lincoln: University of Nebraska Press, 1996), 87, 203, 226–227, 277; Greg Grandin, *The End of the Myth: From the Frontier to the Border Wall in the Mind of America* (New York: Henry Holt, 2019), 21–22; J. C. Guice, *Frederick Stump: The Rest of the Story* (Biloxi, Miss., 1991). Rather incredibly, the elder Frederick Stump seems to be the same man who had been jailed (and escaped) after murdering a number of Indians in Pennsylvania in 1768.
36. Guice, *Frederick Stump*, 71.
37. Paul I. Wellman, *Spawn of Evil: The Invisible Empire of Soulless Men Which for a Generation Held the Nation in a Spell of Terror* (New York: Doubleday, 1964), 39.
38. He appears in Logan County tax records with stock listed as property even before he owned any land. See Logan County Tax List, 1792–1800 (Logan County Genealogical Society, 1991), Kentucky Historical Society, Frankfort, Ky.
39. "Andre Michaux's Travels (1793–1796)," in Williams, *Early Travels in the Tennessee Country*, 338.
40. Louis-Philippe, *Diary of My Travels in America* (1797; repr., New York: Delacorte Press, 1977), 110–111.
41. James Ross, *Life and Times of Elder Reuben Ross* (Philadelphia: Grant, Faires & Rodgers, 1882), 214.
42. Reuben Gold Thwaites, ed., *Travels West of the Alleghanies: Made in 1793–96 by André Michaux; in 1802 by F. A. Michaux; and in 1803 by Thaddeus Mason Harris* (Cleveland: Arthur H. Clark, 1904), 215–222. Contains Michaux's descriptions of the Barrens (quote on p. 217).
43. Maj. William Stewart recollections, Draper Manuscripts, WHS, 30S, 191–192.
44. Coates, *The Outlaw Years*, 41.
45. Coroner's inquest of Frederick Stump, Jr., Warren County Court Minute/Order Book A, 146, Warren County Records, microfilm roll 7031530, KDLA.
46. Multiple sources suggest this sinking with stones in the river. Col. John Stump recollections, Draper Manuscripts, WHS, 31S, 55; Major William

Stewart recollections, Draper Manuscripts, WHS, 30S, 191. Micajah later confessed to this murder, according to newspapers. Young, *Westward into Kentucky*, 147 (gun).

47. Coroner's inquest of Frederick Stump, Jr., KDLA.
48. "Lexington, April 25," *Kentucky Gazette*, April 25, 1799.
49. *Warren County Kentucky Circuit Court Book 1, 1797–1801*, compiled by Sandra K. Gorin (Gorin Genealogical Publishing, 1993), 20, KHS, Frankfort, Ky.
50. "Lexington, March 28," *Kentucky Gazette*, March 28, 1799.
51. Young, *Westward into Kentucky*, 147 ("bad chance"); "Mercer County," *Palladium* (Kentucky), March 21, 1799, clipping, Draper Manuscripts, WHS, 1Q, 34 (locks); "Lexington, March 28," *Kentucky Gazette*, March 28, 1799.
52. Young, *Westward into Kentucky*, 147.
53. Young, *Westward into Kentucky*, 149.
54. "By the Governor, a Proclamation," April 22, 1799, repr. in Rothert, *The Outlaws of Cave-in-Rock*, 88.
55. "Winchester May 22," *Claypoole's American Daily Advertiser*, May 30, 1799.
56. Personal communication with Laura Edwards, July 16, 2025, and Kate Haulman, October 11, 2023. See also Laura F. Edwards, *Only the Clothes on Her Back: Clothing and the Hidden History of Power in the Nineteenth-Century United States* (New York: Oxford University Press, 2022), and Kate Haulman, *The Politics of Fashion in Eighteenth-Century America* (Chapel Hill: University of North Carolina Press, 2011).
57. Young, *Westward into Kentucky*, 147.
58. "Lexington, July 25," *Kentucky Gazette*, July 25, 1799.
59. Harrison, "John Breckinridge and the Kentucky Constitution of 1799," 221–223; Coward, *Kentucky in the New Republic*, 115–123.
60. Coward, *Kentucky in the New Republic*, 126–129.
61. [Mr. Lewis?] to John Breckinridge, July 18, 1799, Breckinridge Family Papers, series 1, vol. 17, Manuscript Division, Library of Congress, Washington, D.C.
62. John Breckinridge notes on the 1799 Kentucky constitutional debates, Breckinridge Family Papers, series 1, vol. 18, Manuscript Division, Library of Congress, Washington, D.C.
63. Harrison, "John Breckinridge and the Kentucky Constitution of 1799," 233. There were a few exceptions: Instead of being chosen by electors (as under the 1792 constitution), the governor and senators would now be elected directly by the people. But Kentuckians lost the ability to elect sheriffs and judges. The senate's existence was untouched. And to balance the concession of direct election, the delegates discarded ballot voting and instated *viva voce* voting—ensuring that every man would have to vote aloud. Finally, slavery was protected, with no move toward emancipation.
64. A small hullabaloo arose when, after signing his name, Thomas Clay wrote, *I protest against it*. The clerk removed the note. Harrison, "John Breckinridge and the Kentucky Constitution of 1799," 232.

65. Breckinridge, "To the Voter," Breckinridge Family Papers.
66. "The Story of the Harps," *Port Folio,* August 1825, 123.
67. "From Esqr. James Leeper of Henry Co.—Tennessee," 124–125.
68. Draper, "A Sketch of the Harpes," 169.
69. "Lexington, August 16," *Centinel of Freedom* (Newark, N.J.), September 10, 1799.
70. "The Harpes—from Col. Sevier," 306.
71. Young, *Westward into Kentucky,* 147.
72. Trabue account in the *Centinel of Freedom* (Newark, N.J.), September 10, 1799; this also appeared in Pennsylvania, New York, and Kentucky newspapers.
73. Breazeale, *Life as It Is,* 142; "The Harpes—& Their Murders," Rutledge, Tenn., August 31, 1844, Draper Manuscripts, WHS, 32S, 250; "Founding of Knoxville: Letter of Hugh Dunlap," *American Historical Magazine and Tennessee Historical Society Quarterly* 9, no. 2 (1904): 182.
74. "The KNOXVILLE GAZETTE, Wednesday *Evening, August* 7," *Knoxville Gazette,* August 7, 1799.
75. See, for example, Robert Love to John Sevier, September 18, 1799, Governor John Sevier Papers, Box 2, Folder 4, TSLA. "It's probable that he will make to his father in laws John Rice's where he was harbored," Love wrote about Wiley.
76. "Founding of Knoxville: Letter of Hugh Dunlap," 182. Another writer, the son of the Knox County deputy sheriff, later repeated this story: "Dunlap had been very vigilant in endeavoring to arrest them, and they had threatened him," he wrote. Breazeale, *Life as It Is,* 139.
77. "The Harpes—from Col. Sevier," 308; September 22, 1797, entry in Indian Department Expense Book, Knoxville, 1797–98, Microfilm 83, TSLA (Dunlap rides with proclamation); David Henley to Gabriel DuVoll, Esq., March 3, 1808, David Henley Papers, Microfilm 625, TSLA.
78. Breazeale, *Life as It Is,* 142; Young, *Westward into Kentucky,* 147.
79. "Lexington, January 8," *Stewart's Kentucky Herald,* January 8, 1799; "Lexington, April 25," *Kentucky Gazette,* April 25, 1799.
80. Young, *Westward into Kentucky,* 149.
81. Richard Miller Hadsell, "John Bradford and His Contributions to the Culture and the Life of Early Lexington and Kentucky," *Register of the Kentucky Historical Society* 62, no. 4 (1964): 267 ("by the flickering"); Daniel A. Yanchisin, "John Bradford, Public Servant," *Register of the Kentucky Historical Society* 68, no. 1 (1970): 63 ("dig into").
82. "Lexington, January 9," *Kentucky Gazette,* January 9, 1799; "Lexington, April 18," *Kentucky Gazette,* April 18, 1799; "Lexington, April 25," *Kentucky Gazette,* April 25, 1799.
83. On newspapers and printing in this era, see Eric Burns, *Infamous Scribblers: The Founding Fathers and the Rowdy Beginnings of American Journalism* (New York: Public Affairs, 2006) (quote "as spices" on p. 189); Uriel Heyd, *Reading Newspapers: Press and Public in Eighteenth-Century Britain and America*

(Oxford: Voltaire Foundation, 2012); Carol Sue Humphrey, *The American Revolution and the Press: The Promise of Independence* (Evanston: Northwestern University Press, 2013); Pasley, *The Tyranny of Printers;* and Jordan E. Taylor, *Misinformation Nation: Foreign News and the Politics of Truth in Revolutionary America* (Baltimore: Johns Hopkins University Press, 2022).

84. As of 1794, Roulstone was also the federal postmaster in Knoxville, further boosting his position as a node of newsgathering in town. George F. Bentley, "Printers and Printing in the Southwest Territory, 1790–1796," *Tennessee Historical Quarterly* 8, no. 4 (1949): 336–339. On printers swapping stories, see Taylor, *Misinformation Nation*, 16.
85. Yanchisin, "John Bradford, Public Servant," 63; William Henry Perrin, *The Pioneer Press of Kentucky* (Louisville: J. P. Morton, 1888), 13.
86. Daniel Roe letter, in "The Story of the Harps," *Port Folio,* August 1825, 127.
87. Hall, *Letters from the West*, 269.
88. Breazeale, *Life as It Is*, 138–139.
89. Young, *Westward into Kentucky*, 150.
90. Daniel Roe letter, in "The Story of the Harps," *Port Folio,* August 1825, 124–125.
91. Draper, "A Sketch of the Harpes," 166.
92. Hall, *Letters from the West*, 269.
93. "Rampage killing" is a category now used by crime experts to encompass both spree and mass killing, which share some characteristics. Traditionally, criminology and law enforcement have recognized three categories of multicide: mass killing, serial murder, and spree killing. The Harps meet the classical definition of spree killing—three or more murders at two or more locations in a relatively short time. In 2005, the FBI eliminated spree killing from its own categorizations on the grounds that it was not helpful to law enforcement—though some criminologists still argue for its usefulness. See Mark Safarik and Katherine Ramsland, *Spree Killers: Practical Classifications for Law Enforcement and Criminology* (Boca Raton: CRC Press, 2019), xiii, 1.
94. James Alan Fox, "In Rampages, It's About Revenge," cnn.com, February 9, 2013, www.cnn.com/2013/02/08/opinion/fox-la-rampage/index.html.
95. On the phenomena of mass killing and rampage killing, I have found these works especially helpful: Arnon Edelstein, *Mass Murder and Serial Murder: An Integrative Look* (Stuttgart, Germany: Ibidem Press, 2020); Mark Follman, *Trigger Points: Inside the Mission to Stop Mass Shootings in America* (New York: HarperCollins, 2022); James Alan Fox, Jack Levin, and Kenna Quinet, *The Will to Kill: Making Sense of Senseless Murder*, 4th ed. (Boston: Pearson, 2012); James Alan Fox, Jack Levin, and Emma E. Fridel, *Extreme Killing: Understanding Serial and Mass Murder*, 4th ed. (Los Angeles: SAGE, 2019); Ronald M. Holmes and Stephen T. Holmes, *Mass Murder in the United States* (Upper Saddle River, N.J.: Prentice Hall, 2001); Michael D. Kelleher, *Flash Point: The American Mass Murderer* (Westport, Conn.: Bloomsbury, 1997);

Louis Klarevas, *Rampage Nation: Securing America from Mass Shootings* (Amherst, N.Y.: Prometheus, 2016); Adam Lankford, *The Myth of Martyrdom: What Really Drives Suicide Bombers, Rampage Shooters, and Other Self-Destructive Killers* (New York: Macmillan, 2013); Seamus McGraw, *From a Taller Tower: The Rise of the American Mass Shooter* (Austin: University of Texas Press, 2021); Lee Mellor, *Rampage: Canadian Mass Murder and Spree Killing* (Toronto: Dundurn, 2013); Katherine Ramsland, *Inside the Minds of Mass Murderers: Why They Kill* (Westport, Conn.: Praeger, 2005); and Safarik and Ramsland, *Spree Killers*. Among recent works that try to identify the risk factors and similarities among rampage killers, my thinking has been shaped most deeply by Jillian Peterson and James Densley, *The Violence Project: How to Stop a Mass Shooting Epidemic* (New York: Abrams Press, 2021).

96. See Fox, "In Rampages, It's About Revenge"; Ramsland, *Inside the Minds of Mass Murderers*, 33.
97. Edelstein, *Mass Murder and Serial Murder*, 55.
98. Kelleher, *Flash Point*, 10–11.
99. Holmes and Holmes, *Mass Murder in the United States*, 33–34; Edelstein, *Mass Murder and Serial Murder*, 49.
100. Edelstein, *Mass Murder and Serial Murder*, 49.
101. Edelstein, *Mass Murder and Serial Murder*, 49 ("angry and desperate young men," "glory and a halo"); Ramsland, *Inside the Minds of Mass Murderers*, 33 ("feel that life is becoming overwhelming," "blame others").
102. Richard Estep, "Rampage and Spree Killers," in *Serial Killers: The Minds, Methods, and Mayhem of History's Most Notorious Murderers* (Boston: Credo Reference, 2021). "Most rampage killers are giving the middle finger to the rest of humanity," Estep writes. "They judge their level of success based upon the sheer number of people they kill or injure and the amount of media coverage they get for committing atrocities."
103. Daniel Drake, *Pioneer Life in Kentucky: A Series of Reminiscential Letters from Daniel Drake, M.D., of Cincinnati, to His Children* (Cincinnati: Robert Clarke, 1870), 134.
104. Drake, *Pioneer Life in Kentucky*, 134–136.
105. Young, *Westward into Kentucky*, 147.
106. Trabue account, *Centinel of Freedom*.
107. Interview with Gen. Thomas Love, 116–117; Young, *Westward into Kentucky*, 147.
108. Young, *Westward into Kentucky*, 147.
109. "The Harpes. (from James Givens)," Draper Manuscripts, WHS, 29S, 132.
110. Interview with Gen. Thomas Love, 117.
111. Young, *Westward into Kentucky*, 147.
112. Young, *Westward into Kentucky*, 148.
113. Young, *Westward into Kentucky*, 148.
114. Young, *Westward into Kentucky*, 148 ("Dreadfully"); *Carolina Gazette* clipping, September 26, 1799, transcription, Draper Manuscripts, WHS, 5XX, 7–8 ("much beaten"). Both of these accounts of the Brassels' encounter with

the Harps are likely quite accurate since Robert Brassel survived to tell the tale almost immediately.

7: The Pursuit

1. The Stegall case did not leave behind many court records. The scenario is reconstructed from a few depositions given by Stegall neighbors in the Otto Rothert Papers at the Filson Historical Society, Louisville, Ky.; oral traditions kept by William Love's family and others who knew the Harps (or lived through their escapade), most of which are preserved in the Draper Manuscripts Collection at WHS; and snippets of what the Harp women later told people. The phase of the moon comes from *The Kentucky Almanac, for the Year of Our Lord 1799*.
2. Edmund L. Starling, *History of Henderson County, Kentucky* (1887).
3. Samuel Hopkins to Thomas Hart, April 8, 1799, Samuel Hopkins Papers, KHS, Frankfort, Ky.
4. For a painstaking re-creation of where the Stegall house stood, referencing modern roads and landmarks, see Carl Veazey, "Murder on Deer Creek," in *Sixth Annual Year Book of the Historical Society of Hopkins County, Kentucky* (July 1, 1980), 11–17.
5. Interview with Gen. Thomas Love, 119.
6. Interview with Gen. Thomas Love, 119.
7. John Sevier to Capt. Arthur Crozier, July 25 and 29, 1799, Governor John Sevier Papers, Box 1, Folder 14, TSLA. Emphasis mine. Four days later, he authorized Chesley Coffee, the father of one of the victims, to raise another search party. This time, he named the suspects: "It is supposed," he wrote, "that Micajah Harp and Willie Harp are the perpetrators of the said murders."
8. "The KNOXVILLE GAZETTE, Wednesday *Evening, August* 7," *Knoxville Gazette*, August 7, 1799.
9. J. W. Wells, *History of Cumberland County* (Louisville, 1947), 39 (Tully's estate); "An Act for the Relief of Christiana Tully," December 18, 1800, in *Acts Passed at the First Session of the Ninth General Assembly for the Commonwealth of Kentucky* (Frankfort, 1801), 19.
10. Young, *Westward into Kentucky*, 149.
11. "August 22," *Augusta Chronicle*, Georgia, October 12, 1799; *Palladium* clipping, August 22, 1799, Draper Manuscripts, WHS, 1Q, 37; Young, *Westward into Kentucky*, 150; "From Esqr. James Leeper of Henry Co.—Tennessee," 124–125.
12. *Palladium* clipping, August 15, 1799, Draper Manuscripts, WHS, 1Q, 37.
13. "Mercer County," *Palladium*, Kentucky, March 21, 1799, clipping, Draper Manuscripts, WHS, 1Q, 34.
14. "An Act Respecting Fugitives from Justice, and Persons Escaping from the Service of Their Masters," February 12, 1793, in *The Public Statutes at Large of the United States of America*, ed. Richard Peters (Boston, 1848), 302–305.

15. Trabue account, *Centinel of Freedom.*
16. "The Harpes—from Col. Sevier," 309.
17. Trabue account, *Centinel of Freedom.*
18. George Herridon and Mrs. Herridon recollections, Draper Manuscripts, WHS, 30S, 185.
19. George Herridon and Mrs. Herridon recollections, Draper Manuscripts, WHS, 30S, 185. This detail also reportedly came from Micajah's wife, Susana.
20. Interview with Gen. Thomas Love, Draper Manuscripts, WHS, 30S, 119 (ladder).
21. Isham Sellers deposition, Henderson County Court, September 4, 1799, transcription, Otto Rothert Papers, unprocessed, Filson Historical Society, Louisville, Ky.; Rothert, *The Outlaws of Cave-in-Rock*, 131–132.
22. Young, *Westward into Kentucky*, 150.
23. Interview with Gen. Thomas Love, 118.
24. The Loves owned six bondspeople: adults Sally and Amos and four children, Rhoda, Milly, Ishmael, and Cato. Interview with Gen. Thomas Love, 117–118; Richard Beard, *Brief Biographical Sketches of Some of the Early Ministers of the Cumberland Presbyterian Church*, 2nd ed. (Nashville: Cumberland Presbyterian Board of Publication, 1874), 356–374; William Love estate inventory, in *Livingston County, Kentucky County Court Order Books A–B May 1799–January 1807*, compiled by Brenda Joyce Jerome (1994), 24, KHS, Frankfort, Ky.
25. "From Genl. Jonathan Ramsay," Draper Manuscripts, WHS, 5S, 70. Gen. Ramsay, via Draper, says, "Love was then out surveying" and "was a Deputy Surveyor under Jonus Ewing of a District." Also, William Calhoun Love confirms in his journal: "My father . . . was killed by the Harps while on a tour of surveying in what is now Hopkins County." "The Memoirs of William Calhoun Love," Donald E. Collins, transcriber, accessed at https://sites.rootsweb.com/~kycaldw2/wmclove.
26. Hall, *Letters from the West*, 123.
27. "KNOXVILLE, *September* 18," *Georgetown Gazette* (South Carolina), November 6, 1799.
28. He had likely served as a justice of the peace before this since he swore in several others appointed as such at Livingston County's founding in 1799. Jerome, *Livingston County, Kentucky County Court Order Books*, 1–2.
29. Collins, "The Memoirs of William Calhoun Love."
30. Draper, "A Sketch of the Harpes," 169. This narrative relies on extremely close detail provided directly in an interview with Silas McBee, who was a justice of the peace, a neighbor of Stegall's, one of the first at the scene of the murders, and a member of the posse that pursued the Harps. As it is close to firsthand testimony, I rely on it heavily.
31. George Herridon and Mrs. Herridon recollections, Draper Manuscripts, WHS, 30S, 184.
32. Interview with Gen. Thomas Love, Draper Manuscripts, WHS, 30S, 120.

33. Draper, "A Sketch of the Harpes," 169–170.
34. Neville Lindsey deposition, Henderson County Court, September 4, 1799, transcription, Otto Rothert Papers, unprocessed, Filson Historical Society, Louisville, Ky.
35. "Due process" generally refers to the protections guaranteed by the Fourth, Fifth, Sixth, and Eighth Amendments to the Constitution. Since the passage of the Fourteenth Amendment in 1868, the Supreme Court has considered state and local law enforcement—as well as federal—to be bound by these guardrails. See Jeffrey B. Bumgarner, *Federal Agents: The Growth of Federal Law Enforcement in America* (Westport, Conn.: Praeger, 2006), 7–8.
36. "Probably the single most unique characteristic of American law enforcement," writes Bumgarner, "when compared with law enforcement in other countries—including democratic ones—is its decentralized nature." Bumgarner, *Federal Agents*, 1.
37. Quoted in Bryan Vila and Cynthia Morris, *The Role of Police in American Society: A Documentary History* (Westport, Conn.: Greenwood, 1999), 12.
38. For introductions to the history of American law enforcement and its popular roots, see, for instance, Manfred Berg, *Popular Justice: A History of Lynching in America* (Chicago: Ivan R. Dee, 2011); Laurence Armand French, *The History of Policing America: From Militias and Military to the Law Enforcement of Today* (Lanham, Md.: Rowman & Littlefield, 2018); Sally E. Hadden, *Slave Patrols: Law and Violence in Virginia and the Carolinas* (Cambridge: Harvard University Press, 2001); David R. Johnson, *American Law Enforcement: A History* (St. Louis: Forum Press, 1981); and Adam Malka, *The Men of Mobtown: Policing Baltimore in the Age of Slavery and Emancipation* (Chapel Hill: University of North Carolina Press, 2018).
39. Berg, *Popular Justice*, 12–13.
40. Vila and Morris, *The Role of Police in American Society*, 3.
41. Malka, *The Men of Mobtown*, 37.
42. John Trenchard and Thomas Gordon, *Cato's Letters; Or, Essays on Liberty, Civil and Religious, and Other Important Subjects*, ed. Ronald Hamowy, vol. 1 (1720; repr., Indianapolis: Liberty Fund, 1995), 1:234 (no. 33).
43. Jonathan Elliot, ed., *The Debates in the Several State Conventions on the Adoption of the Federal Constitution as Recommended by the General Convention at Philadelphia in 1787*, vol. 3 (Washington, 1836), 381.
44. Quoted in Richard H. Kohn, *Eagle and Sword: The Federalists and the Creation of the Military Establishment in America, 1783–1802* (New York: Free Press, 1975), 2.
45. Bumgarner, *Federal Agents*, 3.
46. See especially Laura F. Edwards, *The People and Their Peace: Legal Culture and the Transformation of Inequality in the Post-Revolutionary South* (Chapel Hill: University of North Carolina Press, 2009).
47. The Kentucky Resolutions of 1798, repr. in Watkins, *Reclaiming the American Revolution*, 165. These quotes are from the second resolution.

48. Newman, *Fries's Rebellion*, 29–30.
49. On Fries's Rebellion, see Terry Bouton, "'No Wonder the Times Were Troublesome': The Origins of Fries Rebellion, 1783–1799," *Pennsylvania History* 67, no. 1 (2000): 21–42; Churchill, "Popular Nullification, Fries' Rebellion, and the Waning of Radical Republicanism," 105–140; W.W.H. Davis, *The Fries Rebellion* (Doylestown, Pa., 1899); Jeffrey S. Dimmig, "Palatine Liberty: Pennsylvania German Opposition to the Direct Tax of 1798," *American Journal of Legal History* 45, no. 4 (2001): 371–391; Newman, *Fries's Rebellion;* Paul Douglas Newman, "The Federalists' Cold War: The Fries Rebellion, National Security, and the State, 1787–1800," *Pennsylvania History* 67, no. 1 (2000): 63–104; and Whitman H. Ridgway, "Fries in the Federalist Imagination: A Crisis of Republican Society," *Pennsylvania History* 67, no. 1 (2000): 141–160.
50. Davis, *The Fries Rebellion*, 8–12.
51. Newman, *Fries's Rebellion*, 15.
52. Davis, *The Fries Rebellion*, 65–66.
53. "To John Adams from James McHenry, 5 April 1799," *Founders Online*, National Archives, https://founders.archives.gov/documents/Adams/99-02-02-3409.
54. On March 2, 1799—less than a week before Fries and his men rescued the prisoners from the Sun Inn—Congress passed the Eventual Army Act, giving "eventual authority to the President of the United States to augment the army" by activating the militia of several states in case of domestic rebellion or invasion. Under the new law, the president could do so without Congress's consent. This may explain the proclamation's overheated definition of Fries's actions as "treason." Had the offense been less serious, Newman argues, Adams might have called only for the activation of Pennsylvania forces—and would have left open the possibility of pressure to use the "New Army," a federal force of regular troops that was being built, even at this moment, in response to the French threat. Adams, Newman posits, likely wanted to deploy only the Eventual Army—that is, "federalized" militia—and not regular troops. But because Adams left Philadelphia days after issuing the proclamation, suppression of the resistance was left to his secretary of war, James McHenry. McHenry moved beyond the letter of the Eventual Army law and activated regular troops as well as state militias—without the approval of Congress or the president. See Newman, *Fries's Rebellion*, 146–148.
55. Davis, *The Fries Rebellion*, 93–94.
56. Davis, *The Fries Rebellion*, 127, 142.
57. Draper, "A Sketch of the Harpes," 170.
58. For an introduction to salt making in early Kentucky, see Robert E. McDowell, "Bullitt's Lick: The Related Saltworks and Settlements," *Filson Club Historical Quarterly* 30, no. 3 (1956); also see Sachs, *Home Rule*, chap. 2.
59. Draper, "A Sketch of the Harpes," 170.
60. *Georgetown Gazette* (South Caroline), November 6, 1799.

61. In federal records, we can see him "ranging on the frontiers of Washington County, Territory of the South," in mounted militia under Corporal James Hazlett in 1793, and in 1794, part of the mounted infantry mustered "for the protection of the frontiers" under James White. "Compiled Service Records of Volunteer Soldiers Who Served from 1784 to 1811," RG 94, Records of the Adjutant General's Office, 1762–1984, series M905, roll 28, National Archives and Records Administration, Washington, D.C.
62. Interview with Gen. Thomas Love, 121.
63. The Government v. Moses Stegall case file (1794), docket no. 21/204, Knox County Court of Pleas and Quarter Sessions Files, KCA (trespass, assault, and battery); The Government v. Moses Stegall (1795), docket no. 131/64, Hamilton District Superior Court Minute Book, vol. 3, 20–21, KCA (horse theft). One man actually thought Stegall had "run away from Knoxville," while another thought he recalled the man being jailed for horse stealing and then using an auger to bore out the bolt on the door and escape. See "The Harpes (from James Givens)," 135 (auger), and "From Esqr. James Leeper of Henry Co.—Tennessee," 128 ("run away").
64. Don Simmons, *Tax Lists Christian County, KY: 1797, 1798, 1799* (1974), 5, KHS, Frankfort, Ky.
65. McBee had recruited Grisson and Tompkins before Stegall secured his men, it appears. Draper, "A Sketch of the Harpes," 170.
66. I owe this to personal communication with Kelly Hyberger, at the Filson Historical Society, Louisville, Ky., May 26, 2022.
67. Draper, "A Sketch of the Harpes," 170.
68. Chesley Coffee commission to pursue the Harps, July 29, 1799, Governor John Sevier Papers, Box 1, Folder 14, TSLA; Robert Love to John Sevier, September 18, 1799; John Sevier to Major David Campbell, September 19, 1799, in Military Order Book of John Sevier 1796–1804, Governor John Sevier Papers, Box 2, Folder 8, TSLA (Robert Love). Judge Samuel Burks's promise that anyone provisioning Coffee's men would be reimbursed by the state is written on the back of a copy of Sevier's July 29 proclamation, in Governor John Sevier Papers, Box 5, Folder 6, Miscellaneous Papers 1799, TSLA.
69. Draper, "A Sketch of the Harpes," 170.
70. "The Harpes—from Col. Sevier," 309.
71. Draper, "A Sketch of the Harpes," 175.
72. "Another Revolutionary Soldier Gone!," *Mississippi Advertiser*, February 8, 1845.
73. Dunkerly, *The Battle of Kings Mountain*, 64.
74. Draper, "A Sketch of the Harpes," 168.
75. Good discussions of the signs men looked for while scouting can be found in Roseann R. Hogan, ed., "Buffaloes in the Corn: James Wade's Account of Pioneer Kentucky," *Register of the Kentucky Historical Society* 89, no. 1 (1991): 1–31. Also see Everett Dick, *The Dixie Frontier: A Social History of the Southern Frontier from the First Transmontane Beginnings to the Civil War* (1948;

repr., Norman: University of Oklahoma Press, 1993), 265: "In the wooded sections of Kentucky and Tennessee cane, weeds, and small bushes grew up in such profusion that two or three men even on foot could not pass through without leaving a trace. Out on the barrens the grass and nettles revealed to the discerning woodsman the route of those passing."

76. Young, *Westward into Kentucky*, 150; "Lexington, September 5," *Kentucky Gazette*, September 5, 1799.
77. On the history and evolution of slave patrols, see especially Hadden, *Slave Patrols*.
78. See Isaac Shelby Papers, Filson Historical Society, Louisville, Kentucky.
79. Draper, "A Sketch of the Harpes," 170.
80. Draper, "A Sketch of the Harpes," 171.
81. Draper, "A Sketch of the Harpes," 172.
82. Collins, *Collins' Historical Sketches*, 2:351–352.
83. Draper, "A Sketch of the Harpes," 172.
84. Draper, "A Sketch of the Harpes," 172.
85. Draper, "A Sketch of the Harpes," 172. Three men lagged behind with the women: McBee had Sally, and Tompkins and Lindsey took Betsy and Susana. Stegall, Leeper, Christian, and Grisson pursued Micajah, with Leeper eventually breaking out ahead of the others.
86. Draper, "A Sketch of the Harpes," 173.
87. "From Genl. Jonathan Ramsay," Draper Manuscripts, WHS, 5S, 70.
88. "From Esqr. James Leeper of Henry Co.—Tennessee," 126; "From Genl. Jonathan Ramsay," Draper Manuscripts, 5S, 70.
89. Draper, "A Sketch of the Harpes," 172–173; Collins, *Collins' Historical Sketches*, 2:350.
90. John Leeper and Matthew Christian depositions, Henderson County Court, September 4, 1799, Otto Rothert Papers, unprocessed, Filson Historical Society, Louisville, Ky.; Rothert, *The Outlaws of Cave-in-Rock*, 132; Draper, "A Sketch of the Harpes," 173.
91. "KNOXVILLE, *September* 18," *Claypoole's American Daily Advertiser*, October 12, 1799; "Knoxville, September 18," *Georgetown Gazette* (South Carolina), November 6, 1799, which printed the number as "37."
92. "The Harpes—from Col. Sevier," Draper Manuscripts, WHS, 30S, 311. This came from one of Leeper's relatives.
93. Collins, *Collins' Historical Sketches*, 2:351. This came from Stewart, who had custody of the Harp women.
94. "The Harpes—from Col. Sevier," Draper Manuscripts, WHS, 30S, 311.
95. Collins, *Collins' Historical Sketches*, 2:351. This came from the Logan County sheriff, William Stewart, who had custody of the Harp women ("war against all mankind"); Breazeale, *Life as It Is*, 146 ("agreed with each other").
96. Breazeale, *Life as It Is*, 146.
97. Draper, "A Sketch of the Harpes," 167.
98. Estep, "Rampage and Spree Killers."

99. Collins, *Collins' Historical Sketches*, 2:350.
100. Collins, *Collins' Historical Sketches*, 2:347.
101. Draper, "A Sketch of the Harpes," 173.
102. Rothert, *The Outlaws of Cave-in-Rock*, 55–56.
103. James Fitzjames Stephen, *A History of the Criminal Law of England*, 3 vols. (London: Macmillan, 1883), 3:25–26.
104. Blackstone, *Commentaries on the Laws of England*, 4:5.
105. On the shifting attitudes toward punishment in this era, see Rebecca M. McLennan, *The Crisis of Imprisonment: Protest, Politics, and the Making of the American Penal State, 1776–1941* (New York: Cambridge University Press, 2008); David J. Rothman, *The Discovery of the Asylum: Social Order and Disorder in the New Republic* (Boston: Little, Brown, 1971); and Cesare Beccaria, *An Essay on Crimes and Punishments* (1764; repr., Stanford: Academic Reprints, 1953), 97 (quote).
106. Paul Knepper, "Thomas Jefferson, Criminal Code Reform, and the Founding of the Kentucky Penitentiary at Frankfort," *Register of the Kentucky Historical Society* 91, no. 2 (1993): 129–149, especially 144–146.
107. Warfield, *The Kentucky Resolutions*, 62–63; "An Act to Amend the Penal Laws of This Commonwealth," February 10, 1798, in William Littell, *The Statute Law of Kentucky*, vol. 2 (Frankfort, Ky., 1810), 10–11. The change applied to crimes committed by "any free person"; enslaved Kentuckians were excepted.
108. Benjamin Rush, *An Enquiry into the Effects of Public Punishments upon Criminals and upon Society* (Philadelphia, 1787), 16.
109. Halttunen, *Murder Most Foul* (quote on p. 4).
110. Halttunen, *Murder Most Foul*, 41–46.
111. Thomas Speed, *The Political Club, Danville, Kentucky, 1786–1790* (Louisville: John P. Morton, 1894), 125–127.
112. The Constitution defines treason as "levying War" against the United States or "adhering to their Enemies."
113. Starling, *History of Henderson County*, 104–105.
114. Henderson Circuit Court Order Book, 1799–1811, 4–5, Henderson County Records, Microfilm Reel, 7036587, KDLA.
115. Rothert, *The Outlaws of Cave-in-Rock*, 133, fn. 14.
116. Edward Coffman, *The Story of Logan County* (Nashville: Parthenon Press, 1962), 38–39; Collins, *Collins' Historical Sketches*, 2:482.
117. Major William Stewart recollections, 188–190.
118. John Leeper and Neville Lindsey depositions, September 4, 1799, Henderson County Court, Otto Rothert Papers, unprocessed, Filson Historical Society, Louisville, Ky.
119. Major William Stewart recollections, 188–190.
120. Collins, *Collins' Historical Sketches*, 2:348; James Alves notes, Draper Manuscripts, WHS, 2CC, 34.
121. On the origins and evolution of lynching in America, see, for example,

Berg, *Popular Justice;* James Elbert Cutler, *Lynch-Law: An Investigation into the History of Lynching in the United States* (New York: Longmans, Green, 1905); Michael J. Pfeifer, *The Roots of Rough Justice: Origins of American Lynching* (Urbana: University of Illinois Press, 2011); Ashraf H. A. Rushdy, *American Lynching* (New Haven: Yale University Press, 2012); and Christopher Waldrep, *The Many Faces of Judge Lynch: Extralegal Violence and Punishment in America* (New York: Palgrave Macmillan, 2002).

122. "KNOXVILLE, *September* 18," *Georgetown Gazette* (South Carolina), November 6, 1799.

123. Draper, who interviewed Silas McBee, wrote that the three hundred dollars in reward money was sent in silver to all seven men. It was delivered by Joseph Kirkendall, "the then representative of their District in the Kentucky Legislature." Draper, "A Sketch of the Harpes," 175.

124. "An Act Directing the Payment of Money to John Leiper and Others," in *Acts Passed at the First Session of the Eighth General Assembly for the Commonwealth of Kentucky* (Frankfort, 1800), 199; Rothert, *The Outlaws of Cave-in-Rock,* 139. For one scholar who points out the illegitimacy of Micajah's death, see Waldrep, *The Many Faces of Judge Lynch,* 24.

125. Rothert, *The Outlaws of Cave-in-Rock,* 139. Tennessee declined altogether to pay out any reward money. Leeper and the others petitioned its legislature, but a committee found that their claim was "unreasonable and ought not to be granted." See *Journal of the Senate at the First Session of the Fourth General Assembly* (Knoxville, 1801), 119.

126. Hall, *Letters from the West,* 276–277; Collins, *Collins' Historical Sketches,* 2:347–348; Rothert, *The Outlaws of Cave-in-Rock,* 142.

127. Rothert, *The Outlaws of Cave-in-Rock,* 142; Interview with Gen. Thomas Love, Draper Manuscripts, WHS, 30S, 121.

128. Perhaps the most famous example of this is the South Carolina Regulator Movement: When gangs terrorized the backcountry in the 1760s, planters banded together as an ad hoc police force and refused to disband until the government raised courts and jails and sent sheriffs to keep peace. See especially Richard Maxwell Brown, *The South Carolina Regulators* (Cambridge: Harvard University Press, 1963).

129. Rushdy, *American Lynching,* 25–26.

130. "A Hint for Attention to Be Paid to Lynch's Law," *Augusta Chronicle* (Georgia), June 14, 1794, quoted in Rushdy, *American Lynching,* 24.

131. Draper, "A Sketch of the Harpes," 175; Starling, *History of Henderson County,* 529. This story appears a little differently in Rothert, *The Outlaws of Cave-in-Rock,* 142–143, and John Reynolds, *The Pioneer History of Illinois* (Belleville, Ill.: N. A. Randall, 1852), 72, 239.

132. They had intended to use Micajah's head for "getting the large rewards" but found they could not preserve it well. Collins, *Collins' Historical Sketches,* 2:345, 350–351, 757.

133. "Knoxville, June 11," *Kentucky Gazette,* July 10, 1800.

8: The Trace

1. On flatboat travel on the Mississippi River during these years, see Michael Allen, *Western Rivermen, 1763–1861: Ohio and Mississippi Boatmen and the Myth of the Alligator Horse* (Baton Rouge: Louisiana State University Press, 1990); William C. Davis, *A Way Through the Wilderness: The Natchez Trace and the Civilization of the Southern Frontier* (New York: HarperCollins, 1995), especially 35–41; Charles Henry Ambler, *A History of Transportation in the Ohio Valley* (Glendale, Calif.: Arthur H. Clark, 1932); and Joseph Hartley, *The Economic Effects of Ohio River Navigation* (Bloomington: Indiana University, 1959).
2. Quoted in John Francis McDermott, "Travelers on the Western Waters," *Proceedings of the American Antiquarian Society* 77, pt. 2 (1967): 265.
3. Hall, *Letters from the West*, 90, 92; Allen, *Western Rivermen*, 112–113.
4. Hall, *Letters from the West*, 181–183 (Old Pap and "marvellous tales").
5. Eberhard L. Faber, *Building the Land of Dreams: New Orleans and the Transformation of Early America* (Princeton University Press, 2015), 51–55; Thomas Ashe, *Travels in America* (London, 1808), 333–341; James Pitot, *Observations on the Colony of Louisiana, from 1796 to 1802*, trans. Henry C. Pitot (1802; repr., Baton Rouge: Louisiana State University Press, 1979).
6. See Pitot, *Observations on the Colony of Louisiana*, 165–180.
7. Ashe, *Travels in America*, 331.
8. Pitot, *Observations on the Colony of Louisiana*, 110; Pierre Clément de Laussat, *Memoirs of My Life*, ed. Robert D. Bush (Baton Rouge: Louisiana State University Press, 2003), 41–42.
9. Faber, *Building the Land of Dreams*, 51–56; Ashe, *Travels in America*, 333–341.
10. See Davis, *A Way Through the Wilderness.* The Trace bore through Choctaw and Chickasaw country (in Natchez, the locals called it "the Path to the Choctaw Nation"), with a few lonely stations along the way. Most of it was sandy, rough, and gravelly. At some points, it disappeared almost entirely. In 1801, as Baker contemplated his homeward journey, the United States government was concluding treaties with both the Choctaws and Chickasaws to improve the road. (The Indians granted only the right-of-way; they maintained control of ferries and stopping places.) Soldiers started cutting and clearing soon after. But progress was slow. Eight years later, in 1809, they were still working.
11. "Lexington, September 14," *Kentucky Gazette*, September 14, 1801; Guild, *Old Times in Tennessee*, 96–97.
12. "Lexington, September 14," *Kentucky Gazette*, September 14, 1801.
13. Laussat, *Memoirs of My Life*, 70. Sugar was first grown in Louisiana in 1795, but by 1802, there were seventy-five sugar plantations in the colony, producing five million pounds of sugar annually. Julien Vernet, *Strangers on Their Native Soil: Opposition to United States' Governance in Louisiana's Orleans Territory, 1803–1809* (Jackson: University Press of Mississippi, 2013), 4.
14. Mark Twain, *Adventures of Huckleberry Finn* (New York, 1885), 25–26.

15. William Faulkner, *Requiem for a Nun* (New York: Random House, 1951), 101–102.
16. Laussat, *Memoirs of My Life*, 17.
17. Faulkner, *Requiem for a Nun*, 249.
18. *Mississippi Gazette*, November 24, 1801, microfilm roll 35649, Mississippi Department of Archives and History, Jackson, Miss. (hereafter cited as MDAH).
19. Laussat, *Memoirs of My Life*, 87.
20. Nathaniel Herbert Claiborne, *Notes on the War in the South* (Richmond: William Ramsay, 1819), 92–96.
21. Joseph T. Hatfield, *William Claiborne: Jeffersonian Centurion in the American Southwest* (Lafayette: University of Southwestern Louisiana, 1976); Robert V. Haynes, *The Mississippi Territory and the Southwest Frontier, 1795–1817* (Lexington: University Press of Kentucky, 2010), 49–50 (quote on p. 49); Robert D. Bush, *The Louisiana Purchase: A Global Context* (New York: Routledge, 2014), 89.
22. Joseph T. Hatfield, "Governor William Claiborne, Indians, and Outlaws in Frontier Mississippi 1801–1803," *Journal of Mississippi History* 27, no. 4 (1965): 323–350.
23. Dunbar Rowland, ed., *Official Letter Books of W.C.C. Claiborne, 1801–1816*, 6 vols. (Jackson, Miss., 1917), 1:45.
24. Rowland, *Official Letter Books of W.C.C. Claiborne*, 1:44–45.
25. McCoy, *The Elusive Republic*, 196.
26. Rowland, *Official Letter Books of W.C.C. Claiborne*, 1:45.
27. Rowland, *Official Letter Books of W.C.C. Claiborne*, 1:61–62. Salcedo may have been worried about how the United States government, not just his own subjects, would perceive the action of apprehending Americans. In the same letter, he wrote, "It is impossible for me to do anything with this class of People without giving room for complaints, or my motives being wrongly interpreted" (62).
28. "Juan Manuel de Salcedo (1801–1803)," in Walter Greaves Cowan and Jack B. McGuire, *Louisiana Governors: Rulers, Rascals, and Reformers* (Jackson: University Press of Mississippi, 2008), 54; Raymond J. Martinez, *Rousseau: The Last Days of Spanish New Orleans* (Gretna: Pelican, 2003), 97–98.
29. Rowland, *Official Letter Books of W.C.C. Claiborne*, 1:91.
30. John James Audubon, *Audubon and His Journals*, ed. Maria R. Audubon, 2 vols. (New York: Scribner's Sons, 1897), 2:232.
31. On Mason, see especially Raymond Martin Bell, *Samuel Mason, 1739–1803: Captain in Virginia, Judge in Pennsylvania, River Pirate in Kentucky, Desperado in Mississippi* (1985); Mark J. Wagner and Mary R. McCorvie, "Going to See the Varmint: Piracy in Myth and Reality on the Ohio and Mississippi Rivers, 1785–1830," in *X Marks the Spot: The Archaeology of Piracy*, eds. Russell K. Skowronek and Charles R. Ewen (Gainesville: University Press of Florida, 2006), 230–234; and Rothert, *The Outlaws of Cave-in-Rock*, 157–266.
32. McBee, *The Natchez Court Records, 1767–1805*, 418.

33. *Palladium*, August 12, 1802; Rothert, *The Outlaws of Cave-in-Rock*, 204.
34. George Willey, "Natchez in the Olden Times," in Claiborne, *Mississippi, as a Province, Territory, and State*, 531.
35. Guild, *Old Times in Tennessee*, 96.
36. "Trial of Samuel Mason at New Madrid, 1803," English translation, 98, MDAH (hereafter cited as "Mason transcript").
37. In Britain, the bandits of the eighteenth century were often former butchers who had once relied on neighborhood customers and old-fashioned credit but fell out of the economy as it transitioned to capitalism. This is precisely what was happening in the borderlands of the United States: new routes of exchange, newly capitalist. "Banditry is a notable feature of the transition to capitalism," wrote historian Peter Linebaugh. See Linebaugh, *The London Hanged: Crime and Civil Society in the Eighteenth Century* (Cambridge University Press, 1992), 184–185, 195.
38. Other reports characteristic of predation on commerce: *Palladium*, August 12, 1802; *Mississippi Gazette*, November 24, 1801, microfilm roll 35649, MDAH.
39. Wagner and McCorvie, "Going to See the Varmint," 228–229. On the exaggerated tales of river piracy, see Allen, *Western Rivermen*, 80–83.
40. Claiborne to Daniel Burnet, April 27, 1802, in Rowland, *Official Letter Books of W.C.C. Claiborne*, 1:91. Emphasis original.
41. Ashe, *Travels in America*, 295–296.
42. Mason transcript, 1.
43. Mason transcript, 3.
44. In criminal cases, the general practice under Spanish law was for the commandant of the district to hold hearings first and then, if justified, send the accused to New Orleans for further trial. See Jack D. L. Holmes, "Law and Order in Spanish Natchez, 1781–1798," *Journal of Mississippi History* 25, no. 3 (1963): 186–201.
45. Mason transcript, 108.
46. Faber, *Building the Land of Dreams*, 61–62; Pitot, *Observations on the Colony of Louisiana*, 26. See also Derek Noel Kerr, *Petty Felony, Slave Defiance, and Frontier Villainy: Crime and Criminal Justice in Spanish Louisiana, 1770–1803* (New York: Garland, 1993).
47. Pitot, *Observations on the Colony of Louisiana*, 8.
48. Pitot, *Observations on the Colony of Louisiana*, 29.
49. Each district also had a police deputy appointed by the governor-general. New Madrid's commissioner of police was also present at the Mason hearings.
50. Mason transcript, 13–14.
51. Mason transcript, 30–31.
52. Mason transcript, 27–29.
53. Mason transcript, 26–29.
54. Mason transcript, 30.

55. Mason transcript, 31.
56. Mason transcript, 32 ("without any body"), 33.
57. Mason transcript, 34.
58. "The Harpes. (from James Givens)," Draper Manuscripts, WHS, 29S, 137.
59. William Claiborne to Daniel Burnet, April 27, 1802, in Rowland, *Official Letter Books of W.C.C. Claiborne*, 1:91. Emphasis mine.
60. Robert Love to John Sevier, September 18, 1799; John Sevier to Major David Campbell, September 19, 1799.
61. Other people from Tennessee and Kentucky were pouring into the lower Mississippi River valley in these years. Even an early contingent of Cherokee migrants had settled in, on the St. Francis River. See David Campbell to Thomas Jefferson, October 27, 1803, in Barbara B. Oberg et al., eds., *TPTJ*, vol. 41, *11 July to 15 November 1803* (Princeton University Press, 2014), 614–615.
62. "The Harpes—from Col. Sevier," Draper Manuscripts, WHS, 30S, 317.
63. Col. John Stump recollections, Draper Manuscripts, WHS, 31S, 56.
64. See, for instance, Col. John Stump recollections, Draper Manuscripts, WHS, 31S, 56 ("mold," toe); Guild, *Old Times in Tennessee*, 98 (knife fight); "The Story of the Harps," *Port Folio* (August 1825), 116. "He was identified by several marks," a direct witness informed James Hall.
65. Mason transcript, 35–36.
66. Peyroux sent them downriver with an armed guard of militiamen, each of whom was paid fifty pesos. He actually purchased a pirogue to transport the criminals, which was to be sold in New Orleans or returned to New Madrid afterward. See Ronald R. Morazán, "Records of the Cabildo: Miscellaneous Documents Relating to River Pirates," *Louisiana History: Journal of the Louisiana Historical Association* 42, no. 2 (2001): 212.
67. Despite his earlier tepid attitude toward the brigands, Salcedo seemed to have decided with certainty by March 1803 that Mason's men were a very serious threat. "These pirates had practically blockaded the navigation of the river," he wrote to the Cabildo, the city government. "It is safe to conclude that, if this band of criminals had not been captured, the navigation on the river and travel to upper Louisiana would not have been possible without the protection of an armed guard." Morazán, "Records of the Cabildo," 212. See also Nicholas Maria Vidal to Gov. Claiborne, March 3, 1803, series 488, RG 1 (Administration Papers), doc. 144, MDAH ("continued infamous").
68. Salcedo to the Cabildo, March 3, 1803, details Salcedo's rationale for suspending the Spanish trial. "I have resolved to send the criminals and [a transcript of] the judicial proceedings to the honorable governor of Natchez, so that he may bring the case to a conclusion and pronounce sentence," Salcedo wrote. Morazán, "Records of the Cabildo," 212–213.
69. *Western Spy* (Cincinnati), May 4, 1803, transcription, Draper Manuscripts, WHS, 7S, 19–20.

70. Mason transcript, 50 and passim.
71. *Western Spy* (Cincinnati), May 4, 1803; Salcedo letter to Claiborne, May 18, 1803, series 488, RG 1 (Administration Papers), doc. 160, MDAH (recounts the escape and asks for reimbursement for his expenses in apprehending and imprisoning the criminals).

9: The Two Faces of John Setton

1. Laussat, *Memoirs of My Life*, 14 (quote); Allen, *Western Rivermen*, 42–43.
2. Nicholas Maria Vidal to Gov. Claiborne, March 3, 1803.
3. Quoted in Robert W. Tucker and David C. Hendrickson, *Empire of Liberty: The Statecraft of Thomas Jefferson* (New York: Oxford University Press, 1990), 3. On Jefferson's life and character, see Joseph J. Ellis, *American Sphinx: The Character of Thomas Jefferson* (New York: Vintage, 1998); Kevin J. Hayes, *The Road to Monticello: The Life and Mind of Thomas Jefferson* (New York: Oxford University Press, 2008); Hayes, *Jefferson in His Own Time* (Iowa City: University of Iowa Press, 2012); Thomas S. Kidd, *Thomas Jefferson: A Biography of Spirit and Flesh* (New Haven: Yale University Press, 2022); and Peter S. Onuf, *The Mind of Thomas Jefferson* (Charlottesville: University of Virginia Press, 2007). On Jefferson's "Anas," his memoranda of private conversations, and the role of gossip in early national politics, see Joanne B. Freeman, *Affairs of Honor: National Politics in the New Republic* (New Haven: Yale University Press, 2001), 62–104.
4. John Adams to Abigail Adams, October 25, 1799, in *AFC*, 14:38.
5. See "Letter from Alexander Hamilton, Concerning the Public Conduct and Character of John Adams," 934–971 (quote on p. 941).
6. On the election of 1800, see John Ferling, *Adams vs. Jefferson: The Tumultuous Election of 1800* (New York: Oxford University Press, 2004); James Horn, Jan Ellen Lewis, and Peter S. Onuf, eds., *The Revolution of 1800: Democracy, Race, and the New Republic* (Charlottesville: University of Virginia Press, 2002); and Freeman, *Affairs of Honor*, 199–261.
7. Thomas Jefferson to John Taylor, June 4, 1798, in *TPTJ*, 30:389.
8. Ellis, *American Sphinx*, 169–170. Ellis notes that the lore around Jefferson's unassuming arrival has been somewhat exaggerated.
9. James Thomson Callender, *The Prospect Before Us*, 3 vols. (Richmond, 1800), 1:167. James L. Roark et al., eds., *Understanding the American Promise: A Brief History* (Boston: Bedford/St. Martin's, 2011), 252–253.
10. Ellis, *American Sphinx*, chap. 4 (quote on p. 197).
11. Thomas Jefferson to Robert Livingston, April 18, 1802, in Bush, *The Louisiana Purchase*, 148.
12. Thomas Jefferson to Samuel Adams, February 26, 1800, in Barbara B. Oberg et al., eds., *TPTJ*, vol. 31, *1 February 1799 to 31 May 1800* (Princeton University Press, 2004), 395; Thomas Jefferson to James Madison, August 27, 1805, in Mary A. Hackett et al., eds., *The Papers of James Madison*, Secretary of State Series, vol. 10, *1 July 1805–31 December 1805* (Charlottesville: University

of Virginia Press, 2014), 247–248. On Napoleon's North American dreams, see Alexander DeConde, *This Affair of Louisiana* (Baton Rouge: Louisiana State University Press, 1978).

13. Thomas Jefferson to Robert Livingston, April 18, 1802, in Bush, *The Louisiana Purchase*, 148.
14. Ellis, *American Sphinx*, 207.
15. For an overview of the Louisiana Purchase, see Bush, *The Louisiana Purchase.* Quotes here come from Francois Barbé-Marbois, *The History of Louisiana, Particularly of the Cession of That Colony to the United States of America*, which is excerpted in Bush, *The Louisiana Purchase*, 155.
16. "Louisiana Ceded to the U. States," *Columbian Courier, and Weekly Miscellany* (Massachusetts), July 1, 1803.
17. "London, May 17," *American Citizen* (New York), July 1, 1803.
18. Horatio Gates to Thomas Jefferson, July 18, 1803, in *TPTJ*, 41:87; Andrew Jackson to Thomas Jefferson, August 7, 1803, in *TPTJ*, 41:156; Wilson Cary Nicholas to Thomas Jefferson, September 3, 1803, in *TPTJ*, 41:313.
19. Thomas Jefferson to John Dickinson, August 9, 1803, in *TPTJ*, 41:170, contains much of Jefferson's initial reasoning.
20. Thomas Jefferson to Levi Lincoln, August 30, 1803, in *TPTJ*, 41:290. Emphasis original.
21. See, for instance, "American," *American, and Baltimore Gazette*, July 30, 1803.
22. "Entry 9: Letters Sent to Civilians, 1800–1817," vol. 1, 513–514, RG 107, Records of the Office of the Secretary of War, National Archives and Records Administration, Washington, D.C.
23. Barbara Fifer and Martin Kidston, *Wanted! Wanted Posters of the Old West: Stories Behind the Crimes* (Helena: Farcountry Press, 2003); Seth Ferranti, "The History of the Most Wanted Poster," *Huffington Post*, December 14, 2016, www.huffpost.com/entry/the-history-of-the-most-wanted-poster_b_5851ba70e4b0865ab9d4e8d7.
24. Frederick S. Calhoun, *The Lawmen: United States Marshals and Their Deputies, 1789–1989* (New York: Penguin Books, 1991), 3; Oliver, *The Birth of the FBI*, 12.
25. For overviews of early American criminal justice, see Samuel Walker, *Popular Justice: A History of American Criminal Justice*, 2nd ed. (New York: Oxford University Press, 1998), especially 25–27; Elizabeth Dale, *Criminal Justice in the United States, 1789–1939* (New York: Cambridge University Press, 2011), especially 7–25; and Friedman, *Crime and Punishment in American History*.
26. *Western Spy*, July 20, 1803, transcription, Draper Manuscripts, WHS, 7S, 21–22.
27. Morazán, "Records of the Cabildo," 212.
28. William C. C. Claiborne to Thomas Jefferson, July 13, 1803, in *TPTJ*, 41:46.
29. Thomas Jefferson to Henry Dearborn, July 12, 1803, in *TPTJ*, 41:33.
30. Henry Dearborn to Governor Archibald Roane, July 18, 1803, in *Alexandria Expositor*, September 19, 1803.

31. Henry Dearborn to Governor Archibald Roane, July 18, 1803; Thomas Jefferson to Henry Dearborn, July 13, 1803, in *TPTJ*, 41:34 (see editorial note); Henry Dearborn to William C. C. Claiborne, "Extract—War Dept. July 18, 1803," Draper Manuscripts, WHS, 1Q, 40. This letter was widely reprinted in newspapers nationally.
32. Henry Dearborn to William C. C. Claiborne, "Extract—War Dept. July 18, 1803." When *Western Spy* ran an update a few weeks later, it mentioned Claiborne's offer of a reward. (See *Western Spy* [Cincinnati], August 3, 1803, transcription, Draper Manuscripts, WHS, 7S, 21–22.)
33. Mason allegedly sought out intelligence on what people knew of his exploits. According to one account, he sometimes stopped mail carriers on the Natchez Trace, "always anxious to know what was said of him by the public." Guild, *Old Times in Tennessee*, 94–95.
34. "The Robber of the Wilderness," *Wheeling Gazette*, December 10, 1829, clipping, Draper Manuscripts, WHS, 29CC, 75–76.
35. Zadok Cramer, *The Navigator* (Pittsburgh, 1808), 115.
36. "Committee Report on Petition of Elisha Winters," April 17, 1810, in James F. Hopkins and Mary W. M. Hargreaves, eds., *The Papers of Henry Clay, Volume 1: The Rising Statesman, 1797–1814* (Lexington: University Press of Kentucky, 1959), 468.
37. Jeff Truly to Otto Rothert, September 6, 1917, Otto Rothert Papers, unprocessed, Filson Historical Society, Louisville, Ky.
38. *Kentucky Gazette*, November 22, 1803.
39. This description is the traditional version of how Mason met his end. It is repeated in countless nineteenth-century sources. But no contemporary documents, to my knowledge, confirm that May and Setton killed him or even that the head they presented was Mason's. He was never seen again, at least not publicly. Meanwhile, Setton and May did come to trial in Mississippi after being caught, but they were charged with robbery and piracy, not murder. One newspaper report suggested that May took credit on the gallows for killing Mason; he "spoke of the benefit he had rendered to society by destroying old Mason" ("Natchez, February 6," *Poulson's American Daily Advertiser* [Philadelphia], March 10, 1804). There are some indications that they had been tried earlier for Mason's murder, but I have found no records to confirm that. Mississippi territorial court records are spotty for these years.
40. Hall, *Letters from the West*, 279.
41. Jeff Truly to Otto Rothert, September 6, 1917, Filson Historical Society.
42. Jeff Truly to Otto Rothert, September 6, 1917, Filson Historical Society. This detail is also given in Claiborne, *Mississippi, as a Province, Territory, and State*, unsourced, suggesting it may really have come from local court records.
43. Jeff Truly to Otto Rothert, September 6, 1917, Filson Historical Society.
44. Quoted in Rothert, *The Outlaws of Cave-in-Rock*, 253.

45. Jeff Truly to Otto Rothert, September 6, 1917, Filson Historical Society.
46. Jeff Truly to Otto Rothert, September 6, 1917, Filson Historical Society (Ker catching cold).
47. William Baskerville Hamilton, *Anglo-American Law on the Frontier: Thomas Rodney and His Territorial Cases* (Durham: Duke University Press, 1953), 72–74; William S. Coker, "Peter Bruin: Record as Soldier, Judge, Settler," *Natchez Democrat* (1968), 8–10 ("unhappy propensity"); Coker, "Peter Bryan Bruin of Bath: Soldier, Judge and Frontiersman," *West Virginia History* 30, no. 4 (1969): 579–585. Useful biographical information about Bruin and David Ker can be found in their subject files at MDAH.
48. Hamilton, *Anglo-American Law on the Frontier*, 4–5, 62–64.
49. Mack Swearingen, *The Early Life of George Poindexter: A Story of the First Southwest* (New Orleans: Tulane University Press, 1934) (quotes on pp. 69–70).
50. Transcription, September 15, [1803?], possibly from *Palladium*, Draper Manuscripts, WHS, 1Q, 40.
51. Hamilton, *Anglo-American Law on the Frontier*, 92. Poindexter himself acknowledged in a letter to the governor that the robbery had occurred "in the tract of Country assigned to the Choctaw nation." See George Poindexter to Acting Governor Cato West, January 14, 1804, RG 1, series 488, doc. 290, MDAH.
52. On the Choctaws in this period, see especially James Taylor Carson, *Searching for the Bright Path: The Mississippi Choctaws from Prehistory to Removal* (Lincoln: University of Nebraska Press, 1999), and Greg O'Brien, *Choctaws in a Revolutionary Age, 1750–1830* (Lincoln: University of Nebraska Press, 2002).
53. As president, Thomas Jefferson had mulled this particular bit of coastline very deeply. He was uncomfortable that so much of the nation's western flank was occupied by Indians. He wrote about trying to purchase it. "I think it also all important to press on the Indians, as steadily and strenuously as they can bear, the extension of our purchases on the Missisipi from the Yazoo upwards," he wrote in May 1803. See Thomas Jefferson to W.C.C. Claiborne, May 24, 1803, in Barbara B. Oberg et al., eds., *TPTJ*, vol. 40, *4 March to 10 July 1803* (Princeton University Press, 2013), 422 (quotes); Thomas Jefferson to Henry Dearborn, May 13, 1803, in *TPTJ*, 40:365; and DeConde, *This Affair of Louisiana*, 132–133. Dearborn ("most powerful") is quoted in Carson, *Searching for the Bright Path*, 65.
54. See the Treaty of Hopewell (1786) and the Treaty of Fort Adams (1801).
55. George Poindexter to Acting Governor Cato West, January 14, 1804.
56. See "An Act for the Punishment of Certain Crimes Against the United States," April 30, 1790, in *The Public Statutes at Large of the United States of America, from the Organization of the Government in 1789, to March 3, 1845*, ed. Richard Peters (Boston: Charles C. Little and James Brown, 1845), 112–119. William Baskerville Hamilton deduced that this must be the law under

which Setton and May were charged; see Hamilton, *Anglo-American Law on the Frontier*, 93. A contemporary letter written by William Claiborne all but confirms this theory; Claiborne wrote that they were convicted of "Piracy and Felony" for "offences committed without the limits of the Territory against the Laws of the [United States]." See Claiborne to James Madison, March 15, 1804, in Rowland, *Official Letter Books of W.C.C. Claiborne*, 2:40–41. The word in brackets is an educated guess for a blank space in the document.

57. Acting Governor Cato West, Washington, to Governor William Claiborne, February 16, 1804, RG 1, series 488, doc. 311, MDAH.
58. Thomas Rodney to Caesar A. Rodney, February 14, 1804, in Simon Gratz, ed., "Thomas Rodney," *Pennsylvania Magazine of History and Biography*, vol. 43, no. 4 (1919): 334–335.
59. Hamilton, *Anglo-American Law on the Frontier*, 91.
60. Thomas Rodney to Caesar A. Rodney, February 14, 1804, in "Thomas Rodney," 334–335.
61. Thomas Rodney to Caesar A. Rodney, February 14, 1804, in "Thomas Rodney," 335.
62. "Report of House Committee: Extent of Federal Jurisdiction," March 14, 1804, in Clarence Edwin Carter, ed., *Territorial Papers of the United States*, vol. 5, *The Territory of Mississippi 1798–1817* (Washington: Government Printing Office, 1937): 311, quoted in Hamilton, *Anglo-American Law on the Frontier*, 93–94; David M. Hargrove, *Mississippi's Federal Courts: A History* (Jackson: University Press of Mississippi, 2019), 21, 29.
63. "Committee Report on Petition of Elisha Winters," April 17, 1810, *The Papers of Henry Clay*, 468–469.
64. George Poindexter to Acting Governor Cato West, January 14, 1804.
65. "Committee Report on Petition of Elisha Winters," April 17, 1810, 469.
66. Vic Gatrell, *The Hanging Tree: Execution and the English People, 1770–1868* (New York: Oxford University Press, 1994); Halttunen, *Murder Most Foul*; Laussat, *Memoirs of My Life*, 96–97 (swallows).
67. Laussat, *Memoirs of My Life*, 88.
68. Col. John Stump recollections, Draper Manuscripts, WHS, 31S, 55–56.
69. Claiborne, *Mississippi, as a Province, Territory, and State*, 227.
70. "Frankfort, February 29," *Kentucky Gazette*, March 6, 1804.
71. See, for example, "Natchez, February 6," *Poulson's American Daily Advertiser* (Philadelphia), March 10, 1804, p. 3.
72. Col. John Stump recollections, Draper Manuscripts, WHS, 31S, 56.
73. "The Story of the Harps," *Port Folio*, August 1825, 116. Poindexter believed for the rest of his life that he had prosecuted Wiley Harp. This quote is taken from a periodical published in the 1820s, in which Poindexter pointedly told someone that the man with Mason was Wiley—no doubt.
74. "The Harpes—from Col. Sevier," 317.

75. "The Harpes—from Col. Sevier," 317; "Natchez, February 6," *Poulson's American Daily Advertiser* (Philadelphia), March 10, 1804.
76. Franklin L. Riley, "Extinct Towns and Villages of Mississippi," in *Publications of the Mississippi Historical Society*, ed. Riley, vol. 5 (Oxford, Miss., 1902), 346–347.

Epilogue: The Ashes of the Grave

1. Douglas L. Winiarski, "Shakers and Jerkers: Letters from the 'Long Walk,' 1805, Part 1," *Journal of East Tennessee History* 89 (2017): 90–110; quotes ("They laugh, they sing") are from "The Jerks," *Virginia Argus*, October 24, 1804, reproduced in Winiarski, "Shakers and Jerkers," 91.
2. Benjamin Seth Youngs Diary, February 28, 1805, ASC 859, Winterthur Library, Delaware ("high ridges," "deep gullies"); "A Concise Sketch of the Life and Experience of Issachar Bates, Written By Himself," item R* 289.8 B32, History Room, 36–37, Dayton Metro Library, Ohio. I am immensely grateful to Douglas Winiarski for sharing these sources with me.
3. "A Concise Sketch," 36.
4. "A Concise Sketch," 36–37. For more on Bates's life, see Carol Medlicott, *Issachar Bates: A Shaker's Journey* (Hanover, N.H.: University Press of New England, 2013). This episode appears on pp. 76–77.
5. "From Esqr. James Leeper of Henry Co.—Tennessee," 129; Edward Coffman, *The Story of Logan County* (Russellville, Ky., 1962), 72; Draper, "A Sketch of the Harpes," 174. The marriage bond is listed in *Logan County, Kentucky Marriages, 1790–1865* (Russellville, Ky., 1981), American Antiquarian Society, Worcester, Mass. (though Betsy is mis-transcribed here as "Patsey").
6. George Herridon and Mrs. Herridon recollections, Draper Manuscripts, WHS, 30S, 186–187; *Logan County, Kentucky Marriages, 1790–1865*, 14. Given that she was living on Col. Anthony Butler's plantation, it seems fairly clear that this is Susana Roberts aka Harp.
7. William Calhoun Love diary, https://sites.rootsweb.com/~kycaldw2/wmclove, accessed July 22, 2019.
8. George Herridon and Mrs. Herridon recollections, Draper Manuscripts, WHS, 30S, 186–187; Coffman, *The Story of Logan County*, 72.
9. Maj. William Stewart recollections, Draper Manuscripts, WHS, 30S, 190 ("prodigal"); Breazeale, *Life as It Is*, 150; "From Genl. Jonathan Ramsay," Draper Manuscripts, 5S, 70–72; Collins, *Collins' Historical Sketches*, 2:351.
10. Sally Rice vs. Ephraim Walker & Betsey his wife, in *Records of Roane County: Minute Book A, 1801–1805*, WPA transcription (1937), Calvin M. McClung Historical Collection, Knox County Public Library. The associated file papers for this case, which are still held in the Roane County Archives, do not reveal anything further about the "words spoken."
11. Collins, *Collins' Historical Sketches*, 2:351.

12. "I asked the Major the name of the man she married. He could not be induced to divulge it," Collins wrote. Collins, *Collins' Historical Sketches*, 2:351.
13. Maj. William Stewart recollections, Draper Manuscripts, WHS, 30S, 190–191.
14. See Breazeale, *Life as It Is*, 146; Hall, *Letters from the West*, 277. This story is also repeated in James Alves notes, Draper Manuscripts, 2CC, 34.
15. Collins, *Collins' Historical Sketches*, 2:351–352.
16. Knox County Court Minutes, Book 2, 51, microfilm roll 139, TSLA.
17. Willie Harp to Jesse Parker, sheriff's sale, February 8, 1800, Knox County Warranty Deed Book F1VI, 300–302, KCA; Jesse Parker to Martha Bradley et al., October 11, 1842, Knox County Warranty Deed Book H2, 86–89, KCA.
18. Bamman, "This Land Is Our Land!"
19. Thomas Blount to John Gray Blount, May 17, 1798, in *The John Gray Blount Papers*, 3:225.
20. Albert Bruce Pruitt, *Glasgow Land Fraud Papers, 1783–1800* (1988), iv–v.
21. Koonts, " 'An Angel Has Fallen!' " 301–328; Pruitt, *Glasgow Land Fraud Papers*.
22. Stockley Donelson to Andrew Jackson, October 2, 1800, in *The Papers of Andrew Jackson*, 236–237.
23. Smith and Owsley, *The Papers of Andrew Jackson*, 37.
24. Andrew Jackson to John Overton, January 22, 1798, in *The Papers of Andrew Jackson*, 168–169.
25. Alfred Moore to James McHenry, June 30, 1799, in Bernard C. Steiner, *The Life and Correspondence of James McHenry: Secretary of War Under Washington and Adams* (Cleveland: Burrows Brothers, 1907), 446.
26. Quoted in Cumfer, *Separate Peoples, One Land*, 82.
27. McLoughlin, *Cherokee Renascence in the New Republic*, 46.
28. Steiner, *The Life and Correspondence of James McHenry*, 446.
29. Brown, *Old Frontiers*, 451–453.
30. Collins, *Collins' Historical Sketches*, 1:25.
31. Hall, *Letters from the West*, 272–273.
32. Donald G. Mathews, "The Second Great Awakening as an Organizing Process, 1780–1830: An Hypothesis," *American Quarterly* 21, no. 1 (1969): 23–43.
33. Young, *Autobiography of a Pioneer*, 109–110.
34. Daniel Blake Smith, "Introduction," in *Westward into Kentucky*, 10.
35. Young, *Autobiography of a Pioneer*, 95–97; this story is also recounted in Collins, *Collins' Historical Sketches*, 2:695.
36. Young, *Autobiography of a Pioneer*, 96–97.
37. Smith, *Legends of the War of Independence*, 326–328.
38. Smith, *Legends of the War of Independence*, 326–328.
39. William Calhoun Love diary, https://sites.rootsweb.com/~kycaldw2/wmclove, accessed July 22, 2019; Beard, *Brief Biographical Sketches*, 357–358.

40. Faulkner, *Requiem for a Nun*, 103, 104, 249.
41. Crews and Starbuck, *Records of the Moravians Among the Cherokees*, 1:104–105.
42. Venable, *Beginnings of Literary Culture in the Ohio Valley*, 361–385.
43. HISTORY OF THE HARPS appears in bold relief on its original title page as a selling point; see Breazeale, *Life as It Is*, in which their tale is narrated on pp. 136–151.
44. In some cases, Smith describes real events and real characters but with slightly altered names and details. He calls the Harps "Bill" and "Joshua," though he is obviously referring to Wiley and Micajah. He claims to have drawn most of his stories from firsthand testimony—from people he met or knew—but he waited to publish, conveniently, until no one was alive to dispute his stories. "The *facts* are vouched for as given by old soldiers, their wives, pioneers and their contemporaries . . . but who are now believed to all be in their graves," Smith wrote (*Legends of the War of Independence*, vi–vii).
45. Draper, "A Sketch of the Harpes," 175.
46. "Another Revolutionary Soldier Gone!," *Mississippi Advertiser*, February 8, 1845.
47. "Man of Five Worlds," *Courier-Journal* (Louisville), magazine section, December 7, 1952, clipping, Otto Rothert Papers, Filson Historical Society, Louisville, Ky.
48. A letter to Mr. LL Goldberg, possibly from Maurice Alvares, April 22, 1924, Otto Rothert Papers, Filson Historical Society, Louisville, Ky.
49. Paul Allen, *A History of the American Revolution; Comprehending All the Principal Events Both in the Field and in the Cabinet*, 2 vols. (Baltimore, 1822), 1:v.
50. Richard Bushman, *From Puritan to Yankee: Character and the Social Order in Connecticut, 1690–1765* (Cambridge: Harvard University Press, 1967), 288 ("release of energy," "sorrows").
51. Holmes and Holmes, *Mass Murder in the United States*, 33–34.
52. Fox, "In Rampages, It's About Revenge."
53. Hall, *Letters from the West*, 277.
54. Faulkner, *Requiem for a Nun*, 102–104.

INDEX

ABOUT THE AUTHOR

KATHERINE GRANDJEAN is an associate professor of history at Wellesley College, where her research explores early American and Native American history, environmental history, and violence in American history. Her first book is *American Passage: The Communications Frontier in Early New England.* She has been the recipient of several major research fellowships from the National Endowment for the Humanities, the American Antiquarian Society, and the American Council of Learned Societies, among others.

ABOUT THE TYPE

This book is set in Van Dijck. Known for its sharp contrast, refined strokes, wide capitals with strong thick/thin contrast, and large x-height, it offers excellent legibility. It is a classic Dutch Old Style revival, named after Christoffel van Dijck (1601–1669), a leading Dutch typefounder during the seventeenth-century Golden Age of Dutch printing. His work represented a crucial transition from calligraphic types toward more modern, structured letterforms and significantly influenced English typefounders, especially William Caslon. Van Dijck's designs were revived digitally by Jan van Krimpen and the Monotype Design Studio in the 1930s, creating the widely recognized Van Dijck font family.